Politics, Economics, and Inclusive Development

The Politics, Economics, and Inclusive Development series examines the challenges and progress in promoting humanistic development. The complex tasks of simultaneously pursuing economic growth, broad participation and equity, democratic peace, and sustainability require scholarship that merges in-depth analysis of the many factors that influence development outcomes with contextually rich experiences. The single- or multiauthored monographs use an interdisciplinary methodology to explore diverse experiences of individual nations, world regions, or the entire global system in their quest for more democratic, technically sound, and sustainable development. The publications from the Politics, Economics, and Inclusive Development series will be valuable to students, scholars, policymakers, and international development practitioners.

William Ascher · Shane Joshua Barter

Moving within Borders

Addressing the Potentials and Risks of Mass Migrations in Developing Countries

palgrave
macmillan

William Ascher
Claremont McKenna College
Claremont, CA, USA

Shane Joshua Barter
Soka University of America
Aliso Viejo, CA, USA

ISSN 2945-6436 ISSN 2945-6444 (electronic)
Politics, Economics, and Inclusive Development
ISBN 978-3-031-37548-4 ISBN 978-3-031-37549-1 (eBook)
https://doi.org/10.1007/978-3-031-37549-1

Cover illustration: Ser Amantio di Nicolao/Transferred from Flickr via Flickr2Commons

This Palgrave Macmillan imprint is published by the registered company Springer Nature Switzerland AG
The registered company address is: Gewerbestrasse 11, 6330 Cham, Switzerland

Paper in this product is recyclable.

Acknowledgements

Seeing this book come to print has been a long process. The authors would like to thank the participants from the internal migration workshop hosted by the East-West Center and Pacific Basin Research Center, whose many insights heightened our understanding of internal migration (see Barter and Ascher, eds, 2019). Thank you also to Natalia Mirovitskaya as well as the reviewers and editors at Palgrave Macmillan. We would also like to thank several student research assistants at the Claremont Colleges (Tania Gray, Caroline Jenkins, Andrea Medina, Laura Mora, Charlotte Reinnoldt, Isabella Smith, and Cloe [Fio] Wibawa) as well as from Soka University of America (Mahesh Kushwaha, Nikita Sukmono, Mukesh Bastola, Wren Biggers, and Mira Peregud), along with Kayo Yoshikawa and the Pacific Basin Research Center. We would also like to thank Shabbir Cheema for constructive comments and support.

Prologue

Across the world, news broadcasts and policy debates underscore the urgency of international migration. In the United States, migration from Latin America as well as the Middle East involves pitched battles between those wishing to keep migrants out and those hopeful for a more humanitarian approach. Thousands of Africans drown as their overloaded boats capsize in the Mediterranean en route to Europe. European leaders debate how to react to the arrival of some five million Syrian migrants fleeing a brutal civil war. These migration crises have fueled the rise of right-wing parties, seeking to secure their borders against migrant threats. In South America, Venezuelans fleeing crime and hunger languish in Colombia; in the Middle East, hundreds of thousands of Iraqis live in overcrowded conditions in Jordan and Egypt. In Southeast Asia, hundreds of thousands of Myanmar's Rohingya have fled to Bangladesh and throughout Southeast Asia; seemingly echoing the fears of Western governments, Asian leaders have framed Rohingya as threats, bringing the possibility of Islamic radicalism and a strain on public spending (Straits Times 2018). And following Russia's invasion of Ukraine, millions of Ukrainians have fled to Europe and beyond. No wonder we are tempted to conclude that international migration represents the defining migration issue of our era.

The reality is that, despite a relative lack of attention, internal migration is far more expansive, and is at least as deserving of international cooperation, as international migration. The International Organization for Migration (IOM 2018a, 2) estimates that there are some 740 million internal migrants worldwide, about three times the number of international migrants. In terms of forced displacement, it is estimated that over two-thirds are internally displaced, while under a third cross borders as refugees or asylum seekers (Sasse 2020, 347).

Internal migration can be a boon or a tragedy. Despite many cases of dire hardship, conflict, and vulnerability, countless people migrate within their home country without incident. Migration may represent a safety or welfare mechanism, helping marginalized farmers gain access to land or helping rural people find jobs in cities. Internal migration represents a key survival strategy for the poor and a key development strategy. Success stories may be difficult to identify, as a lack of conflict may not be visible and one can always find victims in any large-scale process, but many countries have handled large-scale internal migration successfully. This is especially true of large-scale urban migration, but also in state-led resettlement. Indonesian transmigration involved relocating millions of people from densely populated Java to outer islands; contrary to some misconceptions, the program was in many ways successful, with much of Sumatra receiving large-scale migration without substantial conflict and with visible integration. Some governments have channeled urban migration successfully to peripheral "new cities" to take advantage of the benefits of productivity gains while reducing urban slums. Others have successfully restricted internal migration to protect vulnerable indigenous communities or delicate ecosystems.

Yet frequently, internal migration per se and the interactions between migrants and host communities are fraught with hardship for both migrant and host communities. In contrast to headlines about international migration, how much do we hear of camps for internally displaced persons (IDPs) and the deprivations faced by their inhabitants, including sexual violence in and around camps in South Sudan? Is the world aware of inter-province migrants in China lacking documents to enroll their children in school or receive healthcare? Are people outside of India aware of officials justifying resettlements as a means to "civilize" the tribal inhabitants in the target area, or Mumbai police standing idly by while Shiv Sena thugs beat immigrants who do not speak Marathi? How much analysis is provided to the squalid conditions of internal displacement centers in Syria or Guatemala that lead to further relocation efforts and compel IDPs to become refugees? These are the lived realities of many internal migrants.

This book should be of interest to those studying economic development, as many instances of internal migration unleash greater productivity—witness the case of China—as well as access to previously unavailable goods and services. Lamenting the limited number of studies of internal migration compared to international migration, Skeldon (2008, 2), points out that there is more potential "located in home-country populations" in contributing to labor forces. Much more recently, in his extensive study of rural-urban migration, Lucas (2021) emphasizes the lack of attention to internal migration. For fundamental questions related to the outcomes of migration and benefits for migrant families, "Most of the attention has been directed to international migrants" (Lucas 2021, 337). On the other hand, if managed poorly, large-scale internal migration can waste economic resources and fuel destructive conflict.

For those concerned about international migration, it must be recognized that internal migration often precedes and even triggers international migration, either as an opportune jumping-off step or to escape from adverse conditions caused by internal migration. For example, some unknown fraction of the Syrian refugees arriving in Europe are persons who could not find a safe place in their home country. While we focus on Ukrainian refugees arriving into Poland and other countries, there are far more displaced within the country; even before the 2022 Russian invasion, Ukraine had one of the world's highest numbers of IDPs (Sasse 2020, 348). The migration of Central Americans to the United States reflects the same pattern. For Skeldon (2006, 20), intra-state migration from villages to cities is often followed by international migration. Young urban migrants who are unable to achieve their desired success often continue on to cities in other countries. In Morocco, de Haas (2005, 23) observes "the huge significance of rural-to-urban migration … [and] the crucial function of internal migration as a precursor to international migration." Hugo (2016, 651–652) notes that "there are often strong relationships between internal and international migration which remain little understood because the two types of movement are conceptualised, measured and studied separately." Those concerned about city planning must, of course, take into account the urbanization that constitutes the greatest volume of internal migration worldwide. The unforced urbanization by employment-seekers requires different state responses than for migrants fleeing violence in their home areas, who are often whole families with minimal resources. For those committed to contributing to ecosystem sustainability, frontier migration is a pressing concern, as examples in the Amazon, Borneo, Sumatra, and other cases can attest.

While many host communities have benefited from the synergies with new arrivals and greater resources and amenities resulting from a higher population, it is not just migrants who are threatened by internal migration. Internal migrants may represent the national ethnic majority, perhaps relocating with state assistance in what may appear as internal colonialism. Indigenous ethnic minorities, in particular, have been highly vulnerable to migratory threats. Sometimes, migrant and host communities may both be victims of state policy, disaster, or other factors beyond their control, but end up fighting one another.

The host state is *primus inter pares* in handling internal migration in ways that lack a parallel in international migration. While not the only important actor, there is a pressing need to better understand the role of the state in handling internal migration—policy successes, failures, and points in between. Sometimes national and subnational governments help internal migrants. Sometimes they are indifferent or incapable, or perhaps face internal divisions related to migration, especially between national and subnational governments. Sometimes they actively work to exploit or displace their own citizens, in which case there are few options open to internal migrants, many of whom then seek to become international migrants as a result of these failures. Various state agencies and levels of government are key to successfully govern internal migration, but too often fall short.

We may feel complacent if these deprivations do not plague our countries. Yet, we all have a potential role to pressure our governments and intergovernmental organizations to be more active in improving the outcomes of internal migration. Foreign assistance could be a powerful tool to relieve resource pressures in resettlement areas, but also to induce governments of developing countries to better accommodate migrants and host communities. Though controversial, international conventions can justify interventions against governments that oversee egregious maltreatment of migrant or host communities. Only recently has the International Organization for Migration (IOM) turned its attention to internal migration. Only recently have the World Bank and other development assistance agencies emphasized the importance of developing livelihood initiatives for people in camps for internally displaced persons, who otherwise are wasting their lives "warehoused" in squalid camps.

If we are not complacent, then we must understand what drives states to initiate migrations and how they react to migrations that are not state-initiated. This book centers on the obligations of the state at all of its levels, both vertically (from national to subnational levels) and horizontally (across various agencies, such as the armed forces, planning, environmental, and welfare agencies). We must appreciate that neglect or abuse by the state typically rests on complex motives. Officials may feel a profound ambivalence toward the standing of migrants and are therefore uncertain as to how to address migrant-host community conflicts. State motives range from helping migrant and/or host communities, gaining greater control over particular populations, relieving ecological pressures, and more. Sometimes, states initiate migration for strategic ends, as reflected in the Brazilian government's efforts to populate the Amazon to preempt migration from other countries, Iran's program to resettle Persians into Arab-dominated Khuzestan Province bordering Iraq, or Turkey's expulsion of Kurds from their ancestral lands. The state's reactions to what is often called "spontaneous migration" are complicated by uncertainty in assessing and evaluating migrants' motives, ranging from job-seeking and land-seeking to fleeing violence and escaping natural disasters. Since the state's policies toward aiding migrants typically depend on assumptions of whether migrations are "forced" or "voluntary," the uncertainty can be troubling. Whether the state should have an obligation toward families that migrate along with officially sponsored migrants is also ambiguous. It is equally unclear if states should enact policies that limit their citizens' ability to relocate to regions with sensitive ecologies, such as areas with endangered species, or beleaguered minority groups, such as the Uyghurs in western China.

We must be fair: the dilemmas facing the state are frequently daunting, even if officials are well-intentioned. Although sometimes states have the power to support both migrants and host communities, in many cases state power is more limited than leaders (and their critics) believe. Even the most carefully planned resettlement programs cannot provide full control over the volume of migrants, their ultimate locations, and migrant-host interactions. Sponsored resettlement programs may not attract as many takers as officials had hoped, or may be swamped by extended families joining sponsored migrants. Migrants who are settled in particular areas may not remain, or, because of clashes with host communities, may require resettlement.

Leaders often face a delicate balancing act in deciding how dominant state institutions ought to be in the resettlement areas. State obligations to maintain order, protect the vulnerable, and enforce laws call for a significant presence, yet such dominance may well inhibit members of migrant and host communities from working out mutually agreeable arrangements. When state support places migrants as the state's clients, state involvement is likely to be seen as biased. In some cases, leaders find it safer—and easier—to turn their backs on migrants and host communities alike.

How, then, can the international community improve the well-being of migrants and host communities? Institutions dedicated to assisting displaced people and other migrants need to be strengthened and better coordinated. As international organizations shift their focus to internal migration, there is reason for optimism. Foreign assistance agencies, whether international or bilateral, can be more assertive in tying the volume of assistance to the treatment of migrants and host communities. International actors can also target assistance projects to areas made vulnerable because of migration. Some international conventions and treaties (e.g., the African Union's Kampala Convention) directly establish the state's responsibilities for the care of displaced people.

Less provocative ways to influence the state require support for a broad range of seemingly technical challenges. For state-initiated migrations, comprehensive planning, careful formulation of incentives, and support for both the migrants and the anticipated host community, as well as estimating the resources needed to provide sufficient state presence, can be reinforced by the collective wisdom of countries that have wrestled with internal migration. Thus, it is not simply a matter of pressuring states to be responsible in the migrations they instigate or to govern migrant-host interactions fairly—it is a matter of actively contributing to the work of state institutions. There is a pressing need to grasp the many governance challenges and policies related to internal migration, something we hope to provide in the pages that follow.

References

de Haas, Hein. 2005. Morocco's Migration Transition: Trends, Determinants, and Future Scenarios. *Global Migration Perspectives* 28. Global Commission on International Migration, Netherlands.

Hugo, Graeme John. 2016. Internal and International Migration in Eastand Southeast Asia: Exploring the Linkages. *Population, Space, and Place* 22: 651–668.

IOM (International Organization for Migration). 2018a. *World Migration Report 2018*. New York: United Nations.

Lucas, Robert E.B. 2021. *Crossing the Divide: Rural to Urban Migration in Developing Countries*. Oxford: Oxford University Press and KNOWMAD.

Sasse, Gwendolyn. 2020. War and Displacement: The Case of Ukraine. *Europe-Asia Studies* 72 (3): 347–353.

Skeldon, Ronald. 2006. "Interlinkages between Internal and International Migration and Development in the Asian Region." *Population, Space and Place* 12 (1): 15–30.

Skeldon, Ronald. 2008. International Migration as a Tool in Development Policy: A Passing Phase? *Population and Development Review* 34 (1): 1–18.

Straits Times. 2018. Rohingya Crisis Could Pose Security Risk to Region, Najib Warns. March 18.

Contents

1	**Introduction: Success and Failure**	1
	A Roadmap	7
	References	10
2	**Understanding Internal Migration**	13
	Conceptualizing Internal Migration	13
	Voluntary and Involuntary Internal Migration	18
	State-Initiated, State-Managed, and Unmanaged Migration	19
	Victims and Oppressors	20
	Fluid Categories	20
	From Holism to Fragmentation in Studying Internal Migration, and Hopefully Back	22
	Internal and International Migration	25
	References	28

Part I Stakeholders: The State, Migrants, and Hosts

3	**The Primacy of the State**	35
	The State's Discretion	37
	The Complexity of the State	41
	State Motives	41
	Economic Motives	41
	Political Motives	44

Socioeconomic Motives 47
Ecological Motives 49
Psychology of State Interactions 51
Overlap of Identifications 51
Overgeneralization 53
Feelings of Superiority 53
Conclusions 53
References 54

4 The Many Levels of the State 59
Political Decentralization 60
Administrative Decentralization 63
Fiscal Decentralization 63
Clashing Governments 64
Internal Migration Agencies and Offices 65
Conclusions 68
References 69

5 Sympathy for the State: Coping with Internal Migration 71
Uncertainty 71
Volume 72
Location 72
Eligibility 72
Intergroup Relations 73
Vulnerability of State Officials 74
Limits of Capacity 74
Dilemmas 75
Conclusions 82
References 82

6 Migrants in Train: State-Initiated and Managed Migrations 85
State-Coerced Migration 86
Forced, But Not by the State: Evacuation and Resettlement 91
Voluntary State-Managed Migrants: Clients and Pioneers 92
The Clients 93
The Pioneers 94
Conclusions 96
References 96

7	**Unsponsored Migrants: The Enterprising**	99
	The Land Hungry	100
	The Entrepreneurial Land Hungry	103
	Resource Extractors	103
	Merchant Migrants	104
	The Urbanizers	105
	Profiles of Urban Migrants: Bihari Migrants in Mumbai	109
	Deterrence and Expulsion of Urbanizers	111
	Mechanisms of Exclusion	113
	The Edges of Urbanization	116
	Upward Mobility and Remittances	120
	Conclusions	121
	References	121
8	**Unsponsored Migrants: The Expelled**	127
	Development IDPs	128
	Conflict IDPs	133
	Disaster IDPs	136
	Creating Migrant Communities	139
	Conclusions	140
	References	141
9	**Room to Let? Host Community Perspectives**	143
	Migrant-Origin Communities	144
	Solidarity or Solubility: The Importance of Host Cleavages	147
	Exchange Perspectives	149
	Welcome to the Jungle: Rural Host Communities	150
	Welcome to the Big City: Urban Host Communities	151
	Conclusions	153
	References	153

Part II What Can Go Wrong

10	**Migratory Deprivations**	159
	Pre-migration Contexts	160
	Material Deprivations	161
	The Ambiguity of Property	161
	Promising Much, Delivering Little	163
	Economic Competition	164
	Exceeding Carrying Capacity	166

Political Deprivations 167
Host Political Deprivations 167
Migrant Political Deprivations 168
Generating Political Difference 168
Sociocultural Deprivations 169
Cultural & Deferential Deprivations for Hosts 169
Cultural and Deferential Deprivations for Migrants 171
Conclusions 172
References 172

11 Migratory Conflicts 175
Host Violence: Sons of the Soil 176
Migrant Violence: Settler Conflicts 182
Security Deprivations: Processes of Migratory Violence 183
Roles of the State 186
Conclusions 188
References 188

12 State Failures 191
Some Caveats 191
Failures of Planning 193
Failure to Collect Information 194
Failure to Provide Information 195
Failure to Plan Resettlement 196
Failure to Estimate the Volume of Migration 197
Failure to Support Material Well-Being 198
Failure to Manage Property Rights 200
Failure to Recognize Development Opportunities 201
Political Inclusion and Partnerships 202
Failure to Recognize Civic Rights 202
Failure to Partner with Non-state Actors 204
Sociocultural Factors 206
Failure to Consider Compatibility 206
Failure to Respect Migrant/Host Cultures 207
Migratory Insecurity 208
Failure to Provide Order 208
Failure to Remain Neutral 209
Conclusions 210
References 211

Part III What to Do About It

13 State Accountability: Theory, Evasion, and Potential Remedies 217
Degrees of Accountability 218
Identifying the Reasons and Mechanisms for Evading Accountability 219
Self-Accountability Obstacles 219
Low Expectations, Low Accountability 220
Blaming Others 221
Uncertainty of Outcomes 221
Ambiguity of State Obligations 221
Ambiguity of the Degree of Coercion 222
Ambiguity of International Norms 223
Ambiguous Obligations to Host Communities 224
The Temporal Dimension of Accountability 225
Preempting the State's Evasion of Accountability 226
Spreading Accountability as an Incentive for Co-management 226
Conclusions 227
References 227

14 State Responses and Best Practices 229
Restricting Internal Migration 230
Preventing Conflicts 235
Reforming State-led Migration 235
Rewarding Host Communities 239
Resolving Conflicts 242
Separation 242
Integration 244
Conclusions 246
References 247

15 Societal Responses 251
Give Me Shelter: Religion in Internal Migration 252
Conflict IDPs 253
Disaster IDPs 254
Shortcomings of Faith-Based Migratory Aid 256
Making Migration Work: Civil Society Advocacy and Assistance 256

Come Together: Traditional Leaders and Social Integration 259
Conclusions 263
References 263

16 The International Community: A Brief for International Involvement 267
What the International Community can do 269
Increase Support for IDPs 269
Direct Financial Resources to Low-Income Rural Areas or Small Towns 270
Cooperate with Governments to Reform Laws, Regulations, and Practices 271
Support Programs to Reduce Technical Barriers to Work and Social Assistance 272
Support Infrastructure Development to Minimize Displacement and Socioeconomic Distress 272
Facilitate Income-generating Opportunities for IDPs Confined to Camps 273
Managing Difficult Relations with the State 274
Press for Greater Acknowledgment and Support of IDPs 274
Defend Just Compensation for Infrastructure IDPs 276
Offsett Biases in Favor of Migrants 276
Protect Against Problematic Displacements 277
Encourage Recognition of IDP Status 277
Pressure for Reforms 278
Overcome State Restrictions on Information 279
Addressing the Challenges to Effective International Contributions 279
Uncertainty Regarding Future Conflict 279
Collective Action Weaknesses 280
Cooperation Among International Organizations 283
Concern over the Permanence of Resettlement 284
Conclusions: Challenges of Coordination 284
References 285

17 Lessons in Safeguarding the Benefits of Internal Migration 291
Lesson One: Internal Migration can Benefit All 291
Lesson Two: What can go Wrong 293

Lesson Three: The Primacy of the State 293
Lesson Four: Governing Internal Migration 294
Lesson Five: Vertical Coordination 297
Lesson Six: State Officials Evade Accountability 298
Lesson Seven: The Overlapping Forms of Internal Migration 299
Lesson Eight: The Centrality of Ambiguity 300
Lesson Nine: Fair Compensation for the Displaced 301
Lesson Ten: Avoid "Warehousing" IDPs 302
Lesson Eleven: Attention to Host Communities 302
Lesson Twelve: Do Not Overlook Sending Communities 303
Lesson Thirteen: The State is Not Alone 304
Lesson Fourteen: Bring Critics In 305
Lesson Fifteen: Targeted Conditionality 305
Lesson Sixteen: Migration is Only the Beginning 306
Final Thoughts 307
References 307

References 309

Index 341

Abbreviations

AU	African Union
FAO	Food and Agricultural Organization (United Nations)
GPFD	Global Program on Forced Displacement
HTA	Home Town Association
ICCPR	International Covenant on Civil and Political Rights
IDMC	Internal Displacement Monitoring Center
IDP	Internally Displaced Person
IFI	International Financial Institution
ILO	International Labour Organization
IOM	International Organization for Migration
NGO	Non-Governmental Organization
NLSA	National Land Settlement Association (Philippines)
OECD	Organization for Economic Co-operation and Development
SEZ	Special Economic Zone
SLC	Social Land Concession (Cambodia)
SoS	Sons of the Soil
UDHR	Universal Declaration of Human Rights
UN	United Nations
UNHCR	United Nations High Commissioner for Refugees

List of Tables

Table 1.1	Proportion of population migrating from one jurisdiction to another over five years, 2000–2010	4
Table 3.1	State Mechanisms and Motives	38
Table 6.1	State-managed Resettlement Programs during Selected Periods	87
Table 7.1	Urban Population Increases by Region and Country, 2000–2020 (UN Population Division 2018)	106
Table 7.2	Proportions of Migrants According to Urban or Rural Directions, by Sex (Cattaneo and Robinson 2020)	107
Table 7.3	Proportions of Migrants According to Urban or Rural Directions (Rees et al. 2017)	108
Table 8.1	Dams Generating Large Numbers of IDPs (≥50,000) (years approximate)	131
Table 8.2	New IDPs Generated by Conflict and Violence (2017–2022)	134
Table 8.3	New IDPs Generated by Natural Disasters (2017–2022)	137

CHAPTER 1

Introduction: Success and Failure

Following the ouster of long-time President Suharto in 1998, Indonesia was in turmoil. The country saw nearly a dozen violent intergroup conflicts, from separatist wars to Christian-Muslim riots. Many suggested that an underlying cause of conflicts was state-sponsored transmigration, in which millions were relocated from the densely populated "inner islands" to more sparsely populated "outer islands" over several decades. For some, transmigration represented "Indonesia's greatest failure," one that "ended in hatred and bloodshed" (England 2001, 1). Conflicts in Kalimantan, Sulawesi, Ambon, Papua, as well as Timor and Aceh, were indeed linked to internal migration. However, contrary to popular belief, violence typically unfolded between host communities and regional migrants relocating without state support. While criticizing state-led migration, some media reports admitted that "the targets of hostility by local Christians have been spontaneous migrants rather than government assisted transmigrants" (Greenlees 1999, 1). Amidst Indonesian "Sons of the Soil" (SoS) conflicts, natives generally spared state-managed transmigrants from Java. Tens of thousands of persons died and countless more were displaced as a result of conflicts between natives and internal migrants, but the millions of state-managed migrants were not central to hostilities (Barter and Côté 2015; Hedman 2008). Far from state-managed migration causing conflict, violence was a result of the absence of state management among different groups of internal migrants.

W. Ascher and S. J. Barter, *Moving within Borders*, Politics, Economics, and Inclusive Development, https://doi.org/10.1007/978-3-031-37549-1_1

In other contexts, we see laws enacted to protect internally displaced persons (IDPs). For decades, Colombia faced numerous armed conflicts, generating some five million IDPs. Unlike Indonesia, the Colombian government established some of the world's most progressive IDP protection laws. Enacted in 1997, Law 387 lays out rights for displaced persons, including family reunification, state assistance, counseling, non-discrimination, non-refoulment, and the ability to return home. Despite this landmark legislation, Colombian IDPs face familiar challenges. Urban governments "doubt their plight," seeing the migrants not as IDPs, but as poor, job-seeking, potentially troublesome urban migrants (Zea 2019, 34).

Just as Colombian laws designed to help IDPs are contravened by subnational governments, we see some transnational efforts to protect IDPs undermined on the ground. In 2009, the African Union (AU) established the Kampala Convention, one of the first international agreements to support IDPs. The Convention lays out state responsibilities to support displaced persons, tackle the factors that cause displacement, and assist in relocation. Ferris (2014, 6) suggests that this "is the first instrument intended to legally bind an entire region on matters related to preventing situations of mass displacement and to addressing the vulnerabilities and needs of those who have been displaced." Commentators have even argued that the Kampala Convention be adapted elsewhere (Lecamwasam 2014). However, signatories have continued to see mass displacement and have failed to follow the Convention's protocols. In 2019, South Sudan ratified the Convention, although it remains home to tens of thousands of IDPs living in perilous conditions and preyed upon by state forces (Luedke 2019).

India and China are each home to hundreds of millions of internal migrants—some doing far better having migrated, some seriously imperiled. Instead of being IDPs, most are "voluntary" migrants seeking jobs or land in different parts of their respective countries. Despite their very different political systems, governments at various levels in both countries seek to deter internal migration by tying social programs to residency. This means that those migrating to new areas may be denied access to education, healthcare, food rations, and other forms of assistance by being outside of their home district. Some face violent opposition. In India, the far-right Shiv Sena is a violent organization largely concerned with keeping internal migrants out of Maharashtra state. According to an International Labor Organization (ILO) report (2020, 11), while India sends out millions of international migrants, "the magnitude of internal labour migration within the country has been much more staggering," with internal migrants comprising "some of the most vulnerable and disenfranchised groups in India." Meanwhile, in China, internal migration persists despite the limitations set through household registration systems (hukou); by the early 2010s, some 150 million were people considered "floating populations" (Wallace 2014). Many Chinese citizens outside their home district could not work legally in formal, full-time jobs, and thus provided low-paid factory labor in ways reminiscent of undocumented international migrants in the West. This had the socioeconomic consequence of a "quasi-apartheid system," keeping the rural poor away from privileged urban communities (Alexander and Chan 2004, 609). While Chinese policies still restrict urban migration, despite progressive easing of the restrictions, the government celebrates Han migration to border and minority regions, applauding internal migrants for promoting civilization and development (Côté 2019b, 92). India and China both feature what amount to internal immigration regimes, managing millions of people in search of a better life, but with significant human costs.

These are just a few of the many examples that lay bare the importance and urgency surrounding internal migration. As should be clear, internal migration matters. It represents high politics in many countries. Although not granted the policy or media spotlight provided to international migration, internal migration is a much larger phenomenon with similar human, economic, and cultural consequences. The estimated total stock of internal migrants in 2009 was 740 million and may be over one billion as of 2020 (IOM 2020, 19).[1]

Variations in rates of internal migration from one country to another are striking, as shown in estimates of the number of persons living away from their home region for at least five years, a conventional time frame for analyzing internal migration (Bell et al. 2015). Table 1.1 displays estimates of the proportions of populations of a large but not exhaustive set of countries for about 2000–2010.[2]

Here, we see major differences in Asia between Fiji's high of 42 percent changing locations over five years and India's five percent; for Africa,

[1] Due to the pandemic, more recent reliable estimates are unavailable.

[2] The calculations to arrive at these estimates is complicated by the challenge of determining how to define a migration in terms of the passing into a different jurisdiction, when each country has its distinctive set of jurisdictions of different areas.

Table 1.1 Proportion of population migrating from one jurisdiction to another over five years, ~2000–2010

Africa		*Asia*		*Latin America*	
Senegal	35	Fiji[3]	42	Panama	38
Cameroon	33	Mongolia	28	Chile	36
Guinea	22	Kyrgyzstan	23	Paraguay	31
South Africa	22	Cambodia	18	Costa Rica	28
Morocco	21	Malaysia	16	Barbados	27
Uganda	19	China	14	Bolivia	26
Rwanda	18	Vietnam	14	Peru	23
Tunisia	17	Indonesia	13	Uruguay	22
Ghana	15	Thailand	11	Brazil	17
Mauritius	12	Iran	11	Argentina	17
Mali	7	Philippines	9	Guatemala	15
Egypt	5	Iraq	8	Dom. Republic	14
		Nepal	8	Mexico	14
		N. Korea	6	Ecuador	14
		India	5	El Salvador	13
				Cuba	12
				Honduras	12
				St. Lucia	11
				Nicaragua	10
				Haiti	10
				Venezuela	7

Senegal's high of 35 percent and Mali's seven percent; for Latin America, Panama's 38 percent compared to Venezuela's seven percent.[4]

Estimates of the total number of internal migrants are complicated by its many different forms, although estimates of these different types of movement also suggest the scale of the issue. The Internal Displacement Monitoring Centre (IDMC) (2021) estimates that over 33 million persons were forcibly displaced within their countries in 2019. Focusing on urbanization, the United Nations estimates that 77 million people

[3] Though geographically among the countries of Oceania, Fiji is one of the countries served by the UN Economic Commission for Asia and the Pacific.

[4] Venezuela's figure predates the economic and political collapse that has recently driven millions of Venezuelans to migrate, though most internationally to other South American countries.

migrate annually to cities (UN Habitat 2016). According to one estimate, China alone is home to some 200 million internal migrants, more than the world's total number of international migrants (Hamnett 2020, 693). The magnitude of internal migration is extensive, involving a wealth of humanity and having numerous social, economic, political, and other effects.

This book highlights the importance of internal migration, its many forms, why it offers promise, why it often goes wrong, and what can be done to improve it. We seek to bridge disparate approaches to internal migration, noting common challenges and focusing on the primacy of the state in managing internal migration. As will be discussed in Chapter 2, policy and scholarly work on internal migration is found in specialized subfields, such as urbanization, conflict IDPs, or displacement from development projects. Although a division of labor is useful, these and other subtypes are often blurry; for example, many IDPs become urban migrants, or are both conflict and economic migrants, since conflicts typically stymy local economic opportunities. There is a need to study internal migration holistically, including various subfields. To our knowledge, this is the first book to do so, despite long-standing calls by experts in the field to develop a more integrated approach to studying the various forms of internal migration (Skeldon 2018).

Internal migration should be understood as its own broad field, recalibrating concepts and tools derived from international migration. On the one hand, we can demonstrate the importance of internal migration by noting similarities with the more recognized aspects of international migration. For example, people may leave their homes for similar reasons, regardless of their destinations. Indeed, internal and international migration are not separate phenomena, with many international migrants starting as internal migrants but failing to integrate into new homes. It makes sense that many people would initially relocate closer to home, but then cross borders if this initial relocation does not work out. That said, many concepts from international migration are poor fits for the study of internal migration, which contains forms that are less common in international migration such as ecological migrants, urban migrants, and state-induced IDPs. As we will discuss below, an IDP is not simply a refugee who does not cross a border, as IDPs are pushed by especially diverse factors, lack legal recognition, and may expect or be expected to return. Further, internal migration is larger, more common, and more difficult to count. Perhaps most importantly, internal migration features very different roles for the state.

A core contribution of this book is to emphasize the primacy of the host state in managing internal migration, and the multiple levels of the state with varying degrees of responsibility and diversity of motives. Whereas international migration lacks on overarching sovereign, necessitating the role of international organizations, internal migrants remain under the authority of the host state at various levels. In some ways, this could be seen as better, as internal migrants possess citizenship and some protections. On the other hand, things can be worse if the state is the cause of their displacement and blocks external assistance. Government leaders often invoke sovereignty to get away with actions condemned by the international community. In other cases, national governments may want to help migrants, but are unwilling or unable to influence subnational governments that essentially view internal migrants as foreigners. This book seeks to demonstrate that the primary challenge is for state officials to "own" the consequences—and therefore the responsibilities—of managing internal migration, whether or not initiated by the state. State ownership does not mean that the state is alone; part of owning the problem may be to embrace international assistance.

The moral obligation of the state to manage internal migration is not restricted to national governments. In many cases, subnational authorities determine how material resources and participation are distributed among migrants and local people. At all levels of the state, opportunities exist to improve or worsen relations among migrants and host communities.

Given its scale, the vulnerability of many involved, and the absence of protection under international law, anyone interested in human well-being should care about internal migration. This is clearly true for IDPs. When the state forcibly relocates people to populate border areas, encourages assimilation, builds a megaproject, or occupies valuable land, those displaced tend to lack legal recourse, suffer cultural and social losses, and may lack compensation. Another important human aspect relates to the host communities, areas receiving large numbers of internal migrants. Sometimes, host communities enjoy considerable privilege, with disadvantaged migrants living at the edges of established society and exploited by residents. In other cases, migrants may be privileged, arriving with state support or from more developed areas, in effect colonizing less developed areas. Programs may seek to provide land to migrants from densely populated centers, representing welfare for one disadvantaged group while threatening another. Internal migration may be seen as a way to assimilate or disrupt ethnic minorities, including indigenous communities. The result can be violence, but also cultural loss and economic injustice.

In addition to obvious human dimensions, the impacts of internal migration are crucial for economic development. Classical theories of urban migration as well as rural-rural migration note how migration can make up for labor shortages. Internal migration represents a faster, easier way to satisfy labor demands than international migration. Many urbanizers leave behind rural poverty to find employment and provide for their families. For example, the mass migration of people from Thailand's poorest northeast region to Greater Bangkok has enabled industrial expansion while augmenting the incomes of northeasterners through remittances. Some state transmigration programs have led to new agricultural productivity and rising living standards. Done right, internal migration can enrich lives and promote economic development. That said, failures can generate serious losses. Countless states have sunk resources into internal migration schemes, only to see projects fail, migrants return or move to other unsustainable sites, and land remains untilled but already deforested.

A Roadmap

Having introduced the importance of internal migration and previewed its many forms and stakeholders, Chapter 2 provides a deeper conceptual overview and a review of the scholarly literature. Here, we note the difficulties in defining and measuring internal migration, which threatens to be an unwieldy concept. We observe that aside from valuable works on the conceptual connections among different forms of internal migration (Hugo 2006; Skeldon 1990, 2009), studies of internal migration tend to be divided into subfields such as urbanization, violence-driven IDPs, physical infrastructure IDPs, environmental refugees, state resettlement programs apart from assisting IDPs, and so on. There is considerable value in studying internal migration holistically, noting overlapping forms and some common responses.

With this groundwork laid, the chapters of Part I analyze the stakeholders in internal migration. Chapter 3 discusses the primacy of the state, a central difference between internal and international migration. The presence of an overarching sovereign state can make internal migration less of a problem, as migrants are citizens afforded rights and privileges, or it can make their situation far worse than the fate of millions of international migrants. Much depends on the policies, desires, and capacities of the host state. State officials often have the opportunity to evade accountability by ignoring migration conflicts, particularly those in remote areas.

Of course, the state is not monolithic, as national and subnational governments as well as different agencies may have distinct goals in managing internal migration, as examined in Chapter 4. States often fall short of assisting their people, even putting migrants and hosts at risk to achieve their goals. As a rejoinder, Chapter 5 discusses the importance of sympathizing with the state to some extent, as officials may be unable to effectively deal with internal migration.

Chapters 6–8 focus on internal migrants, separated into state-initiated and managed migrations (Chapter 6) and unmanaged migrants, including economic migrants (Chapter 7) and displaced persons (Chapter 8). In state-initiated migration, the state represents the primary catalyst, sending migrants from their homes to pursue economic, political, or strategic gains. Even where the state does not oversee the migration process, various agencies are intimately involved in the well-being of migrants. State-managed migration refers to situations in which communities are relocated for a variety of reasons, perhaps pushed out by natural disasters or choosing to relocate to frontier areas, and from there are managed by the state. In Chapters 7 and 8, we discuss unmanaged migrants, sometimes referred to—misleadingly—as spontaneous migrants. These people migrate on their own accord, with states typically remaining indifferent or hostile. In some cases, namely large-scale urbanization or migration to sensitive areas, we address the significance of states managing flows of migrants. In discussing persons expelled from their homes in Chapter 8, we discuss three primary causes of displacement: development, violent conflict, and ecological disasters.

Chapter 9 highlights groups whose interests are too often overlooked in studies of migration—host communities (and, briefly, sending communities). State attention to the needs of host communities is crucial in making internal migration work. Hosts may seek to exclude or exploit migrants, or may be excluded or exploited by them. The successful management of internal migration demands restricting abusive hosts and protecting abused ones. When migrants are favored by the state, it is essential also to provide for hosts to avoid conflict.

Having identified key stakeholders, Part II looks at what can go wrong, laying out various challenges and potential catastrophes. Chapter 10 examines the many forms of deprivation that often accompany internal migration. Here, we look at some of the social, economic, political, cultural, and ecological costs borne by migrants and hosts. Chapter 11 discusses violent migratory conflicts, the most destructive outcomes of poorly managed internal migration. "Sons of the Soil conflicts," in which groups demand to be dominant by virtue of their prior claims to the area, have a massive human toll and are notoriously difficult to overcome, threatening well-being and development around the world. Chapter 12 addresses state failures. Many state efforts to manage internal migration end in tragedy, as states suffer from various pathologies, with planners lacking proper information, refusing to think long-term, failing to consider other forms of migration, and failing to pay attention to host communities.

Part III examines what to do about the many challenges associated with internal migration. Chapter 13 dissects the accountability issues facing state institutions. An important implication is that state officials may be devious or timid in taking effective action. Overcoming these obstacles opens up opportunities to embrace some "best practices" from around the world, and innovative ways to handle migration and help integrate migrants into host communities. Of course, it is always problematic to detail successes, as any case will surely result in winners and losers. But try we will, documenting more or less successful approaches. Chapter 14 focuses on state policies. Here, we consider ways to improve communication across levels of government, noting that some of the most important policies will be enacted by subnational authorities. We also consider the potential for the decidedly illiberal policy of restricting internal migration to protect ecologically sensitive regions and culturally vulnerable communities. Recognizing limited state capabilities, Chapter 15 goes beyond state-centric analysis to examine how traditional leaders and civil society can help mitigate the worst effects of internal migration, providing governance and encouraging integration. Chapter 16 looks above the state, at the international community. Despite the centrality of the host state in managing internal migration, the international community must play prominent roles in pressuring and assisting the state, as well as advocating for the rights of internal migrants alongside host communities. Chapter 17 concludes with some broad lessons derived from our study.

The time is long overdue for a holistic assessment of strategies to safeguard the benefits of internal migration through an integrated analysis of migration motives and patterns. Of course, for each opportunity or risk, the specific needs of migrants and host communities must be addressed with the context-specific strategies, keeping in mind the migrations that may have preceded and the further migrations that may occur. Mass relocations within borders, be they state-initiated, state-managed, or unmanaged, affect the lives of hundreds of millions of people around the world. Internal migration can bring people to areas of greater prospects of productivity and security. It can reduce the motivation to undertake perilous efforts to migrate internationally. When it goes wrong, internal migration can lead to violence, poverty, ecological destruction, and cultural loss. This is too pressing a topic to ignore. Hundreds of millions of people are on the move, and scholars, NGOs, and policymakers must keep up.

References

Alexander, Peter, and Anita Chan. 2004. Does China Have an Apartheid Pass System? *Journal of Ethnic and Migration Studies* 30 (4): 609–629.

Barter, Shane, and Isabelle Côté. 2015. Strife of the Soil? Unsettling Transmigrant Conflicts in Indonesia. *Journal of Southeast Asian Studies* 46 (1): 60–85.

Bell, Martin, Elin Charles-Edwards Philipp Ueffing, John Stillwell, Marek Kupiszewski, and Dorota Kupiszewska. 2015. *Internal Migration and Development: Comparing Migration Intensities around the World*. Population Council.

Côté, Isabelle. 2019a. 'Adopting Migrants as Brothers and Sisters'—Fictive Kinship as a Mechanism of Conflict Resolution and Conflict Prevention in Lampung, Indonesia. In *Internal Migration: Challenges in Governance and Integration*, ed. Shane Barter and William Ascher, 97–111. New York: Peter Lang.

Côté, Isabelle. 2019b. Internal Migration, Political Liberalization, and Violent Conflict in Authoritarian China. In *People Changing Places: New Perspectives on Demography, Migration, Conflict, and the State*, ed. Isabelle Côté, Matthew I. Mitchell, and Monica Duffy Toft, 86–103. London: Routledge.

England, Vaudine. 2001. Indonesia's Greatest Failure. *South China Morning Post*. 18 July.

Ferris, Elizabeth. 2014. *Ten Years After Humanitarian Reform: How Have IDPs Fared?* Washington, DC: Brookings-LSE: Project on Internal Displacement.

Greenlees, Don. 1999. Unwanted Arrivals. *The Weekend Australian*. March 27.

Hamnett, Chris. 2020. Is Chinese Urbanisation Unique? *Urban Studies* 57 (3): 690–700.

Hedman, Eva Lotta, ed. 2008. *Conflict, Violence, and Displacement in Indonesia*. Ithaca: Southeast Asia Programme Publications, Cornell University.

Hugo, Graeme John. 2006. Forced Migration in Indonesia: Historical Perspectives. *Asia and Pacific Migration Journal* 15 (1): 53–92.

ILO (International Labour Organization). 2020. Road Map for Developing a Policy Framework for the Inclusion of Internal Migrant Workers in India.

IDMC (Internal Displacement Monitoring Center). 2021.*Global Report on Internal Displacement 2021: Internal Displacement in a Changing Climate*. Geneva: Internal Displacement Monitoring Center.

IOM (International Organization for Migration). 2020. *World Migration Report*. New York: United Nations.

Lecamwasam, Menaka. 2014. The Internally Displaced in South Asia: Lessons from Kampala. *Asia-Pacific Journal on Human Rights and the Law* 15 (1–2): 147–173.

Luedke, Alicia. 2019. Preventing and Responding to Sexual and Gender-Based Violence in and Around South Sudan's Protection of Civilian (POC) Sites. In *Internal Migration: Challenges in Governance and Integration*, ed. Shane Barter and William Ascher, 19–31. New York: Peter Lang.

Skeldon, Ronald. 1990. *Population Mobility in Developing Countries: A Reinterpretation*. London: Belhaven.

Skeldon, Ronald. 2009. *International Migration, Internal Migration, Mobility, and Urbanization: Towards More Integrated Approaches*. Geneva: IOM Publications.

Skeldon, Ronald. 2018. International Migration, Internal Migration, Mobility and Urbanization: Towards More Integrated Approaches. IOM Migration Research Series 53.

UN Habitat. 2016. *World Cities Report 2016: Urbanization and Development; Emerging Futures, United Nations Human Settlements Programme*. Nairobi: UN-Habitat.

Wallace, Jeremy W. 2014. *Cities and Stability: Urbanization, Redistribution, & Regime Survival in China*. Oxford: Oxford University Press.

Zea, Juan Esteban. 2019. How IDPs Navigate the Resettlement Process in Bogotá, Colombia. In *Internal Migration: Challenges in Governance and Integration*, ed. Shane Barter and William Ascher, 33–46. New York: Peter Lang.

CHAPTER 2

Understanding Internal Migration

Before moving into this book's core issues surrounding the actors, challenges, and best practices of internal migration, we provide a brief conceptual discussion. Internal migration is an expansive, deceptively tricky research and policy topic. It is notoriously difficult to measure, involves many forms, is rarely studied as a broad phenomenon, and differs in important ways from international migration.

Conceptualizing Internal Migration

Internal migration has the potential to be an unwieldy concept. Lucas (2021, 13) observes the immense complexity of measuring migration, since for any category, there "are no sharp boundaries, but rather continuums" where the author must define a cutoff. Technically, any individual who moves to a new house or down the hall to a new apartment is an internal migrant. Yet, our project is concerned with groups of people and larger patterns, with mass internal migration in which people relocate their primary residence for a substantial period (King and Skeldon 2010). Temporal aspects are important, as migration need not be permanent, but is also different from a local vacation or staying at a friend's house. Skeldon (2018, 4) notes that estimates of internal migration will differ considerably if we require more than four, or eight, or twelve months as

W. Ascher and S. J. Barter, *Moving within Borders*, Politics, Economics, and Inclusive Development, https://doi.org/10.1007/978-3-031-37549-1_2

the minimum of new residency. One way to think about the time horizons is that after a few months, perhaps when a new address is used for official correspondence, movement becomes migration. In terms of distance, early studies differentiated migrants from movers, with migrants crossing borders and movers relocating to familiar surroundings (Kosinski and Prothero 1975, 2). This brings up the question of where internal migration fits, whether those moving within national borders are migrants or movers. Kosinski and Prothero suggest that migration entails moving across major jurisdictions, including internal borders, and into different social contexts.

In this book, we adopt the Kosinski-Prothro focus on internal migration as streams of relocation within a country's national borders, but which cross significant subnational administrative and socio-cultural borders. This echoes Fitzgerald's (2008, 146) understanding of migration as "transborder," not limited to state borders, but also including subnational, administrative, and cultural boundaries. The important point is that internal migrants may find themselves treated differently by a new government or now live in a new cultural environment, considered outsiders by officials and residents.

For readers familiar with international migration, this book identifies some problems with approaching internal migration through the lens of international migration. While it is hardly straightforward to collect data on international migration, it is far more difficult to measure the volume and destinations of internal migration, as the presence of official immigration points, lower volume, and the considerable attention it receives ensure that somewhat reliable data exist for counting those who cross international borders. The difficulty of estimating the quantitative aspects of internal migration has been recognized for decades. For Todaro (1976, 64), "one of the most difficult and persistent problems" in studying internal migration patterns is "adequately measuring the major variables." For Kubát and Richmond (1976, 9), the study of internal migration "is beset with difficulties of proper measurement." Data may come from a national census, subnational residence records, or surveys, but these sources barely touch the realities in informal settlements or conflict zones, or the phenomena of return migration and secondary migration to yet another site. This is compounded by the many forms of internal migration, as specific measures are required and expertise may be useful in assessing urban migrations, IDPs, relocations, and rural-to-rural migration. The complexity of measuring internal migration has led some experts to conclude that "the search for a meaningful and consistent definition of a global estimate for the total number of internal migrants is largely illusory" (Skeldon 2018, 3). Thus, the IOM estimates cited in Chapter 1 of 740 million internal migrants in the world rests on uncertain foundations, and may well be conservative. What is clear, however, is that the scale of internal migration is immense and varied.

The relative complexity of internal migration lies in two facts: the causes of internal migration go beyond the causes of international migration, and the forms of internal migration are more interconnected. The dominant causes of *international* migration are the desire for a better life in a foreign context perceived to offer a stable and known set of opportunities, and flight from violence—refugees claiming a "well-founded fear of persecution" (Martin et al. 2005; Martin 2014; UNHCR 2019). *Internal* migrations can have both of these causes, plus the additional causes of dislocation due to natural disasters, state-directed resettlement, state-instigated changes in opportunities (e.g., highways inducing migration to previously inaccessible areas), and displacement to make way for physical infrastructure projects.

In contrast to the focus of most of the literature on one particular type of internal migration such as urbanization, specific IDPs, or voluntary resettlement, we highlight the need for a broad integrative approach that emphasizes the connections among different forms of migration. This rests on the obvious facts that multiple migrations may have occurred previously in the same area, and for any given individual or family, multiple migrations may occur under different circumstances and potentially for other motives (Lucas 2021, 275).

That internal migrants may fit multiple categories is clear in numerous examples:

- In Ethiopia, voluntary land-seeking rural-to-rural migration by Gedeo farmers led to conflict with local Gujis, forcing many Gedeos into displacement camps, with some poverty-stricken Gedeos migrating to cities.
- In Indonesia, Madurese in the state-directed "*Transmigrasi*" resettlement program migrated to rural West Kalimantan; many Madurese then migrated to urban areas, where conflicts with host communities led to violence that drove Madurese into IDP camps, then some were resettled by the state back to Madura and others to other towns in West Kalimantan.

- Rural Vietnamese urbanizers to Ho Chi Minh City have been expelled from the low-income areas to make way for profitable higher-rent developments; many settle in peripheral areas or return to rural areas.
- Rural Bolivians migrating first to La Paz, then migrate again, along with native Bogotanos, to more promising El Alto, a city built through state-financed physical infrastructure.
- Thai Buddhists, especially from the poor Northeast region, have been supported by the state to migrate to Muslim areas in the South; violence against the migrants has compelled many to return to the Northeast or to migrate to Bangkok or other cities outside of the South.
- In India, Bihari migrants to Mumbai suffer attacks from native Marathis, compelling many to leave Mumbai, migrating back to Bihar or to other states.
- Laotian hillside farmers, coercively resettled in low-land areas, have had reduced earnings, compelling some to move to Vientiane and other Laotian cities.
- Many of the poor drawn to the Brazilian Amazon by state-built highways and modest farming grants had to abandon failing Amazonian farms; prompting another migration: some to other farms, some migrating deeper into the forest as artisanal miners.

Another need for integrative analysis of internal migration's forms and motives is the common occurrence that the migration of one set of people triggers or facilitates the migration of others. An initial state-sponsored or unsponsored migration enables others to use the migratory infrastructure, or to be attracted by the destination and growing opportunities. An expulsion of one group often leads to another group moving into the vacated land. Or the arrival of one group, and the conflict or lack of resources that ensues, compels part of the host community to migrate, often resulting in rural-to-urban migration. Consider the following:

- The Amazonian highways mentioned above also drew miners, merchants, and so on; the old city of Manaus has become the seventh largest city in Brazil, with one of the highest urbanization rates in the country.

- Indonesia's Transmigration Program drew not only the formally enrolled resettlement migrants from the congested inner islands of Java, Bali, and Madura, but also unsponsored migrants. For Papua, it has been estimated that from 1970 to 2000, three unsponsored migrants arrived for every one sponsored transmigration migrant (McGibbon 2004, 23).
- Massive dams in China have displaced millions of rural people, directed by the state into existing and newly developed cities (Heming et al., 2001). While huge numbers of the displaced people have faced long-term hardships, many rural people from other areas have migrated to these better-developed cities.
- The Turkish army's expulsion of Kurds has left abandoned land available for both internal and international migrants.
- An extremely large set of conflicts triggered by the migration of groups to and within India's Northeast states has for decades led to the displacement of groups in the target areas, and then further migrations of these groups when they leave IDP camps.

Another reason to examine internal migration holistically is the potential to gather lessons across different forms of migration that could sensitize policymakers to the broad range of potential opportunities and risks, or to enlighten them in the ways to address other forms. Knowledge of how conflict can arise from resettlement programs can raise awareness of the warning signs of conflict arising from unmanaged migrations. When national policymakers consider whether to allow international agencies to provide assistance for conflict or development IDPs, the lessons of providing assistance to disaster IDPs may very well be relevant. When subnational governments refuse to accept IDPs from other states or provinces, there may be lessons available from the experiences of other forms of migration. By studying exclusion in slices, broader patterns may be obscured. When authorities allow international agencies to provide assistance for disaster IDPs, there may be something to learn in terms of conflict or development IDPs. In conflict cases, community-led cultural ceremonies to integrate new villages may be useful in helping to integrate urban migrants living in diverse slums. There is much to be gained by comparing insights from different subfields of internal migration, with a certain degree of cross-fertilization providing a better understanding of the challenges and solutions associated with internal migration.

Voluntary and Involuntary Internal Migration

Migration research commonly distinguishes between voluntary and involuntary migration. To be sure, some relocate more or less against their will, compelled by war, disasters, development projects, or state policies, while others relocate more voluntarily, such as economic migrants moving to cities or to claim land. But there are few cases where all aspects of migration are entirely forced or where no structural forces compel movement. Generally, when persons migrate within borders for reasons beyond their control, we emphasize the term "displaced," as the dislocation is thrust upon them. We should, however, be wary of terms such as "forced migration." As Turton (2003, 10) observes, "even in the most constrained of circumstances, human beings struggle to maintain some area of individual decision making—and those who succeed are those who survive best." IDPs still make decisions about when and how to leave, what and whom to bring, and where to go. In contrast, it is common to speak of those who migrate more voluntarily as "spontaneous" migrants, a term which makes it sound as if migrants relocate on a whim. We should also avoid framing migration as entirely voluntary, as those moving to find employment are typically pressured by economic need. Connecting these to other common terms, it can be said that migration that is compelled involves "push" factors, while that which is more voluntary involves a greater emphasis on "pull" factors (Petersen 1958).

Regardless of the degree to which internal migration is voluntary for the migrant, the arrival of newcomers is typically not at the discretion of the host communities. Even so, migrants may be welcomed if they bring valued goods and services (Van Der Wijst 1985; Hardjono 1986), and the state commits to provide adequate infrastructure and services to accommodate higher population density and potential clashes. Yet, a host of factors, ranging from occupational complementarity or competition to cultural affinity or antipathy, impact migrant-host community relationships. The relations between the two may be the deciding factor in successful integration (McGhee 2006). Indeed, this is a primary driver of conflict across the developing world, as resettlement is often emphasized over the long-term process of integration.

State-Initiated, State-Managed, and Unmanaged Migration

Related to the degree to which migration is voluntary, we can also recognize different degrees of state involvement. It is sometimes assumed that any instance of large-scale internal migration involves the state, or that any time the state is involved in managing migrants, its policies are responsible for the migration. In fact, the role of the state in internal migration can take many different forms. Sometimes, we can speak of state-initiated migration, where state agencies represent the cause of migration, the primary push factor. Here, if not for state policy, migration would not have occurred. As detailed in Chapter 3, this is carried out for a variety of reasons, including nation-building, national security, ethnic cleansing, economic development, ideological visions, ecological protection, and more. One should not, however, always equate state-initiated migration with involuntary migration. Many state resettlement programs relocate voluntary recruits from the landless poor, standing as a form of welfare.

A huge middle ground exists between state-controlled and so-called spontaneous, or voluntary, migration. Studying internal migration in Vietnam, Zhang et al. (2006) reject dichotomies of forced and voluntary, state and non-state migration, noting how internal migrants skirt state policies and gain indirect forms of state support. What we refer to as "state-initiated" migration involves state policies shaping flows, destinations, and ethnic relations in internal migration, but not formal resettlement programs.

Another potential level of state involvement is unmanaged migration, where migrants relocate independently of state programs. Whether the impetus to relocate is out of state hands due to natural disasters, armed conflict, economic opportunity, and so on, the state may be indifferent or hostile to such migratory flows or may benefit in some way from them. Initially, the state may play a minimal role in shaping the movement, scale, and well-being of migrants and host communities. Yet, very often the state becomes involved, either because of material deprivations or conflicts between the migrants and host communities.

We can also examine different levels of state involvement in host communities. Host communities facing the arrival of outsiders typically lack much support. It is possible that states initiate and manage migrants very closely, but offer little to host communities, thus stoking resentment. In their study of IDP resettlement in Ukraine, Balueva and Chuprina (2018) lay out the dangers of excluding host communities. Conversely, states may manage all aspects of migration, including programs for host communities that encourage integration.

It is also possible that migration is totally unmanaged by the state, but the state in some way supports host communities. Some migrations go against state policies, such as when Indian land-seekers without an "Inner Line Permit" illegally enter areas reserved for particular hill tribes. This is especially pronounced for rural-to-urban migration, resulting in squatter settlements in such countries as Brazil (Requia et al. 2016) and India (Doshi 2011; Datta 2012). More generally, for China and Vietnam with their hukou and ho khau home registration systems, individuals registered in their ancestral birthplace have been denied social services if they move to new areas (Fan 2008; Chan 2010; Wallace 2014; Anh et al. 2016; Quang et al. 2016).

Victims and Oppressors

An important part of conceptualizing internal migration is the relative power of migrant and host communities. Migrants and host communities may have positive synergies, yet depending on the cases that one has in mind, one might perceive migrants as oppressors, for example if economically advantaged communities with state support colonize peripheral minority or indigenous territories. Alternatively, migrants may be victims, such as rural poor arriving in cities or conflict IDPs facing persecution at the hands of established host communities. Established residents may use the tenuous status of migrants to their advantage, as sources of cheap labor. We should be wary of seeing either community as "good" or "bad," as migrants or hosts can be victims, aggressors, or both, depending on case-specific dynamics. That said, just because one group has power over another does not mean that its interests should be disregarded. A focus on the needs and insecurities of the dominant group is essential to avoiding conflict.

Fluid Categories

Another aspect of the complexity of internal migration is that the types involved are fluid. Situations can be complicated when there are different layers of migration and/or cross-cutting divisions. It is unclear how much time must pass before one is no longer considered a migrant, nor is it clear what conditions are necessary or how long must pass before one is considered part of the host community, or even native. In many cases, the migrant/native distinction is contested, as older migrant communities may make nativist claims against more recent migrant groups. Jackson (2006) observes that being native is a slippery category, allowing multiple degrees and meanings. In Malaysia, Malays and the native clans of Malaysian Borneo are formally classified as "indigenous" (Bumiputera, Sons of the Soil), even though the ancestors of the current "Orang Asli" clearly arrived earlier, but are designated as "original" but not indigenous. Long-standing migrant communities may align with indigenous peoples as newer migrant groups arrive. Many communities claim to be native but are perceived by indigenous communities as migrants (Madhavan and Landau 2011). Sometimes, native communities feature internal divisions, with some mixing with migrants, thus blurring native/migrant lines. Temporal factors are not everything, though, as the newest migrant group might be the most welcome if it shares religious or ethnic affinities with the indigenous group.

Categories of internal migrants are also fluid. For example, IDPs may be relocated to a new site, but then opt to move a second time to a nearby city, making them both involuntary IDPs and voluntary urban labor migrants. Refstie et al. (2010) note that many conflict IDPs in Uganda migrate to urban areas, so may no longer be recognized as IDPs and are denied assistance (see also Crispet al. 2012). Long (2008) notes that in Peru and beyond, migration is often multi-sited, with migrants moving back and forth, shifting between national and international, and being pushed out by mixed factors. It is common for people to be several types of migrants; once they have severed ties to their homes, a failure to integrate and find security may motivate secondary migration. As noted below, this is one of several reasons why internal migration should be approached holistically, alongside specialized subfields.

The fluid nature of internal migration can be illustrated with an anecdote from Indonesia, in one of several cases we will revisit throughout the book. In the 1970s, the Indonesian government undertook extensive *transmigrasi* policies, relocating people from the crowded islands of Java, Bali, and Madura to sparsely inhabited outer islands such as Sumatra, including the restive province of Aceh. Javanese migrant identities were complicated by the presence of Dutch-era Javanese communities as well as local intermarriage, the arrival of unsponsored Javanese migrants, and the fact that many state transmigrants returned to Java within a few years. Amidst Aceh's separatist conflict, rebels routinely exaggerated the scale of Javanese migration as well as tensions with migrants, championing a nativist Acehnese nationalism. In the early 2000s, the rebel movement began attacking Javanese migrants. State-sponsored Javanese migrants now became conflict IDPs, fleeing in many directions. In the provincial interior, Javanese IDPs allied with indigenous communities to form anti-rebel militias. Those fleeing to Aceh's coasts were soon forced to flee again as the conflict expanded, and again after the 2004 tsunami destroyed many IDP camps. At that point, some Javanese were simultaneously state transmigrants, conflict IDPs, and disaster IDPs. Those fleeing to neighboring provinces were met with combative local governments that turned them away; many eventually formed informal squatter communities in urban Medan or in rubber plantations. Others fled to Malaysia or Singapore, becoming international migrant laborers. Aceh's Javanese have existed as multiple forms of internal migrants, failing to fall neatly into a single category (Barter 2014).

From Holism to Fragmentation in Studying Internal Migration, and Hopefully Back

There are precedents to consider migration holistically. A classic demographic literature examined migration at the broadest level, encompassing internal and international flows. Many studies take E.G. Ravenstein's authoritative 1885 "laws of migration" as their point of departure, with internal migration carried out through a series of smaller moves instead of a larger leap all currents of migration produce "counter-currents" (Ravenstein 1885, 198–199). Lee (1966) posited a "Theory of Migration" that outlined the importance of push and pull factors, as well as intervening structural variables presumed to hold across the whole range of migrations: "no restriction is placed upon the distance of the move or the voluntary or involuntary nature of the act, and no distinction is made between external and internal migration" (Lee 1966, 49).

In the 1970s, scholars shifted toward more specialized studies of internal migration, particularly rural-urban migration in the pursuit of employment (Fields 1975). One of the major contributions, as well as limitations, of these studies was the use of neoclassical market models. Todaro (1976) borrows from economics in developing general laws of internal labor migration. The "Todaro migration model" emphasized that "migration can be explained primarily by the influence of economic factors," namely migrants' expected economic costs and benefits, such as employment opportunities. The "New Economics of Labor Migration" (Stark and Bloom 1985) provided a more fine-ingrained analysis of both internal and international migration, particularly with respect to urbanization, by positing that families can diversify their migration to reduce risk by having different family members take on different roles, often through young urbanizers sending remittances back home.

The market-based explanation for migration was later criticized for downplaying traits of specific migrant groups, including attitudes and culture (Stahl 1995), and for excluding the state. Fan (2008) notes that many studies of internal migration lack an emphasis on the role of the state, with the exception of centralized systems such as China. Neoclassical theories emphasize market forces to explain motivations for migration, with inadequate appreciation of how the state shapes motivations, as well as direct state resettlement. Crucially, many early case studies focusing on migration in the developing world did emphasize the centrality of the state—the state's role was so important, they had little choice. Bock and Rothenberg (1979) examine Mexico's state-planning agencies in creating new towns outside of Mexico City, noting that market-based models from developed countries are of limited use in understanding urban planning and internal migration in poorer, authoritarian countries. Jones and Richter (1982, 3) suggest that, unlike in the West, a considerable portion of internal migration in Southeast Asia is "either government-sponsored or indirectly promoted." Studies of China, India, and South Africa have focused both on state-managed migration and on state efforts to limit migration to certain places and for certain groups. For Oberai (1983), state internal migration policies are often ineffective, but it remains true that many states are intimately involved in managing internal migration.

The fragmentation of migration research into various subfields is a partial reflection of the very different motives behind migrations, as urbanization and export processing zones involve migration through economic incentives, while efforts to populate remote, ethnic-minority areas or displace people for megaprojects involve state policies. This also has been informed by differences between developed and developing countries, as migration in developed countries is primarily marked by labor migration, with pull factors, while the developing world has been home to many different forms of internal migration, including some primarily due to push factors, including state actions. As a result, we see specialized subfields.

Urban migration is a massive academic field, studying informal settlements/slums, urban sprawl, primary and satellite cities, and more. One of the most comprehensive studies of urban migration is Lucas' *Crossing the Divide* (2021), a book that uses extensive survey data to better understand the nature of internal migration to cities in developing countries. The study of forced displacement also has become specialized. In particular, the post-Cold War shift to study internal conflicts also spawned a new subfield focused on conflict IDPs. Cohen and Deng's *Masses in Flight* (1998) is one of the best-known comparative studies, noting that many conflict IDPs lack the protections and assistance provided to many refugees. IDP studies are typically policy-driven and case-specific, with many connected to research undertaken by international organizations such as the International Labor Organization (ILO), International Organization for Migration (IOM) and United Nations High Commissioner for Refugees (UNHCR). Since the 1990s, IDPs have received significant academic and policy attention, but migration research remains dominated by concerns with international migration, not surprising given the prestige of such journals as the *International Migration Review, International Migration,* and the *Journal of Refugee Studies*, though they do accept some articles on internal displacement. For Mooney (2005, 9), the perspectives on internal displacement have been too narrow: "For some, the term 'internally displaced persons' refers only to people uprooted by conflict, violence, and persecution, that is, people who would be considered refugees if they crossed a border." Below, we will return to the ways that internal migration rests uneasily alongside concern for international migration.

The study of internal migration through specialized subfields is especially true for urban migration and IDPs, whose experts talk to each other only rarely. The lack of communication, despite real-world overlap and similar concepts, has been noted by a handful of studies. Crisp et al. (2012, S23) observe that IDPs are increasingly "found not in camps or among host communities in rural areas, but in the towns and cities of developing and middle-income countries," demanding greater engagement with urban governments to provide assistance to IDPs, who may otherwise be seen as squatters.

Thus, although the more specialized studies of different forms and cases of internal migration are useful to illustrate specific dynamics, there is also good reason for the broad study of internal migration.

Internal and International Migration

Just as we assert in this book that internal migration should be studied holistically, one could also make the case that migration as a whole should be. Early studies, particularly by the geographers who synthesize socioeconomic aspects across regions (e.g., Pelzer 1945), did precisely this, demonstrating how push and pull factors can explain movement within as well as across borders. We agree that there is much to be learned from comparing internal and international migration, especially in terms of integration with host communities and the life cycle of migration (international migrants beginning as internal ones). This said, forms of internal migration are already studied in comparison with and through theories derived from international migration. Crucially, there are also underappreciated differences between internal and international migration, namely the centrality of the state.

Internal migrants are not entirely different from those crossing international borders. Nor are the sources of internal migration entirely different from international migration, as migrants may be pushed by violence, disasters, or state policies, or pulled by various opportunities to cities or special economic zones (SEZs) (Adepoju 1998). Although they do not cross international borders, internal migrants may cross significant internal borders, finding themselves in alien cultures or ecosystems. Many internal migrants are essentially undocumented migrants, lacking recognition by authorities and living in the shadows of local society. Perhaps most importantly, some of the humanitarian challenges faced by internal migrants are no less severe than for many international migrants. Although in theory, internal migrants are citizens protected by host states, in reality, governments—particularly on the subnational levels—may be indifferent or even hostile toward the migrants. International law and organizations extend protections to international migrants in ways that internal migrants do not enjoy. This is not to say that internal migrants are worse off than those relocating across borders, but, rather, that we have no reason to believe their conditions and needs are fundamentally different.

As a result of these similarities, it may not be surprising that the concepts, organizations, and scholarship dedicated to international migration often extend their mandate to internal migrants (Cohen and Deng 1998, 2–5). The UNHCR often deals with conflict IDPs, although it prioritizes international migrants. The organization and operation of IDP camps are typically modeled on refugee camps. Academic subfields such as migration studies and refugee studies often include research on internal migration and IDPs. Many of the organizations and concepts that deal with IDPs and other internal migrants are borrowed from international migration.

Despite some similarities with international migration, internal migration is distinctive in several ways. As noted, there are far more internal migrants than there are international migrants. Some forms of internal migration lack equivalent international forms. Although we do not consider moving within a narrow jurisdiction (e.g., a district) to constitute internal migration, the borders can be blurry, whereas international migration is more straightforward. An IDP is not the internal equivalent of a refugee, as a refugee is pushed out by a fear of persecution or violence, while IDPs may be pushed by a range of forces. Disaster and development IDPs generally lack international equivalents, as such migrants are typically expected to be relocated within their countries (Cernea 2006). Even focusing just on wars, scholars have found that IDPs and refugees flee in response to distinctive forms of violence (Moore and Shellman 2006). And while return migration is important for international migrants, internal migrants may be more likely to return home or repeat the same form of migration.

The differences between internal and international migration are most apparent when considering the stakeholders. Each of these actors is discussed in more detail in the chapters to come, but it bears noting how their situations vary in comparison with international migration. For the migrants themselves, internal migration and return migration may be easier, but humanitarian assistance may be less available and there is limited recourse to international law (Barutciski 1998). Internal migrants face distinctive challenges in dealing with authorities and are especially likely to relocate several times (Cattaneo and Robinson 2020; Rees et al. 2017).

The challenges facing the host communities are different as well. International migrants, although they may impose great burdens on host communities, may be less politically threatening to host communities than internal migrants, as their scale is often limited and flows regulated. Many host communities fear that internal migrants will bring further migration, with few laws available to limit further arrivals, and often state officials who actively promote new arrivals. Therefore, local communities may feel the need to be preemptively combative when internal migrants arrive, sparking conflicts (World Bank 2017).

Another key difference is in the role of the international community. Refugees face a precarious existence, but in theory, are protected by international law and various organizations. Mason (2018) notes that "unlike refugees, internally displaced persons do not have a universal convention to call their own." For Cohen (2006, 88), some groups displaced from the same place and for the same reasons receive different degrees of support, creating a "glaring disparity." In Chapter 16, we note the development of various regional and state-level agreements to protect IDPs, but they remain limited. International actors display only sporadic interest in internal migrants; Betts (2009) acknowledges that international migrants garner the vast majority of international attention, despite a need for focusing on conflict, development, and environmental IDPs. His study, however, focuses on international refugees. When international actors do look at internal migrants, they tend to be conflict IDPs.

One important reason for the limited attention to internal migrants from the international community is the presumption that each sovereign state has the responsibility to provide assistance to its internal migrants. Yet, in many circumstances, states lack the motivation, capacity, or both to safeguard internal migrants and the groups that they encounter. Muggah (2000, 213) suggests that assistance to IDPs should be "state-centric," "designed with the implicit recognition that states have a constitutional and international obligation to preserve and maintain the basic rights of its civilian population." The behavior of the state—at various levels from national to village jurisdictions—is the most important, fundamental difference between international and internal migration.

As this book shows, the roles of various state agencies and levels of government make internal migration distinctive and in need of dedicated research. As citizens, internal migrants have some claim to jobs and social services, which could make their situation more positive—unless the host community regards the migrants as serious economic threat. In addition, where host states cause distress that compels migration, or where they block international assistance efforts, internal migrants may face more challenges than do international migrants. As noted by Barutciski (1998, 11–12), some scholars suggest that refugees and IDPs should be approached similarly, but they are "forgetting one critical distinction in the plight of these two groups…by being outside of their country, refugees are in a fundamentally different situation according to the international legal order." He goes on to explain why the role of the state can be a complicating factor for IDPs: "One important consequence…is that the international community's access to IDPs can be limited or qualified. This is not the case with refugees."

The stakeholders described above will be discussed in more detail in the chapters of Part I, focusing on the roles of the state, the motivations of various types of internal migrants, and host communities. For now, the important takeaway is that these actors experience internal migration differently than do international migrants, again making the case for the dedicated study of internal migration. This chapter has discussed internal migration as a concept—definitions, data, and types—as well as provided a brief glimpse into the study of internal migration and made a case for the dedicated, holistic study of internal migration. With these foundations laid, we can move on to discuss the actors involved, the challenges, and then some ways to better manage internal migration.

References

Adepoju, Aderanti. 1998. Linkages between Internal and International Migration: The African Situation. *International Social Science Journal* 50 (157): 387–395.

Anh, Dang Nguyen, Gabriel Demombynes, and Linh Hoang Vu. 2016. Reforming Vietnam's Household Registration System. World Bank & Vietnam Academy of Social Sciences (VASS).

Balueva, Olga, and Elena Chuprina. 2018. Strategic Processes for the Internal Migration Processes Regulation in Ukraine. *Baltic Journal of Economic Studies* 4 (1): 16–24.

Barter, Shane Joshua. 2014. *Civilian Strategy in Civil War: Insights from Indonesia, Thailand, and the Philippines*. New York: Palgrave Macmillan.

Barutciski, Michael. 1998. Tensions between the Refugee Concept and the IDP Debate. *Forced Migration Review* 3: 11–14.

Betts, Alexander. 2009. *Forced Migration and Global Politics*. London: Wiley-Blackwell.

Bock, P.G., and Irene Fraser Rothenberg. 1979. *Internal Migration Policy and New Towns*. Champaign: University of Illinois Press.

Cattaneo, Andrea, and Sherman Robinson. 2020. Multiple Moves and Return Migration within Developing Countries: A Comparative Analysis. *Population, Space and Place* 26 (7): 1–21.

Cernea, Michael. 2006. Development-Induced and Conflict-Induced IDPs: Bridging the Research Divide. *Forced Migration Review* 261: 25–27.

Chan, Kam Wing. 2010. Crossing the 50 Percent Population Rubicon: Can China Urbanize to Prosperity? *Eurasian Geography and Economics* 53 (1): 63–86.

Cohen, Roberta. 2006. Developing an International System for Internally Displaced Persons. *International Studies Perspectives* 7 (2): 87–101.

Cohen, Roberta, and Francis Deng. 1998. *Masses in Flight: The Global Crisis of Internal Displacement*. Washington: Brookings Institution Press.

Crisp, Jeff, Tim Morris, and Hilde Refstie. 2012. Displacement in Urban Areas: New Challenges, New Partnerships. *Disasters* 36 (S1): S23–S42.

Datta, Ayona. 2012. *The Illegal City: Space, Law and Gender in a Delhi Squatter Settlement*. Burlington, VT: Ashgate.

Doshi, Sapana. 2011. *The Right to the Slum? Redevelopment, Rule, and the Politics of Difference in Mumbai*. Diss. Berkeley, CA: University of California.

Fan, C. Cindy. 2008. Migration, Hukou, and the Chinese City. In *China Urbanizes: Consequences, Strategies, and Policies*, ed. Shahid Yusuf and Tony Saich, 65–89. Washington, DC: World Bank.

Fields, Gary S. 1975. Rural-Urban Migration, Urban Unemployment and Underemployment, and Job-Search Activity in LDCs. *Journal of Developmental Economics* 2 (2): 165–187.

Fitzgerald, David. 2008. Colonies of the Little Motherland: Membership, Space, and Time in Mexican Migrant Hometown Associations. *Comparative Studies in Society and History* 50 (1): 145–169.

Hardjono, Joan. 1986. "Transmigration: Looking to the Future." *Bulletin of Indonesian Economic Studies* 22 (2): 28–53.

Heming, Li, Paul Waley, and Phil Rees. 2001. "Reservoir Resettlement in China: Past Experience and the Three Gorges Dam." *Geographical Journal* 167 (3): 195–212.

Jackson, Stephen. 2006. Sons of Which Soil? The Language and Politics of Autochthony in Eastern DR Congo. *African Studies Review* 49 (2): 95–124.

Jones, Gavin W., and Hazel V. Richter. 1982. Introduction. In *Resettlement Programs in Southeast Asia*, eds. Gavin W. Jones and Hazel V. Richter. Canberra: Australian National University.

King, Russell, and Ronald Skeldon. 2010. 'Mind the Gap!' Integrating Approaches to Internal and International Migration. *Journal of Ethnic and Migration Studies* 36 (10): 1619–1646.

Kosiński, Leszek A., and R. Mansell Prothero. 1975. Data and Measures in Migration Research. In *People on the Move: Studies on Internal Migration*, eds. Leszek Kosiński and R. Mansell Prothero, 1–17. New York: Taylor & Francis.

Kubát, Daniel, and Anthony H. Richmond. 1976. Introduction. In *Internal Migration: The New World and the Third World vol. 4*, eds. Daniel Kubát and Anthony H. Richmond. Beverly Hills, CA: Sage Publications.

Lee, Everett S. 1966. A Theory of Migration. *Demography* 3 (1): 47–57.

Long, Norman. 2008. Translocal Livelihoods, Networks of Family and Community, and Remittances in Central Peru. In *Migration and Development Within and Across Borders: Research and Policy Perspectives on Internal and International Migration*, eds. Josh DeWind and Jennifer Holdaway, 39–70. Geneva: IOM.

Lucas, Robert E.B. 2021. *Crossing the Divide: Rural to Urban Migration in Developing Countries*. Oxford: Oxford University Press and KNOWMAD.

Madhavan, Sangeetha, and Loren B. Landau. 2011. Bridges to Nowhere: Hosts, Migrants, and the Chimera of Social Capital in Three African Cities. *Population and Development Review* 37 (3): 473–497.

Martin, Susan F. 2014. *International Migration: Evolving Trends from the Early Twentieth Century to the Present*. New York: Cambridge University Press.

Martin, Susan F., Patricia Weiss Fagen, Kari M. Jorgensen, Andrew Schoenholtz, and Lydia Mann-Bondat. 2005. *The Uprooted: Improving Humanitarian Responses to Forced Migration*. Lanham, MD: Lexington Books.

Mason, Elisa. 2018. Internally Displaced Persons: Guide to Legal Information Resources on the Web. Forced Migration Current Awareness. https://fm-cab.blogspot.com/p/idps.html.

McGhee, Derek. 2006. Getting 'Host' Communities on Board: Finding the Balance between 'Managed Migration' and 'Managed Settlement' in Community Cohesion Strategies. *Journal of Ethnic and Migration Studies* 32 (1): 111–127.

McGibbon, Rodd. 2004. Plural Society in Peril: Migration, Economic Change, and the Papua Conflict. *East-West Center Policy Studies* 13.

Mooney, Erin. 2005. The Concept of Internal Displacement and the Case for Internally Displaced Persons as a Category of Concern. *Refugee Survey Quarterly* 24 (3): 9–26.

Moore, Will H., and Stephen M. Shellman. 2006. Refugee or Internally Displaced Person? To Where Should One Flee? *Comparative Political Studies* 39 (5): 599–622.

Muggah, H.C.R. 2000. Conflict-Induced Displacement and Involuntary Resettlement in Colombia: Putting Cernea's IRLR Model to the Test. *Disasters* 24 (3): 198–216.

Oberai, A.S. 1983. *An Overview of Migration-Influencing Policies and Programmes*. New York: St. Martins Press.

Pelzer, Karl J. 1945. *Pioneer Settlement in the Asiatic Tropics*. New York: American Geographical Society Special Publication No. 29.

Petersen, William. 1958. A General Typology of Migration. *American Sociological Review* 23 (3): 256–266.

Quang, Binh Bui, Thi Thu Ha Nguyen, and Chuong Ong Nguyen. 2016. Internal Migration in the Context of Trade Liberalisation in Vietnam. *Malaysian Journal of Economic Studies* 53 (2): 195–209.

Ravenstein, Ernst G. 1885. The Laws of Migration. *Journal of the Statistical Society of London* 48 (2): 167–235.

Rees, Philip, M. Bell, Martin Bell, Marek Kupiszewski, Dorota Kupiszewska, Philipp Ueffing, Bernard Aude, Elin Charles-Edwards, and John Stillwell. 2017. The Impact of Internal Migration on Population Redistribution: An International Comparison. *Population, Space and Place* 23 (6): 20–36.

Refstie, Hilde, Chris Dolan, and Moses Chrispus Okello. 2010. Urban IDPs in Uganda: Victims of Institutional Convenience. *Forced Migration Review* 34: 32–33.

Requia, Weeberb J., Henrique Llacer Roig, Petros Koutrakis, and Maria Silvia Rossi. 2016. Mapping Alternatives for Public Policy Decision Making Related to Human Exposures from Air Pollution Sources in the Federal District, Brazil. *Land Use Policy* 59: 375–385.

Skeldon, Ronald. 2018. International Migration, Internal Migration, Mobility and Urbanization: Towards More Integrated Approaches. IOM Migration Research Series 53.

Stahl, Charles W. 1995. Theories of International Labor Migration: An Overview. *Asian and Pacific Migration Journal* 4 (2–3): 211–232.

Stark, Oded, and David Bloom. 1985. The New Economics of Labor Migration. *American Economic Review* 75 (2): 173–178.

Todaro, Michael P. 1976. *Migration and Economic Development: A Review of Theory, Evidence, Methodology and Research Priorities*. Nairobi: University of Nairobi.

Turton, David. 2003. Conceptualising Forced Migration. RSC Working Paper No. 12: Working Paper Series. Oxford: University of Oxford.

UNHCR (United Nations High Commissioner for Refugees). 2019. What is a Refugee? Available at www.unrefugees.org/refugee-facts/what-is-a-refugee/

Van Der Wijst, Ton. 1985. Transmigration in Indonesia: An Evaluation of a Population Redistribution Policy. *Population Research and Policy Review* 4 (1): 1–30.

Wallace, Jeremy W. 2014. *Cities and Stability: Urbanization, Redistribution, & Regime Survival in China*. Oxford: Oxford University Press.

World Bank. 2017. *Forcibly Displaced: Toward a Development Approach Supporting Refugees, the Internally Displaced, and their Hosts*. Washington, DC.

Zhang, Heather X., P. Mick Kelly, Catherine Locke, Alexandra Winkels, and W. Neil Adger. 2006. Migration in a Transitional Economy: Beyond the Planned and Spontaneous Dichotomy in Vietnam. *Geoforum* 37 (6): 1066–1081.

PART I

Stakeholders: The State, Migrants, and Hosts

The following several chapters present the remarkable variety of outlooks and actions of the three most important stakeholders in the drama of internal migration: states, migrants, and host communities. This section emphasizes the multiplicity of motives behind the actions of the state and the migrants, as well as the broad range of circumstances that trigger and accompany migrations. Anticipating the outlooks of migrants and host communities is crucial for understanding feelings of threat and deprivation, and the resulting mobilization to engage in destructive conflict. The outlooks also rest on the psychology of the interactions among migrants, host communities, and state officials.

Chapters 3–6 focus on the state, the dominant but not always coherent actor in governing internal migration.

Chapter 3 clarifies why the state is so central to the fate of migrants and host community members, even when its role is not obvious. The posture of the state is always in play, whether initiating, restricting, managing, or allowing migrations to proceed unchecked. Once migrations have occurred, decisions on the nature of state presence and whether state action will tilt in favor of the migrants or the host communities are then crucial.

Chapter 4 analyzes vertical and horizontal divisions in the state, as different levels of government and state agencies may have competing interests when it comes to migration-related policies. This discussion emphasizes the complexities that stem from the fact that the state is not a unitary actor. Enumerating the roles and failures of the state to govern internal migration provides ample opportunities to criticize the shortcomings of state actions, a necessary diagnosis for guiding reforms in state approaches. However, critiques of state approaches need to be balanced with an appreciation for the difficult challenges that state officials face.

Chapter 5 thus explains why it is worthwhile to have sympathy for the difficulty of managing the bewildering array of migration patterns. Internal migration reflects different circumstances and frequently involves different forms of migration occurring at the same time, as populations flow to and from cities and the countryside, along with rural-to-rural and urban-to-urban migrations at the same time. State institutions often operate under severe resource constraints and poor information regarding migration patterns. All of this makes governance difficult for even the most well-meaning governments.

Chapters 6–8 bring home how the single label "migrant" obscures distinctive migratory contexts. As the most direct link between the state and the migrants, the state-initiated and managed migrations discussed in Chapter 6 place migrants in a position of varying degrees of dependency on the state. This chapter explores the implications of coerced and voluntary migrations, recognizing that the distinction is not as sharp as it seems. Analyzing the implications of state involvement is important because it often means that migrants are state clients and are therefore more likely to be favored when officials arbitrate conflicts. However, migrations sometimes reflect state coercion to move populations against their will. The following two chapters examine the circumstances of migrants whose movements are not overseen by the state. Most urbanization falls into this category, as well as land-hungry and entrepreneurial migrants arriving in rural areas—the enterprising migrants who are the focus of Chapter 7. Chapter 8, then, looks to the expelled, various types of IDPs and the role of the state in shaping as well as responding to their movements.

In unmanaged migrations, relations between migrants and host communities may depend on the compatibility of the groups, their resources, whether the state will intervene if conflicts arise, and, if so, whether the state will favor some over others. Therefore, the circumstances and outlooks of members of the host community are especially important, as explored in Chapter 9. Host communities typically have little say in the decisions on migration flows. Sometimes host community members reject internal migrants, while at other times they may welcome the resources and opportunities that they bring. Even in the latter cases, interactions are dynamic, and initial enthusiasm may sour as competition arises. In extreme cases, this can lead to bloodshed and expulsion. As a result, any discussion of internal migration must also focus on the responses and well-being of host communities.

CHAPTER 3

The Primacy of the State

For fifty years, the Brazilian Amazon has experienced extensive deforestation, stripping away one of the world's largest rainforests and accelerating global warming. At the heart of the Amazon's deforestation has been the rise of agriculture, largely through farms operated by internal migrants. Migration has also brought attention to public health concerns as well as to the user rights of indigenous peoples. Beginning in the 1960s, migration into the Amazon expanded considerably and has continued ever since. The link between deforestation and internal migration is sometimes misunderstood, seen as driven by economic need and market forces. Perz et al. (2010, 459) judged that: "In the 1970s and 1980s, migration to roadside settlement frontiers of the Brazilian Amazon proceeded at a rapid pace… Most such migration was spontaneous, and the demographic flood in many road corridors overwhelmed state agencies."

Yet, Amazonian migration has never been fully "spontaneous," as it was intimately shaped by state policies. Perz et al. (2010) refer to the large number of migrants taking part in direct action land reform, as opposed to those formally resettled by the state. But even those relocating on their own accord do so utilizing roads and other infrastructure created by the state. Massive road-building initiatives into the Amazon began in the 1960s under the military government, motivated by a drive to extract resources, resettle potentially rebellious landless poor, and settle

W. Ascher and S. J. Barter, *Moving within Borders*, Politics, Economics, and Inclusive Development,
https://doi.org/10.1007/978-3-031-37549-1_3

border areas—the latter under the slogan of "occupy it or surrender it." The shift toward settling the Amazon, including deforestation and the loss of indigenous rights, came about through state policy. For Wood (2002, 21), "the exploitation and settlement of the Amazon was aggressively promoted by the federal government, then in the hands of the Brazilian military. Development policies designed to populate the region included credit and tax incentives to attract private capital to the region, the construction of the Transamazon Highway, and the colonization of small farmers on 100-hectare plots." State promotion of Amazonian migration, sometimes with small-holder land titles and modest grants, made the Amazon a more attractive destination than it would have been without state incentives.

That said, opportunities were routinely exaggerated by Brazilian authorities. They had rushed to promote Amazonian migration without undertaking adequate agricultural assessments to know where farming would be suitable. As a result, small-scale farming largely failed in the Amazon's poor soils, leading would-be farmers to take up dangerous prospecting and encroaching into state-protected reserves. Just as state policy accelerated internal migration to the Amazon, some of the many problems associated with this migration have resulted from the absence of state planning. Whether farms succeeded or failed, the result remained massive deforestation and habitat loss driven by internal migration.

This example draws attention to the importance of recognizing how and why the state must be the predominant focus in analyzing internal migration, even if the normative focus of this book is on the well-being of migrants and host communities. It first explains the bases of much greater discretion held by the state than other actors involved in internal migration. It emphasizes the complexity of this discretion by noting that the state is not a unified actor. Because the state's discretion is employed in pursuit of many different objectives in different cases, the chapter then summarizes potential state motives. To understand the stance that state actors take toward migrants and host communities, we review the most important psychological insights into state officials' biases and interactions with migration stakeholders. The chapter then addresses how the range of discretion creates issues of accountability and perverse consequences of state actions.

The State's Discretion

State officials typically have far more discretion than other actors in shaping patterns of migration. Migrants have some discretion in deciding whether and where to move, but frequently this is decided within the constraints established by the state. Host communities typically have even less discretion; if migrants arrive, host community members may decide to accommodate or resist—a narrow set of alternatives. In contrast, state officials may coerce, sponsor, initiate, manage, ignore, or block migrations. They typically decide how much state presence the target areas will have. They decide on whether and how much state resources will be devoted to the migration and the host site. And they decide whether to favor migrants or host communities should conflicts arise.

Unlike migrants and host communities, state actors have, at least in principle, a broad range of options regarding internal migration. Table 3.1 displays these options, ranging from coercive resettlement to blocking migration, and many of the motives behind this array of options. The importance of the state is most obvious for formal resettlement programs or state-initiated displacements. Yet, as the Brazilian case indicates, states may instigate migration through actions short of formal sponsorship. Physical infrastructure provides a greater opportunity to migrate. Providing incentives to some migrants, thereby signaling that the area is attractive, can popularize migration to others. And conveying that the migrants will be favored if clashes with host communities occur can be encouraging as well.

It is true as well that in many circumstances, the state can take decisive action to reduce hostilities among migrants and host communities. Even if groups have the means to reconcile their own conflicts, the state may block or perhaps endorse these initiatives. For example, in 1998, Ethiopian officials from the federal, regional, and local levels participated along with leaders of the Gedeo and Guji ethnic communities in a shared traditional reconciliation process to put an end to a violent conflict (Dagne 2013, 223). While the agreement to cease hostilities was backed by beliefs that violators would be cursed, state involvement helped build confidence that state officials would not subvert the intergroup agreement.

The pervasiveness of the state in population dynamics is even apparent in migrations that do not occur. States also play active roles in limiting migration, despite Article 13 of the Universal Declaration of Human

Table 3.1 State Mechanisms and Motives

State-managed migration	
Coercive	
Expulsion without a specific destination	• Permit physical infrastructure (roads, dams, solar arrays, windmills, nature reserves, and/or manufacturing) (India) • Reduce the power of rival groups • Confiscate assets or jobs from the expelled people • Change the political balance
Coercive resettlement	• Promote economic activity (Ethiopia; Empire) • Permit physical infrastructure (roads, dams, solar arrays, windmills), nature reserves, and/or manufacturing (India) • Consolidate political control (Ethiopian and Tanzanian villagization) • Change the political balance (Ethiopia Derg; Empire)
Non-coercive	
Voluntary state-sponsored resettlement	• Promote economic activity • Reduce population pressures (Indonesian *transmigrasi*; Indian Dandakaranya) • Acculturate host-community members (Indonesia, India; both regarding remote minorities) • Divert migrations from other areas (Brazilian Amazon)
State-initiated migration	
Migration-enabling infrastructure	• Facilitate migrants' transport to sites (Brazilian Amazon road building) • Make living at the migration site more attractive through physical infrastructure improvement (Thailand: housing for Northern and Northeastern Buddhist migrants to the Muslim-populated South) • Divert migrations from other areas (Brazilian Amazon)
Increasing the security risks in the origin site	• Promote flight from the origin site, through state threats of physical harm or permitting non-state actors to threaten or harm

(continued)

Table 3.1 (continued)

Granting access to developers through eminent domain	• Promote infrastructure for economic or environmental projects
Recognizing new land claims	• Encourage land-seeking migration (Brazilian Amazon)
Establishing satellite cities	• Encourage peri-urbanization
Managing migration patterns	
Channeling migration to specific areas and/ or restricting it from other areas	• Avert conflict • Protect ecosystems • Maintain economic activities in the areas of origin • Control the burden of social service provision • Manage political balance

Rights (UDHR), which guarantees free movement of citizens within their country. There is a long history of limiting internal migration. In colonial India, the British restricted migration to tribal regions through the 1900 Hill Tracts Manual, which placed severe restrictions on the settlement of outsiders (Chakma and Maitrot 2016, 4–5). The 1920 Line System strengthened these restrictions, blocking Muslim Bengali migrants from Buddhist and animist regions. With independence, these restrictions were lifted, leading to waves of internal migration and a series of violent conflicts (Chakma and Maitrot 2016, 10). Scriven (2010, 21–22) recounts the problems confronting Brazilian and Peruvian conservation efforts when an unexpectedly large number of migrants poured into the Amazon. In Indonesia, spontaneous migrants relocating alongside Javanese state transmigrants to Papua significantly increased the volume of in-migration. This led to dissatisfaction among native Papuans, as unsponsored migrants, especially entrepreneurs from nearby eastern islands (largely ethnic Bugis, Butonese, and Makassarese), dominated urban economies and some agricultural sectors (Tadjoeddin and Chowdhury 2009, 40). Many states have created restrictions on migration to urban areas or from poorer areas to richer ones, sometimes through internal passports, often to restrict indigenous communities and other minorities, a system infamously applied in the Soviet Union's *propiska* policies and South Africa's pass system. One primary example discussed in later chapters is China's *hukou* system. In Vietnam, the governments of Ho Chi Minh City and Hanoi have restricted urban migration through administrative measures (Quang et al. 2016, 208). New Order Indonesia restricted ethnic Chinese from moving to rural areas. The government of Singapore has created laws to avoid ethnic enclaves, restricting the ability of its people to sell their houses and relocate (Sim et al. 2003).

State officials also typically have the discretion to decide whether to give standing to domestic non-state organizations, such as non-governmental organizations (NGOs), to assist migrants and/or host communities, or to undermine NGO efforts. State actions to muzzle NGOs can range from obstacles to registration, denying them financial assets, expulsion, or violence.

When international actors try to mitigate deprivations suffered by migrants or host communities, they typically operate through the state or at its sufferance. Bilateral or multilateral aid agencies generally have to channel resources through the state bureaucracy, providing opportunities for officials to hold up or divert disbursements. Even when powerful international actors operate on the ground, such as UNHCR IDP camps, the doctrine of national sovereignty limits their discretion. In South Sudan, the UNHCR is not permitted to send guards to protect women who must venture beyond the boundaries of IDP camps (Luedke 2019). International NGOs are even more beholden to state officials than are intergovernmental organizations. After the 2004 tsunami in Aceh, Indonesian authorities allowed NGOs to assist disaster IDPs but blocked them from assisting conflict IDPs (Barter 2019; Zeccola 2011). In 2009, international NGOs were expelled from Darfur IDP camps by the Sudanese government.

No wonder state agencies and levels of government bear so much responsibility when migrations go poorly. Many activists rightly criticize state officials for initiating unsound migrations, resorting to coercion, maltreating migrants or host communities, infringing on people's rights to migrate, or turning a blind eye to problems that migrations create. They can be unwilling to devote adequate resources to relieve the resource strains in resettlement areas or unwilling to place sufficient staff in contentious areas. And, as some of the motivations listed in Table 3.1 indicate, state officials may use migration as a means to strengthen their control vis-à-vis either the area of origin or the target area, reduce the power of rival groups, manipulate political balances, weaken challenges to state authority, and appropriate resource revenues that otherwise would be captured by residents.

State officials at different levels often contend over who should have how much authority to gain these advantages. Thus, we need to take an open-minded view in assessing state actions. Conceiving of the state as multiple actors with multiple interests is crucial for going beyond equally naïve views: that state officials are trying to maximize the well-being of migrants and host communities or that state actors only care about their own interests.

The Complexity of the State

When we say that the state is not monolithic, we mean that state actors serve at different levels of government and different agencies within each level. The shorthand of speaking of the "the state" (or "the government") masks different mandates, interests, viewpoints, capacities, and potentials. State agencies often feature distinct roles and motivations regarding internal migration. Some, such as those related to the environment or indigenous peoples, may oppose migration promoted by security or business officials. Even more likely is that levels of state administration often have different stances toward migration, leading to vertical clashes within the state. National governments typically are more likely to promote migration, with subnational governments opposing migrations that challenge the local ethnic balance and put greater stress on local resources. The inverse also may be true, as national governments may be indifferent, while subnational governments support various forms of migration to promote development and alter demographics.

State Motives

Having demonstrated the striking range of state involvement, it is important to highlight the intricate range of state motivations—listed but not elaborated in Table 3.1.

Economic Motives

The motives to enhance economic productivity may focus on either the migrants' original location or the resettlement location. Motives also differ in terms of whether they focus on the productivity of the area once people are expelled or on the productivity of the resettled people.

To Control Land. Expelling people from their original location may be motivated by a desire to transform their home region and generate profits. Physical infrastructure projects such as hydroelectric dams or SEZs often entail the removal of residents. Whether the state provides compensation or relocation assistance, and to what degree, is a major issue in many countries.

Controversies over the displacement of people from SEZs or areas with equivalent designations often center on accusations of corruption because of limited or absent compensation for displaced people. In India, Yadav (2019) shows that despite the presence of state-mandated compensation, the creation of SEZs often does not provide for displaced poor communities that are left to mobilize in defense of their rights. Controversies over SEZ displacement often center on unjust compensation or outright expropriation, sometimes involved with corruption. This vulnerability is heightened by the fact that many areas are home to people without formal property rights.

States may displace communities to provide infrastructure and energy. The final report of the World Commission on Dams (2000) proposes guidelines for dealing with displaced people, but many problems persist. Because of the magnitude of financial commitments required to construct major hydroelectric dams, financing often involves bilateral and multilateral foreign assistance agencies. In such cases, these agencies, representing individual donor countries or the international community more broadly, take on obligations to treat displaced people fairly. Controversies over hydroelectric dams rarely fail to mention the inadequacy of efforts to leave the displaced people no worse off than their pre-displacement situation.

States may compel forced migration from urban areas as well, removing informal settlements as a means to seize precious property. In many countries, few adequately remunerative economic opportunities exist outside of capital cities, stimulating migration from rural areas. As migrants arrive in urban areas, they inhabit the few urban spaces not currently used—marginal geographies such as steep slopes, swamps, edges of infrastructure or rivers, underneath highways, graveyards, and similar locations. As local police accept bribes and protection fees, urban "squatters" often pay de facto rent and may inhabit land for significant periods. They may even improve their land, and as surrounding land becomes more valuable, their presence may become tenuous. This can lead to mass expulsions in the form of arrests, raids, fires, and bulldozing, as local governments and developers seek to control urban space. As squatters resist expulsion, states then face dilemmas regarding how to respond. Hardoy and Satterthwaite (2014) examine "squatter citizens" across the Global South, observing the policy dilemmas facing city and national governments, but also the disastrous outcomes of slum removal. Among many examples, they note clashes between local government removal teams and informal communities in Buenos Aires in the 1980s, in which 20,000 residents successfully resisted violent raids and state exclusion (Hardoy and Satterthwaite 2014, 12).

One policy question the state must consider is whether expulsion should or should not be accompanied by a detailed resettlement plan for one or more targeted areas. Of the three options facing states intent on expelling people—simply expelling them without compensation, expelling them with compensation, or providing support for relocation to resettlement locations—a specific resettlement initiative obviously entails greater state involvement.

To Control Resources. The most aggressive motive for expulsion is to expropriate belongings, jobs, or firms. Whether state leaders try to justify seizures as "spoils of war" or invoke the perceived disloyalty of the expelled people, whatever is left behind by mass relocations can be taken by the state or by other residents. Some of the best-known cases involve postcolonial transitions. In the former Rhodesia, Mugabe's government forcibly evicted white settlers and confiscated their property, in which initially more regulated and compensated seizures of land gave way to more violent, militia-led attacks (Shaw 2003). In many former colonies, independence leaders nationalized colonial properties and businesses ruled by settlers, forcing the dispossessed to relocate. It is also common for states to remove indigenous peoples from lands to seize property or to control resources such as timber or gems.

To Stimulate Economic Productivity. While productivity may be pursued (though not always successfully) through the above-mentioned projects, other productivity-seeking initiatives focus on the gains expected away from the migrants' home area. State leaders may believe that productivity can be enhanced by bringing people to other, specific sites. These are typically, at least to begin with, rural regions.

Agricultural productivity has been a dominant concern for many postcolonial leaders, often involving radical re-engineering of agricultural systems. Some populations in drought or flood-prone areas have been resettled to regions where agriculture is believed to be more sustainable. The Derg, Ethiopia's Marxist military government (1974–1987), decided to resettle one and a half million people from the drought-prone north to the South and Southwest, with more than 600,000 resettled by 1986 (Ofcansky and Berry 1991). The fact that many people fled from the government's resettlement effort greatly complicated the overall program. Farming by scattered populations has sometimes been seen as inadequately productive, either because of a lack of marketing economies of scale or the difficulties of farming cooperatives. Similarly, Nyerere's villagization in post-independence Tanzania aimed at concentrating populations to engage in collective production (Lofchie 2014, 80–83). In both cases, ideological orientations played large roles. Not only did the Derg resettle people out of climatic concern, it also "used [common] lands to undertake resettlements, villagization and socialist agriculture in the forms of state farms and producer cooperatives" (Srur 2013, 21).

When state leaders believe that an area has potential for higher productivity through additional population, regardless of where the settlers originate, the resettlement approach may range from active sponsorship, such as Indonesia's *transmigrasi* and India's Dandakaranya, to less direct enabling actions such as Brazil's Amazonian highway expansions.

Providing capital and infrastructure for regional development through industrial zones in economically underdeveloped areas also may induce migration. Whether or not the state intends to provide employment for locals, job opportunities may attract migrants from other areas. For example, efforts at industrial decentralization in Greater Bangkok have created a magnet for jobseekers to move to newly established development zones outside of the Bangkok core. For Mills (2012, 90), "Communities in the vicinity of such development zones have experienced forms of rural 'suburbanization' as formerly agricultural villages become service and dormitory centers for new factories whose employees are typically migrants from more distant areas."

Political Motives

It is difficult to disentangle economic from political motives for state-managed migration. Clearly, economic programs that benefit particular groups can increase support for the government and strengthen the resources of these groups in political competition with others. However, when states encourage migration that sacrifices economic gain, we may more clearly recognize political motivations for such policies. Politically motivated state-managed migration may be carried out for several, often complementary reasons.

Rewarding Supporters. Insofar as migration is seen to benefit migrants, the state might sponsor migration to reward existing supporters or attract new support. Fearon and Laitin (2011, 207) point out that states may "want to appease their support base" by providing access to land. They cite the example of Bangladeshi President Ziaur Rahman, who in 1979 provided land for tens of thousands of Bengali families in the Chittagong Hill Tracts. In this case, the migrants entered an area occupied by indigenous peoples who lost some of their land rights (Roy 2000). Ahsan and Chakma (1989, 960) refer to postcolonial "government-initiated internal migration" as an example of internal colonialism, with governments rewarding the Bengali non-tribal majority, who "reap most of the benefits accruing from development projects."

Controlling Conflict Areas. Resettlement programs can be a vehicle for state control, involving the establishment or expansion of state institutions and to restive areas. Resettlement also may involve incentives and/or coercion that bring migrants to areas where they would be under stricter state control. For example, Ethiopian villagization under the Derg not only addressed drought, but also gave the Derg more direct control over migrants and host communities. Keller (1985, 7) describes the Derg's "statist tendencies" in terms of its "vigorous promotion of villagization," which the government claimed was to concentrate rural communities to increase service provision. The north-to-south resettlement targeted conflict areas; "villagization is most common in the south and southeast, areas hotly contested by Somali irredentists and Oromo secessionists" (Keller 1985, 7).

This is not a unique example, as migration may dilute rebellion through exile or dilute rebellious areas. During Indonesia's Darul Islam Rebellion in the 1950s, "villagers who had supported the rebels were resettled thousands of miles across the archipelago" (Amrith 2011, 139). In Turkey, the military expelled Kurds from Eastern and Southeastern Anatolia after 1987 to undermine their numerical strength in potentially secessionist areas (Çelik 2005, 139).

In the Philippines, state-led internal migration has played an important role in pacifying one conflict, while also stoking discontent elsewhere. In the 1950s, the government responded to the communist Huk Rebellion in part by granting land to rebel families in the country's periphery, especially in Mindanao. This served to provide land for poor farmers and undermine the communist conflict, but also generated conflict with Muslim communities, part of a broader pattern of state-supported Christian migration to Muslim areas (Kerkvliet 1971). In China, state-led migration to Xinjiang has evolved from coerced to incentivized Han migrants, encouraging the arrival of millions of persons to the restive province, including the development of special police and militia forces employing migrants (Becquelin 2000).

It is important to note, though, that observers may overpredict the extent to which states utilize this strategy of diluting rebellion through migration. In Indonesia, commentators regularly charged that Suharto's New Order used state-led internal migration to dilute rebellion in separatist regions (see Brown 2008, 267). In fact, the vast majority of state transmigrants were settled in central and southern Sumatra, regions lacking rebellions. Separatist areas such as Aceh and Timor were never major transmigrant recipients, and Papua became one only by the mid-1980s (Barter and Côté 2015). States certainly use migration to dilute rebellion, but we must be careful not to level this charge where it is not warranted.

Changing Ethno-Political Balances. Resettlement may bring in loyalists to dilute potential opposition, or simply expel people to undermine them politically or economically. Increasing or decreasing the percentages of particular groups within a given area can serve the state by creating new majorities, demoting oppositional groups from a majority to a minority, or eroding the mobilization capability of specific groups through ethnic removal/cleansing. One example was Stalin's massive relocations or expulsions of over twenty ethnic groups (Martin 1998; Polian 2004). Ejecting people from their home area can undermine their ability to pursue their Sons of the Soil claims or sustain guerilla resistance. The strategy may be expulsion, as in the case of Saddam Hussein's government's ejection of Kurds from Kirkuk, or attraction, as in the Iranian government's resettlement of Persians in Khuzestan to reduce the demographic dominance of Arabs in that province.

Providing Symbolic Gestures. Political leaders sometimes maximize the scope of resettlement programs to convey state strength and ambition. Sending and protecting migrants to peripheral areas may be part of broader nation-building strategies. Once there, the return of migrants may be especially symbolically damaging for authorities, who may even limit the right of return as they extend further support to their investment. Physical infrastructure projects are often scoped to impress—grandiose hydroelectric dams, massive airports, athletic venues for international competitions, and so on. The enlargement of these projects entails greater displacement. The concern is that this political motive may amplify initiatives beyond what is socially and economically optimal, pushing the volume of migration beyond the carrying capacity of the areas where migrants arrive.

Serving Geopolitical Strategy. Officials may also wish to increase populations in regions contested by other countries. This may serve functional aims, of having loyal groups in a contested region, or it may serve symbolic ends, allowing states to argue that they are already in possession of a given territory. One of the motives of the Brazilian military government's promotion of Amazonian expansion was to counter the growing Peruvian, Colombian, and Bolivian populations in Amazonia. In India, the government initiated the Prime Minister Rehabilitation Plan of 2008 with financial incentives to attract Kashmiri Pandits back to Kashmir, although the instability and hostility between Muslims and Hindus in Kashmir have thwarted this resettlement initiative. In the Caucasus, Seymour and Brzezinski (2019) note that governments have purposely failed to integrate displaced peoples, maintaining their displaced status with hopes of using them to repopulate lost territory.

Socioeconomic Motives

Reducing Landlessness. Resettling landless people—or those with minimal holdings—has frequently been an alluring initiative where land in remote regions is believed to have room for productive cultivation. Despite ample potential criticisms, it should not be forgotten that state-led migration can serve as a welfare mechanism for landless peasants. The prevalence of resettlement to reduce landlessness is driven both by land fragmentation and consolidation. Land becomes fragmented when it is divided among offspring, often resulting in plots too small to sustain livelihoods; inheritance by only one child (commonly the eldest male) leaves other offspring landless. Land is often consolidated when small farms are not viable or farmers without secure property rights are subject to expulsion to make way for large-scale agriculture. Even when user rights have not been challenged, the competitive advantages of large landowners frequently enable them to buy out smallholders. This leaves the potentially explosive context in which the poor press for redistribution, while the landowners are protective of their assets.

The least controversial approach is for the state to offer fair compensation for the landholdings. For example, in Costa Rica, resettlement as part of the land reform under the *Instituto de Desarrollo Agrario* (previously the *Instituto de Tierras y Colonización*) was propelled by the state's purchase of such landholdings, largely of forest land, beginning in the 1970s. The *Instituto* served as a land bank, providing titles but with the requirement that the farmers would have to pay back the cost of the land. However, because the land was not fertile—which was why it was not already cultivated—the cost of fertilizer to make the land productive was often prohibitively high. Thus, many farmers leased the land to agribusinesses and moved again (Reimer 2010, 16–21).

In Brazil, addressing landlessness has been one motive for opening the Amazon for settlement. Since the Brazilian government first encouraged Amazonian settlement in the 1970s, nearly a million people have migrated there. However, with an estimated 30 million landless rural people toward the turn of the century (Petras 1998, 130), Amazonian resettlement has had only a relatively modest impact on this fundamental problem. Moreover, leaders of the landless people's movement (*Movimento dos Trabalhadores Rurais Sem Terra*—MST) have criticized resettlement initiatives on the grounds that better agricultural prospects exist elsewhere, which also have a lower incidence of diseases such as yellow fever and malaria.

Reducing Congestion. The rising population in specific areas—cities or rural regions—has led many states to encourage resettlement into less populated areas. Population control measures take decades and may generate social resistance (e.g., from religious groups), making it easier to relocate the problem. The socioeconomic deprivations and potentially explosive political risk of population congestion have triggered rural-targeted resettlement efforts to establish new towns away from major population centers, or satellite cities on the periphery of major urban centers.

Three long-standing patterns have impelled resettlement programs to relieve congestion. First, straightforward urbanization reflects population growth and, often, farm consolidation. When urbanization is gradual, the congestion might not mobilize the attention of policymakers until the problem is so serious that state leaders see large-scale resettlement as imperative. A second pattern is growing rural congestion due to population growth, which in many instances threatens greater urban congestion. The challenge lies in how to relieve rural landlessness without triggering compelled urbanization to congested cities. This may be addressed by channeling residents of congested areas to less populated rural areas or secondary cities. The third pattern is urban or rural congestion due to the massive influx of expelled or violence-fleeing populations from other areas. This was one reason why, following the India-Pakistan partition, the Indian government resettled displaced Bengalis in rural areas of the Andaman Islands, Andhra Pradesh, Assam, Madhya Pradesh, Odisha, and Tripura.

Civilizing "Backward" Peoples. Some state-sponsored resettlement initiatives seek to alter the host population's cultural composition, modes of production, or both. This state strategy may involve relocating indigenous people or sending "more sophisticated" migrants to remote regions in the hope that the "less sophisticated" local people will emulate the newcomers. Duncan's edited volume, *Civilizing the Margins* (2004), emphasizes how state-led migration represents a core tool to promote cultural change among indigenous peoples, providing several examples from across Asia. Davidson (2008, 96) quotes a Javanese governor of West Kalimantan as needing "migrants to civilize the Dayaks." Bose (2006, 64) reports that the rationales for resettling Bengalis included helping the refugees as well as "the 'civilization' of a local tribal group through enforced contact with the newcomer." To the degree that the local population sees manifestations of such heavy-handed "projects," the potential for the local population's clashes with the migrants, the state, or both, is obvious.

Ecological Motives

States also may compel migration to protect sensitive rural or urban environments: protecting forests and biomes, or protecting cities from mudslides originating in hillside shanty towns. That said, states frequently use environmental concerns to mask some of the motives mentioned above, such as "civilizing" local people or promoting development (Duncan 2004).

Expelling Urban Squatters. As noted, the expulsion of urban informal settlements is a common phenomenon throughout the world. Squatter expulsions typically take place as developers want access to precious urban land, but there may also be health, safety, and ecological concerns at play. States frequently cite such factors to justify land grabs. However, it is sometimes true that squatters occupy land that puts them or others in danger (e.g., along rail lines, highways, or flood-prone waterways) or create ecological concerns (e.g., settling along sensitive waterways or vulnerable habitats). By using the rhetoric of health and safety, states thus implicitly use the language of helping urban squatters, implying possibilities for more humane resettlement.

Instead of simply evicting and bulldozing squatter sites, local governments may resettle migrants in less environmentally sensitive areas within the local area or try to improve sites to reduce environmental risks. In Mumbai, state and city governments that earlier had undertaken coercive slum clearances then developed more accommodating policies. Doshi (2011, 34) describes the shift in new policies, including the Slum Improvement Program (SIP), which worked to change how authorities saw slums, which are "not just encroachments but also substandard housing in need of environmental improvement through the provision of services such as water, sanitation, roads and lighting." This change in perspective entailed an emphasis on improving informal settlements among urban migrants, not relocating them and forcing them into further migrations.

Establishing and Protecting Nature Reserves. Nature reserves represent particularly pervasive rural conservation initiatives. The triple objectives of conservation, economic gains from ecotourism or carbon credits, and the possibility of attracting foreign assistance have propelled the enclosure of populated areas for such reserves in several developing areas (Galvin and Haller 2008). Whether labeled "protected areas," "national parks," or "nature reserves," the establishment of such areas typically involves either complete expulsion or substantial limitations on the local peoples' user rights. In cases of expulsion, whether to nearby or distant sites and whether state assisted or not, resettlement is coerced. In the case of limited user rights, the need to migrate depends on how strictly the income-earning activities are limited by enforced regulation, with severe restrictions on permissible activities compelling displacement. In addressing whether the expansion of protected areas throughout Central Africa would exacerbate poverty, Cernea and Schmidt-Soltau (2006, 1813) argue that this "concern is triggered by the fact that no explicit policy, guidelines or strictures against forced population displacements (physical or economic) have been adopted by any of the Governments in the region nor by the international NGOs promoting the extension of protected areas." Not only does forced displacement from nature parks in Cameroon, the Central African Republic, Equatorial Guinea, Gabon, Nigeria, and the Republic of Congo present humanitarian concerns, but the presence of ecological IDPs also threatens the sustainability of the parks themselves.

People forcibly relocated from nature reserves by states may have been recent migrants seeking new opportunities in natural areas. In other cases, they are indigenous people with long histories of inhabiting remote areas. In these cases, removing indigenous peoples from their lands may be carried out in the name of conservation, but also may represent an effort to establish control. In Thailand, there are long-standing debates regarding swidden/shifting agriculture among highland peoples (Delang 2002). The Thai state has worked to relocate highland communities and force them to settle, using ecological arguments that growing indigenous populations make swidden unsustainable, destroying sensitive ecological areas. Many highland communities, though, perceive the ecological argument as another pretext to resettle their people, opening the doors for outsiders to exploit local resources.

Psychology of State Interactions

Having described the varied motives of the state in overseeing migration, including economic, political, social, and ecological considerations, we now consider how state officials may perceive these processes. Officials overseeing migration base their decisions in part on their perceptions of potential and actual migrants as well as host communities. These perceptions, in turn, are based on the officials' identifications with the presumed identifications and attributions of potential or actual stakeholders. The three obvious dimensions relevant for understanding officials' attributions are the degree of overlap of identifications with migrants or host community members, the likelihood that state officials will over-generalize the attributes of migrants and host communities, and the degree to which the officials feel superior to either group.

Overlap of Identifications

For non-coercive resettlement programs, state officials have to persuade individuals to migrate, communicating (validly or not) the state's concern for their well-being. For mandatory displacements for which the state takes responsibility, the same sense of responsibility to the migrants is often present. This direct attachment has the potential to generate sympathy for migrants compared to host communities. Such attachment would reinforce the accountability considerations of favoring the migrants because their well-being more directly conveys the success of the resettlement program.

Favoritism toward migrants also is likely to be enhanced when states encourage migration to areas where the presence of migrants strengthens state control. Thai Buddhists from the north and northeast were favored with housing in the South to help deepen state control in Muslim regions. This echoes the bias of Philippine state officials in Mindanao, who often collaborated with Christian migrants to capture the best land and dilute the weight of the Muslim population (McKenna 1998, 120). Similarly, Persians have been resettled in the western Iranian province of Khuzestan to tilt the population balance against local Arab speakers (Elling 2013, 55–70). In such cases, state officials may identify with migrants, feeling compelled to support co-ethnics; their presence in the target area is, in a sense, a state investment.

The situation is different when coerced resettlement or straightforward expulsion is motivated by the state's fear that leaving people in their home areas would lead to opposition to the state, or even secession. In such cases, expelled migrants may be viewed as disloyal troublemakers. Turkish military leaders expelled "disloyal" Kurds without being able (nor desiring) to test the loyalty of the expelled people. Stereotyping that exaggerates the number of disloyal people worsens the state leaders' antagonism. Here, the targeted population is viewed as a problem rather than an investment or responsibility.

The dynamics for state officials who interact directly with migrants and host communities at the sites of migration are likely to be different from those sitting in the capital formulating resettlement programs. Front-line administrators are likely to identify more closely with those who share common traits. This raises an important tactical issue: should the resettlement program or other migratory policies rely on local authorities, assign staff from the migrating people, or, as in the case of the Indian Administrative Service, bring in administrators with no strong identifications with either community? Differences in identifications may give rise to clashes between national and local officials. Except for expulsions of people seen as threatening the state, national leaders typically favor migrants involved in state resettlement programs, especially if their reputation rests on the sustainability of the resettlement. If officials present at the target site are local, their shared identifications with the host community increases the risk of conflicts among levels of the state.

Overgeneralization

Some degree of overgeneralization or stereotyping of a sizable group of people is inevitable, because individual variations are largely unknown. Yet, the degree of stereotyping depends on such factors as physical distance, cultural differences, and previous interactions. Top-level resettlement policymakers, far from migration sites and interacting with migrants and host communities through intermediaries, are likely to think of these stakeholders in overly broad terms. This means that these distant policymakers are less prepared to understand what proportion of migrants and host community members are culturally open-minded, adaptable, educated, overly aggressive, rebellious, and so on. Intelligence from sources closer to both the potential migrants and the people at resettlement sites therefore can be crucial to avoid poor site selection and unnecessarily provocative management of the migration patterns.

Feelings of Superiority

Except when the targets of expulsion are opposition leaders, the stereotypes that top-level state officials attribute to migrants and host communities also reflect the likelihood that these officials are of higher social status and are better educated than either migrants or host communities. Officials may rationalize the heavy-handed treatment of either group on the grounds that the government knows what is best for all concerned, failing to account for the specific needs of migrant or host communities. Especially for indigenous host communities, protests against demands for change may be interpreted as opposition to development.

Conclusions

This chapter has detailed the centrality of the state, emphasizing its importance in overseeing various stages and forms of internal migration. The expansive presence of the host state sets internal migration apart from international migration. The state is the primary actor in governing migration, or else failing to do so. We noted that the state typically enjoys some degree of discretion in terms of migratory policies and psychological dispositions. We also emphasized the complexity of the state and its motives, explained in part by the fact that states are not unitary actors, with various agencies and levels of a government possessing divergent policies. Yet, it is a dangerous over-simplification to assume that the state is in control of migratory processes, even if it always plays some role and sometimes wishes to appear in control.

References

Ahsan, Syed Aziz-al, and Bhumitra Chakma. 1989. Problems of National Integration in Bangladesh: The Chittagong Hill Tracts. *Asian Survey* 29 (10): 959–970.

Amrith, Sunil S. 2011. *Migration and Diaspora in Modern Asia*. Cambridge: Cambridge University Press.

Barter, Shane, and Isabelle Côté. 2015. Strife of the Soil? Unsettling Transmigrant Conflicts in Indonesia. *Journal of Southeast Asian Studies* 46 (1): 60–85.

Barter, Shane Joshua. 2019. Displacement and Reintegration in Aceh, Indonesia. In *Internal Migration: Challenges in Governance and Integration*, eds. Shane Barter and William Ascher, 113–128. New York: Peter Lang.

Becquelin, Nicolas. 2000. Xinjiang in the Nineties. *The China Journal* 44: 65–90.

Bose, Pablo. 2006. Dilemmas of Diaspora: Partition, Refugees, and the Politics of 'Home.' *Refuge: Canada's Periodical on Refugees* 23 (1): 58–68.

Brown, Graham K. 2008. Horizontal Inequalities and Separatism in Southeast Asia: A Comparative Perspective. *Horizontal Inequalities and Conflict: Understanding Group Violence in Multiethnic Societies,* ed. Frances Stewart, 252–281. London: Palgrave Macmillan.

Çelik, Ayşe Betül. 2005. 'I Miss My Village!': Forced Kurdish Migrants in Istanbul and their Representation in Associations. *New Perspectives on Turkey* 32: 137–163.

Cernea, Michael, and Kai Schmidt-Soltau. 2006. Poverty Risks and National Parks: Policy Issues in Conservation and Resettlement. *World Development* 34 (10): 1808–1830.

Chakma, Nikhil, and Mathilde Maitrot. 2016. How Ethnic Minorities Became Poor and Stay Poor in Bangladesh: A Qualitative Enquiry. *EEP/Shiree*.

Dagne, Shibru Abate. 2013. Conflict and Conflict Resolution Mechanisms in Ethiopia: The Case of Gedeo and Guji Ethnic Groups. Master's Thesis: Andhra University.

Davidson, Jamie S. 2008. *From Rebellion to Riots: Collective Violence on Indonesian Borneo*. Madison: University of Wisconsin Press.

Delang, Claudio O. 2002. Deforestation in Northern Thailand: The Result of Hmong Farming Practices or Thai Development Strategies? *Society & Natural Resources* 15 (6): 483–501.

Doshi, Sapana. 2011. *The Right to the Slum? Redevelopment, Rule, and the Politics of Difference in Mumbai*. Diss. Berkeley, CA: University of California.

Duncan, Christopher, ed. 2004. *Civilizing the Margins: Southeast Asian Government Policies for the Development of Minorities*. Ithaca: Cornell University Press.

Elling, Rasmus. 2013. *Minorities in Iran: Nationalism and Ethnicity After Khomeini*. New York: Palgrave Macmillan.

Fearon, James D., and David D. Laitin. 2011. Sons of the Soil, Migrants, and Civil War. *World Development* 39 (2): 199–211.

Galvin, Marc, and Tobias Haller, eds. 2008. *People, Protected Areas, and Global Change: Participatory Conservation in Latin America, Africa, Asia, and Europe*. Bern: Geographica Bernensia.

Hardoy, Jorge E, and David Satterthwaite. 2014. *Squatter Citizen: Life in the Urban Third World*. New York: Routledge.

Keller, Edmond J. 1985. State, Party, and Revolution in Ethiopia. *African Studies Review* 28 (1): 1–17.

Kerkvliet, Benedict J. 1971. *The Huk Rebellion: A Study of Peasant Revolt in the Philippines*. Berkeley, CA: University of California Press.

Lofchie, Michael F. 2014. *The Political Economy of Tanzania: Decline and Recovery*. Philadelphia: University of Pennsylvania Press.

Luedke, Alicia. 2019. Preventing and Responding to Sexual and Gender-Based Violence in and Around South Sudan's Protection of Civilian (POC) Sites. In *Internal Migration: Challenges in Governance and Integration*, eds. Shane Barter and William Ascher, 19–31. New York: Peter Lang.

Martin, Terry. 1998. The Origins of Soviet Ethnic Cleansing. *Journal of Modern History* 70 (4): 813–861.

McKenna, Thomas M. 1998. *Muslim Rulers and Rebels: Everyday Politics and Armed Separatism in the Southern Philippines*. Berkeley, CA: University of California Press.

Mills, Mary Beth. 2012. Thai Mobilities and Cultural Citizenship. *Critical Asian Studies* 44 (1): 85–112.

Ofcansky, Thomas and LaVerle Berry, eds. 1991. *Ethiopia: A Country Study*. Washington: GPO for the Library of Congress. Resettlement and Villagization, http://countrystudies.us/ethiopia/.

Perz, Stephen G., Flavia Leite, Cynthia Simmons, Robert Walker, Stephen Aldrich, and Marcellus Caldas. 2010. Intraregional Migration, Direct Action Land Reform, and New Land Settlements in the Brazilian Amazon. *Bulletin of Latin American Research* 29 (4): 459–476.

Petras, James. 1998. The Political and Social Basis of Regional Variation in Land Occupations in Brazil. *The Journal of Peasant Studies* 25 (4): 124–133.

Polian, Pavel. 2004. *Against their Will: The History and Geography of Forced Migrations in the USSR*. Budapest: Central European University Press.

Quang, Binh Bui, Thi Thu Ha Nguyen, and Chuong Ong Nguyen. 2016. Internal Migration in the Context of Trade Liberalisation in Vietnam. *Malaysian Journal of Economic Studies* 53 (2): 195–209.

Reimer, Tanya. 2010. Brazil's Landless Movement (MST) and the Changing Culture of Property. *On Politics* 2 (1): 1–41.

Roy, Rajkumari Chandra Kalindi. 2000. *Land Fights of the Indigenous Peoples of the Chittagong Hill Tracts, Bangladesh*. Document No. 99. Copenhagen: International Work Group for Indigenous Affairs.

Scriven, Joel. 2010. *Markets & Payments for Ecosystem Services: Engaging REDD+ on Peru's Amazonian Frontier*. Diss. Oxford: Oxford University.

Seymour, Lee, and Marek Brzezinski. 2019. Unsettled States: Displacement, Governance, and Integration in the Southern Caucasus. In *Internal Migration: Challenges in Governance and Integration*, eds. Shane Barter and William Ascher, 47–62. New York: Peter Lang.

Shaw, William H. 2003. They Stole Our Land: Debating the Expropriation of White Farms on Zimbabwe. *Journal of Modern African Studies* 41 (1): 75–89.

Sim, Loo Lee, Shi Mang Yu, and Sun Sheng Han. 2003. Public Housing and Ethnic Integration in Singapore. *Habitat International* 27 (2): 293–307.

Srur, Muradu. 2013. Rural Commons and the Ethiopian State. *Law, Social Justice & Global Development* 2 (1): 1–47.

Tadjoeddin, M. Zulfan, and Anis Chowdhury. 2009. Socioeconomic Perspectives on Violent Conflict in Indonesia. *The Economics of Peace and Security Journal* 4 (1): 39–47.

Wood, Charles H. 2002. Introduction: Land Use and Deforestation in the Amazon. In *Deforestation and Land Use in the Amazon*, eds. Charles H. Wood and Roberto Porro, 1–40. Gainesville: University of Florida Press.

World Commission on Dams. 2000. *Dams and Development: A New Framework for Decision-Making: Final Report of the World Commission on Dams*. London: Earthscan.

Yadav, Vineeta. 2019. The Political Economy of Special Economic Zones and Internal Displacement in India. In *Internal Migration: Challenges in Governance and Integration*, eds. Shane Barter and William Ascher, 77–95. New York: Peter Lang.

Zeccola, Paul. 2011. Dividing Disasters in Aceh, Indonesia: Separatist Conflict and Tsunami, Human Rights and Humanitarianism. *Disasters* 35 (2): 308–328.

CHAPTER 4

The Many Levels of the State

Although it is commonplace to speak of "the state" as if it were a monolithic entity, many levels of state exist in any country, not to speak of the myriad ministries, agencies, commissions, and the like that exist across governmental levels. The "state" at subnational levels has grown in power and relevance throughout the developing world through a wave of decentralization in recent decades. Malesky and Hutchinson (2016, 126) note that in the 1990s, "a wave of decentralization spread across the world with almost every sizeable country devolving some sort of responsibilities to sub-national units." Decentralization initiatives in unitary systems[1] (e.g., Chile, Indonesia, the Philippines, and Uganda) have added to long-standing decentralization built into federal systems (e.g., Argentina, Brazil, India, Mexico, and Nigeria), which have themselves undergone further decentralization. The trend toward decentralization has been complicated with further changes through special autonomous and administrative regions enjoying new powers, even in otherwise unitary systems.

[1] In principle, in "unitary" systems the national government reserves all governance rights except for those delegated to subnational jurisdictions, in contrast to "federal" systems.

W. Ascher and S. J. Barter, *Moving within Borders*, Politics, Economics, and Inclusive Development,
https://doi.org/10.1007/978-3-031-37549-1_4

This downward shift in political power further complicates interactions among migrants, host communities, and state officials. Often advocated as a democratic pursuit of "self-governance" and enacted without adequate appreciation for its limitations, decentralization should not be considered an end in itself, but rather a means to optimize the provision of state services, some of which (e.g., defense against external aggressors or environmental protection) would not be optimized through subnational control. The decisions as to which services ought to be decentralized should hinge on effectiveness, efficiency, responsiveness, equity, contributions to self-determination and self-reliance, and avoidance of destructive conflict (Rondinelli 2006).

Decentralization can have both positive and negative consequences for migrants and host communities. Typically, though, decentralization tips the balance of political power away from internal migrants and toward host communities. National governments may find themselves with limited ability to support sponsored migrants (in terms of sending new migrants or supporting existing communities) or protect the rights of unsponsored migrants. Meanwhile, host communities may enjoy new powers over migrants, sometimes meaning a resurgence of native culture, at other times meaning the exclusion and exploitation of poorer groups, including efforts to disenfranchise migrants to protect this power. The risks for the migrants are present in all three of the main components of decentralization: political, administrative, and fiscal (see Anderson 2009; Schneider 2003).

Political Decentralization

Decentralization is often accompanied by democratization at multiple subnational levels (Thede 2009). Insofar as the combination of decentralization and democratization puts decision-making in the hands of elected subnational officials who owe their positions to voters, disenfranchised migrants face a greater disadvantage than when the national government is responsible for providing services. Even if migrants possess formal voting rights, they may be ineffective in contesting elections if they are numerically weak, poorly mobilized, or face voter suppression. Boone and Duku (2012, 672) note that as a consequence of Ghana's political decentralization, "decentralized, democratic local government does not provide a forum in which migrants can overcome the structural political disadvantage that currently leaves them vulnerable to chiefs' and indigenes' efforts to roll back their acquired property rights."

Political decentralization particularly undermines the standing of migrants who are not members of a powerful group in the area. When subnational officials at any level owe greater accountability to the more powerful groups within their jurisdiction, the fair treatment of migrants as outsiders who do not belong to those groups is at risk. Even a dominant national group, such as ethnic Russians in the Russian Federation, can be subjected to severe hazards in areas formally controlled by other groups. For example, during the collapse of the Soviet Union, Yeltsin granted power to ethnic republics to gain their support for Russia's exit of the Soviet Union. Hagendoorn et al. (2008, 354–355) report that ethnic leaders

> Reestablished control over regional economic assets and, covertly, enhanced the privileged status of the titulars in the ethnic republics...In the Caucasus, Avars in Dagestan are in conflict with returning Chechens who were deported in 1944, they are in conflict with the Nogai who are attempting to establish their own national territory, and with Kumyks who want to establish their own national autonomy... In the Volga-Ural region, there are tensions between Tatars and Russians in Tatarstan; there is also antagonism between Tatars and Bashkirs in Bashkortostan and between Bashkirs and immigrating Russians. In eastern Siberia, titulars in Tuva have been openly anti-Russian since their annexation by the Soviet Union in 1944 and there were violent conflicts between them in 1990. In Sakha-Yakutia, control over the rich resources creates tensions between Russians and Yakuts.

Note that Russian migrants, who presumably would not face discrimination from the federal government, may face discrimination in Tatarstan and Bashkortostan, and conflict in a semi-autonomous region politically dominated by Yakuts. Kolstø (2019) bases the relative absence of conflict despite anti-migrant, titular nationalism on the idea that many Russian migrants accepted the principle of native rule, taking care not to provoke natives in ethnic republics.

Political decentralization thus increases the responsibility of the national government to channel migration away from areas where subnational authorities are likely to feel little obligation toward the migrants, and even more so if the groups have had antagonistic histories.

Just as national trends toward decentralization may imperil migrant groups, asymmetrical devolution of power in the form of territorial autonomy may negatively impact migrants whose ethnicities do not define the distinctiveness that is the basis for establishing the area's autonomy. Ghai (2000, 8) defines territorial autonomy as "a device to allow ethnic or other groups claiming a distinct identity to exercise direct control over affairs of special concern to them, while allowing the larger entity those powers which cover common interests." Many areas are granted greater autonomy by national leaders to forestall restiveness and even secession. Once subnational leaders gain these powers, they often use them to embark on something resembling nation-building, taking actions similar to those employed by the centralized power (Keating 1996). One consequence is new pressure on various minorities within autonomous regions, including migrant groups (Barter 2018).

Numerous examples exist of newly empowered regional majorities using autonomous powers to pressure domestic migrant groups, often generating exclusion, conflicts, or new patterns of out-migration. Examples include Anglophones in Québec, Castilian Spanish in Catalonia or Basque Euskadi, Christian Filipinos in Mindanao, Javanese in Aceh, and many more. In Nicaragua, political power is highly centralized except for the Afro-Indigenous Moskito coast. There, mestizo Spanish migrating to local towns report dissatisfaction with local government power, reporting fear of separatism and economic exclusion (Sánchez 2007). In a sense, granting power to natives in their own territories may contribute to righting historical wrongs. That said, this may also generate new forms of exclusion, conflict, and out-migration.

For national minorities granted greater control over an area where they are in the majority, other groups within that area may be compelled to migrate out, because of new language policies, the imposition of religiously based behavioral restrictions, or discriminatory economic policies. Ghai (2001, 25) observes that "ethnically based autonomy will create new minorities; the position of these minorities may be worse than in a non-ethnic state, since they may be subjected to discrimination or have to acknowledge the symbols and cultures of the regional majority." For established autonomous areas, people living outside of the area who wish to migrate to the area, perhaps to join with family or pursue occupations, may be formally prohibited from doing so, even in countries observing the general principle of free movement.

Administrative Decentralization

With decentralization comes more responsibilities and employment opportunities related to subnational governments. Administrative decentralization adds to the burden of typically under-resourced subnational agencies (Ahmad et al. 2005), and newly selected local administrators often face a steep learning curve to reach competence. These limitations often reduce the effectiveness of services on which both migrants and host communities depend, thereby increasing tensions over accessing state programs. Further, competition for services and jobs may stoke tensions or enable a host or migrant group to capture the local state. In many cases, sudden decentralization stokes migratory conflicts, discussed more in Chapter 11.

To be sure, administrative decentralization can have positive impacts. It can reduce the risks that distant state officials would impose inappropriate regulations and resource allocations to the frequently delicate situations of migrant-host community interactions. Local control may also increase the likelihood that representatives of migrant groups and host communities could resolve conflicts through respected traditional reconciliation mechanisms, with which local authorities may have some familiarity. If migrants are permitted to participate in local decision-making, both they and host communities might feel a greater stake in the broadened community.

Fiscal Decentralization

As political and administrative decentralization inevitably means that subnational officials must assume greater responsibility, fiscal decentralization is imperative, either through secure commitments of the allocation of monies collected by the national government, or through feasible taxation capability by subnational authorities (Prud'homme 1995; Litvack et al. 1998; Tanzi 2001; Anderson 2009).

Insofar as fiscal decentralization increases the taxing capacity of subnational governments at the expense of national government revenues, subnational jurisdictions with larger tax bases will enjoy more funding, while poorer areas see a reduced influence over financial allocations, which would increase inequality across these jurisdictions. However, in other countries, the income levels of wealthier and poorer regions converge due to more effective governance or continued transfer payments (Martinez-Vázquez et al. 2017, 1112).

In many cases, subnational governments do not receive adequate transfers from the national government, lack the authority or capability to collect sufficient revenues, or both. National government agencies, resistant to losing authority and resources, may drain the budget resources that are supposed to be devoted to subnational transfers. Weak administrative decentralization may hamper the subnational efforts to collect revenues despite its increased taxing authority. In addition, while it is often taken for granted that fiscal decisions at more local levels enhance the efficiency of public spending, this depends on the competence, honesty, and fairness of the political leaders and administrators overseeing public spending (Liu et al. 2017, 248).

The combination of resource constraints and local officials' typically greater accountability to the host community frequently exacerbates problems for migrants. Protection for poor migrants can be undermined by the shift of spending authority to subnational authorities to the degree that the poor are less favored by the subnational authorities. Martínez-Vázquez et al. (2017, 1112) suggest that "Normative public finance traditionally has reserved redistribution goals to the central government and, actually, many programs affecting income distribution and the poor have been increasingly devolved to sub-national governments." Thus, perhaps the most dramatic weakness of decentralization has been the shirking by national state officials who fail to follow through with sufficient fiscal transfers to the next level of subnational government. From the perspective of national officials, decentralized responsibility reduces their accountability even if a portion of the resources are transferred from the central government. If migrants are denied services due to rationing by subnational authorities, these authorities are more likely to be held accountable.

Clashing Governments

In a centralized system, we may see the state as a rather unitary, cohesive actor. This is never entirely the case, as there will always exist competing agencies and factions. However, such states are especially likely to develop cohesive internal migration policies, for better or worse. With decentralization, providing new powers to subnational governments may generate clashes between governments related to internal migration. This may involve central governments clashing with subnational governments, often with central governments supporting migrants and subnational governments supporting hosts. This is not always the case though, as sometimes subnational governments (especially in cities) may welcome migrants as a source of cheap labor, while central governments may wish to reduce migration levels.

Other potential conflicts may arise between subnational governments, with migrant-sending states at odds with migrant-receiving states, perhaps owed to restrictions on migration, perceived excessive migration, the treatment of migrant groups, or the return of migrants. For example, there have long been clashes between the Mumbai city and Maharashtra state governments, on one hand, and migrant-sending state governments of Bihar and Uttar Pradesh on the other. During the 2020–2021 COVID-19 pandemic, officials of Mumbai and Maharashtra pushed migrants out of the region, while officials in Uttar Pradesh and Bihari criticized the decision to deport groups during lockdowns, seeking to avoid hundreds of thousands of migrants returning home (Priyadarshini and Chaudhury 2020).

Temporal dynamics may also invite clashes between governments. It is possible that a newly democratic regime may inherit problems created by state-led migration under previous autocratic regimes. It is also possible that centralized autocratic systems tolerate limited subnational resistance, but with greater liberalization, subnational governments may finally be able to voice opposition against national policies.

Internal Migration Agencies and Offices

The assignment of state agencies to oversee internal migration varies according to the nature of the migration. The multi-faceted issues involved in security, social services, economics, and politics typically call for numerous state agencies to be involved. Nevertheless, a lead agency often has enough control to shape the management of migration according to its institutional interests. And the choice of lead agency is, in some cases, a fascinating window onto the state's preoccupations with the risks and opportunities of migration.

Often it is difficult to designate which government agency ought to be mandated to oversee internal migration, with responsibilities spread across multiple agencies according to their own mandates which are often focused on specific forms of migration. Dedicated offices can play important roles in gathering data, overcoming problems, and supporting migrants. For example, the Philippines' prioritizing of international migration and the remittance economy is centered in the Office of Migrant Workers Affairs, located within the Department of Foreign Affairs, as well as various other offices tasked with the reintegration of overseas workers, training, and voting (Rodriguez 2010). It seems that all countries feature agencies tasked with international migration, but it is rarer to find a single agency overseeing the full range of internal migration policies. Indonesia is unique in that it long featured a Ministry of Transmigration, tasked with planning and executing state-led migration across the country, including long-term monitoring and support for migrant communities (Fearnside 1997). The presence of a dedicated government agency demonstrates how transmigration has represented high politics in Indonesia for decades. The Transmigration Ministry was downgraded after the 1990s, and its functions collapsed within related offices (after 2014, part of the Ministry of Villages, Development of Disadvantaged Regions, and Transmigration).

For the most part, state agencies dealing with internal migration are related to specific events and migrant groups, such as resettling IDPs from a specific conflict or disaster or managing labor migrants in urban areas. The efforts to manage unsupported migrations are often placed in the hands of the Interior Ministry, in many countries the dominant state entity for internal administration and security. For example, in Colombia, with a long history of pervasive violence and hence massive migration, the Interior Ministry directs the Internal Coordinating Group for Armed Conflict Victims Policy (*Grupo de Articulación Interna para la Política de Víctimas del Conflicto Armado*). Specialized displacement ministries often reflect recent levels of violence within a given country, but also political symbolism. In 1996, the government of Georgia created the Ministry of Internally Displaced Persons from the Occupied Territories, Accommodation and Refugees of Georgia. This ministry existed for 18 years, tasked with overseeing policies relating to IDPs and repatriation. Similarly, since 2016, Ukraine has had a Ministry of Reintegration of Temporarily Occupied Territories (MTOT) to coordinate support for IDPs from Crimea and Donbas, as well as prepare for a hoped-for return to Russian-occupied territories (evident in the title "temporary").

In the absence of one dominant agency, the essential task of the "lead agency" is to try to coordinate the efforts of multiple state entities. In Ghana, the National Migration Unit under the Ministry of the Interior develops the institutional structure to implement, monitor, and evaluate both state and non-supported internal migrations, assisted by an Inter-Ministerial Steering Committee on Migration with participation by nine other ministries and six additional government entities (Government of Ghana, 2016). The National Migration Unit within the Ministry of the Interior "spearheads" the coordination. Given the often-conflicting mandates of the other entities, this coordination may not amount to much more than convening committees and task forces to share information and perspectives.

In some cases, the assignment of responsibility for overseeing internal migration furthers broad governance initiatives. In Kenya, for example, although the Interior Ministry has coordinative responsibility over executive agencies (its formal title is "Ministry of Interior and Coordination of National Government"), the responsibility for internal displacement is assigned to a Directorate of Special Programmes of the Ministry of Devolution of Planning. The "devolution" label reflects the decentralization initiative to place more authority in the hands of the governors of Kenya's 47 counties.

In other cases, the assignment carries out economic restructuring. In Zimbabwe, the expropriation of white-held land and the resettlement of black farmers in the 1980s was managed by the Department of Rural Development, the Department of Co-operative Development, and the Agricultural and Rural Development Authority. These three agencies were tasked with "coordinating and administering beneficiary selection" (Gonese and Mukora 2003, 211). The process of land re-appropriation was a central policy of the Zimbabwe government for two decades, with various classification schemes and agencies resettling black farmers. The institutional instability contributed to mismanagement, leading to many policy failures.

Sri Lanka features revealing ministry titles in terms of the government's preoccupations and objectives, reflecting the dislocation of Tamils in northern Sri Lanka during the civil war and the halting repatriation of those who had fled to India. The names of these government bodies change regularly, including the Ministry of Nation Building and Development as well as the Ministry of Resettlement in 2005 (Muggah 2008, 261). At least part of migration oversight has been situated within what from 2010 to 2015 was designated as the Ministry of Resettlement, Reconstruction and Hindu Religious Affairs. In 2016, it was designated the Ministry of Prison Reforms, Rehabilitation, Resettlement and Hindu Affairs. As of 2018, it is the Ministry of National Policies, Economic Affairs, Resettlement and Rehabilitation, Northern Province Development, Vocational Training & Skills Development, and Youth Affairs.

Administrative authority over state-directed resettlement resulting from infrastructure development presents a distinctive pattern, in that the financing and construction coordination of these initiatives often place the technical initiative manager as the lead agency of the entire range of considerations, including resettlement. Even so, multiple agencies inevitably are involved, because of mandates for financial control, security, environmental protection, commerce, and so on. For example, the Mumbai Urban Transport Project, launched in 2002 with World Bank support, was coordinated by the Mumbai Metropolitan Region Development Authority, but multiple entities were required in the stages from planning to financing to expulsion and resettlement (Roquet et al. 2015, 16–17). Similarly, because the Costa Rican state electricity company *Instituto Costarricense de Electricidad* (ICE) conceived the construction of the Arenales Hydroelectric Project in the 1950s, ICE was given responsibility for the resettlement. Stocks (2014, 21) notes that "agricultural communities totaling approximately 2500 people were displaced by the new reservoir. ICE's Office of Resettlement...was charged with creating a viable resettlement plan for the displaced communities." In both cases, the lead agencies lacked the intrinsic mandate and institutional expertise to manage the migration. Because multiple agencies with different mandates are involved, inter-agency rivalry and conflicts are the norm.

Conclusions

The state is no monolith, a fact that is exceptionally important in understanding internal migration governance. Although there have been some efforts to create state bodies to coordinate policies related to internal migration, governance remains scattered across horizontal and vertical levels of government. The frequent lack of coherence of the state will be a recurring theme in the chapters to come, as varied subnational authorities struggle to coordinate, and sometimes contribute to migratory conflicts. This challenge, then, may lead to some degree of sympathy for the state officials seeking to best manage internal migration.

References

Ahmad, Junaid, Shantayanan Devarajan, Stuti Khemani, and Shekhar Shahet. 2005. Decentralization and Service Delivery. World Bank Policy Research Working Paper 3603. World Bank, Washington, DC.

Anderson, George. 2009. *Fiscal Federalism: A Comparative Introduction*. Oxford: Oxford University Press.

Barter, Shane Joshua. 2018. Rethinking Territorial Autonomy. *Regional Studies* 52 (2): 298–309.

Boone, Catherine, and Dennis Kwame Duku. 2012. Ethnic Land Rights in Western Ghana: Landlord-Stranger Relations in the Democratic Era. *Development and Change* 43 (3): 671–693.

Fearnside, Philip. 1997. Transmigration in Indonesia: Lessons from Its Environmental and Social Impacts. *Environmental Management* 21 (4): 553–570.

Ghai, Yash. 2000. Ethnicity and Autonomy: A framework for Analysis. In *Autonomy and Ethnicity: Negotiating Competing Claims in Multi-Ethnic States*, 1–27. Yash Ghai. Cambridge: Cambridge University Press.

Ghai, Yash. 2001. *Public Participation and Minorities*, vol. 1. London: Minority Rights Group.

Gonese, Francis T, and Charles M. Mukora. 2003. Beneficiary Selection, Infrastructure Provision and Beneficiary Support. In *Delivering Land and Securing Rural Livelihoods: Post-Independence Land Reform and Resettlement in Zimbabwe*, eds. Michael Roth and Francis Gonese, 205–235. Centre for Applied Sciences, University of Zimbabwe, and Land Tenure Center, University of Wisconsin-Madison.

Government of Ghana, Ministry of the Interior. 2016. *National Migration Policy for Ghana*. Accra, Ghana.

Hagendoorn, Louk, Edwin Poppe, and Anca Minescu. 2008. Support for Separatism in Ethnic Republics of the Russian Federation. *Europe-Asia Studies* 60 (3): 353–373.

Keating, Michael. 1996. *Nations against the State: The New Politics of Nationalism in Quebec*. Catalonia and Scotland: Springer.

Kolstø, Pål. 2019. The Concept of 'Rootedness' in the Struggle for Political Power in the Former Soviet Union in the 1990s. In *People Changing Places: New Perspectives on Demography, Migration, Conflict, and the State*, eds. Isabelle Côté, Matthew I Mitchell, and Monica Duffy Toft, 107–127. London: Routledge.

Litvack, Jennie, Junaid Ahmad, and Richard Bird. 1998. *Rethinking Decentralization in Developing Countries*. Washington, DC: World Bank.

Liu, Yongzheng, Jorge Martinez-Vazquez, and Alfred M. Wu. 2017. Fiscal Decentralization, Equalization, and Intra-Provincial Inequality in China. *International Tax and Public Finance* 24:2; 248–281.

Malesky, Edmund J., and Francis E. Hutchinson. 2016. Varieties of Disappointment: Why has Decentralization not Delivered on Its Promises in Southeast Asia? *Journal of Southeast Asian Economies* 33 (2): 125–138.

Martínez-Vázquez, Jorge, Santiago Lago-Peñas, and Agnese Sacchi. 2017. The Impact of Fiscal Decentralization: A Survey. *Journal of Economic Surveys* 31 (4): 1095–1129.

Muggah, Robert. 2008. *Relocation Failures in Sri Lanka: A Short History of Internal Displacement and Resettlement*. London: Zed Books.

Priyadarshini, Anamika and Sonamani Chaudhury. 2020. The Return of Bihari Migrants After the COVID-19 Lockdown. In *Borders of an Epidemic: Covid-19 and Migrant Workers*, ed. Ranabir Samaddar, 66–75. Kolkata: Calcutta Research Group.

Prud'homme, Remy. 1995. The Dangers of Decentralization. *World Bank Research Observer* 10 (2): 201–220.

Rodriguez, Robyn Magalit. 2010. *Migrants for Export: How the Philippine State Brokers Labor to the World*. Minneapolis: University of Minnesota Press.

Rondinelli, Dennis. 2006. Government Decentralization and Economic Development: The Evolution of Concepts and Practices. *Research in Public Policy Analysis and Management* 15: 433–445.

Roquet, Vincent, Luciano Bornholdt, Karen Sirker, and Jelena Lukic. 2015. *Urban Land Acquisition and Involuntary Resettlement: Linking Innovation and Local Benefits*. World Bank, 2015.

Sánchez, Luis. 2007. Splitting the Country: The Case of the Atlantic Coast of Nicaragua. *Journal of Latin American Geography* 6 (1): 7–23.

Schneider, Aaron. 2003. Decentralization: Conceptualization and Measurement. *Studies in Comparative International Development* 38 (3): 32–56.

Stocks, Gabriela. 2014. *Assessing the Long-Term Effects of Development-Forced Displacement and Resettlement: The Case of Nuevo Arenal, Costa Rica*. Doctoral Dissertation, University of Florida. Gainesville, FL.

Tanzi, Vito. 2001. Pitfalls on the Road to Fiscal Decentralization. Working Paper No. 19. Carnegie Endowment for International Peace, Washington DC. April. http://www.carnegieendowment.org/files/19Tanzi.pdf.

Thede, Nancy. 2009. Decentralization, Democracy, and Human Rights: A Human Rights-Based Analysis of the Impact of Local Democratic Reforms on Development. *Journal of Human Development and Capabilities* 10 (1): 103–123.

CHAPTER 5

Sympathy for the State: Coping with Internal Migration

With the state's dominance in managing internal migration comes the problems, and even vulnerability, of being in charge. In contrast to the generally unsympathetic critiques of the state's actions concerning internal migration, our analysis of the state's roles and motivations recognizes that officials face enormous uncertainty and dilemmas. Due to their power in overseeing internal migration, states are typically held accountable for outcomes over which they have at the most only partial control. Appreciating that the actions of state officials must be understood in terms of how they try to cope with uncertainty and dilemmas is crucial in providing insights into their priorities and actions.

Uncertainty

Whether or not internal migration is state-sponsored, officials face high levels of uncertainty regarding the volume of migrants, settlement locations, eligibility for assistance, and likely outcomes of intergroup relations. Without sufficient knowledge of these factors, officials may be unable to plan effectively how many migrants to encourage or permit to migrate, where they should be channeled, who should receive benefits, and how to anticipate and preempt intergroup conflict.

W. Ascher and S. J. Barter, *Moving within Borders*, Politics, Economics, and Inclusive Development, https://doi.org/10.1007/978-3-031-37549-1_5

Volume

There is no guarantee that state-sponsored resettlements will attract the planned number of migrants, and typically even greater uncertainty exists as to the volume of unsponsored migrants who would accompany formally sponsored migrants. The volume of state-initiated migration, such as those facilitated by infrastructure development into frontier areas, is often even more uncertain, as in the case of the Brazilian Amazon. Whether state officials can predict the volume of migrations that are neither sponsored nor instigated is challenged by the uncertainties of natural disasters, outbreaks of violence, and so on. Urbanization patterns are subject to perceptions of job opportunities that can result in a flood of migrants whether or not the job opportunities actually exist, narratives over which the state lacks control. Even when volumes initially appear to resemble estimated numbers, subsequent new arrivals or return/ secondary migration may change these numbers, frustrating even the best predictions.

Location

The likelihood that migrants will remain in the planned areas is also uncertain. Agricultural migrants, such as those in the Amazon, often move multiple times, coming into contact with different host communities. States may effectively manage an initial migration, but then lack control over subsequent relocations, blurring state responsibility for migrant welfare. The difficulty of tracking migrants is especially great when—as is typical—the sustainability of the migrants' livelihoods in the planned areas has not been adequately assessed in advance to ensure that the first location will serve for a long time. Migrants to cities, who are rarely part of planned programs, may relocate to other areas within the city or to other cities altogether as job opportunities, living conditions, and intergroup relations prove disappointing. Once an initial move has taken place, a migrant's roots are somewhat severed and they may be especially mobile, with further moves not uncommon (Lucas 2021, 275).

Eligibility

When states create programs to assist internal migrants such as IDPs, it is immensely difficult to ensure that this support reaches the intended recipients. Eligibility for assistance programs targeting people displaced due to violence is uncertain because of the subjective nature of such fears. Migrants leaving violent areas, as in Colombia, have the incentive to claim that they are fleeing violence regardless of the actual level of risk they faced. Granting eligibility indiscriminately may exhaust assistance budgets, while denying eligibility will antagonize those denied and may exclude deserving recipients. Officials in relevant agencies may have vastly underestimated the scale of victimization, especially since during conflicts victims may be unlikely to come forward unless provided with incentives and protection.

Intergroup Relations

Levels of cooperation and conflict among migrants and host communities are highly unpredictable, with even the most organized states unable to know if economic and cultural compatibilities will result from migration. State planners may relocate a community from a disaster area, bringing them to an area with people of the same faith, but then ethnic differences or seemingly small religious differences may become salient as tensions mount. In terms of economic complementarity, it is difficult to know if migrants are best off when they feature relatively similar or relatively different economic niches with host communities. Even when groups appear complementary for some time, shifting economic or ecological conditions could change this. Consider the case, mentioned earlier, of Ethiopia's Gedeos and Gujis in Guji areas. The groups largely cooperated for decades, based on the symbiosis of Gedeos supplying grains and vegetables to Gujis in exchange for milk and meat. This changed in the 1990s, when more Gujis took up sedentary farming, unleashing competition over land (Dagne 2013; Debelo 2007). In 2018, clashes between these groups led to tens of thousands displaced, mostly Gedeo farmers. For the state, it is very difficult to know if migrants and hosts will get along, as there are myriad economic, political, and social factors at play that may be very difficult to predict, such as whether pastoralists would give up centuries-old lifestyles for sedentary farming. Salient cleavages between migrants and hosts may only appear clear in hindsight.

Vulnerability of State Officials

In addition to the general vulnerability that state officials face when blamed for any of their actions, the fact that they often find themselves in the middle of conflicts between migrants and host communities poses no-win—and frequently dangerous—situations. When disputes arise that require state arbitration, the losing side often will conclude that state favoritism is at play. A common psychological reaction to adverse decisions is to attribute malicious intent to decision-makers (Dodge 2006). Frontier areas often lack sufficient security infrastructure to protect frontline officials from reprisals. In Northeast India's "Naxalite Belt" (Guha 2007) and in Assam (Baruah 1986), police and other state officials have been attacked due to anger toward migration, even involving officials who had nothing to do with migration. One result is that an already limited state presence may weaken even further as officials flee for safety. Local officials might be accused of bias in their dealings with migrants or host communities. When local officials arbitrate conflicts in favor of the host community, higher officials may see this as undermining the sponsored migration. Often it is easy for higher-level state officials to blame the failure of poorly designed programs on the local officials required to implement them.

Limits of Capacity

In addition to the impact of uncertainty on control, the state inevitably has limitations in its administrative capacity to address problems among migrants and host communities even in relatively high-certainty situations. State leaders may know what actions would further their goals, but face legal and political constraints. Insofar as they are beholden to international actors, state actions may be further constrained by the demands of aid agencies, commitments to international agreements, and concerns over international reputation.

In cities, the potential for confrontations among hundreds or thousands of people that could result in conflicts escalating to riots is notoriously difficult to predict. Even in the United States, with high certainty as to population composition in particular locales and a huge amount of research on intergroup relations, Myers (2000, 174) concludes that "predicting riots turned out to be a notoriously difficult task, and even retrospective analyses have had difficulty explaining rioting using the social and economic conditions presumed to be at issue." This is compounded by the seemingly mundane triggers of intergroup conflicts. In Indonesia from 1990 to 2003, 35 percent of sectarian collective violence was triggered by traffic accidents (Varshney 2004, 36). Elsewhere, migratory violence may be triggered by elections, the timing of holidays, university admissions, or athletic competitions. States have limited control over such conflict-triggering events.

State control in frontier areas is especially challenging, due to the constraints of telecommunications and transportation and the difficulty of attracting competent staff to low-amenity areas. Areas with extensive ethnic and linguistic diversity face communication challenges among state officials, migrants, and natives. This may amplify small disagreements and misunderstandings, along with undermining the ability to address conflicts that arise.

Dilemmas

The many objectives that the state is expected to fulfill in the face of uncertainty and vulnerability give rise to chronic dilemmas faced by officials. Because there are no easy answers, officials are vulnerable politically for whatever position they take, and therefore may be tempted to duck accountability through various means.

Expulsion: How Much Compensation? When the state expels people to make way for physical infrastructure, the question of how much compensation, if any, inevitably arises. This is particularly important in terms of the duty to care for the most deprived people, who are most likely to be displaced because placing the projects in the areas of the lowest land values—slums and wastelands—typically increases the economic viability of the project. If one of the costs is compensating the displaced, and if the basis of compensation is leaving expelled people no worse off, this is more economical than displacing people with more valuable property.

Furthermore, more infrastructure projects are economically viable if expelled people are deemed as not deserving compensation. Particularly in cities, the residents of appropriated areas frequently are urban migrants who settled where they could, without formal authorization. Some may have resided there for weeks, others for years. Whether current residents all deserve compensation is an open question that depends on local property laws, the time elapsed since settlement, and other factors.

Whatever formal guidelines exist, inconsistencies and arbitrariness in how these guidelines are applied may lead to serious deprivations for IDPs. In India, the formal compensation policy for infrastructure-displaced people seems progressive on paper. World Bank analysts Reddy and Talwar (2014) report that the 2013 Right to Fair Compensation and Transparency in Land Acquisition, Rehabilitation and Resettlement Act "provides for up to two times market value, against one time in the previous act and this figure is then doubled by applying a one hundred percent "solatium" against 30% in the previous act." However, the practicalities yield different results:

> Though people get more compensation under [the] new act, an increase in multiplier does not address the fundamental question of determining 'market value' in a country where registered values under-represent land purchase price to evade high stamp duties. The challenge is exacerbated in rural areas where there are fewer land transfers, and therefore fewer registered sales deeds to use as reference points.

Expulsion Plus Resettlement? Beyond the obligation to compensate people displaced by infrastructure development, the state may bear the obligation to resettle these IDPs. This extends the state's accountability and liability concerning the well-being of both migrants and host populations. What otherwise may have been considered a measure confined to one point in time in terms of the state's explicit obligations, becomes an ongoing obligation.

In the rush of clearing land for infrastructure development, it is challenging to carry out proper consultation, identify proper resettlement sites, gauge the needs for state services, and organize entries into the new area. Therefore, the more straightforward and temporally limited approach of simply paying the expelled people is often very attractive from the perspective of state officials in the local area. The problems of integrating the migrants wherever they arrive from such unmanaged migration would then have to be addressed by other officials.

Endorsing Traditional Conflict Resolution Mechanisms? Sometimes officials have to decide whether to yield control to migrants and host community members to find ways to resolve conflicts, even if resolution mechanisms clash with existing policies and state control. The Gedeo-Guji case provides a compelling example, where state-led efforts to bring the groups together failed, only for more bottom-up efforts to find more success for several years before the return of conflict in 2018.

The conflict occurred in the southern state of Oromia, the homeland of various Oromo peoples including the Guji, and the diverse "Southern Nations" state, in which ethnic Gedeo are a small minority concentrated in the district bordering the Guji area. Over several decades, Gedeo farmers migrated into under-cultivated Guji areas, intending to expand their cultivation of traditional crops and varieties of high-value coffee (Debelo 2007; Dagne 2013). Yet, Gujis, under state pressure to become sedentary, also shifted to coffee cultivation, asserting their land rights. By the 1990s, tensions mounted with the creation of firm federal ethnic district borders, rising Gedeo populations, and land shortages. These tensions exploded into violence in 1995, killing thousands and displacing hundreds of thousands. State and national authorities attempted to intervene, but in the context of a weak state, this had little effect.

The two groups are closely connected, with Guji and Gedeo sharing an origin myth but speaking different languages. Both communities are impoverished and largely illiterate, but occupy different economic niches. Historically, Guji people were mostly herders, highly mobile across the region, while Gedeo were, and remain, mostly farmers. This provided the groups with a level of complementarity, exchanging meat and other animal products for fruits, vegetables, produce and grains. Debelo (2007, 58) observes that, for the most part, Guji and Gedeo lived harmoniously, with their "deep-rooted economic interdependence" explained by the fact that "Gedeo did not share similar ecological niches with the Guji, which in turn limited the possibility of competition over resources." Another factor was that Guji herders have historically looked down on Gedeo farmers. Guji men were known to view farmers as less brave and manly, making violence against them seen as cowardly. As a result of this taboo, as well as economic complementarity, Guji elders could invoke a curse on anyone attacking Gedeo people.

As Gujis increasingly turned to farming, these norms changed, leading to violence. In the wake of this failure, elders stepped in to officiate disputes in the IDP camps, invoking several traditional processes such as clan partnerships between the two communities (*gada*), symbolic tribute (*qallu*), and curses against those attacking the other side (*gondoro*). National and state-level authorities recognized the effectiveness of traditional systems. Instead of controlling the peace process, officials facilitated traditional systems. Dagne (2013, 240) explains that the government "recognized the need to collaborate with customary intuitions so as to bring about lasting peace and security in the area." Guji and Gedeo elders were encouraged to lead ceremonies, attended by government officials and regional tribal leaders. State officials wisely helped to facilitate the ceremonies, even releasing an incarcerated Guji spiritual leader to participate. Both sides pledged to avoid violence, cursing anyone attacking the other side. Even though many may not believe in curses, the ceremony emphasized the importance of peace and stigmatized those who violated it and risked excommunication (Debelo 2007, 66).

The gondoro approach found some success where official channels failed. It must have been galling for Ethiopian officials to release the Guji leader from prison to officiate at the Gedeo-Guji ceremony of reconciliation in 1998, after state-led 1995 reconciliation efforts failed. State officials may not wish to empower religious or traditional leaders to help resolve conflicts between migrants and natives, perhaps because such groups will then challenge state power or may promote other forms of conflict down the road. State leaders recognized their limited reach and played a supporting role in a societal mechanism; "there is a general understanding that the intervention of elders ended the 1998 conflict, while government structures made the progress of traditional institutions of intervention smooth" (Kinfemichael 2014, 81). That said, given rising populations and economic competition, this region again experienced violent clashes in 2018–2019, displacing over 70,000 people (Gardner 2019). The government struggled to establish control, with various international agencies stepping in to provide aid and calm tensions. It remains to be seen if traditional approaches to social integration can once again help improve tensions between these communities.

Which Lead Agency? The choice of a lead agency will shape whether migration initiatives are viewed as "social engineering" with an open-ended commitment to managing economic, political, and social interactions, or a one-shot, contained action. It is useful to point out that the rough distinction between displacement policies ("clearing out people in the way") and resettlement programs ("placing migrants in selected areas") typically reflects quite different mindsets, as well as the state entities involved in planning and execution.

Many displacement actions are propelled by infrastructure initiatives, often with construction and economic agencies taking the lead: it is essentially physical engineering. The fate of the displaced people is likely to be a secondary consideration. In sharp contrast, resettlements designed to restructure the ethnic, cultural, or political composition of target areas represent sociopolitical engineering on a grand scale. The primacy of social engineering as the heart of site-targeted resettlement programs typically puts the initiative in the hands of resettlement agencies separate from the standard sectoral agencies such as the agricultural ministry, defense ministry, environmental agency, and so on. These integrated agencies are often in conflict with production-oriented agencies, as in the case of Costa Rica's *Instituto de Desarrollo Agrario*. In addition to the difficulties of deciding on how to approach these tradeoffs, top leaders have to cope with what are often inter-agency conflicts. In Laos, Mahaphonh et al. (2007, 1, 23) note that land conflicts expanded "due to government induced programs such as resettlement and village re-location," concluding that land conflicts were exacerbated by limited "inter-agency cooperation" as well as inter-agency rivalry. It seems reasonable to create broader migration agencies with diverse expertise, but this still may not ameliorate tensions among various experts and ministries.

Scale Back the Resettlement to Contain Budget Risks? The impacts of the decisions to launch resettlement programs, expel people from particular areas, or develop migration-stimulating physical infrastructure last far into the future—the communities involved may be changed forever. As is typical of policy impacts, uncertainty about the consequences of instigated migration increases over time. Interactions among migrants and host communities evolve, often in complex ways, as unanticipated economic consequences emerge and cultural changes are extremely difficult to assess. In many cases, the costs of effective management have been unexpectedly high, burdening successive governments.

More modest plans would reduce the likelihood that successor governments—or the current government given changing economic contexts—would eliminate the program or cut it drastically, leaving migrants stranded. However, scaling back the initial resettlement funding may hobble the program in terms of research and monitoring to ensure that appropriate sites are chosen, the economic support needed by migrants and/or host populations is provided, and governance capability is adequate.

Extend State Presence? Particularly when state-initiated migration extends to a frontier, state leaders face the dilemma of whether to intensify the state presence in the resettlement areas. On the one hand, this may strengthen the state's capacity to maintain order in resettlement areas, but it also may embroil the state in the conflicts that arise, requiring open-ended, unpredictable budgetary commitments. Recruiting willing officials may be challenging, and placing state officials in remote areas puts them farther from the support base on which they typically rely. One possible consequence is that state officials, beyond official monitoring by higher-level officials, will engage in corruption. For example, in China, "corruption among the officials and the sale of urban hukou seen as a lucrative area to earn money by the local authorities has further heightened the suspicions and angst of the rural migrants" (Hasija 2012, 9).

Another risk is that state officials may be beholden to particular elites or factions within the settlement area, and are especially likely to cooperate with state-sponsored co-ethnics in frontier regions. Some state leaders may opt for an "out of sight, out of mind" strategy, and permit migrants and indigenous populations to work out their issues with minimal state involvement.

Favor Sponsored Migrants Even If Host Populations Are More Vulnerable? In principle, a national government is responsible for the well-being of all of its citizens. However, no state can attend fully to the well-being of everyone. A compelling normative principle is that the state should prioritize the care of the most vulnerable groups, whether they are migrants or members of the host communities. Insofar as the expelled migrants are the most vulnerable, they should be favored; in other cases, host communities should have priority. Yet the principle of supporting the neediest frequently clashes with the state's accountability to make sponsored resettlement successful. Generally, this means that migrants are the "clients" of the program, and their well-being and stability of residence are the criteria by which the program will be evaluated by the state leaders held accountable. This client status puts resettled migrants in an advantageous position vis-à-vis hosts, for whom leaders also have an obligation of care. In some instances, state leaders will invoke—obviously controversially—the "improvement" of the host population by its contact with supposedly more modern migrants.

Limit the Right to Migrate? Article 13 of the Universal Declaration of Human Rights enshrines the right to freedom of movement.[1] There may, however, be good reasons to ignore this right, such as protecting vulnerable populations or ecosystems, or reducing the likelihood of destructive conflict. Yet, the restrictions may represent an

[1] Similarly, the International Covenant on Civil and Political Rights (ICCPR) states in Article 12 that "Everyone lawfully within the territory of a State shall, within that territory, have the right to liberty of movement and freedom to choose his [sic] residence" (ICCPR 1966).

illiberal strategy if needy people are denied opportunities that would not have serious adverse impacts. National officials may wish to keep particular people of particular ethnicities, religions, or partisan loyalties in or out of particular areas for political balance or to maintain a presence in a region potentially contested by other countries. Thus, instead of taking the free movement doctrine as an imperative, the state officials have a more complicated imperative: to decide (a) whether potentially destructive migrations should be allowed or blocked; and (b) whether encouraged or discouraged, how to accomplish either at an acceptable socioeconomic cost. Either way, officials at various levels face the risk of dissatisfaction on the part of erstwhile migrants if the migration is blocked by the opposition of people in the target area.

Accommodating Illegal Urban Settlements? Urbanization of low-income people poses an accommodation dilemma: should the state destroy the environmentally hazardous shanties at the risk of antagonizing squatters and blocking their efforts to be more productive? Costello (1987, 441) succinctly summarizes "the thorny issue of government accommodationist policies vis-a-vis urban squatters." From a social justice and human capital perspective, it makes good sense to provide members of this group with such basic services as potable water, electricity, schools, and sanitation facilities. The point is sometimes made, however, that such policies serve to intensify the urban crisis by attracting additional immigrants to already overcrowded cities. Should the state invest scarce resources in upgrading the slums, which could attract more migrants to the city? In the cases of voluntary urbanizers, discouraging low-income migration is frequently preferred by local authorities, but national leaders who understand the productivity gains of urbanization (see Chapter 7) would be more disposed to oppose the expulsion of the squatters and support the upgrading.

How Forceful Should State Control Be? Because state-initiated migration typically generates consequences that deviate from the planned impacts, state leaders face the dilemma of coping with the prospect of limited control, often exacerbated by limited resources. One consequence, especially for infrastructure-driven migration to remote regions, is that not all migrants fit the state's preferred profile. Migrants may move from target areas to other areas that state leaders deem inappropriate. The sociopolitical interactions among migrants and host populations evolve, sometimes in destructive ways. Therefore, states often find themselves enmeshed in remedial actions: addressing the environmental consequences when resettlement sites suffer from serious environmental degradation, policing conflicts between migrants and indigenous populations, trying to reverse migration patterns when the volume of migrants exceeds the planned level, extending state presence in frontiers into which migrants have gone beyond the planned extent of the resettlement, or addressing migrations into the areas (such as protected areas) from which other people have been expelled. For example, protected areas in Guatemala have been occupied by migrants fleeing violence (Aguilar and Morgera 2009, 19). Authorities thus face dilemmas of protecting vulnerable ecologies versus protecting vulnerable peoples.

When migration is unpredictable and difficult to control, state leaders may resort to more heavy-handed approaches to cope with otherwise spontaneous behavior on the part of migrants and/or host communities. Stricter regulations, greater state presence, and direct coercion may be how the state attempts to control when more subtle instruments seem too weak. Officials thus face the vicious cycle that while containing unintended consequences requires coercive instruments, coercion often generates resistance, which in turn presses the state to even more coercive actions to put down the resistance. This spiral of hostility may involve migrants, local populations, or both.

Conclusions

It is easy to damn the state regarding internal migration policies. There are bound to be groups that are perceived to lose out in any major state action, generating grievance and resistance even when policies are carried out in good faith. Officials may be criticized for supporting migration or for blocking it, condemned as authoritarian social engineers either way. Officials may be criticized for failing to remove poor communities from flood-prone regions after disaster strikes, or may be criticized by the same groups for pushing poor people out beforehand or for failing to relocate them to suitable locations. This chapter focused on the many dilemmas faced by state officials in governing internal migration, hopefully creating a degree of sympathy for at least some of the cases and policy failures reviewed in the following chapters.

References

Aguilar, Soledad, and Elisa Morgera. 2009. Wildlife Law and the Empowerment of the Poor in Latin America. *FAO Legal Papers Online* 80. Rome: UN Food and Agriculture Organization.

Baruah, Sanjib. 1986. Immigration, Ethnic Conflict, and Political Turmoil—Assam, 1979–1985. *Asian Survey* 26 (11): 1184–1206.

Costello, Michael A. 1987. Slums and Squatter Areas as Entrepots for Rural-Urban Migrants in a Less Developed Society. *Social Forces* 66 (2): 427–445.
Dagne, Shibru Abate. 2013. Conflict and Conflict Resolution Mechanisms in Ethiopia: The Case of Gedeo and Guji Ethnic Groups. Master's Thesis: Andhra University.
Debelo, Asebe Regassa. 2007. Ethnicity and Inter-ethnic Relations. The 'Ethiopian Experiment' and the Case of the Guji and Gedeo. Master's Thesis: Universitetet i Tromsø.
Dodge, Kenneth A. 2006. Translational Science in Action: Hostile Attributional Style and the Development of Aggressive Behavior Problems. *Development and Psychopathology* 18 (3): 791–814.
Gardner, Tom. 2019. Shadow Falls Over Ethiopia Reforms as Warnings of Crisis Go Unheeded. *The Guardian*, March 14.
Guha, Ramachandra. 2007. Adivasis, Naxalites and Indian Democracy. *Economic and Political Weekly*: 3305–3312.
Hasija, Namrata. 2012. *Migrant Unrest in China*. New Delhi: Institute of Peace and Conflict Studies China Research Programme. www.ipcs.org/issue_briefs/issue_brief_pdf/SR119-CRP-MigrantUnrestinChina.pdf.
ICCPR (International Covenant on Civil and Political Rights) 1966.
Kinfemichael, Girum. 2014. The Quest for Resolution of Guji-Gedeo Conflicts in Southern Ethiopia: A Review of Mechanisms Employed, Actors and Their Effectiveness. *Ethiopian Journal of the Social Sciences and Humanities* 10 (1): 59–100.
Lucas, Robert E.B. 2021. *Crossing the Divide: Rural to Urban Migration in Developing Countries*. Oxford: Oxford University Press and KNOWMAD.
Mahaphonh, Nouphanh, Pheuiphanh Ngaosrivathana, Meena Phimphachanh, Sysaweui Chittasupha, Serntai Pasay, and Peter Jones. 2007. *Study on Land Conflicts and Conflict Resolution in Lao PDR*. Vientiane: Lao-German Land Policy Development Project Land Policy Study 9.
Myers, Daniel J. 2000. The Diffusion of Collective Violence: Infectiousness, Susceptibility, and Mass Media Networks. *American Journal of Sociology* 106 (1): 173–208.
Reddy, I.U.B., and Smrithi Talwar. 2014. How Fair is 'Fair Compensation' under India's New Land Acquisition Act? *World Bank End Poverty in South Asia Blog*. Washington, DC: World Bank.
Varshney, Ashutosh, Mohammad Zulfan Tadjoeddin, and Rizal Panggabean. 2004. *Patterns of Collective Violence in Indonesia, 1990–2003*. Jakarta: United Nations Support Facility for Indonesian Recovery.

CHAPTER 6

Migrants in Train: State-Initiated and Managed Migrations

Given the multiple reasons for states to promote migration, and different circumstances in which migrations occur, many forms of migration exist as the result of state actions. This variation makes it extremely difficult to generalize about those who migrate because of state decisions to facilitate, instigate, formally sponsor, or coerce migrations. It certainly makes sense to distinguish between voluntary and coerced migrations, the latter further distinguishable between resettlement *to* specific areas and displacement *from* specific areas. Greater fuzziness exists in distinguishing among migration patterns that are triggered or instigated by state action short of demanding that people move. It is difficult to determine whether building a highway into an area that would seem attractive to land-hungry farmers, along with providing agricultural extension services to the area, is "state-sponsored," or if a state-funded social assistance program for people displaced by violence or natural disasters should also fit within this category. Or should extended family members who tag along with sponsored migrants be considered "sponsored" migrants—especially if they are seen as such by host communities?

This chapter presents the range of profiles and perspectives of migrants who move because of state actions—many of these would not have relocated if not for the state initiative. The magnitudes and durations of state

W. Ascher and S. J. Barter, *Moving within Borders*, Politics, Economics, and Inclusive Development, https://doi.org/10.1007/978-3-031-37549-1_6

resettlement initiatives vary enormously, from resettling less than a thousand people to make way for a utility-scale solar array, to many millions relocated to highland areas. As Table 6.1 indicates, many resettlements have been truly massive. This chapter is organized beginning with the most coerced migrations, then cases where states relocate migrant groups to help them, and then state-promoted, voluntary migrants. This will lead into Chapters 7 and 8, on non-state, unmanaged migrants.

State-Coerced Migration

States often force their people to migrate. This may be driven by considerations at the point of departure, such as wanting land for development or pushing out a certain group, or else it may be focused on the destination areas, promoting development, assimilating remote populations, or securing borders. This distinction is important, as states that simply want people out may coerce displacement with little regard for resettlement, whereas if the focus is on the destination, states are more likely to manage the entire process. If they are resettled in state-selected locations, the migrants' circumstances will depend on several factors, including how much state support they receive (and for how long), the reactions of local communities, and the area's economic viability.

Migrants forced to move may or may not be brought to state-selected locations. They may be displaced by the state, but not managed by it. This could involve urban or rural peoples whose lands are prized by state planners, creating development IDPs. Prominent examples include those displaced to make way for infrastructure projects such as dams. Sometimes, urban populations forced out by the state are already voluntary migrants from rural areas now living in informal settlements in the city. As the state displaces them from their new homes, they thus face different challenges as migrants. It may also be the case that a given area is overpopulated, with officials driving out groups to reduce congestion or dilute rebellion.

With its coercive capability, the state often can reduce the weight of ethnic or political groups in particularly sensitive areas through expulsion. States may displace their own citizens as part of counterinsurgency measures. In the 1980s, the Turkish army began expelling Kurds from Eastern and Southeastern Anatolia (Çelik 2005, 139). At the same time, many Kurds fled the areas due to fear of violence involving Kurdish insurgents and the army. The Burmese army expelled Karen, Shan, and

Table 6.1 State-managed Resettlement Programs during Selected Periods

Country	*Period*	*Total national population*	*Resettled people*	*Resettled families*	*Estimated people (~3 per family)*	*Source*
Farmer Relocation						
Brazil	1981–2010	200,000,000		1,500,000	4,500,000	Navarro (2009, 276–278)
China (a)	1980–2010	1,100,000,000	20,000,000		20,000,000	Lo and Wang (2018, 34)
Indonesia	1905–1950	38,000,000		222,000	666,000	Oberai (1983, 142–143)
	1950–1977	15,000,000		771,000	2,313,000	Oberai (1983, 142–143)
Laos (b)	1989–2000	5,000,000	900,000		900,000	Evrard and Goudineau (2014, 944)
Philippines	1972–2000	50,000,000		4,000,000	12,000,000	Borras (2009, 230)
Zimbabwe	2000–2007	12,000,000		160,000	480,000	Binswanger-Mkhize and Deininger (2009, 69)
Rural to Villages ("Villagization")						
Ethiopia (c)	1984–1986	42,000,000	600,000		600,000	Gebre (2003, 50)
Tanzania	1967–1974	11,000,000	2,560,000		2,560,000	Barker (2019, 95)
Nomads to Farming and Fishing Areas						
Somalia	1975–1977	4,000,000	120,000		120,000	Tsui et al. (1991, 131)

(a) "Poverty Alleviation Resettlement" (b) Upland swidden (c) Upland farmers

Rohingya from rebellious areas (Falla 1991; Grundy-Warr and Wong Siew Yin 2002). During the Guatemalan civil war, the army forced hundreds of thousands of indigenous Guatemalans out of the highlands to sever rebel support (Delli Sante 1996). Another case is Saddam Hussein's efforts to drain the marshes of Iraq, turning river estuaries into desert to drive out outlaws and Marsh Arabs suspected of resisting the regime, but with little concern for their destination (Ahram 2015). It is also possible that a given ethnic group is subject to expulsion, or barred from residing near borders, specific ethnic territories, or urban areas. These cases all involve political expulsion, with the state wanting people out with little concern for helping them relocate.

Casting political IDPs as disloyal and disruptive allows state leaders to deny compensation. To make matters worse, these migrants often carry this reputation into the areas to which they migrate. When political IDPs are expelled from areas where they had numerical strength and thrust into areas dominated by others, they are likely to strengthen their in-group identity, perhaps through the dynamic of shared victimization (Bar-Tal et al. 2009; Confino 2005). Many such state-led displacements stand as eventual drivers of international migration, with IDPs weary of living under hostile states.

It is also possible that states may remove people from a given location by force, then dictate and thus manage their relocation. They may do so for a desire to control the displaced community, block them from returning, or achieve development goals in the receiving area. This could include entire ethnic minority communities relocated by rulers, such as the Tatars under Stalin, who were deported suddenly and en masse to Central Asia due to suspected links to Germany (Uehling 2004). Another example is found in counterinsurgency programs, with villagers not only being pushed from their homes, but also being relocated into "strategic hamlets" to monitor them and sever civilians from rebel groups. This strategy evolved from British counterinsurgency operations in the Boer War (1899–1902) and during the 1950s in Kenya and peninsular Malaya, with the Americans expanding the tactic in Vietnam in the 1960s. Forced resettlement into state-controlled villages was utilized in Latin American conflicts in the 1970s and 80s. Taylor (1998, 48) notes that in Peru, the army forced communities to "pack up their belongings and move" to government villages. Most of the new settlements failed, as "inter-community rivalries and uncertainty surrounding how they would be able to earn a living and protect their possessions" led to conflicts among civilians, resentment toward the state, and greater support for the rebels. Within three years, government villages had been largely abandoned, with civilians returning to their homes or living with rebel groups.

Other forms of state-coerced resettlement are typically presented as aiding the people required to move, assimilating host communities, or securing borders. Here, states typically invest considerable attention and resources in the destination areas, managing the entire internal migration process, and sometimes monitoring migrants long into the future.

It is hard to imagine that migrants who are directly coerced by the state to resettle in a specific area would do so happily. Regardless of whether the state's primary focus is on conditions of the migrants' home area or the state's advantage in bringing populations to where they can be controlled more effectively, migrants may see the state as forcing change onto the most fundamental aspects of their lives.

It is conceivable that coercion might be justified if it is in the interests of the migrants, and coercion is the only way to relocate them. People may live in flood-prone or otherwise ecologically sensitive areas. This presumes not only that the state officials have the migrants' welfare at heart, but also that officials know better than migrants. Even if officials can demonstrate that communities are at risk, it does not always follow that the people will be better off elsewhere. For example, a prolonged drought in the 1970s led the Ethiopian government to begin ambitious, coercive resettlement programs. One program involved resettling over a million rural northerners to more densely populated sites in the country's south. The result was disastrous, with migrants suffering from disease and famine. Prothero (1994, 659) recounts that

> People were moved from higher altitudes in the north and centre of the country to lower-lying areas in the west and south west; from the relatively malaria-free Ethiopian plateau above 2000m to lower altitudes where malaria was endemic. Settlers lacked immunity and were at risk of high morbidity and mortality. Risks of malaria infection were increased further in settlements with irrigation which extended in space and time the habitats favourable for vector breeding.

In addition to health challenges, the economies at relocation sites fared poorly, with farmers taking years to attain self-sufficiency in basic foods and pastoralists remaining dependent on the state for decades. Relocation, sickness, economic challenges, and dependency also led to psychological problems among migrants. Migrants defied orders and returned to their former homes, especially as drought conditions improved and authorities were unable to effectively monitor relocation sites (Prothero 1994, 660).

Migrants suffering from such misfortunes are prone to be resentful when state promises prove false, especially if migrants believe that state interests, rather than migrant welfare, were the driving motive. For Arnall (2019, 257), "Development narratives…can be so powerful that relocated people might consent to, or even appear to support, resettlement in spite of it leading to very poor living conditions." When such narratives fall short, the result can be widespread discontent. Arnall cites Tanzanian "villagization" (*sogeza*) schemes (1967–1974) as a case in point. Under President Nyerere, Tanzania forced millions of peasants into centralized government villages of several hundred households. State-coerced village resettlement was partly carried out to encourage development, as authorities believed that dense, centralized settlements would allow for agricultural modernization and better provision of government services (Wenban-Smith 2015, 7). It was also carried out for ideological reasons, namely Nyerere's quasi-socialist concept of Ujamaa (extended family), which necessitated one-party, paternalistic political power as well as glorifying tight-knit rural villages. Wenban-Smith (2015, 7) reports that although Tanzanian villagization started "as something to be encouraged on a voluntary basis, slow progress led to a hardening of official attitudes and increasing use of coercion." The turning point was in 1973, when officials forced thousands of people to move from flood-prone river plains to hilltop state villages. The new villages lacked water and the soils could not grow the crops that thrived along the river. For those forced to relocate, "a widespread feeling of having been herded together into close proximity with a large number of strangers" led to tensions, fears of witchcraft and theft, and contradicted the state's mission of cooperation in developing new communities (Schneider 2004, 357).

States also compel migration through less direct coercion. Rulers may use intimidation, restrictions of access to land, the denial of services at the original site, and the promise of services in a new site to compel migration. In Laos, Bird (1992, 5) summarizes the ambiguity of resettlement as "nominally voluntary rather than forced." The Lao government banned shifting cultivation and took over forests, severing highland peoples from primary resources. Authorities also placed "resettlement agents" in highland villages to compel relocation, as well as to dismantle services and infrastructure. Such high-pressure tactics did not always involve direct coercion, but may be considered as migration forced upon communities by the state.

Forced, But Not by the State: Evacuation and Resettlement

A subset of state-managed migration is found when violence, natural disasters, and other emergencies make it unsafe to remain in a home area. People may be forced out by non-state factors, but their evacuation and resettlement are managed by the state. Authorities may also forcibly relocate communities tha t do not wish to go, but, at least in the eyes of state authorities, must leave for their own good. This can, of course, be a pretext used by states wishing to achieve other goals, but may also involve ensuring people's welfare.

Unlike many forms of coerced state migration, in cases of evacuation and resettlement, those involved are less likely to represent groups favored or targeted by the state. Natural disasters often trigger immediate evacuations that do not imply that migrants are favored clients. In such circumstances, the relationships between migrants and host communities may be supportive initially, as local people sympathize with the displaced. Over time, however, as resources dwindle, relations may fray, depending on tangible factors such as whether support can be replenished by the state, NGOs, or international aid, and intangible factors such as the cultural and political compatibility of the groups.

Whereas more voluntary forms of migration may primarily involve young migrants, sudden evacuations typically involve entire communities. States may try to keep communities together, transplanting them into new homes. This may slow integration into new communities, but offers benefits for migrants who are kept together with those they know and trust. Of course, evacuations are typically rushed. Resettlement sites may not be well prepared and little research may have been done to ensure compatibility with host communities. Resettlement may also involve multiple movements, perhaps first placing evacuees in temporary sites, then relocating them to better-planned homes.

In some cases, the state's reaction to unavoidable evacuation is not resettlement in a particular location, but rather social assistance to people compelled to evacuate, going wherever they find promising or safe. Such migrants have the incentive to demand recognition of their IDP status.

In other cases, IDPs regard officials as threats, therefore seek to minimize contact and remain hidden. Bullock (2017, 11) notes that in El Salvador, a country with one of the world's highest levels of violence, many migrants fear the state as much as they fear gangs; "In general, internally displaced people (IDPs) don't want to be found and counted, and families and individuals often move without informing neighbours or even close relatives where they are." Many IDPs prefer kinship support networks, resisting state assistance, and may be better off as a result, but may also then be disqualified from eventual assistance.

In cases of evacuation, the question of whether and when to return is a difficult dilemma, hinging on whether the migrants' home area is sufficiently safe and can be restored. State officials, host communities, and IDPs may wish to see a return to sites that are not ready or will never be safe. One risk that IDPs face is that states may suspend assistance if they declare that returning home is feasible, essentially forcing repatriation. If migrants disagree and feel compelled to remain, they may mobilize, perhaps with NGO assistance, to remain and retain whatever the state had been providing in social assistance. The inverse may also be true, with IDPs wanting to return to homes that the state declares off-limits. In the aftermath of the 2004 Indian Ocean tsunami, many states and Western NGOs rebuilt villages further from the ocean as a means to protect people from future disasters. Many survivors, however, did not like the new sites because, as fishers, they needed to be closer to the ocean. Relocating to safer areas would thus threaten livelihoods, prompting disaster IDPs to defy orders, adopt new vocations, or get around new laws by building sleeping dorms on the beaches (Sina et al. 2019). Many IDPs deemed the low probability of a major disaster preferable to being far from their livelihoods, resisting state efforts to force them into safer areas.

Voluntary State-Managed Migrants: Clients and Pioneers

Other forms of state-initiated migration are more voluntary, with authorities providing incentives to those willing to relocate. Here, migrants are typically young and poor, and often represent dominant ethnic groups. This may involve young men, young families, or extended families. The opportunity for needy families to come voluntarily under the sponsorship of the state to seek improved conditions can be alluring, even if the new locale is unfamiliar and perhaps forebidding. Putting one's fate in the hands of the state or using state-provided physical infrastructure is an act of faith. Sometimes this is rewarded, with migrants supported by the state and enjoying new levels of wealth. In other cases, however, this faith is betrayed. Thus, the perspectives and behaviors of voluntary state-sponsored migrants vary dramatically, depending on how much support they receive from the state and whether that support is effective.

It is useful to think of the relationship between the state and sponsored migrants as an implicit contract. Like many contracts, some difficulties arise because of differences in interests. Whereas state officials often want sponsored migrants to settle in the designated areas and abide by various rules, migrants may wish to settle where they can maximize their well-being, following rules only insofar as they are deemed beneficial. When state officials' motives for promoting migration are dominated by reducing the potential for conflict, the productivity potential of the resettlement area may be of secondary concern. In countries with extensive frontiers, state resettlement may focus on these areas to minimize conflicts with local people. Yet, there are reasons why migration areas are so often sparsely populated, with land not suitable for high-density agriculture. In many cases, migrants are disappointed in the resettlement locales.

The Clients

State-incentivized, voluntary migration programs often proceed as planned, with states managing migrants and ensuring the long-term sustainability of their programs. We will return to relatively successful migration policies in Chapter 14. For now, one danger in even relatively successfully managed migrations is that migrants, whether or not loyal to the state, may become dependent on it. In some cases, resettlement succeeds only because new villages maintain state support for many years, with migrants remaining clients. Such migrants may also be confident about pressing their interests vis-à-vis the local community, insofar as they think of themselves as protected by the state. In the political triangle of state, migrants, and host communities, indulged migrants have a strong interest in maintaining good relations with state officials.

For example, in Thailand, the state encouraged Buddhist settlers from the North and Northeast to the Malay Muslim south. The state-provided settlers with new homes and economic support. But the settlers arrived amidst unrest, with many Malays perceiving the arrivals as state colonialism. This was not necessarily a religious conflict, as established ethnic

Thai and Chinese families were not viewed in the same light as the new migrants. Here, state clientelism represented a double-edged sword, as embittered hosts recognized that the migrants and the state were allied. As the conflict intensified, with militants seemingly trying to push migrants out of the Pattani region, migrants fled, despite state efforts to force them to remain. When Thai migrants left Pattani, they remained largely dependent on the state, insisting that authorities relocate them to safer areas (Olthof 2016, 30). Those who remained continued to be dependent on the state for security and other forms of support.

The Pioneers

In many cases, states promote internal migration, but then migrants are left to their own devices. Migrants could be promised much, with states failing to deliver either by accident or design. As migrants are left to make their own way, such pioneers are often hostile toward the state, clashing with host societies and presenting new governance challenges.

The travails of migrants into the Brazilian Amazon epitomize this pattern. In terms of disconnects of interests, the state's objectives entailed moving land-hungry people away from agriculturally promising regions and complying with conditions of World Bank loans for Amazonian highways. Launched in 1981, the *Polonoroeste* Program granted land in the Amazon to 5,000 families per month. Each sponsored migrant was granted 100 hectares, half of which was to be kept forested as per conditions specified in World Bank loans (Fearnside 1985). The plan was to establish towns along the new highways, with the administrative and social service infrastructure to match the populations entering what had been a near vacuum in these respects.

The reality degenerated into a free-for-all. This was due to the rushed implementation of formal resettlement programs, the low capacity of relevant agencies to provide administrative infrastructure, and the huge number of unsponsored migrants who followed official state migrants. Having been granted land titles and promised assistance, most migrants were left to fend for themselves. The promised agricultural extension services, crucial for the farmers to adapt to the different soil and climatic conditions, lagged far behind. MacMillan (1995, 21) reported that migrants "found that the infrastructure they had been promised was seldom provided in full…Health care, education, credit lines, technical advice and transport facilities were all scarce, reflecting a widely recognized shortfall in Amazonian colonization." What had been billed as an all-embracing resettlement program left migrants as fend-for-yourself pioneers. Fraud and violence marked the struggle for land, with areas such as Pará becoming notoriously dangerous frontiers (Simmons et al. 2007). Many sponsored migrants felt betrayed by the state's failure to keep its promises. Whether these migrants considered state plans to be naïve or insincere in terms of the magnitude of resources required, they certainly did not consider themselves state clients bound to the commitments by any "contract." Migrants frequently defied the provision of maintaining 50 forested hectares, and many migrants moved multiple times to other areas as their farms failed, or took up illegal mineral prospecting or logging.

The case of the Brazilian Amazon is by no means unique in leaving sponsored migrants underserved. Another prominent case relates to Mindanao, in the southern Philippines, a sparsely-populated island that has seen considerable migration from more populous nearby islands. After a series of failed, small-scale settlement programs in the first decades of the twentieth century, US colonizers ceded greater political authority to the Commonwealth government in the 1930s. At this time, migration to Mindanao expanded dramatically, overseen by the National Land Settlement Administration (NLSA). The NLSA worked to screen prospective migrants and manage flows, however "many of these requirements were disregarded" as word spread across the country, leading to the arrival of tens of thousands of families at their own expense, who then benefited from state support (Pelzer 1945, 139). Large-scale internal migration grew again in the 1960s. Settlers rushed to register for state-sanctioned tracts of land and take up farming, but many settlements failed "partly because of the lack of necessary support infrastructure," leading desperate settlers to "relentlessly encroach on to Muslim and Lumad territories" (Villema et al. 2011, 306). The result was decades of separatist and intergroup conflict, costing thousands of lives.

Also in Southeast Asia, a 2016 assessment of Cambodia's Social Land Concession (SLC) program concluded that most sites lacked clinics and schools, or else were missing the requisite doctors and teachers (Richter 2016, 16). Education deficits are particularly concerning, in that the typical pattern of sponsored migrations in all developing regions is that migrants are enticed from more developed areas where education services are considerably more established than in the resettlement site. An additional problem is that migrants may find that schools lack teachers capable of teaching their language. Such cases resemble those discussed at the beginning of the chapter in terms of coerced migration; although voluntary, the state is primarily interested in getting people out, perhaps directing them toward a specific area, but then cutting them loose.

Conclusions

This chapter examined migrations initiated and/or managed by the state. It established varied contexts, including migrations coerced by state authorities, state support for those displaced by other factors, and state-managed voluntary migration. Although most migrations are not sponsored by the state, recent decades have seen a bewildering range of examples of a state being highly involved in internal migration, with tremendous ecological, economic, and human consequences. Even where states are not the primary actors in pushing people out or directing where they go, the following chapter suggests that the state plays a myriad of indirect roles in shaping migratory patterns and well-being.

References

Ahram, Ariel I. 2015. Development, Counterinsurgency, and the Destruction of the Iraqi Marshes. *International Journal of Middle East Studies* 47 (3): 447–466.

Arnall, Alex. 2019. Resettlement as Climate Change Adaptation: What Can be Learned from State-Led Relocation in Rural Africa and Asia? *Climate and Development* 11 (3): 253–263.

Barker, Jonathan. 2019. The Debate on Rural Socialism in Tanzania. In *Towards Socialism in Tanzania*, ed. Bismarck Mwansasu and Cranford Pratt, 95–124. Toronto: University of Toronto Press.

Bar-Tal, Daniel, Lily Chernyak-Hai, Noa Schori, and Ayelet Gundar. 2009. A Sense of Self-perceived Collective Victimhood in Intractable Conflicts. *International Review of the Red Cross* 91 (874): 229–258.

Binswanger-Mkhize, Hans, and Klaus Deininger. 2009. History of Land Concentration and Redistributive Land Reforms. In *Agricultural Land Redistribution: Toward Greater Consensus*, eds. Hans Binswanger-Mkhize, Camille Bourguignon, and Rogier van den Brink, 45–86. Washington, DC: World Bank.

Bird, Kate. 1992. 'Voluntary' Migration in Lao People's Democratic Republic. *Indicators* 93 (Overseas Development Institute).

Borras, Saturnino M, Jr. 2009. Land Redistribution in the Philippines. In *Agricultural Land Redistribution: Toward Greater Consensus*, eds. Hans Binswanger-Mkhize, Camille Bourguignon, and Rogier van den Brink, 215–240. Washington, DC: World Bank.

Bullock, Noah. 2017. Towards a Response: Addressing Forced Displacement by Violence in El Salvador. *Humanitarian Exchange* 69: 9–12.

Confino, Alon. 2005. Remembering the Second World War, 1945–1965: Narratives of Victimhood and Genocide. *Cultural Analysis* 4: 46–75.

Çelik, Ayşe Betül. 2005. 'I Miss My Village!': Forced Kurdish Migrants in Istanbul and Their Representation in Associations. *New Perspectives on Turkey* 32: 137–163.

Delli Sante, Angela. 1996. *Nightmare or Reality: Guatemala in the 1980s*. Amsterdam: Thela.

Evrard, Olivier, and Yves Goudineau. 2004. Planned Resettlement, Unexpected Migrations and Cultural Trauma in Laos. *Development and Change* 35 (5): 937–962.

Falla, Jonathan. 1991. *True Love and Bartholomew: Rebels on the Burmese Border*. Cambridge: Cambridge University Press.

Fearnside, Philip. 1985. Deforestation and Decision-Making in the Development of the Brazilian Amazonia. *Interciencia* 10 (5): 243–247.

Gebre, Yntiso. 2003. Resettlement and the Unnoticed Losers: Impoverishment Disasters among the Gumz in Ethiopia. *Human Organization* 62 (1): 50–61.

Grundy-Warr, Carl, and Elaine Wong Siew Yin. 2002. Geographies of Displacement: The Karenni and the Shan Across the Myanmar-Thailand Border. *Singapore Journal of Tropical Geography* 23 (1): 93–122.

Lo, Kevin, and Mark Wang. 2018. How Voluntary Is Poverty Alleviation Resettlement in China? *Habitat International* 73: 34–42.

MacMillan, Gordon. 1995. *At the End of the Rainbow? Gold, Land, and People in the Brazilian Amazon*. New York: Columbia University Press.

Navarro, Zander. 2009. Expropriating Land in Brazil. In *Agricultural Land Redistribution: Toward Greater Consensus*, eds. Hans Binswanger-Mkhize, Camille Bourguignon, and Rogier van den Brink, 267–290. Washington, DC: World Bank.

Olthof, Douglas Allan. 2016. Compounding Fractures: State-Society Relations and Inter-Ethnic Estrangement in Thailand's 'Deep South'. PhD diss., Simon Fraser University. Burnaby, BC.

Pelzer, Karl J. 1945. *Pioneer Settlement in the Asiatic Tropics*, New York: American Geographical Society Special Publication No. 29.

Prothero, Mansell. 1994. Forced Movements of Population and Health Hazards in Tropical Africa. *International Journal of Epidemiology* 23 (4): 657–664.

Richter, Iris. 2016. Experiences from the Implementation of Social Land Concessions in Cambodia. Bonn: Deutsche Gesellschaft für Internationale Zusammenarbeit. January.

Schneider, Leander. 2004. Freedom and Rural Development: Julius Nyerere, Ujaama Vijijini, and Villagization. *Canadian Journal of African Affairs* 38 (2): 344–392.

Simmons, C.S., R.T. Walker, E.Y. Arima, S.P. Aldrich, and M.M. Caldas. 2007. The Amazon Land War in the South of Pará. *Annals of the Association of American Geographers* 97 (3): 567–592.

Sina, Dantje, Alice Chang-Richards, Suzanne Wilkinson, and Regan Potangaroa. 2019. A Conceptual Framework for Measuring Livelihood Resilience: Relocation Experience from Aceh, Indonesia. *World Development* 117: 253–265.

Taylor, Lewis. 1998. Counter-Insurgency Strategy, the PCP-Sendero Luminoso, and the Civil War in Peru, 1980–1996. *Bulletin of Latin American Research* 17 (1): 35–58.

Tsui, Amy O., Tod A. Ragsdale, and Aden I. Shirwa. 1991. The Settlement of Somali Nomads. *Genus* 47: 131–152.

Uehling, Greta L. 2004. *Beyond Memory: The Crimean Tatars' Deportation and Return*. London: Springer.

Villema, Sietze, Saturnino M. Borras, Jr, and Francisco Lara Jr. 2011. The Agrarian Roots of Contemporary Violent Conflict in Mindanao, Southern Philippines. *Journal of Agrarian Change* 11 (3): 298–320.

Wenban-Smith, Hugh. 2015. *Population Growth, Internal Migration and Urbanisation in Tanzania, 1967–2012: Phase 2 (Final Report)*. London: International Growth Centre.

CHAPTER 7

Unsponsored Migrants: The Enterprising

Most internal migration is not through state-sponsored resettlement programs. State-sponsored migration is more common than we tend to think, and many unsponsored migrants may trail along with sponsored communities, however most people move for reasons not driven by the state, sometimes doing so against state preferences. They may find that living in their home areas is no longer viable, perhaps because of declining agricultural productivity, poverty, landlessness, violence, or the risk of natural disaster, but are unable to obtain state assistance. They may be part of a culture that calls for young people to go out into the world. They may wish to be closer to extended family or other people with whom they identify. Or they may believe that moving to another area would simply improve their lives, expecting job opportunities and a better life, especially as word spreads of opportunities enjoyed by other migrants.

The following two chapters focus on unsponsored migration, movements not primarily driven by the state, even if various officials and policies shape its contours. This chapter focuses on what may be understood as economic migrants—persons who tend to be poor and, to acquire jobs or land, relocate from one region to another. Like many state-sponsored migrants, economic migrants relocate voluntarily to improve their well-being, although the mechanisms are very different and uncertainty perhaps greater. Chapter 8, then, focuses on the expelled, various

W. Ascher and S. J. Barter, *Moving within Borders*, Politics, Economics, and Inclusive Development, https://doi.org/10.1007/978-3-031-37549-1_7

forms of IDPs moving against their will. In a sense, this reflects division between voluntary and involuntary migration. This is a useful distinction, although one that should not be applied too strictly. The idea of "forced" migration suffers from ambiguity, as even those pushed out by immediate violence still make important choices, and economic migration is compelled by structural factors such as unemployment or landlessness. It is essential to remember that many economic migrants are also IDPs, for instance, persons pushed out by war who migrate to cities in search of safety, support, and employment. Still, we can see economic migration more in terms of "pull" factors, while IDPs—many of whom may not be formally recognized as such—are driven more by "push" factors.

For the various forms of unsponsored migration, the state does not primarily oversee movement, but its policies nonetheless shape the volume and well-being of migrants. State actions and policies may range from causing migration (e.g., driving out civilians in wars or clearing out communities for dams), to managing migrants (e.g., IDP camps), making migration easier or more difficult (e.g., land-tenure policies), or even resisting migration (e.g., regulating urban migration).

This chapter on unsponsored economic migrants is organized into three parts. It begins with a discussion of rural migration, under-studied migrant flows from urban and rural regions to new rural areas in search of arable land. It then shifts to merchant migration, where current or erstwhile traders and shopkeepers move primarily to smaller towns, but also to rural and urban areas, in search of business. Finally, we focus on the most studied form of unsponsored population movements—urban migration.

The Land Hungry

For many farmers, each year the crops seem thinner. They wilt in the greater heat and are stunted by brackish water. They leave less surplus to sell, barely enough for growing families. Land-seeking migrants may be dispossessed as another sibling, often the eldest male, inherits the land, or because the division of land among inheritors has left the holdings too small to be viable. Not too far away, rumor has it, are uncultivated lands.

Rumors of available land may also beckon city dwellers to venture into the countryside. Such migration, which one might expect to be relatively unimportant given the trend toward urbanization, is significant in many countries. An estimated nine percent of Indian migrants relocate from cities to the countryside (Hnatkovska and Lahiri 2015, S259), and 19 percent in Ethiopia (Schewel and Bahir 2019, 10). Rees et al. (2017) estimate that, in a selection of developing countries, about ten percent of internal migration is urban to rural. Perhaps we should not be surprised that migration to and from rural and urban areas is a two-way street, especially given the numerous deprivations faced by migrants in urban areas. Lucas (2021, 283) insists that we should not see rural return migrants as "failures" though, as some might have never planned to remain in cities permanently or may return as a sort of retirement. However, it is not clear what proportion of such migrants are seeking land, since the motives, as with any migration, may be mixed: Seeking labor in extractive industries, venturing out as merchants or entrepreneurs, escaping crime-ridden neighborhoods, evicted from informal settlements, a desire for leisure and cleaner air, and so on (Gosnell and Abrams 2011).

A large proportion of urban-to-rural migration is caused by state efforts to decrease urbanization and/or clear out slums, especially in times of upheaval, economic downturns, or in public health emergencies. For instance, the 2008 recession in China led 20–40 million migrant workers to return to their home regions, often in rural areas, due to job losses and heightened costs for temporary urban residency passes (Wallace 2014, 174). During the COVID-19 pandemic, cities around the world saw massive returns of urban migrants to rural areas, sparking fears of contagion as well as rural unrest (Samaddar et al. 2020).

Whether leaving crowded rural farms or cities, rural migrants are typically in search of land. Land-hungry migrants face two distinct scenarios. One is that a potential area for migration is thinly populated, almost exclusively by sedentary farmers, where land is seen as "vacant." This would seem promising, but untilled land where people have tried to farm for centuries is unlikely to be very productive. Land-hungry migrants still may migrate to these areas because they have little choice, are misinformed about its potential, or are simply overly optimistic. The second scenario is that the area is occupied by herders, shifting cultivators, or hunter-gatherers. The land may have agricultural potential that current occupants have not utilized. The herders may be happy to share the area in the prospect of exchanging meat and milk for vegetables and grains, as well as benefit from new investment.

Sometimes farmers had been kept out by residents, through force of arms or state protection. This may have been because of historical animosity, cultural differences, or concern for resources such as water. Officials may have had reasons to keep the area clear of newcomers, perhaps to avoid conflict. But, with consistent pressure, migrants may prevail. For example, Kenyan and Tanzanian governments have prevented pastoralist Maasai from excluding migrant farmers. In Kenya, changing land-tenure policies in the 1970s permitted the Maasai elite to gain private ownership over what had been communal land; some of this land was sold to Kipsigi farmers facing land shortages in their traditional areas. In Tanzania, the *ujamaa* ideology of "one nation and no tribes" permitted any Tanzanian to live in any part of the country, opening up areas that had been reserved for the Maasai to low-income Iraqw and Mbulu migrants seeking agricultural work, prosperous Chagga and Mbulu tradesmen, and state officials intent on developing business initiatives (Homewood et al. 2004, 578–583).

Farmers in need of land would likely prefer to settle near their home area to maintain ties with co-ethnics and to maximize the likelihood that their farming practices will remain appropriate for the new land. However, nearby land may not be available, demanding that agricultural migrants go further afield. They typically possess some agricultural expertise, yet new areas may have different soils, topography, hydrology, and other characteristics that render their traditional farming techniques ineffective. Ecological knowledge may be ill-suited to new contexts, with hosts possessing different property systems or use of land different from those of migrants. Often, such areas are remote, lacking in technology and fertilizer, facing unreliable irrigation, and far from markets.

In many cases, urban-to-rural land-hungry migrants have particularly difficult times. In addition to the baseline challenges facing anyone who ventures into areas occupied by different people, some of the services and amenities that are taken for granted in cities are in short supply in rural areas. Urban-to-rural migrants intending to farm often lack the skills to engage in agriculture. Zezza and Tasciotti (2010) show that urban agriculture is surprisingly common throughout the world, a source of additional nutrition and revenue, perhaps practice for potential future farming. However, even those with urban agriculture experience may lack the expertise and/or capital for rural-scale agriculture or may be unfamiliar with local ecology. Failure is not uncommon; a study of urban residents of Nigeria migrating to rural areas found that four-fifths of them returned to cities within ten years (Adewale 2005).

The Entrepreneurial Land Hungry

Not all land-hungry migrants are poor. Some may migrate to increase their wealth through entrepreneurship. Farmers who are finding success in new crops may set their sights on areas that seem to offer under-utilized land.

Entrepreneurial farmers are likely to maintain connections beyond migration sites for the procurement of supplies and to market their products. Insofar as they bring capital from their home areas, they may be able to establish plantations, employ local people, and purchase more property. They may also introduce new crops, especially those previously not profitable due to a lack of infrastructure. For example, in Indonesia, various internal migrant communities have focused on coffee production, as the crop grows well in mountainous regions not suited to other crops. In Sumatra and Sulawesi, migrants have expanded coffee as well as maize production by encroaching on indigenous and wildlife reserves, leading to new ecological and social pressures (Arifin 2010). The businesses of entrepreneurial migrants may attract more migrants as their laborers. At some point, successful entrepreneurial migrants may become more powerful than the local elite, generating tensions and conflict.

Resource Extractors

The motivation for migration into rural areas to extract minerals, forest resources, or animal products may be either the basis for the initial migration or may represent a fallback if initial plans fail, especially for frustrated agricultural migrants with no place to go. The case of Brazilian gold prospectors in the Amazon exemplifies the transition from failed farmer to artisanal miner (Wood 2002). When resource extraction is large-scale, jobs in commercial mines, oil fields, plantations, and logging companies can attract both low-income laborers and entrepreneurs. In some cases, resource extraction also may benefit local communities, providing jobs, infrastructure, and new goods. Resource extraction generally occurs in remote areas, as high concentrations of minerals render soils infertile, and exploitable forests remain where agriculture has not attracted substantial populations.

That said, natural resource extraction typically faces boom and bust cycles, exposing laborers to layoffs. Extractive industries may stoke tensions with host communities, as the products of such trades may not be marketed locally and may degrade local ecosystems. The arrival of lucrative resource extraction industries may also bring inflation, with basic goods now unaffordable for local communities who suffer from localized externalities. Jobs may not be available to natives with limited education and connections, or else available jobs may be lower-status than those available to migrants.

Merchant Migrants

Merchant migrants are entrepreneurs who relocate for business reasons. Their motivation typically is to fill an underserved niche that is likely to exist when locals lack connections with markets for buying or selling relevant goods, or because the merchant role is considered undesirable for host societies. Merchant migrants may be welcomed, bringing in previously scarce goods and services, but may also upset local socioeconomic orders.

This category tends not to be as well-known as other types of migrants. Migrants intending to engage in entrepreneurship may be ethnically different from existing residents. Historical studies often use this term to refer to Armenian, Jewish, Lebanese, and Chaldean (Nestorian) migrant networks from Europe, across the Ottoman Empire, and throughout eastern Asia (Norris 2013). In colonial systems, merchant migrants were typically international, especially ethnic Indians or Chinese, such as Chettyar moneylenders or Chinese shopkeepers and rice merchants in Southeast Asia. Many countries are also home to domestic merchant classes and groups that may expand through internal migration to small towns and distant cities. This may include the local descendants of migrant Chinese or Indian groups, or perhaps their mixed families. Or they may be more local groups, such as Bugis in Indonesia or Chagga in Tanzania. Some groups may have benefited from historical trade linkages or access to colonial education, providing them marketplace advantages.

Unlike other internal migrants, entrepreneurial migrants typically have reasonably good information about opportunities. In selecting the areas with sufficient perceived potential to have their initiatives work, merchant migrants gather information about the area and assess whether their assets—capital, skills, and connections—could be deployed profitably. In addition, merchant migrants frequently maintain connections in their home areas, if only to preserve their access to inputs and markets. This is often reinforced through kinship connections in other areas.

Merchant migrants frequently face ambivalent or even hostile attitudes among host communities. Often the corollary of the local community's shunning of entrepreneurial occupations is disdain for people who engage in these occupations, sometimes accompanied by the perception that the migrants are exploitative, as in the case of ethnic Chinese merchants in Southeast Asia. Where local people do occupy these roles, migrant businesses often out-compete local firms through lower prices and greater efficiency enabled by their connections and capital, frustrating local competitors. Such migrants may then buy up local assets, leaving hosts more impoverished and generating conflict. Indonesia alone has numerous examples, including across eastern Indonesia, where migrants such as Bugis "sought fortune in agriculture or as traders and owners of small businesses" and clashed with native elites (Ammarell 2002, 61).

The Urbanizers

The most prominent structural economic trend worldwide in the twentieth century, continuing into this century, has been the declining weight of agriculture in both the share of gross domestic product and employment. Unsurprisingly, this coincides with the remarkable pace of urbanization (Haase et al. 2018). Generating non-farm rural employment has become a mounting challenge, and although there may exist other non-farm jobs in rural areas, those without access to land often make their way to cities.

The pace of urban migration in recent decades has been considerable. Table 7.1 shows the rising rate of the urban population in the past twenty years. The urban population proportion over the past two decades has increased from 46.7 percent to 56.2 percent, meaning that over half of the world's people now reside in urban areas.

Although an immensely important form of internal migration, the scale of urban migration should not be exaggerated. Contrary to the conventional wisdom that urbanization accounts for the lion's share of migration, two assessments involving 41 developing countries (see Tables 7.2 and 7.3) found that rural-to-urban migration does not represent the majority of migration in any of these countries.

The apparent anomaly of more rapid urban growth, despite no clear rural-to-urban migration dominance, can be explained by the underappreciated scale of rural migration, international migrants' predisposition to settle in urban areas, and the re-designation of densely populated

Table 7.1 Urban Population Increases by Region and Country, 2000–2020 (UN Population Division 2018)

	% Urban Population		*% Increase (2000–2020)*
	2000	*2020 (est.)*	
WORLD	46.7	56.2	9.5
Eastern Asia	42.0	64.8	22.8
Western Africa	34.5	47.7	13.1
South-Eastern Asia	37.9	50.0	12.1
Middle Africa	39.7	50.6	10.9
Southern Africa	53.8	64.6	10.8
Caribbean	62.8	72.2	9.4
Western Asia	63.8	72.3	8.5
Eastern Africa	21.0	29.0	7.9
Southern Asia	29.0	36.6	7.6
South-Central Asia	29.6	37.1	7.4
Central America	68.7	75.4	6.7
Southern Europe	66.4	72.1	5.7
South America	79.6	84.6	5.0
Northern Europe	77.9	82.6	4.8
Western Europe	76.0	80.2	4.2
Northern Africa	48.3	52.5	4.1
Micronesia	65.6	69.2	3.6
North America	79.1	82.6	3.5
Central Asia	45.7	48.3	2.7
Australia/NZ	84.5	86.3	1.8
Polynesia	42.7	44.4	1.7
Eastern Europe	68.2	69.9	1.7
Melanesia	18.9	19.6	0.7
China	35.9	61.4	25.6
Thailand	31.4	51.4	20.0
Indonesia	42	56.6	14.6
Colombia	74.0	81.4	7.4
India	27.7	34.9	7.2
Brazil	81.2	87.1	5.9

areas as urban, particularly those on the periphery of cities. Lucas (2021) emphasizes that, while important, rural-to-urban migration contributes less to urbanization than does reclassification of rural areas into urban ones. If the estimate that 40 percent of the urban population increase from rural-to-urban migration is accurate, the number of rural-to-urban internal migrations over the past two decades has been nearly 600 million.

Table 7.2 Proportions of Migrants According to Urban or Rural Directions, by Sex (Cattaneo and Robinson 2020)

Country	*Rural–Rural*		*Rural–Urban*		*Urban–Urban*		*Urban–Rural*	
	Male (%)	*Female (%)*	*Male (%)*	*Female (%)*	*Male (%)*	*Female (%)*	*Male (%)*	*Female (%)*
Average	35	48	33	27	22	18	10	8
Benin (1996)	40	57	34	27	11	8	11	8
Burkina Faso (2003)	71	81	17	13	5	3	5	3
Cameroon (2004)	40	41	30	34	13	16	16	8
Ethiopia (2000)	62	68	21	22	12	3	6	5
Madagascar (2004)	59	70	23	16	3	4	15	11
Malawi (2004)	74	72	17	17	3	5	6	6
Mali (2004)	51	58	32	28	7	7	10	9
Mozambique (2003)	55	54	33	31	5	8	8	5
Niger (2006)		71		18		6		6
Nigeria (1999)	45	48	28	23	9	11	19	18
Senegal (1993)		63		24		10		5
South Africa (1998)		25		29		40		8
Tanzania (1999)	63	67	27	23	4	4	4	5
Togo (1998)	52	62	25	20	13	9	8	9
Zambia (1996)	47	47	24	23	15	14	14	14
Bangladesh (2004)	52	75	44	16	4	5	4	2
Nepal (2001)	78	89	17	8	0	2	3	1
Egypt (2003)		24		31		31		14
Jordan (1997)		14		45		37		6
Morocco (2004)		29		42		25		4
Brazil (1996)	12	16	42	40	42	38	5	6
Dominican Rep. (2002)	12	20	50	47	22	20	14	13

(continued)

Table 7.2 (continued)

Country	*Rural–Rural*		*Rural–Urban*		*Urban–Urban*		*Urban–Rural*	
	Male (%)	*Female (%)*	*Male (%)*	*Female (%)*	*Male (%)*	*Female (%)*	*Male (%)*	*Female (%)*
Haiti (2000)	32	43	41	31	18	14	12	10
Nicaragua (2001)	21	19	36	38	26	21	17	21
Paraguay (1990)		29		36		19		17
Peru (2000)	14	8	23	29	47	40	15	23
Philippines (2003)	29	29	35	35	25	24	13	12
Vietnam (2002)		67		13		9		9
Kazakhstan (1999)	24	35	42	33	21	21	11	10
Uzbekistan (1996)		49	33	22		16		14

Table 7.3 Proportions of Migrants According to Urban or Rural Directions (Rees et al. 2017)

Country	*Rural–Rural*	*Rural–Urban*	*Urban–Urban*	*Urban–Rural*
Cambodia (1998)	56	20	15	9
Cameroon (2005)	14	15	54	17
Egypt (2006)	16	26	44	14
India (2001)	54	22	16	8
Indonesia (1995)	18	29	36	17
Iran (2006)	10	19	53	18
Iraq (1997)	14	10	62	14
Kyrgyzstan (1999)	19	43	21	17
Nicaragua (2005)	34	15	31	20
Swaziland (1997)	53	8	34	6
Timor-Leste (2004)	70	10	18	2
Turkey (2000)	5	18	57	20
Vietnam (1999)	33	31	27	9

The number of urbanizers over the past two decades can be estimated by applying the Stecklov (2008) estimate that in the 1990s, 38.5 percent of the growth of cities worldwide was due to rural-to-urban migration. This is consistent with the report by Farrell (2017, 4) that from the 1950s through the 1980s, estimates are all around 40 percent. Thus, if one assumes that the Stecklov ratio estimate has held since the 1990s, the number of new rural-to-urban migrations from 2000 to 2020 would be 582 million.

While some economic migrants enjoy state support, perhaps as part of resettlement projects, urban migrants in search of jobs and money are rarely state-sponsored. This form of migration is often actively resisted by the state, most notably city governments. States may seek to reduce urban migration to reduce slum populations, for fear of concentrating unemployed youths and dissidents, or to reduce strains on infrastructure. Local businesses and authorities may seek to profit from the presence of poor migrants, but in general, those in power typically seek to restrict urban migration through various measures.

Although mostly motivated by a desire for employment opportunities, the motivations of urban migrants may be mixed. Some may be IDPs with nowhere else to go, arriving to cities in search of security. Others may crave the perceived excitement of the city, with youths leaving rural areas and seeking modern urban life. They may arrive to cities for education, hopeful for entrance into universities. Some may leave for reasons related to personal security, fleeing domestic abuse or bullying. For example, persons identifying as LGBTQI may face pressures in conservative rural areas, hopeful to find safety and partners in large cities. Although noting more complex patterns, Lewis (2012) analyzes urban migration among young gay men, a phenomenon common in the West as well as developing countries. Cities may promise economic opportunities, but also excitement, identity networks, anonymity, and security. That said, rural migrants may arrive to cities and be disappointed with the new risks and pressures of urban life.

Profiles of Urban Migrants: Bihari Migrants in Mumbai

To help provide a sense of the great range of identities, opportunities, and risks related to urban migrants, we turn to Deshingkar et al.'s (2006) profiles of Bihari migrants to Mumbai in Maharashtra state. Bihar is India's poorest state, with huge numbers of landless rural people.

Although the two states are 800 miles apart, Bihar accounts for the largest group of non-Marathi migrants to Mumbai (Chadha and Chadda 2018). While most Bihari migrants are desperately poor, some are not. The motives and circumstances of migration to Mumbai are mixed.

Low-income Biharis come to Mumbai seeking employment as domestic helpers or manual laborers. Yet they, like other employment-seeking migrants, typically possess limited information about their prospects. Information about the cities is generally anecdotal, often based more on hopes than sober analysis. Additional uncertainty arises from the unknown number of other migrants pouring into the city, many competing for the same jobs. Migrants may see their contracts end or an economic downturn stunt their employment opportunities. Therefore, chances are high that some labor migrants will be left stranded without adequate employment, which helps explain why many migrate again or return home. Because employment-seeking migrants were earning subsistence incomes or even less before moving to cities, they frequently are willing to accept lower wages and to work harder, often more compliantly, than local workers (Bhagat 2010). Local populations therefore typically resent these migrants as economic threats (Gaikwad and Nellis 2017).

Just like international migration, remittances are a core component of internal migration (Mueller and Shariff 2011). Here, younger or more mobile migrants may earn money from work, but as loyal sons and daughters, are expected to send income home to support their families. Remittances are crucial for many Bihari families, poor and prosperous, who send their sons and daughters to Mumbai. For the poorest families, remittances can make the difference between malnutrition and food sufficiency. Deshingkar et al. (2006, 5) conclude: "migration and remittances have improved the standard of living of thousands of families in the poorest districts of Bihar [...] In the case of the poorest unskilled laborers, migration helps to smooth incomes and improve food security." Remittances are also important for better-off families, enabling them to finance investments such as agricultural expansion or small businesses. Remittances may also enable youths to continue their education, reaching universities with the hope of entering professional classes.

Young urban migrants, whether or not intending to send remittances home, may migrate to escape the socioeconomic conditions at home. Deshingkar et al. (2006, 12) report that "young people are now consciously opting to migrate to explore other areas and in the case of lower castes to break away from caste oppression in the village." In addition to being poor, a large proportion of Bihari urbanizers are Dalits, Adivasi, or Muslim minorities,[1] for whom migration may provide opportunities to escape persecution in some areas of Bihar. Whether they find comparable security risks after migrating is difficult to predict; the incidence of Marathi gangs attacking non-Marathis varies over time and across which groups are seen as more threatening to Marathi jobs. Bihari migrants face tremendous uncertainty far from home in Mumbai, yet conditions at home make this option preferable for thousands of youths.

Deterrence and Expulsion of Urbanizers

While state policies encourage many forms of migration, they typically discourage or even block urban migration. This is typically out of a fear of major cities being inundated with rural migrants. Fox and Goodfellow (2016, 26) note that the number of African countries with policies to discourage urbanization grew to 45 in 2013, from only 18 in 1976; the number of Latin American countries with urbanization-discouraging policies was 26 in 2013, compared to only seven in 1976. By 2013, "fully 88% of least developed countries (as classified by the UN) had in place policies to lower migration from rural-to-urban areas—up from 53% in 1996" (Fox 2017, 4). Officials frequently fear that migrants from rural areas may represent a drain on urban resources or fuel instability with locals.

Several studies, though, point out that urban population growth has important economic advantages. The World Bank (2009, 161–162) emphasizes how urban migration drives growth and wealth redistribution, pointing to a growing consensus that "governments should not see voluntary internal population movements as a threat. Indeed, internal migration offers societies an opportunity for economic growth and the convergence of welfare."

Long-run economic considerations for a country as a whole may compel the state to permit citizens to relocate to cities. Insofar as urbanizers move from low-income rural areas, their higher urban incomes, the increased productivity from agglomeration, and the remittances they send back home may increase national prosperity. In China, rural-to-urban

1 "Dalits" are not part of the caste system, formerly termed "untouchables"; also known as "scheduled castes." "Adivasi" are hilltribe members, beyond the major religious groups; also known as "scheduled tribes."

migration has been seen as heralding the creation of a new middle class, as China seeks to "urbanize to prosperity" (Chan 2010). Some convergence in prosperity between poorer and more advanced areas is predicted from economic theory. From this economic perspective, the state should be passive with respect to voluntary urbanization—but only if the migration is voluntary. As Calderón-Mejía and Ibáñez (2016) demonstrate in the wake of violence-induced urbanization, IDPs may not expect higher employment opportunities and higher wages, and they frequently depress wages of existing urban residents. Voluntary urban migration may be especially economically productive due to its flexible nature, with migrants returning to rural areas during economic downturns or to meet seasonal labor demands.

It is also important to note that the positive economic consequences of voluntary urbanization are long-term and difficult to anticipate with confidence. The obvious dilemma is that state officials typically are held accountable for short-term consequences. These typically include the possibility of intergroup conflict, crime, environmental degradation, disease, and so on. When decentralization has put subnational officials in authority, they often have a straightforward interest in benefiting their existing urban constituents by keeping poor migrants out and expelling recent migrants, thereby "cleaning" the city.

Thus, despite potential economic benefits, leaders and scholars may see urban migration as a sociopolitical threat. Focusing largely on urban migration in China, Wallace (2014) argues that non-democratic countries typically exhibit an "urban bias," extracting resources from rural areas to fund major cities. However, this is also often true of democratic countries (Roberts 2020). Wallace explains China's authoritarian stability in part by its efforts to avoid this outcome, with policies prohibiting and then reducing urban migration, as well as pushing migrants to smaller secondary cities and later investing in rural areas. Although for some, this may overestimate the importance of urban populations for regime instability, it demonstrates the importance of migratory policies and the role of the state, in this case reducing urban migration.

Mechanisms of Exclusion

Various countries have enacted policies that seek to reduce urban migration. The deterrence or expulsion of urbanizers has been accomplished through many measures. Harms (2016) posits six broad categories: (1) lack of documentation required for access (paperwork); (2) economic and market-based exclusion (money); (3) forceful exclusions through violent threats and actions (violence); (4) environmental enforcement and health (environment); (5) urban order and spatial exclusion (space); and (6) community- or self-exclusion (civility).

Paperwork: The lack of documentation limits access to benefits and serves as a rationale for expulsion. In Nigeria, Agunbiadeet al. (2015, 1055) note that "[l]ack of formal land title has been the reason used by the Lagos State government to justify demolition and forced eviction." The lack of documents in India leads to even greater deprivations. Bhagat (2011, 93–94) concludes that migrants' lack of identity and official residence "turns out to be the biggest barrier to their inclusion." The absence of paperwork generates various forms of exclusion, including the inability to open a bank account, obtain a ration card and driving license, vote, go to school, and more. Refusing to provide paperwork is thought to diminish urban migration and sustain the vulnerable positions of those that do relocate.

Money: Government officials, from the municipal to the national level, can discourage urban migration by raising costs and reducing income opportunities. When social services are largely provided by the state in a home area, denying this coverage to would-be migrants can be paralyzing. Some countries charge significant fees for urban migrants, either through bribes or permits. Wallace (2014, 140) describes how China's hukou system shifted from repressive measures to incentive-based pressures, including fees to reside outside of one's home region. Vietnam's ho khau system parallels hukou in the objective of restraining urbanization: "A primary motivation for maintaining a restrictive ho khau system, expressed by citizens and policymakers alike, is to reduce migration to urban cities. Local officials worry in particular about the burden that new migrants place on public services" (Anh et al. 2016, n.p.). While these restrictions on internal migration emulate an earlier Soviet model, they often carry over to post-Communist countries. For example, in Bishkek, the capital of Kyrgyzstan, "internal migration continues to be monitored by an administrative system of registration… required to officially access basic state services" as well as voting, banking, employment, and more (Hatcher and Thieme 2016, 2176–2177). In Mongolia, people are required to register when they relocate, but many do not do so in the capital city of Ulaanbaatar, where a 2017 ban on migration led many to remain undocumented. Without registering, urban migrants are unable to access social and welfare services or access their legal rights (IOM 2018, 36).

In addition to these national policies, subnational restrictions can discourage migration by subverting the coverage of national economic and social services designed for all citizens. In India, Kone et al. (2017, 4) identify state-level mechanisms to deter urban migrants; "many social benefits are not portable across state boundaries since they are administered by the state governments—even when they are federally funded." This means that internal migrants are unable to access food subsidies, hospitals, or schools. Kone further explains how access to jobs and education is limited by state governments. By withholding benefits from urban migrants, officials seek to conserve state resources, but also essentially raise the costs of urban living.

The economic deterrence approaches at the disposal of subnational governments can extend even further, through restrictions on languages that can be used to apply for jobs or benefits, fines on illegal housing, high fees to gain property titles, or other fees applied in migrant-dominated neighborhoods. Subnational governments may even limit migrants' access to private-sector jobs. Kadalayil (2021, n.p.) reports that in India, "the Haryana legislature passed a law directing employers to reserve 75 per cent of jobs that pay a gross monthly salary of up to 50,000 rupees (almost $700) for locals." This growing trend is especially evident in BJP strongholds, demonstrating a marked preference for host communities.

Violence: Urban migrants, especially poorer groups, often are physically confronted and controlled by host communities, whether in the competition for resources or out of sheer animosity. State officials, typically at the local through provincial/state levels, frequently have the discretion to look the other way when host community members strike against migrants. In Maharashtra State, the militant nativist Shiv Sena Party goads young Marathis to harass migrants (Khairkar 2008). Would-be urbanizers may be deterred from entering a city if they become aware that evictions, whether through eminent domain or "beautification" often entail violence, as Harms (2013) documents for Ho Chi Minh City.

The state's powers of either expulsion for illegal residence, or eminent domain in collaboration with private-sector developers, supplant low-income residents, triggering their migration either to other parts of the same city or elsewhere. Describing the techniques of expropriation in Kigali in Rwanda and the adverse impacts on the displaced, Manirakiza (2014, 171) reports that "the centrality of private sector actors in the city's development means that estate developers are given expropriation capacity, since expropriation is made legal and in the public interest as long as it takes place in the context of urban plans being implemented."

Environment: Property values of environmentally sound areas within a city are likely to make these areas out of reach for low-income migrants, necessitating a turn to unsafe, marginal lands. This not only exposes migrants to environmental hazards, but also a greater risk of expulsion on environmental-protection grounds. Harms (2016, 51) notes that "[a]cross South Asia, urban cleanup projects, especially along riverfronts or other urban water features, regularly demand the mass eviction of marginalized populations...[G]reen urbanism is increasingly used as an excuse for exclusionary urbanism." This is typically popular among higher-income residents in terms of their property values as well as the health and aesthetic benefits of clearing out "slums." Conservation, a common rationale for displacing people from rural areas, has been invoked for expulsion from cities as well. In Mumbai, for example, informal settlements have been bulldozed on charges that they encroached on mangroves (Pol 2020). Progressive movements frequently are split in prioritizing low-income populations and conservation.

Space: Formal planning establishes what can be built where; this often restricts the informal settlements that low-income urbanizers might be able to afford, thus providing a rationale for eviction (Harms 2016, 48). Joshi and Kono (2009, 502) assert that in general, zoning regulation has been used explicitly to deter urban migration. Minimum lot-size regulations, restrictions on house size, and designating areas as commercial or industrial rather than residential can exclude settlers. Manirakiza (2014, 171) argues that Rwandan leaders' efforts to "modernize" Kigali impose plans that preclude legal residence for the majority of the population, thus facilitating expropriation of areas promising for development, because "in line with the implementation of urban plans [...] the stipulations for constructing a legally acceptable house in Kigali are so demanding that between 75 and 80 per cent of all households risk being excluded from the urban space."

In Colombia, moving from a poorer urban neighborhood to a wealthier one, with the likelihood of lower crime and better services, is deterred by the artificially elevated cost of living in the higher-income neighborhoods. Utility rates increase according to the "stratum" designation of each neighborhood, from Stratum 1 (the poorest) to Stratum 6 (the wealthiest) (Alzate 2006; Bonilla et al. 2014; Jessel 2017). The irony is that the progressive policy of lower costs in poorer neighborhoods reinforces the impediments of lower-income people from improving their living conditions through movement to better-served neighborhoods.

Civility. Migrants are often trapped in the poorest urban areas through self-segregation, often in reaction to socioeconomic discrimination. For the many migrants with minimal resources, their initial settlement is typically in poor neighborhoods or city outskirts. These neighborhoods are often defined by the region from which the migrants originate; in the Maharashtra cities of Mumbai and Pune, migrants from Rajasthan, Gujarat, Tamil Nadu, and other states live in largely separate neighborhoods (Chadha and Chadda 2018; Khairkar 2008). This is hardly surprising, given linguistic and cultural differences among Indian states, but segregation can occur with far less distinctiveness among rural-to-urban migrants. Spanish-speaking migrants in Bogotá, Colombia also congregate in neighborhoods settled by those from the same regions (Uribe-Mallarino 2008, 162).

Reinforcing this economic segregation is the self-segregation of attributions of social class. In the case of Colombia's capital, Bogotá, Jessel (2017) cites a taxi driver living in a relatively low-income stratum 3: "Strata 4 and 5 are boring, he says, since fewer people dance, drink, party and fight. He thinks [...] the city works better when people stick to their own level." Jessel highlights the euphemisms involving urban strata; "He got out of the strata" for upward mobility and "You can notice his strata" to signify bad character.

The Edges of Urbanization

The above methods to restrict urban migration may dampen the arrival of migrants, but adverse rural conditions may compel continued arrivals and limit returns. Conversely, those living in cities may opt to leave to avoid urban migrants. Either urban migrants or hosts may then relocate to urban edges, inhabiting various satellite cities and planned new urban centers.

The degree of state involvement in the development of satellite cities/new towns varies a great deal. Insofar as the motive of moving low-income settlers out of slums is to enhance their well-being, states are often involved in providing the conditions needed for affordable housing, employment opportunities, and other aspects to attract and maintain these people in the new area. However, the alternative—which is not only less costly for state resources but also reduces state accountability—is to expedite private-sector initiatives to reduce population pressures on the existing city. For instance, private developers were awarded the contract to build the Thu Thiem New Urban Zone at the edge of Ho Chi Minh City. Douglass and Huang (2007, 26) explain the attraction of development completely financed by the private sector:

> For most Vietnamese policymakers, the city is smart in supporting the grand project because the local government can exchange underutilized and undeveloped land use rights for the complete construction of a huge edge city accomplished totally through the private sector, which also pays taxes on its various types of development projects and lease sales. This also lends an appearance of taking enormous pressure off the government to deal with problems such as slum upgrading, affordable housing, water source cleaning, urban flooding, traffic jam, air pollution, and greening the city.

However, developing satellite cities to absorb domestic migrants may generate IDPs. Planning for the new city entailed "evicting 14,600 households, completely razing all built construction, filling in marshes and streams, and then reconstructing 737 hectares of land to create office space, luxury high-rise apartment housing, new public squares, riverfront walks, and pedestrian promenades framed by commercial storefronts" (Harms 2012, 736).

Despite clear problems related to displacement, creating satellite cities adjacent to metropolitan areas offers clear benefits. Some peripheral developments create new urban areas near existing cities to house settlers otherwise trapped in the slums or expelled without another safe destination. They may provide a sufficiently urban environment for new migrants coming from the countryside to provide the benefits of agglomeration and higher-income opportunities.

One of the most notable new town initiatives to pursue affordable housing, in terms of both the volume of residents and the empowerment of its residents, is the Bolivian city of El Alto, now of nearly a million people adjacent to La Paz. As an outlet for families that had migrated from the countryside and had suffered extremely substandard housing in La Paz, and for newly urbanizing people, El Alto became a site with access to employment, property ownership, and support for self-help home construction. Bredenoord and van Lindert (2010, 283) chronicle its remarkable emergence:

> From the 1980s onward, La Paz' population growth increasingly concentrated in the new settlements of El Alto, which gained administrative independence as a separate municipality in the year 1985... In the built-up areas of El Alto, land values steadily rose as more and more people moved into the consolidating settlements. Self-help construction activities increased spectacularly in the 1990s, when water and sewerage systems were installed. In the 2000s, many neighbourhoods were further serviced with gas piping. New construction activities are booming, not in the least because the huge plot sizes made it possible that the owners split their property and sell part of it to new residents.

Another illuminating case can be found in Iran, demonstrating common pitfalls of new towns designed for affordable housing. Andisheh, a new town in the Tehran urban complex, has successfully attracted population from Tehran proper. However, Taghados et al. (2021, 772) deem it the lone successful satellite city around Tehran, reaching 75 percent of its planned population. Meanwhile, other efforts to create satellite towns around Tehran have attracted only 2.4 percent of the capital's population. Manouchehriet al. (2015) attribute the success of Andisheh to affordable housing, opportunities for land ownership, and employment opportunities in smaller cities closer than Tehran, which is 30 kilometers away, requiring a much longer commute than the median commute of roughly 40 minutes.

Despite some real and potential benefits of creating new towns to attract urban migrants, many projects have failed and squandered resources. Three common patterns have undermined efforts to relocate low-income urban residents in satellite cities: Inadequate investment of resources for planning, infrastructure, or social services; poor location; and subversion of affordable housing projects to increase revenues.

New urban areas targeted for affordable housing frequently lack incentives for the private sector to provide decent housing or urban amenities. Left to the state, required resources are often inadequate. Ramakrishnan (2014, 70) describes substandard conditions for poor migrants forcibly displaced to the Bawana resettlement colony in response to "slum upgrading" in Delhi. The site absorbed "close to 120,000 people evicted from squatter settlements," but has left migrants no better off, as "The combined shock of home destruction and inability to access casual labor has depleted hard-earned savings accumulated by residents." Even worse, Bawana's isolation, coupled with the opportunities for industrialists to gain land in the same area, left residents not only exposed to industrial pollution, but only able to seek low-paying jobs near the relocation site. As Ramakrishnan (2014, 70) concludes: "Currently, plans are in progress to transform Bawana into a massive industrial hub; already, many factories have sprung up and are highly dependent on the labor of colony residents, though many residents feel cheated by the owners who severely underpay them."

The locations of new peripheral settlements for lower-income families are often opportunistic, reflecting land prices, the ease of land consolidation, and, in many cases, providing a windfall to well-connected landowners. These factors are unlikely to coincide with the optimal location for settler employment prospects and living conditions. In Bawana outside of Delhi, Ramakrishnan (2014, 70) notes that residents "have been relocated at a considerable distance from former livelihoods, as the colony is on average 35 kilometers away and necessitates a three-hour commute due to the disconnected transport links." The location problems are exacerbated by inadequate investments in physical infrastructure.

Private-sector capture is another common outcome of initiatives ostensibly intended to provide affordable housing in peripheral areas. State agencies motivated by rent-seeking or tax base increases may subvert projects by selling land to developers and setting regulations to maximize the tax base, civic pride, or rent-seeking opportunities. For instance, although new town development near Shanghai and Kolkata was intended to relieve over-crowding, it instead functioned as an "instrument for capturing the exchange value of farmland through attracting wealthy and mobile investors from downtown and overseas" (Wang et al. 2010, 343). Filling in the new towns around Shanghai with low-income residents had been delayed due to limited transit options, with the poorest migrants relegated to the edges of new towns.

Sub-Saharan African cases highlight problems of inadequate preparation for receiving migrants. Abubakar and Doan (2017) assess satellite town development in the capital areas of Abuja (Nigeria), Dodoma (Tanzania), Gaborone (Botswana), and Lilongwe (Malawi), concluding that the emphasis on physical design neglected provisions for adequate housing and basic urban services. Poor-quality informal housing followed rapid urbanization in these areas. However, Abubakarand Doan (2017, 15) do not dismiss the possibility of better public-private partnerships, outlining "useful roles for private sector led investments in new satellite cities as long as they are better planned and implemented." Recognizing that the state's control over development opportunities gives government officials bargaining power, they conclude: "As private property developers are rarely interested in social housing, national and municipal governments should interact with property developers to get the plans of the new satellite towns amended to include provision of affordable housing as a condition for government support."

A different variant emerges when an area becomes more valuable because of changes in physical infrastructure. Chakrabartiet al. (2021, 1014) elaborate on the case of a marginal area in what had been the outskirts of Kolkata:

> In 2005, a city-level Kolkata Environment Improvement Project was launched to make Kolkata slum-free [...] These developments made Nonadanga and the adjoining areas lucrative for real estate investment. According to a Land Use and Urban Development Plan (LUDCP), the Kolkata Metropolitan Development Authority (KMDA) was considering giving a 99-year lease to a private developer for a comprehensive development plan for Nonadanga [...] An increasing squatter settlement in Nonadanga was an impediment to such a move by the government. In 2013, there was a massive eviction drive by KMC, met with a long-drawn protest by the migrants of Nonadanga, which eventually forced KMC to provide resettlement and stall future evictions.

Upward Mobility and Remittances

Despite the many potential problems associated with internal migration, it is important to emphasize that internal migration is such a widespread phenomenon because it benefits many people. Although many urban migrants find themselves living in perilous informal settlements, perhaps no better off than their lives in rural areas, others find employment and improve their lives. Urban migrants may obtain employment, saving enough funds to send remittances back home to provide for their families (Lucas 2021, 336). Migrants may even coordinate to help each other, forming Home Town Associations (HTAs, see Chapter 9) to provide mutual assistance and facilitate new arrivals. In NigeriaBarkan et al. (1991) show that early urban migrants formed HTAs, and with time, became powerful actors in Lagos. Within a few decades, migrants became influential political and economic leaders, sending funds to promote infrastructure development in their home regions. In Mexico, Fitzgerald (2010) shows how migrants moving from Arandas to Guadalajara created powerful student organizations and business groups, soon expanding to transborder activities and encouraging development in their home region. Even those less fortunate may manage to earn a better living and help their home communities.

Conclusions

This chapter has discussed unsponsored, more or less voluntary and enterprising internal migrants. State officials and international actors have to appreciate not only the great diversity of motives and circumstances of unsponsored economic migrants, but also the orientations that they bring to their interactions with host communities. Although some unsponsored migrants prosper along with the communities to which they bring welcomed goods, services, or capital, many of the scenarios outlined above point to disappointment, vulnerability, distrust, and conflict. We turn now to the parallel, and often even more challenging, plight of displaced people who are not supported by state programs.

References

Abubakar, Ismaila Rimi, and Petra Leisenring Doan. 2017. Building New Capital Cities in Africa: Lessons for New Satellite Towns in Developing Countries. *African Studies* 76 (4): 1–20.

Adewale, J. Gbemiga. 2005. Socio-economic Factors Associated with Urban-Rural Migration in Nigeria: A Case Study of Oyo State, Nigeria. *Journal of Human Ecology* 17 (1): 13–16.

Agunbiade, Muyiwa E., Oluwafemi A. Olajide, and Hakeem Bishi. 2015. The Limit of Land Regularisation as Poverty Alleviation Strategy in Informal

Settlements: Empirical Evidence from Lagos, Nigeria. *Journal of Construction Project Management and Innovation* 5 (1): 1045–1063.

Alzate, Maria. 2006. *La Estratificación Socioeconómica para el Cobro de los Servicios Públicos Domiciliarios en Colombia: ¿Solidaridad o Focalización?* Bogotá: CEPAL.

Ammarell, Gene. 2002. Bugis Migration and Modes of Adaptation to Local Situations. *Ethnology* 41 (1): 51–67.

Anh, Dang Nguyen, Gabriel Demombynes, and Linh Hoang Vu. 2016. Reforming Vietnam's Household Registration System. World Bank & Vietnam Academy of Social Sciences (VASS).

Arifin, Bustanul. 2010. Global Sustainability Regulation and Coffee Supply Chains in Lampung Province, Indonesia. *Asian Journal of Agriculture and Development* 7 (2): 67–89.

Barkan, Joel D., Michael L. McNulty, and M.A.O. Ayeni. 1991. 'Hometown' Voluntary Associations, Local Development, and the Emergence of Civil Society in Western Nigeria. *Journal of Modern African Studies* 29 (3): 457–480.

Bhagat, Ram. 2010. Internal Migration in India: Are the Underprivileged Migrating More? *Asia-Pacific Population Journal* 25 (1): 27–45.

Bhagat, Ram. 2011. Migrants' (Denied) Right to the City. In *Urban Policies and the Right to the City in India: Rights, Responsibilities and Citizenship*, ed. Faetanini Marina, 86–99. New Delhi: UNESCO.

Bonilla, Jaime, Denis López, and Carlos E. Sepúlveda. 2014. Estratificación Socioeconómica en Colombia: Contexto General y Diagnóstico. In *Los límites de la Estratificación: En Busca de Alternativas*, eds. Carlos E. Sepúlveda, Denis López, and J. Gallego, 23–40. Bogotá: Editorial Universidad del Rosario.

Bredenoord, Jan, and Paul van Lindert. 2010. Pro-poor Housing Policies: Rethinking the Potential of Assisted Self-Help Housing. *Habitat International* 34 (3): 278–287.

Calderón-Mejía, Valentina, and Ana María Ibáñez. 2016. Labour Market Effects of Migration-related Supply Shocks: Evidence from Internal Refugees in Colombia. *Journal of Economic Geography* 16 (3): 695–713.

Cattaneo, Andrea, and Sherman Robinson. 2020. Multiple Moves and Return Migration Within Developing Countries: A Comparative Analysis. *Population, Space and Place* 26 (7): 1–21.

Chadha, Vikram, and Ishu Chadda. 2018. Policies and Performance of Social Sector in India Since Independence: A Critical Evaluation. *International Journal of Social Science and Development Policy* 4 (2): 64–90.

Chakrabarti, Anuradha, Reena Tiwari, and Haimanti Banerji. 2021. Migrants' Narratives on Urban Governance: A Case from Kolkata, a City of the Global South. *Sustainability* 13 (2): 1009–1025.

Chan, Kam Wing. 2010. Crossing the 50 Percent Population Rubicon: Can China Urbanize to Prosperity? *Eurasian Geography and Economics* 53 (1): 63–86.

Deshingkar, Priya, Sushil Kumar, Harendra Kumar Chobey, and Dhananjay Kumar. 2006. *The Role of Migration and Remittances in Promoting Livelihoods in Bihar*. London: Overseas Development Institute.

Douglass, Mike, and Liling Huang. 2007. Globalizing the City in Southeast Asia: Utopia on the Urban Edge–the Case of Phu My Hung, Saigon. *International Journal of Asia Pacific Studies* 3 (2): 1–42.

Farrell, Kyle. 2017. The Rapid Urban Growth Triad: A New Conceptual Framework for Examining the Urban Transition in Developing Countries. *Sustainability* 9 (8): 1407.

Fitzgerald, David. 2008. "Colonies of the Little Motherland: Membership, Space, and Time in Mexican Migrant Hometown Associations." *Comparative Studies in Society and History* 50 (1): 145–169.

Fox, Sean. 2017. *Neglected Drivers of Urbanisation in Africa*. London: International Growth Centre.

Fox, Sean, and Tom Goodfellow. 2016. *Cities and Development*, 2nd ed. Abington, UK: Routledge.

Gaikwad, Nikhar, and Gareth Nellis. 2017. The Majority-Minority Divide in Attitudes Toward Internal Migration: Evidence from Mumbai. *American Journal of Political Science* 61 (2): 456–472.

Gosnell, H., and J. Abrams. 2011. Amenity Migration: Diverse Conceptualizations of Drivers, Socioeconomic Dimensions, and Emerging Challenges. *GeoJournal* 76 (4): 303–322.

Haase, Dagmar, Burak Güneralp, Bharat Dahiya, Xuemei Bai, and Thomas Elmqvist. 2018. Global Urbanization. In *The Urban Planet: Knowledge Towards Sustainable Cities*, ed. Thomas Elmqvist, et al., 19–44. Cambridge: Cambridge University Press.

Harms, Erik. 2012. Beauty as Control in the New Saigon: Eviction, New Urban Zones, and Atomized Dissent in a Southeast Asian City. *American Ethnologist* 39 (4): 735–750.

Harms, Erik. 2013. Eviction Time in the New Saigon: Temporalities of Displacement in the Rubble of Development. *Cultural Anthropology* 28 (2): 344–368.

Harms, Erik. 2016. Urban Space and Exclusion in Asia. *Annual Review of Anthropology* 45: 45–61.

Hatcher, Craig, and Susan Thieme. 2016. Institutional Transition: Internal Migration, the Propiska, and Post-socialist Urban Change in Bishkek, Kyrgyzstan. *Urban Studies* 53 (10): 2175–2191.

Hnatkovska, Viktoria, and Amartya Lahiri. 2015. Rural and Urban Migrants in India: 1983–2008. *The World Bank Economic Review* 29 (1): S257–S270.

Homewood, Katherine, Ernestina Coast, and Michael Thompson. 2004. In-Migrants and Exclusion in East African Rangelands: Access, Tenure, and Conflict. *Africa* 74 (4): 567–610.

IOM (International Organization for Migration). 2018. *Mongolia: Internal Migration Study*. New York: United Nations.

Jessel, Ella. 2017. 'If I'm Stratum 3, That's Who I Am': Inside Bogotá's Social Stratification System. *Guardian*, November 9.

Joshi, Kirti Kusum, and Tatsuhito Kono. 2009. Optimization of Floor Area Ratio Regulation in a Growing City. *Regional Science and Urban Economics* 39 (4): 502–511.

Kadalayil, Chitrabhanu. 2021. Is India's Federalism Facing Needless Stress Tests? *The National*, April 5. https://www.thenationalnews.com/opinion/comment/is-india-s-federalism-facing-needless-stress-tests-1.1196245.

Khairkar, Vijaya P. 2008. Segregation of Migrants Groups in Pune City, India. *Anthropologist* 10 (2): 155–161.

Kone, Zovanga L., Maggie Y. Liu, Aaditya Mattoo, Çağlar Özden, and Siddharth Sharma. 2017. Internal Borders and Migration in India. World Bank Policy Research Working Paper 8244. Washington, DC: World Bank.

Lewis, Nathaniel M. 2012. Remapping Disclosure: Gay Men's Segmented Journeys of Moving Out and Coming Out. *Social & Cultural Geography* 13 (3): 211–231.

Lucas, Robert E.B. 2021. *Crossing the Divide: Rural to Urban Migration in Developing Countries*. Oxford: Oxford University Press and KNOWMAD.

Manirakiza, Vincent. 2014. Promoting Inclusive Approaches to Address Urbanisation Challenges in Kigali. *African Review of Economics and Finance* 6 (1): 161–180.

Manouchehri, Bahar, Masoumeh Tork, and Hossein Vahidi. 2015. Motivations for Settlement in New Towns in a Developing Country: A Case Study of Andisheh New Town, Iran. *International Journal of Development and Sustainability* 4 (4): 461–478.

Mueller, Valerie, and Abusaleh Shariff. 2011. Preliminary Evidence on Internal Migration, Remittances, and Teen Schooling in India. *Contemporary Economic Policy* 29 (2): 207–217.

Norris, Jacob. 2013. Exporting the Holy Land: Artisans and Merchant Migrants in Ottoman-era Bethlehem. *Mashriq & Mahjar: Journal of Middle East and North African Migration Studies* 1 (2): 14–40.

Pol, Megha. 2020. We Didn't Know Our Home Was Illegal: Diva Residents. *Hindustan Times*, January 9.

Ramakrishnan, Kavita. 2014. Cosmopolitan Imaginaries on the Margins: Negotiating Difference and Belonging in a Delhi Resettlement Colony. *Contemporary South Asia* 22 (1): 67–81.

Rees, Philip, Martin Bell, Marek Kupiszewski, Dorota Kupiszewska, Philipp Ueffing, Bernard Aude, Elin Charles-Edwards, and John Stillwell. 2017. The Impact of Internal Migration on Population Redistribution: An International Comparison. *Population, Space and Place* 23 (6): 20–36.

Roberts, Bryan R. 2020. *The Making of Citizens: Cities of Peasants Revisited.* New York: Routledge.

Samaddar, Arghadip, Ravisekhar Gadepalli, Vijaya Lakshmi Nag, and Sanjeev Misra. 2020. The Enigma of Low COVID-19 Fatality Rate in India. *Frontiers in Genetics* 11 (854): 1–9.

Schewel, Kerilyn, and Asmamaw Legass Bahir. 2019. Migration and Social Transformation in Ethiopia. *International Migration Institute Working Papers Series* No. 152. Oxford: IMI.

Stecklov, G. 2008. *The Components of Urban Growth in Developing Countries.* Unpublished manuscript. New York: United Nations.

Taghados, Mostafa Javaheri, Mahin Nastaran, Esfandiar Zebardast, and Maysam Basirat. 2021. A Future Study on the Role of New Towns in Establishing Balance in the Spatial-Physical Structure of the Metropolitan Regions Based on the National Spatial Planning Approaches and Policies. *Quarterly Journal of the Macro and Strategic Policies* 8 (4): 772–794.

UN Population Division. 2018. *World Urbanization Prospects: The 2018 Revision.* New York: United Nations.

Uribe-Mallarino, Consuelo. 2008. Estratificación Social en Bogotá: De la Política Pública a la Dinámica de la Segregación Social. *Universitas Humanística* 65: 139–171.

Wallace, Jeremy W. 2014. *Cities and Stability: Urbanization, Redistribution, & Regime Survival in China.* Oxford: Oxford University Press.

Wang, Lan, Ratoola Kundu, and Xiangming Chen. 2010. Building for What and Whom? New Town Development as Planned Suburbanization in China and India. *Suburbanization in Global Society* 10: 319–345.

Wood, Charles H. 2002. Introduction: Land Use and Deforestation in the Amazon. In *Deforestation and Land Use in the Amazon*, eds. Charles H. Wood and Roberto Porro, 1–40. Gainesville: University of Florida Press.

World Bank. 2009. *World Development Report*. Washington, DC.

Zezza, Alberto, and Luca Tasciotti. 2010. Urban Agriculture, Poverty, and Food Security: Empirical Evidence from a Sample of Developing Countries. *Food Policy* 35 (4): 265–273.

CHAPTER 8

Unsponsored Migrants: The Expelled

As noted in Chapter 6, state-managed and initiated migrants are typically more voluntary than is often understood, with migrants joining state programs in the pursuit of better lives. Chapter 7 focused on unsponsored economic migrants, those seeking land, jobs, and money largely outside of state programs. These categories are hardly perfect; state-initiated migration may be involuntary (e.g., communities being forcibly resettled for ideological or security purposes) and many urban migrants may be pushed from their homes unwillingly. Migration is often a choice, an extremely important one for the lives of tens of millions of people around the world. However, internal migration is also a means of survival, with external forces compelling flight and resettlement. This chapter focuses on the expelled—migrants pushed by various factors to leave their homes as IDPs. In a sense, these groups are unsponsored, at least initially, as some might benefit from state support in the resettlement process.

The scale of displaced persons around the world is immense. The IOM (2020, 10) estimates that the number of newly internally displaced persons was 41.3 million in 2019, compared to 21 million in 2000. It is estimated that IDPs are twice as common as those that cross borders, with two-thirds of the world's 68 million displaced people remaining in their countries (Sasse 2020). Displacement is principally due to development initiatives, conflict and violence, and natural disasters. The gray area is the

W. Ascher and S. J. Barter, *Moving within Borders*, Politics, Economics, and Inclusive Development, https://doi.org/10.1007/978-3-031-37549-1_8

displacement of people who reluctantly leave their home area because of shrinking incomes (e.g., crop declines due to desertification, encroaching salinity, population pressure, or market collapse). Some of these displaced persons may be considered "environmental refugees." They are rarely counted as displaced, yet they are all migrants.

In contrast to the migrants discussed in Chapter 7, involuntary migrants are typically in direr circumstances. They often lack both the material and the symbolic benefits of official recognition. From a humanitarian perspective, efforts to assist involuntary migrants are the most compelling of any migration challenge: their expulsion often is coercive and is much more likely to involve entire families, and, if the state is involved, the displacement and resettlement are only by-products of the state's principal goals. Like the voluntary migration previously examined, various agencies and officials ought to play crucial roles in shaping movements, helping to resettle, and providing humanitarian support for IDPs.

In many ways, the well-being of IDPs depends on whether they receive recognition as well as compensation or other forms of financial support, namely from the state. Relations with host communities are strikingly different if migrants possess some wealth, allowing them to purchase land, enrich local merchants through commerce, and avoid criminal activities. Arriving destitute in an unfamiliar rural area may make migrants into supplicants. Uncompensated or under-compensated displaced migrants are often more likely to cast their lot in cities, with their lack of relevant skills and money to secure decent housing relegating them to shantytowns. A key question is whether displaced people are recognized as deserving protection. This often varies across types of IDPs, discussed below in terms of those displaced by development, violent conflict, or natural/ecological disasters (Betts 2009, 7–10).

Development IDPs

Chapter 6 highlighted IDPs whose displacement and/or relocation was driven by the state, including political IDPs removed or relocated for strategic, ideological, or economic reasons. However, the role of the state in driving infrastructure/development IDPs can sometimes be unclear, with state agencies often representing the principal drivers of dislocation, and sometimes playing supporting roles for private contractors, for a host of land uses requiring the removal of residents—hydroelectric and irrigation dams, solar arrays, windfarms, highways, seaports, airports, shopping complexes, and nature reserves. A large proportion of development projects are state-supported, through direct state operation, public–private partnerships, zoning rule changes, or concessions to the private sector on public lands. Many of the displacements involve state-directed resettlement, yet in many other cases, families are expelled with little or no compensation.

When experts speak of IDPs, they tend to focus on conflict and disaster IDPs, neglecting the category of development IDPs. Among the most important resources in understanding displacement is the IDMC's annual Global Report on Internal Displacement (GRID). The IDMC reports bifurcate IDPs into conflict (armed conflict, communal violence, criminal violence, and political violence) and disaster (geophysical, storms and floods, wildfires, droughts, landslides, and extreme temperatures), each of which discussed in terms of stocks and flows (IDMC 2022, 6). That said, the IDMC has also published reports focusing on what we understand as development IDPs, namely those displaced by dams and related megaprojects (IDMC 2017). Mooney (2005, 9) suggests that narrow approaches might focus only on conflict IDPs, the type that would constitute refugees if they crossed an international border, while expansive approaches include disaster and development IDPs. She suggests that development IDPs are equally in need of assistance, citing reports that development may displace more persons than war, creating migrants whose plight may go unnoticed.

Among development displacements, many large-scale hydroelectric dams are known to displace thousands of persons, along with threatening local ecology. The effects are often so great that the state is compelled to be involved in the displacement even if the developers are private. Displacements forced by dam construction and operation have led to roughly 80 million people still displaced as of the mid-2010s (IDMC 2017, 2). There is enormous variation in the number of people displaced by the largest hydroelectric dams; roughly 59,000 people were eventually displaced by the Brazilian-Paraguayan Itaipu Dam, second in generating capacity only to China's the Three Gorges Dam, which displaced more than a million people. In recent decades, dams in East and South Asia have generated by far the most IDPs, reflecting the need for electricity driven by industrialization demands and made possible by the enormous hydro potential in both regions, along with large, dense populations.

Table 8.1 provides estimates for those displaced by the dam projects responsible for the greatest volume of resettlement. The numbers provided are rough estimates, intended to illustrate the tremendous scale of development-induced displacement due to this single form of development initiative.

Involuntary migration triggered by state-initiated or state-facilitated infrastructure involves convoluted state-IDP interactions. Infrastructure IDPs often obtain some compensation, since their removal is caused by specific projects. Yet, the terms are typically ambiguous regarding how much compensation will be provided and to whom. Much depends on whether the state is committed to the principle that the displaced must be left no worse off, a doctrine developed in 1980 by the World Bank in its operational principles for physical infrastructure projects requiring displacement (World Bank 1994).

The first challenge is that authorities must estimate what "no worse off" really means, in light of the intangible losses of leaving one's home area. Claims that being away from sacred places, proximity to cultural sites, and so on are significant deprivations that will be difficult to assess. Another challenge is the pace at which compensation would be meted out. A paternalistic approach may dictate that compensation should be provided gradually to deter recipients from squandering the money, but this limits the capacity of compensated people to invest in new initiatives. It also runs the risk of leaving IDPs resentful, as well as doubtful about receiving future compensation. An additional complication is that groups may require different levels of compensation, triggering resentment among those with less. This has been the conundrum in deciding how much, and when, to compensate families displaced to make way for hydroelectric dams. Regarding those displaced by India's Tehri Dam, Asthana (2012) reports the complaints of women that their husbands wasted compensation funds on drinking and consumer goods. This raises the question of who should control compensation, and, in some instances, how to counter male domination and irresponsibility.

Infrastructure IDPs tend to be very poor. They reside in underdeveloped rural areas where large dams may be seen by planners as economically feasible, in urban slums where property values are low enough to make redevelopment affordable, or along the transportation routes selected to minimize property destruction and compensation to owners. As a result, state compensation is particularly important for their well-being. The main advantages of the appeal for state support

Table 8.1 Dams Generating Large Numbers of IDPs (≥50,000) (years approximate)

Dam	*Country*	*Year*	*IDPs*
Sanxia (3 Gorges)	China	2010	1,260,000
Shuikou	China	1960	410,000
Danjiangku	China	1973	383,000
Sanmenxia	China	1960	370,000
Sardar Sarovar	India	2017	360,000
Ertan	China	1958	278,000
Xinanjiang	China	1960	280,000
Miyun	China	1960	200,000
Narmada Sagar	India	2017	200,000
Xiaolangdi	China	2001	181,600
Kuybyshev	Russia	1957	150,000
Pong	India	1974	150,000
Basagar	India	2006	142,000
Zhaxi	China	1961	141,000
Kangsabati Kumari	India	1965	125,000
Aswan High Dam	Egypt/Sudan	1970	120,000
Rybinsk	Russia	1955	116,700
Balimela	India	1990	113,600
Mangla	Pakistan	1967	110,000
Wuqiangxi	China	1966	107,000
Xinfengjiang	China	1969	106,000
Tehri	India	2018	105,000
Rihand	India	1962	102,000
Srisailam	India	1984	100,000
Somasila	India	2004	100,000
Kaptai	Bangladesh	1962	100,000
Gibe I	Ethiopia	2004	100,000
Kiri	Nigeria	1982	100,000
Changma	China	2000	96,000
Tarbela	Pakistan	1967	96,000
Son La	Vietnam	2011	91,000
Xiangjiaba	China	2015	89,800
Xijin	China	1970	89,000
Akosombo	Ghana	1965	82,000
Longtan	China	2010	75,000
Kossou	Ivory Coast	1973	75,000
Baihetan	China	2017	69,000
Sobradinho	Brazil	1982	65,000
Hualiangting	China	2001	61,000

(continued)

Table 8.1 (continued)

Dam	*Country*	*Year*	*IDPs*
Votkinsk	Russia	1965	61,000
Itaipu	Brazil/Paraguay	1982	59,000
Kariba	Zambia/Zimbabwe	1959	57,000
Merowe	Sudan	2009	55,000
Paolo Afonso I-IV	Brazil	1979	52,000

Sources Terminski (2013, 52–53, 56) and International Commission on Large Dams (2021)

made by infrastructure IDPs are that their displacement is obvious and their need to migrate is forced upon them by powerful actors, negating the dismissive argument that migrants ought to be responsible for their outcomes. Even here, state compensation may be selective, often reflecting the influence of more powerful community members. In India, the Ahmedabad -Vadodara Expressway project's compensation went to only the 10,000 landowners, refusing compensation for landless agricultural workers (Fernandes 2017, 9).

An infrastructure initiative may or may not involve detailed resettlement plans, or denying compensation to residents without recognized titles. State decisions on compensating state-displaced persons may be badly miscalculated, leaving migrants worse off. In addition, because adequate state efforts to compensate and/or resettle IDPs may be expensive, officials intent on promoting development initiatives may underspend to make infrastructure projects profitable. A project will be even more profitable if some or all displaced people are denied compensation on the grounds that they lack land titles or are deemed disloyal. As migrants, then, they are doubly disadvantaged due to the lack of compensation and because they are cast as problematic people undeserving of state concern and care.

In addition, some people may be indirectly displaced by infrastructure projects, such as fishers who can no longer subsist in their present locations as hydroelectric dams degrade downstream areas, or farmers blocked from trading routes by new projects. In such cases, identifying and compensating those affected may be especially difficult, more so if the impacts are indirect or slow-acting. These indirectly expelled people might not be designated as displaced; the migrants may be viewed simply as failed fishers or farmers choosing to migrate for economic reasons.

Conflict IDPs

Perhaps the most prevalent motive for unsponsored migration, after employment-seeking, is the fear of violence. Conflict IDPs resemble international refugees, suffering from violence and trauma. Humanitarian assistance is crucially important, yet conflict IDPs sometimes cannot depend on the state, which may itself represent the threat causing displacement. This is a clear difference from the situation for international migrants. And in some instances, migrants are clearly fleeing ongoing violence, in simmering, low-level conflicts, so it may be unclear whether migration was forced, as opposed to seeking better economic and living conditions. Of course, festering conflict will bring economic underperformance and poverty, so these logics reinforce.

The number of displacements due to fear of violence is considerable, difficult to count, highly variable, and growing. According to IDMC estimates, 28.3 million people were displaced by political violence in 2022 (IDMC 2023). Over one million were found in Syria, Congo, and Ethiopia. This number is misleading though, as it refers to new conflict IDPs, not those who remain IDPs from conflicts before 2019. Compared to development and disaster IDPs, this category is the slowest to see resettlement and the end of IDP status. This may be due to the continual nature of violence, the state's culpability in committing violent acts, state strategic interests, or what is almost by definition a limited state presence in conflict areas. Overall, it is estimated that, at the end of 2019, the world was home to 45.7 million conflict IDPs, including 18.3 million children under the age of 15 (IDMC 2020, 2). Worse still, the number of IDPs has grown steadily for 30 years, despite an overall global decline of violent conflicts. The growth is due to violence against civilians as well as the accumulation of conflict IDPs, reflecting the lack of success in resettlement (IDMC 2020, 21).

Important variability exists in the new conflict IDPs generated by year and world region, as revealed in Table 8.2 (IDMC 2018–2023). Here, we see that regional IDP averages can suddenly jump due to the presence of wars. We also see that some regions, especially the Middle East and Africa, have by far the most conflict IDPs, with Ukraine raising the number of European IDPs dramatically in 2022.

Enormous variation also exists in the likelihood that these displacements will be long-lasting. Some people return to their homes when

Table 8.2 New IDPs Generated by Conflict and Violence (2017–2022)

Region	*Year*	*IDPs*
The Americas	2017	457,000
	2018	404,000
	2019	602,000
	2020	238,000
	2021	381,000
	2022	533,000
Middle East & North Africa	2017	4,485,000
	2018	2,137,000
	2019	2,566,000
	2020	2,706,000
	2021	1,011,000
	2022	12,700,000
Europe & Central Asia	2017	21,000
	2018	12,000
	2019	2,800
	2020	85,000
	2021	61,000
	2022	17,100,000
Sub-Saharan Africa	2017	5,472,000
	2018	7,446,000
	2019	4,597,000
	2020	6,780,000
	2021	11,558,000
	2022	9,000,000
South Asia	2017	634,000
	2018	544,000
	2019	498,000
	2020	409,000
	2021	736,000
	2022	35,000
East Asia & Pacific	2017	705,000
	2018	236,000
	2019	288,000
	2020	186,000
	2021	626,000
	2022	1,200,000
Annual Global Average	*2017–2019*	*10,070,000*
Annual Global Average	*2020–2022*	*17,500,000*

IDMC (2018, 2019, 2020, 2021, 2022, 2023)

violence subsides; others find that their homes occupied by others indefinitely, or their villages or towns destroyed. Conflict IDPs share with disaster IDPs the dual misfortune that their expulsion is often sudden, and return uncertain, whereas many development IDPs suffer from the certainty that return is impossible. Many conflict migrants are forced to leave their home areas without notice, arriving without supplies and unable to liquidate their assets before leaving. Alternatively, some conflict flight is anticipatory, with persons fleeing fear of looming violence, but in doing so bringing into question the extent to which they were forced out by war.

Migrants and state officials may believe that displacement will be short term, yet violence and displacement frequently continue for several years. IDMC data shows that conflict IDPs remain unsettled longer than any other IDP group (IDMC 2000 11–12). This creates a further ambiguity for migrants as to whether they should consider themselves as temporary "visitors" or strive to integrate into the local area—if residence in IDP camps even permits them to do so. Conflict IDPs face a further dilemma when officials declare the migrants' home area as safe for return, but migrants remain skeptical. In this circumstance, whatever support the state may have provided the migrants as IDPs may evaporate, and host communities may conclude that the IDPs no longer deserve assistance. This is especially likely when the state has an interest in deeming a conflict resolved. Alternatively, IDPs may wish to return to war-torn areas before the state deems it safe, sometimes pushed by the deprivations suffered in IDP camps such as overcrowding, lack of income-earning opportunities, and crime. One side of the conflict may likely want IDPs to return, while others may want them to remain expelled due to perceived loyalties and ethnic allegiance.

Within a given country, conflict IDPs may vary considerably in their threat levels and subsequent displacement duration. In Ukraine, the IOM estimates that the number of IDPs decreased from a high in August 2022 of seven million persons to about five million six months later (IOM 2023). They found that just over half face protracted displacement, with one-third expecting to return home in the near future. The same survey found that about one-quarter of Ukrainian IDPs were considering going abroad, with most expecting to remain in Ukraine. The varied experiences depended in large part on conflict dynamics and place of origin. Those from Kharkiv were unable to return home, while those from Kiev felt it safer to go back. Still, in January 2023, West Ukraine still produced

130,000 IDPs, despite it being relatively far from the front lines, as people still felt threatened and saw basic services disrupted by war.

Just as ambiguity exists for development IDPs in terms of their status, so too is this true of conflict IDPs. What level of violence is necessary to be considered an IDP? Must IDPs literally be forced out at gunpoint? To what extent do we limit the scope of conflict to civil wars and communal riots, thus excluding organized and endemic violent crime? These are crucially important questions, with state authorities typically providing more conservative definitions, while those in need and their advocates will take a more expansive approach.

Disaster IDPs

Displacement due to natural disasters—earthquakes, hurricanes, tornados, fires, volcanos, tsunamis, and so on—shows even greater variability year-by-year and across regions than displacements caused by conflict and violence. Table 8.3 reveals that displacement due to ecological/natural disasters is substantially higher than displacement due to conflict and violence. That said, natural disasters may be short-lived—as hurricane floods recede, or homes are spared from fires, although in some instances natural disasters such as earthquakes may leave home areas unhabitable for years. Most people displaced by natural disasters return to their homes within a year. In 2018, of the 17.2 million people displaced by natural disasters (including 9.3 million by storms and 5.2 million by floods), only 1.6 million were still classified as displaced by the end of that year (IOM 2020, 45). However, more than development, disasters may be recurring, fluctuating between safe and severe threats over time.

The distinction between natural disasters and straightforward economic decline prodding migration is often fuzzy. Maybank et al. (1995, 197) convey the ambiguity as to whether low rainfall would be considered a drought and hence a natural disaster: "Dryness or absence of rain is not enough to constitute a drought. It must be a deficiency that, for a particular area, falls below the normal or expected amount…for a protracted time that leads to recognition of a drought occurrence." Short-lived flooding that brings seawater into cropland may go unrecognized as a natural disaster, even though salinity may render the land infertile, forcing farmers from their land.

Table 8.3 New IDPs Generated by Natural Disasters (2017–2022)

Region	*Year*	*IDPs*
The Americas	2017	4,476,000
	2018	1,687,000
	2019	1,545,000
	2020	4,500,000
	2021	1,659,000
	2022	2,100,000
Middle East & North Africa	2017	233,000
	2018	214,000
	2019	631,000
	2020	341,000
	2021	233,000
	2022	305,000
Europe & Central Asia	2017	66,000
	2018	41,000
	2019	101,000
	2020	234,000
	2021	276,000
	2022	107,000
Sub-Saharan Africa	2017	2,561,000
	2018	2,611,000
	2019	3,448,000
	2020	4,300,000
	2021	5,554,000
	2022	7,400,000
South Asia	2017	2,840,000
	2018	3,303,000
	2019	9,529,000
	2020	9,200,000
	2021	5,250,000
	2022	12,500,000
East Asia & Pacific	2017	8,604,000
	2018	9,332,000
	2019	9,601,000
	2020	12,100,000
	2021	13,696,000
	2022	10,100,000
Annual Global Average	*2017–2022*	*24,700,000*

IDMC (2018, 2019, 2020, 2021, 2022, 2023)

When natural disasters suddenly displace populations, major humanitarian and logistical challenges arise, but the politics may be straightforward, with disaster IDPs representing clear victims in need of assistance. State leaders may welcome international organizations to assist disaster IDPs, as opposed to infrastructure or conflict IDPs, which the state may see as sensitive. Of course, assisting those displaced by sudden natural disasters still entails many challenges, including property disputes, coordinating foreign assistance, debates over long- or short-term housing, corruption, potential return, and ways to mitigate future disasters. And in some cases, such as in Myanmar after Cyclone Nargis in 2008, authoritarian leaders may even block humanitarian aid to disaster IDPs to avoid letting foreign eyes into the country or to look weak to their citizens.

For slower-acting disasters and ecological changes, the status of IDPs is frequently less clear, and typically, less international assistance is available. For example, climate change has generated health threats as well as declining economic prospects in agriculture and fishing. Persons relocated due to climate change, whether internally or internationally, have often been regarded as economic migrants more than as IDPs or refugees. The uncertainty rests on three factors. First, ecosystem degradation is often gradual, making it difficult to identify causes that are beyond the control of the migrants. Second, given the cyclic nature of environmentally-relevant conditions (e.g., temperature, drought, floods), it may not be clear that the ecosystem is, in fact, irreversibly deteriorating. Third, the state may hold these people responsible for practices that, to an uncertain degree, exacerbate the problems. Perceptions of unsustainable agricultural practices focus blame on residents, weakening the migrants' claims to support. In a survey of state-led climate resettlement, Arnall (2019) warns that states may use this framing to relocate persons to achieve other goals such as undermining rebellion or capturing foreign aid.

Much depends on whether disaster IDPs are deemed permanent or are expected to return to their home areas. Disaster IDPs, like conflict IDPs, frequently face reluctance on the part of host communities and the state to integrate them into the local community, for fear that they will remain as competitors or as burdens on the subnational state institutions. It is often difficult to establish when, if ever, the site of the disaster has recovered sufficiently for the IDPs to return. As with conflict IDPs, disaster IDPs face the additional uncertainty as to whether and when to return home, perhaps pressured to move back before it is safe or economically feasible.

Creating Migrant Communities

In contrast to voluntary migrants, IDPs are more likely to arrive as groups, with young and old, leaders and followers, arriving at new homes together. In some respects, this provides IDPs with opportunities and support systems, as they may be able to take advantage of community ties to adjust and provide counsel. IDP communities may maintain social capital, working together to prosper in their new homes. That said, arriving as more complete societies may bring new problems, appearing more threatening to hosts and slowing integration.

Relations between migrants and host communities are often aggravated by the mental states of IDPs who have suffered physical and psychological traumas from their exposure to personal harm, the loss of relatives and friends, state coercion, economic abandonment, and so on. It is reasonable to expect IDPs will be defensive, and quick to assume the worst in relations with host communities and the state. IDPs also are vulnerable to the "dependency syndrome"; being confined to an IDP camp, they may fall prey to "learned helplessness" (Bosankić et al. 2019). The uncertainty of displaced status for those who may or may not be able to return to their home areas is a limbo that also leads to helplessness and low self-esteem (Havrylchyk and Ukrayinchuk 2016). One report summarizing 56 studies focusing largely on depression, anxiety, and psychosomatic symptoms identified extensive mental health problems among IDPs, especially those living in institutional accommodations and among ethnically dissimilar people (Porter and Haslam 2005). Whereas voluntary migrants exercise some agency, the expelled are victims of circumstance, unable to manage their own fate.

One further point should be stressed about economic migrants arriving in cities or rural areas related to integration and settlement patterns. Voluntary migration typically involves the gradual arrival of young persons to their destinations. While forced displacement might lead entire communities to relocate, arriving as complete societies with varied ages and occupations, voluntary migrants are more likely to arrive slowly and sporadically. This may provide opportunities for integration, perhaps marrying into the host society. Much depends on the attitudes of migrant groups toward host communities. For economically and technologically advanced migrants, as in the cases of farmers entering the lands of herders, shifting cultivators, or hunter-gatherers, it may be a challenge to avoid expressing prejudices against local people. Cambon et al. (2015, 142–143) note that intergroup competition can only be avoided if "some difference between two groups is thought to be stable and legitimate," with more powerful in-groups demonstrating "magnanimity towards the low-status group on the dimension unrelated to the status difference (e.g., warmth)." The implication is that migrants who regard themselves as more sophisticated than host communities may develop stereotypes of local people as easy-going, fun-loving, feckless, and so on.

Given prejudices toward host communities, it is common that migrants maintain separation, developing parallel societies. Voluntary migrants may coordinate with co-ethnics from their home areas, seeking to establish enclaves and recreate their home societies. Cities are typically more patchworks of migrant communities than they are melting pots. In Mumbai, Chadha and Chadda (2018, 84) describe mosaics of migrant ethnic localities:

> Rajasthani and Gujarati communit[ies] are largely concentrated in the western suburbs...[The] Marathi community is mainly concentrated in Central Mumbai...Those living in Chita Camp are mainly South Indians (Andhra Pradesh, Tamil Nadu, Karnataka and Kerala)...People from UP and Bihar are located in Kurla, Sonapur-Bhandup, Govandi, Bandra (East), Mahim, Goregoan, Jogeshwari, Nagpada and Byculla. There is also socio-spatial division in slums - firstly on the basis of religious identities, secondly on the basis of regional identities and third on the basis of caste.

It is not surprising that urbanizers often seek out co-ethnics for security and material assistance. Single-ethnicity enclaves reduce day-to-day interactions with other groups. Although this may insulate migrants from interactions that increase the probability of confrontations, separation may increase stereotyping and thereby magnify the conflicts if they do occur.

Conclusions

This chapter summarized the three primary ways that communities may become migrants through being expelled—by infrastructure development, violent conflict, and ecological disasters. Again, these groups of IDPs may overlap with state and economic migrants, and indeed, with each other. Consider villagers in Java faced with a sudden mudflow, the largest mud volcano in the world, believed by many to be the product of state-affiliated petroleum companies, or IDPs in Sri Lanka pushed out by conflict and then again by natural disasters. Although the three types of IDPs overlap, they are all compelled to relocate for reasons beyond their control.

The migrants described in this chapter are involuntary IDPs, arriving rather suddenly with varying levels of state support to new communities and with uncertain time horizons. Their ability to cope and resettle will depend in large part on state policies, but also on relations with host communities. The latter, often overlooked stakeholders in the drama of internal migration demand a discussion in their own right, the subject of Chapter 9.

References

Arnall, Alex. 2019. Resettlement as Climate Change Adaptation: What Can Be Learned from State-Led Relocation in Rural Africa and Asia? *Climate and Development* 11 (3): 253–263.

Asthana, Vandana. 2012. Forced Displacement: A Gendered Analysis of the Tehri Dam Project. *Economic and Political Weekly* 47 (48): 96–102.

Betts, Alexander. 2009. *Forced Migration and Global Politics*. London: Wiley-Blackwell.

Bosankić, Nina, Enisa Mešić, and Bojan Šošić. 2019. The Floating Pumpkin Syndrome: Forced Migration, Humanitarian Aid, and the Culture of Learned Helplessness. *Journal of Balkan and Near Eastern Studies* 21 (1): 61–73.

Cambon, Laurent, Vincent Yzerbyt, and Sonya Yakimova. 2015. Compensation in Intergroup Relations: An Investigation of Its Structural and Strategic Foundations. *British Journal of Social Psychology* 54 (1): 140–158.

Chadha, Vikram, and Ishu Chadda. 2018. Policies and Performance of Social Sector in India since Independence: A Critical Evaluation. *International Journal of Social Science and Development Policy* 4 (2): 64–90.

Fernandes, Walter. 2017. Internally Displaced Persons and Northern India. *International Studies* 50 (4): 1–19.

Havrylchyk, Olena, and Nadiya Ukrayinchuk. 2016. *Living in Limbo: Economic and Social Costs for Refugees*. Lille: University of Lille.

IDMC (Internal Displacement Monitoring Centre). 2017. Dam Displacement. Geneva.

IDMC (Internal Displacement Monitoring Centre). 2018 *Global Report on Internal Displacement 2018*. Geneva.

IDMC (Internal Displacement Monitoring Centre). 2019 *Global Report on Internal Displacement 2019*. Geneva.

IDMC (Internal Displacement Monitoring Centre). 2020 *Global Report on Internal Displacement 2020*. Geneva.
IDMC (Internal Displacement Monitoring Center). 2021. *Global Report on Internal Displacement 2021: Internal Displacement in a Changing Climate*. Geneva: Internal Displacement Monitoring Center.
IDMC (Internal Displacement Monitoring Center). 2022. *Global Report on Internal Displacement 2022: Internal Displacement in a Changing Climate*. Geneva: Internal Displacement Monitoring Center.
IDMC (Internal Displacement Monitoring Center). 2023. IDMC Data Base. https://www.internal-displacement.org/database/displacement-data.
International Commission on Large Dams. 2021. World Register of Dams. https://www.icold-cigb.org/GB/publications/world_register_of_dams.asp.
IOM (International Organization for Migration). 2020. *World Migration Report*. New York: United Nations.
IOM (International Organization for Migration). 2023. Ukraine Internal Displacement Report: General Population Survey Round 12.
Maybank, J., B. Bonsai, K. Jones, R. Lawford, E.G. O'Brien, E.A. Ripley, and E. Wheaton. 1995. Drought as a Natural Disaster. *Atmosphere-Ocean* 33 (2): 195–222.
Mooney, Erin. 2005. The Concept of Internal Displacement and the Case for Internally Displaced Persons as a Category of Concern. *Refugee Survey Quarterly* 24 (3): 9–26.
Porter, Matthew, and Nick Haslam. 2005. Predisplacement and Postdisplacement Factors Associated with Mental Health of Refugees and Internally Displaced Persons: A Meta-Analysis. *Journal of the American Medical Association* 294 (5): 602–612.
Sasse, Gwendolyn. 2020. War and Displacement: The Case of Ukraine. *Europe-Asia Studies* 72 (3): 347–353.
Terminski, Bogumil. 2013. *Development-Induced Displacement and Resettlement: Theoretical Frameworks and Current Challenges*. Geneva: Ibidem Press.
World Bank. 1994. *Resettlement and Development: The Bankwide Review of Projects Involving Involuntary Resettlement 1986–1993*. Washington, DC.

CHAPTER 9

Room to Let? Host Community Perspectives

The degree to which internal migration is peaceful, successfully achieving various development and security goals, or is conflictual, mired in poverty and violence, depends a great deal on the host community. We can presume that their baseline regarding the arrival of migrants is the perception of whether the new arrivals will improve or detract from local well-being. The early social psychology of intergroup conflict, "realistic group conflict theory," posited the straightforward principle that material threats to jobs, wealth, land, and power lead to ethnocentrism, and negative stereotypes of threatening groups (Sherif 1962; Campbell 1965).

Yet we need to recognize that external, objective measures of well-being, such as economic and educational opportunities, are not the whole story. Do interactions with migrants undermine host community members' self-esteem? Are the characteristics or behaviors of migrants seen as offensive? Such outcomes are difficult to anticipate by distant state officials. Because the reception to migrants can vary, migration planning requires identifying subsets of host communities, their concerns, and their capacities to support or confront migrants and officials.

Despite this complexity, some general orientations can be summarized. It is crucial to recognize that the "host community"—a term that seems to imply a homogeneous set of people—is often differentiated in terms of class, ethnicity, political affiliation, and so on. The nature of cleavages

W. Ascher and S. J. Barter, *Moving within Borders*, Politics, Economics, and Inclusive Development, https://doi.org/10.1007/978-3-031-37549-1_9

within host communities will have important effects on the degree to which segments of host communities can make common cause with new arrivals or else stand united against internal migrants. Migratory outcomes also depend on the magnitude of migration in relation to the carrying capacity of the area.

Migrant-Origin Communities

First, though, some mention should be made of additional stakeholders affected by internal migration. Along with states, migrants, and hosts, internal migration also affects the lives of the communities that send migrants out, the former homes of migrant groups.

On the one hand, we might expect origin communities to suffer losses as young people depart. Just as countries with extensive international migration such as the Philippines suffer from brain drain, a lack of able-bodied workers, and broken families (Parreñas 2005), areas losing large numbers of internal migrants may suffer the same stresses. In Thailand, for example, a quarter of the children in the Northeast—roughly three million—are left behind by migrating parents (UNESCO 2018). In India's mountainous Uttarakhand state, the migration of rural men to cities and other Indian states has left many agricultural plots untilled, with traditional farming techniques lost, and pressures for women to take part in traditionally male physical labor (Joshi 2018). An important risk for origin communities is that when times are bad or projects go awry, large-scale returns of migrants may overwhelm home communities that have been neglected by the state. This neglect often occurs because the lower population reduces the state's incentive to invest in physical infrastructure or upgrade social services. State neglect may result in a continual decline, as worsening conditions prompt even greater migration of young people.

On the other hand, migrants' home communities may benefit greatly from out-migration. The departure of migrants may relieve population pressures, reduce intergroup tensions, and slow environmental loss. This is a stated objective for many state migration projects, although, for the most part, success has been limited in these goals (Fearnside 1997). From a social perspective, the greater burden on women in contexts of male out-migration may be offset by gains in female status. In northern India, Joshi (2018, 10) reports that the departure of males "marginally improved women's access to education, development opportunities, leadership, decision-making power, natural resource management and growing market in some villages…contributing towards social, economic and political empowerment of rural women."

Economic advantages may include networks of chain migration or seasonal labor, or perhaps allow for the expansion of local businesses to migrant areas. Remittances typically bring major economic benefits. While studied extensively for international migration, less has been said of domestic remittances, but not for lack of scale or importance. Lucas (2021, 333) laments that, despite widespread interest in urban migration, the study of domestic remittances "remains far less well covered in the literature." For instance, Thai youths migrating to Bangkok have sent considerable sums home to rural families, especially in the poorer northeastern region of Isan. Gullette (2019) observes that domestic remittances from Bangkok to Isan enabled new investment in rural areas, with funds enabling those that did not migrate to open small businesses, pursue education, or care for extended families. In Morocco, de Haas (2006) finds that internal remittances are typically less than those of international migrants, but provide greater flexibility, and money from internal migration may enable younger family members to later take part in international migration. In the Peruvian highlands, Long (2008) analyzes complex remittance flows, where sometimes origin communities send money or food to migrants, and at other times, migrants send money or processed goods to their home villages. Although sometimes these two-way flows are enabled through in-person visits, it is more common that relatives or migrants would organize by village to send items in bulk via charter microbus (Long 2008, 58). The volume of domestic remittances can be considerable; in China, early estimates in the 1990s place the total value of these transfers at over US$10 billion (Cai 2003). More recent studies have shown that the presence of lineage associations and strong beliefs in ancestral homelands amplify the scale of remittances, as in southern China (Zhang and Yang 2022). While the purchasing power of national currencies may sometimes not be as considerable as foreign currencies, it is typically easier to transfer these funds with few fees. Further, domestic remittances are less dependent on international fluctuations, such as countries closing their borders in times of war, recession, or pandemics.

Compared to international migration, the loss of productive youth through internal migration may be tempered by the relative ease of returning home. The problem of breaking up families may again be offset by easier returns home or by encouraging family members to relocate either permanently or temporarily. Without the barrier of international borders, some of the losses associated with sustained out-migration may be less severe for internal migration.

Connections between out-migration communities and new, often urban communities are frequently sustained through various formal and informal organizations. Migrants in new areas often develop what are known as Home Town Associations (HTAs), alternatively known as Home Village or Home Place Associations. HTAs are community organizations that strengthen connections not just among co-ethnics, but specifically among migrants from the same communities, building solidarity and maintaining linkages to their homes. Such organizations typically form initially to provide welfare to migrants in new surroundings, facilitating the arrival of new migrants by guiding them to employment and housing, and then rotating credit, education, and more. Kin networks can lower the economic as well as psychological costs associated with migration (Lucas 2021, 247). Mutual economic assistance is often the bedrock of HTAs. Agbese (1996, 145) notes that:

> Hometown associations have been an important feature in West Africa for many years...They enable their members to protect themselves against the economic vicissitudes of the urban environment, and the active participants in the associations derive tangible and symbolic benefits from their membership. Hometown associations provide sick benefits, loans, and social and cultural activities for their members, which help reinforce ethnic/hometown identity. In this way, hometown identity is institutionalized and used to cope with economic uncertainties. The financial benefits derived from membership act as a glue in sustaining and maintaining the organizations.

In addition to economic roles, HTAs also typically play important cultural roles for migrants, providing a sense of familiarity. They may organize cultural events, provide education in local languages, and provide funerary rites.

Yet, it is not only migrant communities that benefit from HTAs, which also use place-specific ties to facilitate development in the home region. They may facilitate remittances and home visits, and contribute to developing to promote the development of infrastructure. For example, for Cameroon, Evans (2010, 397) notes: "Mutualism and conviviality remain core activities but associations now often extend their role to the development of the home place, usually through provision of public goods."

With time, HTAs may play important political roles, serving as brokers for urban politicians and linking leaders in major cities to the countryside. Many governments may then partner with HTAs, seeing them as valuable political and economic brokers, perhaps matching remittances to amplify migrant-led development projects. Home towns may encourage this through various celebrations, such as "prodigal son" events to honor generous migrants. That said, they may also become resented by home communities, eventually seen as vehicles for a handful of notable businessmen who think they know what their former homes need (Evans 2010, 407).

HTAs and related organizations are common throughout the world, especially in Africa (Tostensen et al. 2001), but also in Turkey (Özdemir 2014), Latin America (Fitzgerald 2008), and beyond. Juliawan (2010, 40) describes the functions of hometown associations in Indonesian cities: "As Tangerang, a city of 1.4 million in 2006, has become a magnet for people from different corners of Indonesia, hometown associations are thriving as a way of asserting migrant identity and of pooling resources." HTAs may also expand to play similar roles internationally, initially forming to connect and protect migrants, and with time becoming vehicles for development in home regions. As with the study of migration more generally, HTAs have come to be seen mostly in international terms, seen as an instance of transnationalism. As Fitzgerald (2008, 145) observes, such studies of global migrant networks "exhibit a short memory," overlooking the domestic networks upon which global ones are built. He shows that, for one Mexican village, domestic migration to Mexico City and Guadalajara established HTAs that would later serve as foundations for transnational linkage organizations, together serving as sources of development for the home region.

Solidarity or Solubility: The Importance of Host Cleavages

While sending communities can be seen as possessing some agency in terms of migration, host societies typically have less say in the arrival of internal migrants of various stripes. Just as migrant communities may vary in terms of class and ethnicity, the ways that the arrival of migrants to a new area play out vary a great deal on the composition of the host society. In general, a host society with a clear, distinctive sense of identity and group loyalties will be more likely to resist the arrival of migrants compared to a more fragmented local context. When host communities are fragmented, more opportunities and motivations exist to ally with migrant groups. Madhavan and Landau (2011, 477) note that "the evidence from African cities suggests we should be wary of ascribing undue social coherence to the cities' current populations, populations characterized as much by ethnic heterogeneity, economic disparity, and cultural diversity as by solidarity."

There is a long scholarly literature that attributes ethnic conflict or cooperation to the presence of cross-cutting cleavages (Lipset and Rokkan 1967). If groups possess separate faiths, languages, occupations, and other traits, then although there may be fewer opportunities for conflict, when conflicts do occur, they tend to be difficult to moderate (Horowitz 1982, 334). Meanwhile, cross-cutting cleavages, perhaps with some migrants sharing the religion of the host community, can bridge different groups. Selway (2011) argues that unidirectional measures of ethnicity and ethnic fragmentation fall short of explaining various economic and political outcomes, demanding that data should be interactive and multidimensional, essentially measuring the compatibility of given communities. A related approach emphasizes horizontal and vertical inequalities, with the salience of ethnic identity shaped by between-group inequality (hierarchy) and within-group inequality (segmentation) (Siroky and Hechter 2016, 92).

The composition of the host community, and how it intersects with the composition of migrant groups, will thus have important effects on whether internal migration is successful or not. In Mumbai, some occupational sub-castes are threatened by the influx of migrants more adept in their occupations; other residents are happy to see more competition in the provision of goods and services that they consume. Sen (2019) shows how class solidarities can sometimes cut across migrant and native divisions in India, with poor natives finding common cause with poor migrants against elites. In Indonesia, Muslim minorities in Christian areas likely saw the arrival of Muslim migrants very differently than did Christians. In the Philippines, Christian migrants to Mindanao were received differently by native Moro Muslims compared with indigenous Lumad Christians, with the latter more likely to integrate with migrant groups. Crucially, some of these regions would see conflict, but the salient cleavage shifted at least in part from migration to religion.

Exchange Perspectives

Complementarities between hosts and migrants depend not just on societal composition, but also on economic roles. The arrival of migrants initiates a series of exchanges on both material and non-material levels. Host communities may be receptive to filling labor shortages, especially if migrants settle for low wages. Hosts may also be receptive to higher demand for their goods and services from migrants, to sell land at a premium as migrants increase the demand for property, and to enjoy the goods and services that migrants provide. Of course, such hopes may be countered by the fears that local workers will be displaced, that competition for goods and services will raise prices and leave some local people without, migrants will become landowners, and that demand for local people's goods and services decline in the face of competition by migrants.

One particular context is typically quite favorable for host communities, though often at the expense of migrants. If IDPs are confined to refugee camps, provisions for camp residents, whether purchased by the camp management or by the IDPs themselves, provide a market for local producers. Gengo et al. (2018) observe that, while it is often assumed that host communities and IDPs have conflictual relationships, in some cases host communities benefit from goods, customers, personal relationships, and labor related to IDP communities. Based on research in Kenya, they find that the Turkana host community has largely benefited from the presence of IDP and refugee camps, with growing markets for firewood, building supplies, and foods helping local businesses and employing Turkana people. Local producers may even have an incentive to press camp authorities to discourage production within the camp that would compete with the local market, in effective maintaining economic dependency.

Non-material exchanges also can be positive or negative for the host community. Hosts may relish the enhancement of self-esteem if migrants, as supplicants, show gratitude for the noblesse oblige of host community members who help poor migrants. Hosts may also enjoy the status of being able to hire migrants to work for them.

Yet host community members may be intimidated or even humiliated by wealthier, more educated migrants. They may realize that migrants are sent in to assimilate local people. Host communities that find themselves outnumbered by an influx of migrants may lose their cultural dominance. If wealthy entrepreneurial migrants arrive, local people may find themselves in subservient positions.

Welcome to the Jungle: Rural Host Communities

In general, the key to the profiles of rural host community members is their limited economic and technological development. Rural people are likely to be farmers, gatherers, fishers, or woodsmen, proud of their hard work and knowledge of the land, but perhaps sensitive to higher levels of wealth, education, and apparent sophistication of migrants. Some migrants may be similar in livelihoods, but if migrants have greater technical expertise, host community members are vulnerable to insecurity.

Sometimes, rural elites stand to lose the most from the arrival of migrants. The exceptions may be if migrants are mostly uneducated and poor, if rural elites can gain their support, as well as if migrant demand increases the value of the land. One can imagine that if rural elites maintain power through their higher levels of education and economic resources, the arrival of more advanced migrants with more expansive networks could fundamentally disrupt the host society. Although this could be for the better, we should also expect vulnerable elites to respond with nativist claims.

Host community members who are prone to the anxiety of being considered inferior in the face of more technologically and economically advanced migrants may stereotype migrants as arrogant, out of the presumption that the migrants regard themselves as superior. The distress of believing that others look down upon the in-group may be assuaged by looking down upon the out-group. Thus, a destructive dynamic may be triggered by disdain toward out-group members believed to disdain the in-group, whether they do or not. For example, the conflicts that prompted the evacuation from Kalimantan of thousands of Madurese reflected Dayak resentment of perceived Madurese arrogance, a particularly galling perception for the economically less sophisticated, but proudly indigenous Dayaks. König (2013, 127) cites a stereotype that Dayaks hold of the Madurese: "Even if the Madurese associate with the Dayaks…they still like to pretend to be something better." Dayaks often saw Madurese as disrespectful, yet the reaction of some Dayaks was even more visceral, as they were offended by what they perceived as the poor manners, violent nature, and even foul odor of Madurese. Both groups displayed pride and negative views of the other, ultimately leading to considerable violence in the late 1990s (Davidson 2008).

Welcome to the Big City: Urban Host Communities

The profiles of city dwellers who come into contact with recent migrants will vary considerably. This may depend on whether the city is an established metropolis or a new frontier town. In the latter context, many existing residents are likely fairly recent migrants themselves, and the arrival of more population can provide the critical mass for greater urban amenities. Host community members would thus value the greater population. The towns along the Transpacific Highway connecting Brazil to Peru's Pacific ports are becoming more urbane as restaurants and theaters become more viable. Pontianak, the capital of Indonesia's West Kalimantan province, has big-city facilities that would have been impossible without internal migration. At a certain stage of size and development, urban residents may thus welcome internal migrants.

Unlike the rural context, urban residents rarely have to cope with the arrival of sponsored migrants who could claim the backing of the state. In general, urban migrants come of their own accord, whether they left their homes voluntarily or not. Except for the "villagization" of forced settlement of widely scattered rural people into villages, as undertaken in Ethiopia, Laos, Somalia, and Tanzania, urbanization is rarely managed, let alone sponsored.

A very different context exists in large cities where residents, whether long-standing or born elsewhere, may be confronted with unbidden migrants, or they may encourage kin or other co-ethnics to join them. In India, non-Marathi Mumbai residents tend to live in concentrated ethnic settlements. Instead of integrating into Marathi communities, these communities attract co-ethnic migrants into their neighborhoods. Residents whose families hailed from beyond Maharashtra State can find support through the co-ethnic migrants who join their ranks, with a steady stream of arrivals allowing groups to maintain distinct identities where they may otherwise integrate.

Host communities often have the choice either to embrace migrants or marginalize them. Residents may rise to the challenge of aiding migrants, especially if migrants are co-ethnics or have endured similar challenges. In Colombia, low-income women of the outskirts of Medellin have supported migrant women through NGOs and the Catholic Church

(Martinez Portilla et al. 2011). Many residents and migrants also share Afro-Colombian identity. A crucial aspect of the assistance has been the pressure on the Colombian government to recognize migrants as IDPs and therefore entitled to state support. In this case, the social assistance programs are separate from the general programs for residents, such that local women's support does not undermine their prospects for state benefits.

The socioeconomic status of the host community can be a decisive factor in its orientation toward migrants. In Argentina, urban residents' reactions to migrants from poorer northern provinces are split according to class-based political polarization. Wealthier Argentines, largely of European ancestry, may view rural-to-urban migrants of Amerindian or African ancestry as crude, and, in many instances, incorrectly believe that they are immigrants from neighboring countries. The same problem exists for Nepalese who migrate from the Southern Belt. The prejudicial stereotype is particularly insidious because it is not acknowledged as overt racism, but rather conforms to what has been called "subtle" racism: the denial that one is racist, but holding negative attitudes toward behaviors associated with people of a particular race, in this case masked by migratory status (McConahay 1986). In South America, migrants of distinctly non-European features are often blamed for crime and being duped into supporting populist leaders. This stereotype is sustained in part by limited contact between migrants and hosts; they see the migrants, if at all, as workers in menial jobs.

In contrast, rural-to-urban migrants coming to Argentine cities are typically embraced by low-income residents because of the solidarity of class consciousness. A new identity of *villeros* (residents of shantytowns), comprised of both long-standing residents and recently arrived migrants, has emerged in Buenos Aires (Cravino 2002). Lower-income residents not only can share the *villero* identity, but their interactions can also dissolve stereotypes of regional or ethnic differences. The polarization that permits the long-standing and recent *villeros* to bond so well is a deep resentment of the middle-class Argentines. This identity has become a source of mobilization for low-income residents of Buenos Aires and a source of fear among wealthier residents as the percentage of poor voters grows.

Yet, when the solidarity of low-income residents and low-income migrants is absent or erodes, urban residents are prone to resent migrants as their neighborhoods become congested, sanitation systems break down, and lodging is cruder. Hosts may bridle when jobs are hard to come by, education deteriorates from overcrowding, and health facilities are over-stretched. In short, a risk exists that local community members might accept migrants initially, but sour as numbers mount.

Conclusions

Previous chapters focused on the centrality of the state in managing internal migration, as well as the different natures of migrants with and without state support. This chapter has focused on host communities as well as interactions between sending communities and migrants who live within, and may become part of the host community. Hosts may welcome migrants when they bring economic development, play complementary economic roles, and possess shared traits.

On the negative side, we have suggested that host communities with internal divisions and a weak sense of ethnic identity may be less likely to stand up to migrants. In rural areas, hosts may be threatened by more advanced migrant groups, seeing them as arrogant and feeling inferior. In urban areas, residents may chafe at growing congestion and assert dominance over poor migrants, but may also prosper from the arrival of urbanizing migrants.

References

Agbese, Pita Ogaba. 1996. Ethnic Conflicts and Hometown Associations: An Analysis of the Experience of the Agila Development Association. *Africa Today* 43 (2): 139–156.

Cai, Qian. 2003. Migrant Remittances and Family Ties: A Case Study in China. *International Journal of Population Geography* 9 (6): 471–483.

Campbell, Donald T. 1965. Ethnocentrism and Other Altruistic Motives. *Nebraska Symposium on Motivation*, vol. 13, 283–311. Lincoln: University of Nebraska Press.

Cravino, Maria. 2002. Las Transformaciones en la Identidad Villera...la Conflictiva Construcción de Sentidos. *Cuadernos de Antropología Social* 15: 29–47.

Davidson, Jamie S. 2008. *From Rebellion to Riots: Collective Violence on Indonesian Borneo*. Madison: University of Wisconsin Press.

de Haas, Hein. 2006. Migration, Remittances, and Regional Development in Southern Morocco. *Geoforum* 37 (4): 565–580.

Evans, Martin. 2010. Primary Patriotism, Shifting Identity: Hometown Associations in Manyu Division, South-West Cameroon. *Africa* 80 (3): 397–425.

Fearnside, Philip. 1997. Transmigration in Indonesia: Lessons from Its Environmental and Social Impacts. *Environmental Management* 21 (4): 553–570.

Fitzgerald, David. 2008. Colonies of the Little Motherland: Membership, Space, and Time in Mexican Migrant Hometown Associations. *Comparative Studies in Society and History* 50 (1): 145–169.

Gengo, Tieti G., Rahul C. Oka, Varalakshmi Vemuru, Mark Golitko, and Lee T. Gettler. 2018. Positive Effects of Refugee Presence on Host Community Nutritional Status in Turkana County, Kenya. *American Journal of Human Biology* 30 (1): 1–14.

Gullette, Gregory. 2019. Constrained Urban Aspirations: Development, Structural Precarity, and Inequalities within Thai Migration. *Asian and Pacific Migration Journal* 28 (3): 300–323.

Horowitz, Dan. 1982. Dual Authority Politics. *Comparative Politics* 14 (3): 329–349.

Joshi, Bhagwati. 2018. Recent Trends of Rural Out-Migration and its Socioeconomic and Environmental Impacts in Uttarakhand Himalaya. *Journal of Urban and Regional Studies on Contemporary India* 4 (2): 1–14.

Juliawan, Benny Hari. 2010. Extracting Labor from Its Owner: Private Employment Agencies and Labor Market Flexibility in Indonesia. *Critical Asian Studies* 42 (1): 25–52.

König, Anika. 2013. Smelling the Difference: The Senses in Ethnic Conflict in West Kalimantan, Indonesia. In *Senses and Citizenships: Embodying Political Life*, eds. Susanna Trnka, Christine Dureau, and Julie Park, 120–135. New York: Routledge.

Lipset, Seymour Martin, and Stein Rokkan, eds. 1967. *Party Systems and Voter Alignments: Cross National Perspectives*. New York: Free Press.

Long, Norman. 2008. Translocal Livelihoods, Networks of Family and Community, and Remittances in Central Peru. In *Migration and Development Within and Across Borders: Research and Policy Perspectives on Internal and International Migration*, eds. Josh DeWind and Jennifer Holdaway, 39–70. Geneva: IOM.

Lucas, Robert E.B. 2021. *Crossing the Divide: Rural to Urban Migration in Developing Countries*. Oxford: Oxford University Press and KNOWMAD.

Madhavan, Sangeetha, and Loren B. Landau. 2011. Bridges to Nowhere: Hosts, Migrants, and the Chimera of Social Capital in Three African Cities. *Population and Development Review* 37 (3): 473–497.

Martinez Portilla, Isabel, Corona Aguilar, Antonia, and Ianez Dominguez, Antonio. 2011. "Mujeres Desplazadas y Estrategias de Vida: Experiencias de Jefas de Hogar Asentadas en Medellín, Colombia." Departamento de Antropologia Social, Universidad de Sevilla.

McConahay, John. 1986. Modern Racism, Ambivalence, and the Modern Racism Scale. In *Prejudice, Discrimination, and Racism*, eds. John Dovidio and Samuel Gaertner, 91–125. Orlando, FL: Academic Press.

Özdemir, Gürbüz. 2014. "Character of the Pressure Group of Hometown Associations: Case of Cankiri–Turkey." *Review of History and Political Science 2* (2): 63–92.

Parreñas, Rhacel Salazar. 2005. *Children of Global Migration: Transnational Families and Gendered Woes*. Stanford: Stanford University Press.

Selway, Joel Sawat. 2011. The Measurement of Cross-cutting Cleavages and Other Multidimensional Cleavage Structures. *Political Analysis* 19 (1): 48–65.

Sen, Rumela. 2019. Competing Mobilization of Tribal and Class Identity: Politics of Internal Migration in North India. In *Internal Migration: Challenges in Governance and Integration*, eds. Shane Barter and William Ascher, 63–76. New York: Peter Lang.

Sherif, Muzafer, ed. 1962. *Intergroup Relations and Leadership*. New York: Wiley.

Siroky, David, and Michael Hechter. 2016. Ethnicity, Class, and Civil War: The Role of Hierarchy, Segmentation, and Cross-Cutting Cleavages. *Civil Wars* 18 (1): 91–107.

Tostensen, Arne, Inge Tvedten, and Mariken Vaa, eds. 2001. *Associational Life in African Cities: Popular Responses to the Urban Crisis*. Stockholm: Nordiska Afrikainstitutet.

UNESCO. 2018. *Policy Briefs on Internal Migration*. Bangkok.

Zhang, Dong, and Yongjiao Yang. 2022. Internal Migrants' Charitable Giving to Hometowns in China: The Effect of Community Embeddedness. *Population, Space, and Place* 28 (2): e2491.

PART II

What Can Go Wrong

Having unpacked the various actors involved in internal migration—the motivations, dilemmas, and diversity of states, migrants, and host communities—Part II explains what can go wrong. In a sense, this underscores the importance of internal migration as a field of study and why more effective policies to govern internal migration represent such pressing concerns. Internal migration is widespread because it promises those involved to achieve important goals—development, security, or wealth.

Internal migrants may relocate for new opportunities. They may be pushed out by violence or land appropriation, but hope their new home provides safety and stability. Migrants may move to gain access to land in other rural areas or gain employment in towns. Meanwhile, states manage migration for myriad factors—nation-building, economic development, security, and more. Even host communities, groups that typically have migration thrust upon them, may gain economically, as migrants bring investment, and know-how or serve as pools of cheap labor. Fundamentally, internal migration is pervasive—over three times as voluminous as international migration—because it holds promise. Internal migration represents a fundamentally important strategy for economic security among migrants and development for state officials. But as the following chapters make clear, not only can this promise fall short, internal migration can result in situations worse than pre-migration contexts.

In Chapter 10, we focus on various forms of deprivations that often result from large-scale internal migration, with those involved suffering from various economic, political, sociocultural, and security threats and losses. Poorly managed internal migration too often leaves all involved worse off, despite the promise of relocation being to improve livelihoods.

In Chapter 11, we turn our attention to instances in which internal migration leads to violence. In Sons of the Soil conflicts, native groups mount violent resistance against outsiders, leading to riots, pogroms, and other forms of communal conflict. Such migration-related conflicts kill thousands of people every year, a major barrier to well-being across many countries. Finally, with the primacy of the state, leaders may be aware of the potential human cost of mass internal migration, but encourage or allow it anyway because it helps them to achieve their policy goals.

Chapter 12 focuses on state failures, noting how the complexities of internal migration cause leaders to lose control of internal migration, which can have unanticipated, pernicious long-term outcomes.

CHAPTER 10

Migratory Deprivations

It is well understood that "internal migration can play an important role in poverty reduction and economic development" (Deshingkar and Grimm 2005, 5). However, sociopolitical dynamics often impart serious deprivations on both migrants and host communities. Instead of job creation and growth, the results are often poverty, exclusion, ethnic tensions, and violence. This chapter and the next emphasize how internal migration can fail in both the economic and sociopolitical objectives or host communities, officials often communicate that internal migration will create jobs and new economic opportunities. The fact that internal migration often fails in important dimensions represents lost opportunities for human development in many of the world's poorest communities. Thus, this chapter spotlights what can go wrong in internal migrations, documenting various forms of deprivation. These deficits, whether real, anticipated, or simply imagined, may be difficult to avoid, yet state policy, or the lack of it, often exacerbates these deprivations. Therefore, after establishing some contextual aspects and identifying common dynamics, the chapter offers possible reasons for how and why state policies might add to the deprivations that can trigger destructive conflict.

W. Ascher and S. J. Barter, *Moving within Borders*, Politics, Economics, and Inclusive Development,
https://doi.org/10.1007/978-3-031-37549-1_10

Pre-migration Contexts

Any wave of migration, whether part of a resettlement program or not, challenges existing local socioeconomic structures. The existing community within the resettlement area undoubtedly will have particular occupations, cultural practices, political arrangements, and understandings of the history of the area. Although structures are rarely static—previous migrations may have occurred and livelihoods, beliefs, and relationships change over time—the entrance of new migrants is bound to transform the pre-existing socioeconomic ecology. Some groups may find this to be a positive development, especially if they were chafing under the economic, political, or cultural domination of other groups. Even so, the potential for conflict is apparent.

Every pre-migration context has some degree of a hierarchy of wealth, political influence, skill, and deference. This holds from megacities to the smallest villages. As a result, the dimensions of potential conflict can go beyond "migrant versus host community," as the host population often has its own divisions.

We cannot presume that rights are settled before the arrival of migrants; contention over rights is practically universal. A non-obvious insight is that migration not only risks conflict between migrants and host communities, it can worsen conflict within the host community and among the migrants. It can open the opportunity for segments of the host community to press for more rights vis-à-vis more privileged communities. Disadvantaged groups may even seek to ally with the migrants. New arrivals may themselves feature social divisions and conflicts. Resettled communities may arrive with long-standing cleavages, or migrants from different regions may form new divides, to say nothing of tensions with host communities. Sen (2019) documents one example in Bihar, northern India, where the arrival of migrants into tribal areas was, for a time, understood through a class lens. Poor migrants found common cause with poor natives against elites from both groups, temporarily transcending native/migrant divisions.

Unlike host communities, which typically feature rich and poor, young and old, migrants may or may not arrive as whole societies. Although IDPs sometimes arrive as entire villages, especially disaster IDPs, migration is often taken up by young men or a particular class, age, or occupation. The composition of migrant groups represents a crucial component of how migrants will interact with host communities. In

Indonesia, official state transmigrants were mostly poor farmers opening up marginal lands, often entering local patron-client systems. In contrast, conflicts arose from spontaneous migration in the eastern islands, in which traders and businesspeople arrived in new towns and competed with local elites for power (Barter and Côté 2015). In Lampung, poor Javanese farmers arriving as state-managed migrants integrated fairly successfully with native Lampungese. Tensions have instead been with much smaller Hindu Balinese migrant communities, non-Muslim disaster IDPs who arrived as entire villages. While the Javanese joined native villages, families, and power structures, the Balinese stood apart, with Balinese elites clashing with Lampungese for political and economic power. This lack of integration generated animosity and later violence (Côté 2019).

Material Deprivations

It is useful to point out that migrants and host communities alike are vulnerable to intertwined economic risks: clashes over property rights; shortfalls in economic support of resettlement programs; economic competition and the arrival of migrants exceeding the area's carrying capacity, with the consequences of unfulfilled economic prospects, often worsen the carrying capacity problem.

The Ambiguity of Property

Disputes over rights, ranging from land use to employment, frequently exacerbate conflicts following resettlements. For rural natives, land may represent one of the most important forms of wealth and prestige. For many indigenous communities, the arrival of migrants accelerates capitalist understandings of property, displacing communal tenure in favor of ownership. When ownership is challenged by migrants, this can represent a major threat to group identity and native elites. In times of crisis, natives may see themselves as Sons of the Soil, claiming an irreparable connection to the land that is under threat through migration.

Two common conditions complicate these disputes. First, concerning land use, many states claim ownership of huge areas and types of land: "unoccupied" or "under-used" areas (regardless of whether they are occupied by indigenous populations or temporarily fallow as the indigenous groups practice shifting cultivation), land classified as forest (regardless of whether it has forests), or areas deemed as deserving of environmental protection (regardless of whether effective protection occurs). Just as Western countries have a long history of seeing indigenous lands as *terra nullius*, this mentality continues to drive internal migration around the world. An area may be too remote for the state to assert its control, at least until the arrival of settlers. At that point, the state may be compelled to assert its authority to allocate user rights as it sees fit. The possibility that the state would reassign property rights creates the potential for migrants and hosts to contest these rights. However, the government's laws and regulations on land use are by no means universally embraced by migrants or host communities. Clashes among customary (traditional) rights, governmentally-assigned rights, understandings among people, and who controls land uses can create continual contention.

The commodification of land often fuels critiques of internal migration as internal colonialism. Large-scale migration is not simply about the arrival of people, but also about the control of resources and assimilation into capitalist economies. In the Philippines, Muslim areas in Mindanao saw the arrival of Christian migrants, especially from the 1930s through the 1960s. Migrants enjoyed close relations with state officials, allowing them to buy up valuable real estate along new highways. Tuminez (2007, 80) observes: "The Bureau of Lands' policy of prioritizing claims based on filing of paperwork, as opposed to occupancy, spurred further land-grabbing and land speculation… Moros and smaller indigenous groups were the biggest losers in this process." This has led to the exclusion of Moro and indigenous Lumad communities from a migrant-dominated economy, fueling decades of poverty and violence.

Different conceptions of land usage and ownership can cut in several ways. Native customary land ownership may exclude migrants from owning land or other forms of property. Hosts may benefit from controlling property, blocking migrants from owning resources and thus from establishing roots. When poor rural migrants arrive in cities, they typically take over marginal lands, creating squatter settlements. As this land becomes valuable, local authorities may retain formal ownership of land, even when migrants have lived there for decades and have carried out improvements. When planners seek to expel informal communities, the result is often greater poverty and insecurity among already marginalized groups. In these and other ways, migrant communities may find themselves without clear property rights.

Promising Much, Delivering Little

State planners and business leaders typically make exaggerated claims when initiating large-scale migration projects. Transmigration sites and SEZs may promise jobs, education, land, and more, to convince migrants to relocate and hosts to tolerate changes to their homes. State leaders and "infrastructure entrepreneurs" frequently embellish the benefits of migrant-related projects (Flyvbjerg et al. 2009). Quite often, these promises fail to materialize. State promises may fall short in terms of providing infrastructure, technical assistance, capital, or other inputs; productive factories do not materialize; migrants' farms fail; mines or sawmills prove to be less productive than anticipated; companies demand high levels of training or undercut wages; or other initiatives to employ migrants and local populations shrink or collapse. The new abundance of labor must be matched by training, capital, and physical infrastructure for labor to be deployed productively. If not, disappointed migrants, after facing the risks and dislocation of resettlement, may then encroach on the assets of an already frustrated host community.

In pledging support for migrants, states may try to follow through in good faith, but corruption and mismanagement block support from materializing. With state-initiated resettlement to rural areas, the underfunding of rural industrialization requiring physical infrastructure and capital from the state is a major reason for the weakness of rural industries. Poston (1990, 44) reported that across Central Africa, even very small-scale rural industries in metalworking were held back by the lack of basic resources. Inadequate support for obtaining credit, tools, and training may leave migrants ill-prepared to farm the plots they have been given. Both migrants and host populations may be ill-prepared to work in manufacturing or extractive-industries jobs. The lack of physical infrastructure, generally the most obvious obligation of the state, often undermines the potential for productive manufacturing.

When state-corporate partnerships promote SEZs, the result is displacement among host communities alongside the arrival of labor migrants. Leaders tend to promise jobs and infrastructure investments, specifically promising to provide jobs to those displaced by the SEZ. Vineeta Yadav (2019) reports that SEZs in Andhra Pradesh promised far more than was delivered, including water, electricity, roads, job training centers, and high-paying jobs. Not only did these promises fail to materialize, but SEZs and local authorities also clamped down on protest;

"villages were deliberately broken up and scattered to reduce their ability to mobilize against SEZ authorities and governments down the road" (Yadav 2019, 82). In some cases, it is the government that exaggerates job creation and benefits; sometimes it is the private developer, or both. When these promises are broken, host communities are left worse off, and the areas cleared for the SEZs drive residents into IDP status, frequently clashing with migrant workers.

Economic Competition

It is almost certain that migrants will compete with local people and other migrants over jobs, land, and other assets. The question is how intense the competition will be and whether it is accompanied by offsetting economic complementarities. Sometimes a resettlement program is launched with full knowledge that the host community will lose materially. Sometimes authorities may intend to undermine the capabilities of the host community, especially among rebellious minorities. Even if the resettlement design is protective of the local community, migrants are often seen by hosts as economic threats.

Aside from coercively displaced people and those fleeing violence, migrants are often more entrepreneurial than the people who remain in their place of origin, or at least are better connected to national economies and networks. Some migrants are likely to go beyond the economic activities mandated by the resettlement program and formal restrictions (such as bans on outsiders owning land or residing in specific areas). This may not undermine the wealth of host communities, but if migrants grow wealthier, then the inequality itself may cause disruption due to resentment from a sense of relative deprivation (Gurr 1970).

In rural areas, migrants may compete with locals in several ways. Land ownership often represents the most potent symbolic and economic issue, with competing understandings generating disputes. Migrants to rural areas often arrive with knowledge and connections that enable them to establish themselves as small business owners, traders, money lenders, and bureaucrats, coming to dominate lucrative economic sectors. Economic competition may also develop when rural migrants arrive in cities. Although in many ways complementary, as rural migrants may take up low-paid manufacturing jobs and satisfy urban elites, their arrival may also threaten local workers. Poor residents may see their wages undercut by migrants, again generating nativist resistance. In cities, we see groups such as Shiv Sena in India and the Betawi Brotherhood in Indonesia, described in the next chapter, mobilizing to defend native interests. This may even be fueled by local elites, who find that violence toward migrants makes the migrant's existence even more precarious and further drives down wages.

The management of manufacturing wages, which in many contexts is a matter of state control, can aggravate relative deprivation through wage differentials between migrants and hosts. On the one hand, local employees may be favored over migrants. China has been home to separate economies for local and migrant workers. Particularly at the beginning of China's mass urbanization to the coastal provinces, "two discrete labour markets have been created so as to ensure relatively high pay in a fixed number of factory positions for employees from the nearby villages. For performing similar jobs in these same factories, immigrant workers from elsewhere in China earn far less" (Van Luong and Unger 1998, 82–83). More recently, Combes et al. (2020) report that China's impressive gains of urbanization remain highly unequal, with high-skilled natives gaining new opportunities as cities grow, but rural-to-rural migrants remain poor and compete for low-paying jobs. In such cases, it is not surprising that the state does not favor migrants, who may have little choice but to encroach into other land or grasp employment opportunities that threaten the local population.

In contrast, for state-sponsored resettlements, migrants are frequently favored additions that enrich the area in general, but increase disparities with local populations. Host communities not only may face unequal access to jobs and state benefits, but also externalities from growth such as inflation and pollution, and, for some indigenous peoples, exclusion due to the expansion of cash-based economies. Sometimes, frustration toward the state can lead local communities to shun potential opportunities. In Indonesia's North Sulawesi province, various infrastructure programs that came with the arrival of state-managed transmigrants were rejected by local people. Noveria (2002, 9) notes that these people, correctly or incorrectly, "perceived the program as unequal government services for migrants and non-migrants." Because national government spending was seen as primarily benefiting migrants, it sparked jealousy and anger toward migrants. In this case, the relative deprivation is felt keenly by the local population, even though they arguably enjoy increases in absolute levels of development.

Exceeding Carrying Capacity

The constraints on income-earning potential within a given area consist of limitations of resources available: land quality, natural resources, financial and commercial institutions, effective business regulation, education and training infrastructure, healthcare facilities, physical infrastructure, telecommunications, environmental services, and so on. Even if the state is generous in providing resources, the area's capacity to absorb migrants may remain limited. State spending within the resettlement area may not fully overcome the inadequacies of highways, railways, and waterways connecting the resettlement area to other areas needed to provide goods and services. For example, in the Brazilian Amazon, many ranches subsidized by the state as part of the resettlement initiative were abandoned not only because of unfavorable pasture conditions, but also because of "their remoteness from the larger urban markets" (Goulding et al. 1996, 41). With the expansion of roads and rail, as well as the demand for beef as the Amazonian population itself increased, cattle ranching has expanded, yet the early resettlement lacked adequate connectivity with the markets necessary for economic success.

Three major challenges to an area's carrying capacity are the suddenness of the inflow, problems arising from communal differences between hosts and migrants, and the magnitude of migration. Gradual migration may permit synchronized expansion of needed resources and supporting industries, but sudden state-led resettlement programs may take place before the various dimensions of infrastructure can be established. Even well-planned state migration projects may overlook some vital aspects of a new community, such as attracting teachers or providing senior care. The stresses of accommodating a greater population without comparable expansion of physical and social infrastructure risk the decline of living standards, inflation, and rising political tensions. If frustrated migrants then relocate once again, they do so without state oversight.

Carrying capacity is also sensitive to the characteristics of the migrants: the nature of the economic activities they wish to pursue, suitability for these jobs, levels of education, and distinctiveness from the host populations in terms of the feasibility of economic cooperation. If migrants are intent on farming areas with limited agricultural capacity, the arrival of substantial numbers of migrants can undermine agricultural sustainability. If migrants are inadequately trained to undertake available employment opportunities, they remain underemployed until and unless they are trained or new employment opportunities emerge. If migrants' preferred occupations do not suit the local economic needs, or if migrants have difficulty getting along with host communities, the potential of complementarity of economic activities remains unfulfilled.

Finally, economic carrying capacity is a function of the total number of people in relation to existing resource constraints. Presumably, any planned resettlement program would be based on an assessment of the limits of the magnitude of migration that would avoid exceeding the economic carrying capacity of the factors outlined above. The challenges, then, are both whether these assessments are accurate and whether the number of migrants is within this tolerance.

Political Deprivations

In addition to economic promises, internal migration often also holds significant political appeal for the state, with migrants, host communities, or both frequently at risk as migration becomes politicized. Leaders may expect that internal migration can embody nation-building, helping to assimilate troublesome minorities, or at least encourage interconnections across the country (Acharya et al. 2018). Again, the result is often very different, with internal migration deepening political divisions.

Host Political Deprivations

One of the most obvious and important political deprivations is felt among host communities, as the number of settlers grows, and they may come to dominate natives politically. This dominance may be in terms of political sophistication and connections, occupying administrative posts, or electoral strength. Migrants may have strong connections with national or regional authorities. If they have sufficient numbers or other political resources, migrants can tilt political contests in their favor at the expense of the host community. Migrants may staff the ranks of local governments or at least have connections and knowledge of national politics, allowing them to disproportionately benefit from policies. In Iran, the state-sponsored Persian migrants arriving in largely Baloch and Sunni Sistan-Baluchistan Province, and largely Arab Khuzestan Province, have triggered concerns—and violence—by the local groups over their declining political weight (Elling 2013, 55–70). The world is replete with examples in which sustained migration generates new majorities, resulting in the exclusion of natives in non-democratic as well as democratic systems. In such cases, democracy may result in the permanent minority status and thus exclusion of natives in their homeland.

Migrant Political Deprivations

Host communities, powerful or powerless, have cause to worry that migrants will seek a political voice and will undermine established local orders. One response is to deny migrants the right to participate. Even though internal migrants are generally citizens, profound ambiguity often exists as to what civic rights they can exercise outside of their home region. It also may be unclear what duration of residency, if any, is required for these rights to go into effect. In India, even though internal migrants are supposedly provided with rights by the national government, in practice often they are not recognized by state governments. Subnational officials may deny migrants rights to education, identity documentation, social services such as ration cards, and suffrage, privileging locals by disenfranchising the migrants. The rights afforded to citizens may be restricted to the location of origin, rather than in the new area of residence. And even where voting in the new area is a formal right, internal migrants may still be denied. For example, Gaikwad and Nellis (2017, 468) explain the restrictions on Muslim migrant electoral participation in Mumbai:

> Voter ID cards are constituency-specific and are required for Mumbai residents to participate in city, state, and national elections there. Acquiring these cards is no mean feat for India's internal migrant population. Our qualitative interviews revealed that restricting migrant access to voter ID cards is a technique utilized by Mumbai's political elite to curb political participation by disfavored groups.

Migrants who are not afforded voting rights have grounds to challenge any denial of civic rights; if their challenges are continuously denied, conflict is a common response.

Generating Political Difference

If one expected goal of migration is political unity—the fond hope of "nation-building"—the result is often the opposite, as poorly-managed internal migration can generate enduring divisions. As mentioned above, tensions generated by large-scale migration may lead to intergroup tensions between hosts and migrants, but may also deepen divisions among long-time residents. In southern Thailand, Malay Muslims and Thai Buddhists had long histories of coexistence. Communities have a shared heritage, with some more Muslim or Buddhist, but with a common cosmology that survived more gradual migration from Thai and Malay heartlands. State-supported migration of Thai Buddhists, as well as policies of Thaification and centralized political-economic control, has undermined this unity. Policies undertaken to develop a singular Thai national identity across the country eroded common identities in the southern province of Patani, with Muslims and Buddhists severing shared traditions and bifurcating into separate residences (Jory 2011). It is even possible that Malay Muslims in Patani have become less culturally "Thai" in response to nation-building and migration. The result has not only been decades of conflict, but also the erosion of shared political identities.

Sociocultural Deprivations

The deprivations faced by migrants and hosts are not limited to material concerns. Sociocultural factors such as feelings of loss, domination, and inferiority serve to deepen tensions and represent new grievances. When migrants come into contact with a culturally distinctive host community, the possibility of disrespect, contempt, or fear hinges on whether the practices and beliefs of each are regarded as primitive, immoral, or sacrilegious. This triggers what is also known as deference deprivations, with one group's worth denigrated and the other seen as superior (Lasswell and Kaplan 2017/1950).

Cultural & Deferential Deprivations for Hosts

For the host community, the erosion of majority standing may reduce its cultural status, insofar as this loss may undermine the community's influence over education, ceremonies, language, and so on. Powerful migrant groups, especially when supported by the state and representing the cultural influences of a national majority, may displace or assimilate the cultural practices of host communities. Referring again to Iran, Moradi (2014, 66) describes how internal migration has been used to assimilate minorities: "When Persian populations migrate to ethnic minority regions they do not learn the language…it is their ethnic minority hosts that should speak Persian with them." For the host communities, the prestige of migrant groups may diminish the prestige of native cultures. Various state-initiated migration programs are carried out with the expressed goal of taming and civilizing the periphery. Migrants thus arrive with a sense of superiority, with state planners treating natives as backward. Moradi (2014, 66) finds that "Due to better employment and affluence, Persian migrants in minority regions are viewed by some locals as more educated, and more 'up-to-date'," a perspective amplified in the media. Host communities may respond by assimilating, resenting their traditions, or mobilizing resistance.

Cultural tensions may be especially acute when religious differences exist between hosts and migrants. When hosts represent a religious minority in the country as a whole, the arrival of migrants of the majority faith may be seen as an effort to dilute minority faiths. Even when this is not the case, religious differences may represent a source of tensions, as differing cultural expressions are laden with spiritual commitments. Religious differences often provide the fault lines for conflict. In Indonesia, Côté (2019) shows that native Lampungese have established cordial relations with Javanese transmigrants. Both groups share the same faith and many cultural beliefs. However, where conflict has arisen, it has been against smaller, Hindu Balinese communities whose beliefs, art clothing, and practices have been cited as provocative to native Muslims.

The belief that people of another group do not respect one's group is often a particularly potent source of resentment, all the more so because concern over being disrespected by others is often not fully recognized by dominant groups and the perception of disrespect by others frequently motivates disrespect toward them (Techakesari et al. 2015). Host populations encountering migrants unaffiliated with state programs, whether fleeing violence, displaced by infrastructure, or migrating in search of economic opportunity, may be less likely to suffer from significant deference deprivations. However, state-supported resettlement often frames the local populations as of lowly status, as if the area had a vacuum that more capable people could fill. Some bases for denigrating the host population are blatant, such as the Indian government's 1958 Dandakaranya resettlement program in the tribal Bastar district, which was partially motivated by the "'civilization' of a local tribal group through enforced contact with the newcomer" (Bose 2006, 64).

Cultural and Deferential Deprivations for Migrants

For migrants, one potential source of cultural deprivation is separation from the cultural matrix of their home area. In many cases, migrants go from majority to minority status in terms of culturally-relevant identifications. Voluntary migrants may be largely poor youths, arriving without elders or religious leaders. Being severed from their ancestral milieu (e.g., holy sites, burial sites, places of worship, and familiar clergy) can be both distressing and disorienting. Evaluating the plight of rural Chinese who are displaced by construction projects, Shaojun (2006, 29) states that:

> Migrants previously lived in a familiar environment over a long period without much connection or contact with the outside world in a place they inhabited for generations, which gave them a fairly stable social and natural environment, particularly concerning their style of interpersonal interaction and their network of interpersonal relationships. Having this original environment destroyed always leaves them at a loss, in a quandary over their new living environment, new workplace arrangements, and having to put together a new network of interpersonal relationships.

Migrants forcibly displaced from their homes may thus feel a sense of cultural dislocation, as traditions tied to their former home may travel poorly and face challenges in new regions. This may then have pernicious effects on migrant societies. When migrants seek to re-establish cultural institutions in their new homes, this may be opposed by natives, who may block the construction of religious buildings or public cultural symbols.

When ethnic minority migrants are poor, they risk being regarded by the host populations as rootless, unsophisticated, or even childish. One of the informal terms for Chinese urban migrants is equivalent to “vagrant or hooligan” (Nielsen and Smyth 2006, 125). In some state-sponsored resettlements, migrants are caricatured in ways that reflect the anxiety about the loss of assets. For example, rural residents in Papua New Guinea saw state resettled migrants “as thieves and criminals” (Koczberski and Curry 2004, 364). In Indonesia, Malays and Dayaks chafed at Madurese migration, characterizing Madurese behavior as crude and loud, which attackers would later cite when seeking to justify anti-migrant violence (Davidson 2008). In Thailand, Northeasterners migrating throughout the country are reluctant to speak Isan dialects in front of people of the dominant central region. McCargo and Hongladarom (2004, 227) note that: “For the time being, Isan remains mostly the language of personal communication for in-groups of Isan people, and not a language to be used with (or in front of) central Thais. This is the case for many young Isan people, who seek to emulate the behaviour of their Bangkok counterparts, and whose use of local language was declining."

Conclusions

Economic, political, and sociocultural deprivations interact, often undermining human well-being, development, and the goals of state planners. Economic power and political power are closely intertwined, with poverty among migrants or hosts causing a lack of political voice and political marginalization causing economic marginalization. Such power imbalances then amplify sociocultural marginalization, with groups that are excluded seeing their culture, faith, and societies held in lower esteem. Some of the most tangible, headline-grabbing forms of migratory deprivations, though, are related to physical security and violence, the focus of the next chapter.

References

Acharya, Avidit, David D. Laitin, and Anna Zhang. 2018. 'Sons of the Soil': A Model of Assimilation and Population Control. *Journal of Theoretical Politics* 30 (2): 184–223.

Barter, Shane, and Isabelle Côté. 2015. Strife of the Soil? Unsettling Transmigrant Conflicts in Indonesia. *Journal of Southeast Asian Studies* 46 (1): 60–85.

Bose, Pablo. 2006. Dilemmas of Diaspora: Partition, Refugees, and the Politics of 'Home.' *Refuge: Canada's Periodical on Refugees* 23 (1): 58–68.

Combes, Pierre-Philippe., Sylvie Démurger, Shi Li, and Jianguo Wang. 2020. Unequal Migration and Urbanisation Gains in China. *Journal of Development Economics* 142: 1–17.

Côté, Isabelle. 2019. 'Adopting Migrants as Brothers and Sisters'—Fictive Kinship as a Mechanism of Conflict Resolution and Conflict Prevention in Lampung, Indonesia. In *Internal Migration: Challenges in Governance and Integration*, eds. Shane Barter and William Ascher, 97–111. New York: Peter Lang.

Davidson, Jamie S. 2008. *From Rebellion to Riots: Collective Violence on Indonesian Borneo*. Madison: University of Wisconsin Press.

Deshingkar, Pryia, and Sven Grimm. 2005. *Internal Migration and Development: A Global Perspective*. New York: International Organization for Migration.

Elling, Rasmus. 2013. *Minorities in Iran: Nationalism and Ethnicity after Khomeini*. New York: Palgrave Macmillan.

Flyvbjerg, Bent, Massimo Garbuio, and Dan Lovallo. 2009. Delusion and Deception in Large Infrastructure Projects: Two Models for Explaining and Preventing Executive Disaster. *California Management Review* 51 (2): 170–193.

Gaikwad, Nikhar, and Gareth Nellis. 2017. The Majority-Minority Divide in Attitudes Toward Internal Migration: Evidence from Mumbai. *American Journal of Political Science* 61 (2): 456–472.

Goulding, Michael, Nigel J.H. Smith, and Dennis J. Mahar. 1996. *Floods of Fortune: Ecology and Economy Along the Amazon*. Columbia University Press.

Gurr, Ted. 1970. *Why Men Rebel*. Princeton University Press.

Jory, Patrick. 2011. *Muslim Merit-Making in Thailand's Far South*. London: Springer.

Koczberski, Gina, and George N. Curry. 2004. Divided Communities and Contested Landscapes: Mobility, Development, and Shifting Identities in Migrant Destination Sites in Papua New Guinea. *Asia Pacific Viewpoint* 45 (3): 357–371.

Lasswell, Harold D., and Abraham Kaplan. 1950/2017. *Power and Society*. New Haven: Yale University Press; New York: Routledge.

McCargo, Duncan, and Krisadawan Hongladarom. 2004. Contesting Isan-ness: Discourses of Politics and Identity in Northeast Thailand. *Asian Ethnicity* 5 (2): 219–234.

Moradi, Sanan. 2014. Mellat and Qowm: A Political Geography of 'Nation' and 'Ethnicity' in Iran. PhD dissertation. Miami University of Ohio, Oxford, OH.

Nielsen, Ingrid, and Russell Smyth. 2006. Rural Migrants and Public Security. In *Economic Growth, Transition, and Globalization in China*, ed. Yu Yanrui, 121–152. Cheltenham: Edward Elgar.

Noveria, Mita. 2002. *Internal Migration and Heterogeneous Ethnic Groups: Conflict Among Ethnic Groups (A Case Study on Migrant Receiving Areas in the North Sulawesi Province)*. Jakarta: Research Centre for Population-Indonesian Institute of Sciences.

Poston, David. 1990. The Development of Rural Manufacturing Industry in Central Africa: With Special Reference to Metalworking. PhD dissertation, University of Warwick. Warwick, UK.

Sen, Rumela. 2019. Competing Mobilization of Tribal and Class Identity: Politics of Internal Migration in North India. In *Internal Migration: Challenges in Governance and Integration*, eds. Shane Barter and William Ascher, 63–76. New York: Peter Lang.

Shaojun, Chen. 2006. A Study of Poverty Risks Based on Involuntary Migration of Chinese Village Dwellers. *Chinese Sociology & Anthropology* 38 (3): 19–39.
Techakesari, Pirathat, Fiona Kate Barlow, Matthew J. Hornsey, Billy Sung, Michael Thai, and Jocelyn LY. Chak. 2015. An Investigation of Positive and Negative Contact as Predictors of Intergroup Attitudes in the United States, Hong Kong, and Thailand. *Journal of Cross-Cultural Psychology* 46 (3): 454–468.
Tuminez, Astrid S. 2007. This Land is Our Land: Moro Ancestral Domain and Its Implications for Peace and Development in the Southern Philippines. *SAIS Review of International Affairs* 27 (2): 77–91.
Van Luong, Hy, and Jonathan Unger. 1998. Wealth, Power, and Poverty in the Transition to Market Economies: The Process of Socio-Economic Differentiation in Rural China and Northern Vietnam. *The China Journal* 40: 61–93.
Yadav, Vineeta. 2019. The Political Economy of Special Economic Zones and Internal Displacement in India. In *Internal Migration: Challenges in Governance and Integration*, eds. Shane Barter and William Ascher, 77–95. New York: Peter Lang.

CHAPTER 11

Migratory Conflicts

In 2000, the northern Indian state of Assam saw waves of violence as native militias attacked migrants from Bihar and Uttar Pradesh. The attacks killed hundreds and displaced thousands. This is hardly a new problem in the region; in the 1980s, native militias killed four thousand people and displaced 250,000. This led to the creation of an autonomous Bodoland Territorial Region in 2003, but within a few years, the region saw militias again lead attacks on migrant workers, murdering a hundred people over two months (Bhattacharyya and Mukherjee 2018). In 2012 and 2014, Assam saw further violent attacks, with native Bodos targeting Bengali migrants.

Anti-migrant violence is hardly limited to rural northeastern India, as poor migrants have also been targeted in the more developed states of Maharashtra and Gujarat, where harsh rhetoric from the nativist militia Shiv Sena drove violent attacks. Around Bombay, Shiv Sena claimed that Marathi natives are a "superior community" at risk of being "exploited by migrants from other states" (cited in Khairkar 2008, 158). The Shiv Sena's name was derived from a mythical hero who defended Maratha against Mongol invaders. The group originally targeted migrants from southern India before shifting to northern migrants, all the while becoming a mainstream political party. India remains plagued by violent

W. Ascher and S. J. Barter, *Moving within Borders*, Politics, Economics, and Inclusive Development,
https://doi.org/10.1007/978-3-031-37549-1_11

attacks on internal migrants, with nativist militias killing thousands of Indian citizens.

This chapter explores the many forms of violent conflict that all too often result from internal migration. It begins by describing types of migratory violence. Here, we analyze the useful but sometimes vague concept of Sons of the Soil violence, a term that may wrongly frame host communities as the primary instigators, seemingly absolving migrant offensives. Next, we describe how such conflicts unfold, noting how mutual insecurities can develop into deadly violence. As this chapter emphasizes, the state is not typically a primary party to migratory conflicts, but it always plays a crucial role in shaping the form and duration of violence. The roles of subnational governments are especially important here, as they may allow or encourage attacks on migrants, perhaps in defiance of the national government.

When one side is much larger than another, violence can take the form of ethnic cleansing, aiming to eliminate one group from the region or country. When communities are of more equal size and strength, violence may take the form of sustained communal conflicts (Balcells et al. 2016; Montalvo and Reynal-Querol 2005). Either way, we can speak of migratory violence, conflicts resulting from large-scale internal migration.

Host Violence: Sons of the Soil

The study of migratory conflicts was pioneered by Myron Weiner, who observed violence in India in the 1970s between migrants and local communities self-described as Sons of the Soil. His landmark work begins by noting that "migration within a multiethnic society…frequently has destabilizing effects and tends to arouse intense conflicts" (Weiner 1978, 3). Weiner focuses on competition in Indian labor markets, with host communities organizing to keep migrants out through violence, restrictive laws, economic control, and political exclusion. Fearon and Laitin (2011) further popularized the idea of Sons of the Soil conflicts, noting that one-third of all ethnic conflicts "develop between members of a regional ethnic group that considers itself to be the indigenous 'sons of the soil' and recent migrants from other parts of the country" (Fearon and Laitin 2011, 199). Since that time, scholars have developed a deeper understanding of Sons of the Soil conflicts (see Côté and Mitchell 2017). For Côté et al. (2019, 12), Sons of the Soil conflicts sometimes evolve through state-initiated migration, but are especially likely a response to unsponsored migrations.

That said, the concept of Sons of the Soil conflicts remains underdeveloped. Côté and Mitchell (2017) point out that the concept of Sons of the Soil conflict is often unclear and sometimes narrow. Weiner's book focused on political and economic competition more than violence based on, or at least rationalized, by nativism. At times, Weiner suggests a very specific definition of Sons of the Soil conflicts: "middle-class nativist movements in opposition to migrants tend to emerge in those communities where the local population has recently produced its own middle class that aspires to move into jobs held by migrants" (Weiner 1978, 8). It is unclear if this includes international migrants, and, of course, the term is gendered, which Côté and Huang (2020) explain in terms of gendered patterns and perceptions of migration leading to more violence against male migrants.

Weiner's focus on nativism also leaves it unclear if Sons of the Soil conflicts include cases in which hosts attack migrants but do not make explicitly nativist claims, as in many secessionist conflicts. Perhaps most importantly, emphasis on Sons of the Soil seems to suggest that it is natives on the offensive, perhaps excluding violence carried out by migrants trying to usurp control of land and other resources. Fearon and Laitin inflate the number of cases, referring to any conflict linked to internal migration, thus claiming one-third of all ethnic conflicts to be Sons of the Soil conflicts.[1] It remains unclear if Sons of the Soil violence refers to any conflict involving migration or else violence primarily carried out by nativist host communities.

Claiming greater rights on the basis of being the original (autochthonous) or otherwise more authentic residents of an area can

[1] This was probably encouraged by Weiner's original text, which, although focused on nativist violence in India, makes brief reference to several cases, including Burmese and Malays attacking Indians and Chinese, and Latin American settlers attacking indigenous peoples. Another difficulty in defining SoS conflicts is in delineating at which point a community is no longer considered migrant. Fearon and Laitin (2011, 200) suggest a cut-off of one generation. This obscures how a lack of integration may sustain a group's perceived status as migrants for many generations and assumes that migrants arrive all at once. Migration may be drawn-out; ethnic Javanese arrived in Sumatra through transmigration schemes under Dutch colonial rule, with various programs continuing through the 1990s. This means that individual families of a migrant community may feature several generations in a given locale; whereas individuals may be new arrivals, the arrival of the group may be unclear.

be invoked to treat groups present in the area for multiple generations as if they are migrant populations with less claim on power and other resources. However, understandings of autochthony are often ambiguous, leading to arguable claims (Jackson 2006). Rhee (2009) documents how the Merap and Kenyah in Indonesia's East Kalimantan contest claims of indigeneity, labeling other communities as newcomers. The Kenyah engaged in multiple migrations over many decades, although within Kalimantan. Reinnoldt (2019, 96) observes, "Because of this, indigenous groups like the Kenyah, who have migrated to newer areas for various reasons, find themselves in difficult situations wherein they lack strong claims to their new land, yet have left their old land, perhaps without the possibility for return." The Kenyah are indigenous to the region, but does autochthony require continuous residence? Similarly, Jackson (2006, 115) notes in the Democratic Republic of the Congo, "At some level, no one…seems to be sufficiently autochthonous to escape at some point becoming the target for accusations of foreignness."

This fragility of claims of autochthony may account for the extreme positions to defend the Sons of the Soil claim. Jackson (2006, 115) concludes that because of this uncertainty, "The psychological state resulting from this instability is, by definition, paranoia." He emphasizes the risk that to cope with such perilous psychological states, local people may take rigid positions vis-à-vis other groups, whether these groups claim history in the area or are newcomers. These autochthonous stances are typically held by ethnic minorities in remote areas, facing the potential humiliation of backwardness that might be countered by the claim of purity, reinforced by a stereotype of the migrants as "an enemy that, although in the minority, is cunning, ruthless, and engaged in machinations that remain carefully hidden" (Jackson 2006, 115). Insofar as this dynamic holds, local people are not only suspicious of outsiders, but may hold migrants in contempt.

Deadly violence is a graphic consequence of state failures to anticipate this brittleness when state resettlement programs target areas where these extreme orientations are likely to be present. However, the violence that in retrospect can be attributed to resentments against incursions that challenge Sons of the Soil claims often is difficult to predict. Violence is often triggered through small but symbolically potent events such as traffic accidents or youth altercations, spiraling out of control to become riots and pogroms.

Another example of ambiguous but powerful Sons of the Soil claims is seen in violence against Rohingya Muslims in Myanmar's Rakhine state. The Buddhist majority, consisting of ethnic Rakhine and ethnic Burmans (who are mostly migrants), make nativist claims in their attacks on Muslim Rohingya. Buddhists claim to be "sons of the regions" (*taing yin thar*) and claim that Muslims are migrants, making this appear to be a Sons of the Soil conflict (Thawnghmung 2016). However, Muslims have lived in Rakhine state for several generations, recognized as citizens until being stripped of this status by a 1982 law. Buddhists claim the Muslims are international migrants, although both Rohingya and Rakhine Buddhists are largely autochthonous.

Invoking Sons of the Soil claims is clearest when host communities possess some power in relation to migrants, using subnational governments to exclude and mobilizing violence against them. Paradigmatic cases include the migration of poorer communities in India to major cities and tribal areas, cases which inspired Weiner to create the term. Shiv Sena exemplifies nativist violence against vulnerable migrants, similar to the Betawi Brotherhood in Jakarta. Weiner provides an insightful case of India's Assam State, where early British-directed migrations led to successful integration, yet later migrations brought in better-educated Bengalis and merchant Mawaris, groups that would dominate the marketplace, various professions, and land ownership (Weiner 1978, 75–143). To challenge the migrants, an emerging Assamese middle class focused on the state government, winning elections, and slowly taking over the bureaucracy, which they used to restrict immigration and prioritize Assamese natives through new language and education laws. Nativist policies generated Bengali resistance, leading to riots in the late 1960s. Assamese domination led smaller tribal minorities to resist and demand their own states. Weiner observes that Assamese nativism has been violent and conspicuously tied to the local government, with Assamese businesses nurtured by the state to protect them against Bengali competition.

Thus, even the clearest Sons of the Soil conflicts feature considerable complexity. These conflicts may involve long-time residents allying with indigenous peoples against more recent migrants. This is what Sen (2019) finds in northern India, where tribal groups have stood with older migrant "moolvasis" ("those who have grown roots") against newer migrants, dubbed "diku" ("outsider"). Côté and Mitchell (2017, 5) note similar dynamics in western China, where "local Uyghurs have occasionally formed informal inter-ethnic coalitions to ally with 'older' migrants against the recent influx of Han economic migrants." Sometimes, smaller groups ally with natives; in Assam, early migrants integrated and became Assamese. Meanwhile, Muslim Bengalis, once competitors with the Assamese, came to align with natives against Bengali Hindus, even accepting Assamese as their mother tongue (Weiner 1978, 124).

Similarly, in Indonesia's West Kalimantan Province, both indigenous Dayaks and native Malays allied against the Madurese migrants. The Malays, many themselves earlier migrants to West Kalimantan, had established local roots in the province, such that as Dayaks made nativist claims, Malays participated in the anti-Madurese violence (Davidson 2008). Similarly, Vandekerckhove (2009, 543) describes a series of clashes between Dimasa and Karbi communities in northeastern India around late 2005. Once allied against migrants, both groups claimed to be Sons of the Soil, soon "questioning one another's degree of autochthony" and engaging in violent clashes. The conflict generated not only displacement and deaths, but also "a nagging fear that one day even autochthon communities could be classified as insufficiently rooted and evicted" (Vandekerckhove 2009, 539).

Another variant involves natives mounting violence against migrants who arrive with state support or wealth, thus possessing some power. Fearon and Laitin (2011, 199) suggest that, in Sons of the Soil conflicts, "migrants are typically members of the dominant ethnic group who migrate in search of land or government jobs, often supported by the state with economic incentives and development schemes." These cases differ from the Indian cases from which the Sons of the Soil concept was derived, since migrants have the upper hand and state support. Ensuing violence, then, is less one-sided than in classic Sons of the Soil cases, with both sides carrying attacks against the other in sustained communal conflicts.

Sons of the Soil conflicts may not involve just recent migrants, but also persons born in a given area, who are still considered to be migrants due to sustained ethnic differences and a failure to integrate into local society. Fearon and Laitin (2011) highlight Sri Lanka as an example of an SoS conflict, even though it violates their definitional criterion of migrants arriving within one generation. Most Tamils in Sri Lanka were born in the country and most have lived there for several generations, especially "Sri Lankan" Tamils in northern Sri Lanka (Bass 2013; Manogaran and Pfaffenberger 1994). Despite this, many Sinhalese leaders nonetheless cast the Tamils as migrants, accusing them of using violence to capture

Sinhalese native lands. This example becomes complicated in cases of state-managed migration to northeastern Sri Lanka, an area long dominated by older, precolonial Tamil communities. Here, it is the Sinhalese who are migrating to colonize lands, but they perceive their actions as nativist defenses against migrant settlements, an instance that demonstrates the potential complexity of migratory violence (Tambiah 1996, 83–94; Fearon and Laitin 2011, 202).

At the edges of Sons of the Soil conflicts, host communities may utilize violence against communities they perceive as foreign. In numerous countries, colonial-era Chinese and Indian migrants have been targeted with nativist violence, including Tanzania, Uganda, Zimbabwe, Kenya, Trinidad, Fiji, Malaysia, Burma, Indonesia, and Vietnam. These cases appear to be different than Sons of the Soil conflicts due to their international dimensions, even if such communities were locally born, so the conflicts were not generated by recent migration (although they often end in internal migration). In the 1950s and 1960s, Southeast Asian and African governments pushed Indian and Chinese minorities away from the countryside to control capitalists and potential communists. In Indonesia, ethnic Chinese were forced to urban areas due to state policies prohibiting alien groups from owning rural land or businesses, as well as violent attacks, such as Dayak assaults that pushed some 60,000 Chinese from rural West Kalimantan in 1967 (Hugo 2006, 68). Such cases are complex, as they may be framed as "foreign" migrants, even though those targeted are locally born who are forced to become internal migrants.

Finally, secessionist conflicts can also be seen as Sons of the Soil conflicts. Often, rebels frame their struggles in terms of minority nationalism more than indigenous rights. As a result, those fighting for independence are more likely to speak of nationalism than indigeneity, especially since many secessionists face resistance from their own indigenous minorities (e.g., Gayo in Aceh and Lumad in Mindanao). Secessionist rebels also typically fight state security forces more than migrant communities. Despite these points, secessionist conflicts involve a sense of homeland and frequently feature some level of internal migration from the national ethnic majority, with localized communal conflicts often taking place in the shadows of rebel-state clashes. Examples include southern Thailand, the southern Philippines, Aceh, Biafra in Nigeria, Bougainville in Papua New Guinea, Tibet, Xinjiang, and more.

Migrant Violence: Settler Conflicts

History is replete with instances in which migrants, often with state support, attack host communities to colonize their land and establish control. Western settler countries were founded on violence against indigenous peoples; although indigenous peoples mounted Sons of the Soil resistance, the vast majority of violence was from European settlers. Settler violence is not limited to Western settler states, as many countries have expanded through frontier colonies. Around the fifteenth century, Kinh (Viet) settlers worked in tandem with the state to dislodge Cham kingdoms in the center of modern Vietnam. In time, ethnic Kinh migrants represented a "peasant spearhead" for the state to follow (de Koninck 1996). Similarly, Russian settlers violently exploited Siberian natives as they drove east and toward Alaska in the sixteenth century. Such cases are not exactly examples of internal migration, even if patterns of violence are similar, as they are more constitutive of modern borders than occurring within them.

With the advent of the modern territorial state and fixed borders, all corners of the world have experienced internal colonialism, with powerful settlers attacking host communities. As noted in previous chapters, leaders may initiate or manage migration for various reasons: controlling rebellious peripheries, assimilating minorities, obtaining resources, and more. Resulting violent conflicts are not described very well as Sons of the Soil struggles, as the impetus for violence lies with settlers and state officials.

As Côté and Mitchell observe (2017), the SoS literature primarily focuses on Asian conflicts, with limited attention to Africa or Latin America. This reflects the fact that the main aggressors have been state-supported migrants attacking indigenous peoples to gain access to land. The Americas have long histories of settler and state violence against indigenous peoples, provoking resistance. In rural Guatemala, state forces led violence against suspected communist supporters, attacking indigenous Mayan peoples. In parallel with state strikes, mestizo settlers continued to expand in Mayan areas, with violence against indigenous communities continuing long after the communist insurgency (Metz et al. 2010). Similar dynamics are found in the highlands of Peru, Colombia, and the Brazilian Amazon, where state forces and settlers have launched violent attacks on indigenous peoples (Hoefle 2006).

Many cases fluctuate over time, shifting between nativist and settler violence. Conflicts may begin with Sons of the Soil resistance, but the state and settlers prove victorious and continue to use violence against subdued indigenous groups to colonize the area. Some cases move in the other direction. In the Philippines, the Mindanao conflict is traditionally understood as a separatist conflict, with Muslim rebels at war with the state. As mentioned in Chapter 6, the conflict began with the large-scale internal migration of Christians between the 1930s and 1970s, reducing Moros from about 75 to 25 percent of the regional population (Tigno 2006, 29). National and subnational governments encouraged migration, but did not manage it effectively, as most migration from crowded parts of Luzon and the Visayas was "spontaneous" in nature. In the 1950s, Mindanao saw armed settlers arrive to dispossess natives of their lands. Christian militias such as the *ilagas* (rats) attacked Moro and Lumad communities, pushed them from their homes, and then registered the property with state officials. The armed forces often supported Christian gangs in their land seizures, which soon generated violent Moro resistance. Soon thereafter, migratory violence became a separatist conflict. The Moro Islamic Liberation Front has focused primarily on regaining Christian-occupied Maguindanao lands, what it refers to as "Ancestral Domain."

Security Deprivations: Processes of Migratory Violence

Having laid out potential forms of migratory violence, this section focuses on some common processes, charting how internal migration so often ends in violence and describing the features of such violence. When migrants arrive in areas occupied by people of different physical and cultural characteristics, the novelty creates uncertainty for both sides about whether the "others" have peaceful intentions. As Weiner notes, some of the most dangerous situations are found when migrants represent "culturally distinguishable ethnic groups" compared to the host community, especially when middle-class migrants compete for employment (Weiner 1978, 293). Once changes in the economic ecology threaten native livelihoods, property disputes may arise and political balances shift (Côté and Mitchell 2017). Resulting confrontations increase the fear of physical harm even before harm has occurred. Insofar as migrants and host populations are culturally different, the possibility that practices of one group would be regarded as immoral, sacrilegious, or otherwise repugnant by another also increases the perception of physical threat.

This sense of insecurity is itself a deprivation for both sides and can increase the likelihood of destructive conflict over time. When a group feels physically threatened, community members may despair that the state cannot protect them, perhaps witnessing incidents and feeling that not enough was done to protect them. This perceived indifference may compel sectors of migrant or host societies to organize militias, perhaps framed as community defense. As either side does so, this presents a classic security dilemma, as efforts by one side to defend themselves may be perceived by the other side as threatening, leading to counter-mobilization. Militias may lie dormant, but provocateurs may push for preemptive attacks on the other side to demonstrate their willingness and capacity to engage in violence.

Seemingly minor events can expand into sustained violence as tensions lead one side to attach political significance to seemingly minor acts. In deeply-divided societies, events such as traffic accidents, university admissions or grades, speeding tickets, or soccer games take on a wider significance, as one or both sides perceive themselves as under siege, interpreting everyday acts as affronts. Horowitz (2001, 269) refers to these as "flashpoints," seemingly trifling precipitants of large-scale conflicts. The spark that leads to a sustained conflict may be larger events such as an election, the publication of sensitive census data, the passage of a new language law, or an economic crisis. As noted, it may also be something more mundane, such as a traffic accident or dispute in the marketplace. For example, the 1999 riots between Christians and Muslims in Indonesia's Maluku islands began with a dispute between a Christian bus driver and a young Muslim passenger, as did conflicts between Madurese and Dayaks in Kalimantan. Elsewhere, clashes may be sparked by overlapping religious holidays, sporting events, or gambling disputes.

Conflicts typically spread via rumors, as what happened is amplified by hearsay among both sides. As Horowitz (2001, 74) observes, rumors "are satisfying and useful to rioters and their leaders," thus prevailing over accurate information (see also Brass 1997). Lacking shared traditions or institutions, stories can bifurcate into two very separate accounts. Violence can expand quickly as community defense groups are already organized, anticipating clashes. Finally, state forces may be unable to establish peace early on, either because they lack the capacity or because they are partial to one side. If security forces favor a particular side, the state may be pulled into the conflict and become entangled in violence, perhaps with different state agencies warring with each other.

Forms of migratory violence tend to be especially disturbing. The attackers often know the victims, who may be neighbors or classmates. Like other forms of communal conflict, migratory riots typically involve attacks on the other side's women, religious institutions, and other targets intended to shock and assert symbolic dominance. Rape is a shockingly common aspect of migratory clashes, with gangs of young men targeting women. This has been explained in terms of racialized differences and biological domination. In communal conflicts, "women are raped to communicate to other men that they are not masculine and competent enough to 'protect their women'" (Tay 2006, 63). Similarly, religious symbols tend to be targeted to command cosmological dominance. In communal conflicts in India, Singapore, and Malaysia, rumors of pork being thrown at Muslims and beef at Hindus, as well as attacks on butchers and rumors of Muslim violence against cows, are often reported as fueling violence (Yang 1980). In Indonesia, churches were burned down by Muslim militias in Maluku and Poso, with both sides reportedly desecrating the others' holy texts. Although religious symbolism may make conflicts appear cosmological, the centrality of migratory status is often especially salient. In West Kalimantan, Malay Muslim rioters did more damage to Madurese settlers' mosques than did Christian Dayaks (Davidson 2003, 81).

Like other inter-communal conflicts, migratory conflicts involve ethnically-defined targeting and collective security. Those wishing to stand outside of violence may be especially easy to attack by the other side, with conflict dynamics demanding that there are no bystanders. Because they are loosely organized by rival communities, riots tend to flare up without warning, then simmer. Violence predominantly takes the form of brief, chronic riots over several hours or days, only to reappear weeks, months, or years later.

Violent migratory conflict unfolds between warring communities, making this form of violence different than secessionist or revolutionary conflicts, in which organized rebels mount sustained resistance against state forces (Barter 2020). Instead, these conflicts are mostly fought by underequipped gangs, civilians, and various private security forces—what McRae (2013) refers to as "A Few Poorly Organized Men." In migratory conflicts, the state is not typically a combatant. This does not mean, however, that the state is not involved at some level.

Roles of the State

Reflecting a central tenet of this book, the state is intimately involved in shaping the form and duration of migratory violence as well as making conflict more or less likely. Côté and Mitchell (2017, 339) suggest that "state actors tend to play much less prominent roles in SoS conflicts" as opposed to other forms of intrastate conflict. They add, though, that "this should not be misconstrued to suggest that SoS conflict dynamics" lack state involvement. Countless reports of migratory violence recount state security forces enflaming tensions. Sometimes portrayed as masterminds planning violence, it is more common that state officials and agencies encourage tensions for their own gain or are pulled into supporting a particular side.

The role of the state in migratory violence is clearest when state agencies initiate and support internal migration to other parts of the country. This may be done to save citizens from natural disasters, promote development, dilute rebellion, or any number of reasons. When this is the case, migration and migrants represent a state investment, one it seeks to support. States may procure land by force, or at best with limited compensation for natives, setting the stage for later conflicts. As migrants attack hosts, state security forces may defend settlers, courts may refuse to try their crimes, and bureaucracies may recognize their ownership of resources. For example, in the southern Philippines, the national government only sometimes managed internal migration, but on the ground, gave preference to migrants, as settlers had connections with officials and were familiar with property regimes. This constituted "land grabbing by legal means," namely through policies of "prioritizing claims based on filing of paperwork, as opposed to occupancy" (Tuminez 2007, 80). When larger conflicts erupt involving migrants and natives, the state may implicitly or explicitly support migrants, perhaps through the partial application of justice or peacekeeping measures, arming or protecting migrants, or more.

Because national governments will often support migrants in migratory violence, in centralized political systems, subnational governments may follow suit. If this is the case, what explains Sons of the Soil conflicts, in which natives have the upper hand and utilize violence against migrants? In many Sons of the Soil conflicts, national governments avoid involvement, so the primary role of the state in sustained Sons of the Soil violence is found among subnational governments. Especially in decentralized or federal systems, or at least in the face of weak central governments, the state is especially likely to support native violence against migrants at the subnational level, where natives capture local power. Weiner (1978, 344) finds this in India, where migrants are citizens and have the constitutional right to migrate within the country, but states impose regulations and forms of exclusion on migrants, establishing a dual system of citizenship in which states often prevail.

Just as poorer natives may fear competition from migrants for jobs and resources, native politicians may fear their political power threatened by new candidates and voters. Native leaders may respond by mobilizing militias or local security forces against migrants in addition to refusing them the right to social services and voting. Subnational governments may not recognize migrants' civil rights, as this might threaten those in power through electoral competition. When violence flares, hosts may operate with impunity or gain active support from security forces. Many city governments have ruling parties openly aligned with nativist militias, gaining votes by framing themselves as defending native peoples. Meanwhile, national governments are typically notable for their inaction, unwilling to risk political alliances with subnational governance by protecting internal migrants, and with security forces controlled by state-level governments (Wilkinson 2015).

Some of the worst migratory conflicts occur when levels or agencies of the state support different sides, typically with the national government in some way supporting migrants and subnational governments supporting natives. Hosts or migrants may also be connected to state security forces. There are several examples of migrants gaining the support of the military, especially when migrants are co-ethnics or represent a state-managed investment. When natives are more closely tied to police forces, this sometimes generates violence between the military and police. This was the case in eastern Indonesia in the late 1990s when various native Christian communities clashed with Muslim migrants. Violence was exacerbated by the presence of locally recruited police forces, whose ranks were dominated by Christians, and the arrival of the military, whose national recruitment in a Muslim-majority country meant that they were seen as partial to Muslim migrants. As noted in a Human Rights Watch Report (1999), "Muslims accused Christian police in one case of opening fire near a mosque; Christians accused Muslim soldiers in another of helping Muslims attack a Christian village" The perceived partiality of police and military forces both expanded the level of violence and deprived the state of the ability to promote peace as a neutral arbiter.

Conclusions

The chapters in this section thus far have explained how internal migration can go so wrong. While internal migration is carried out with the promise of improving lives, the result sometimes leaves all parties much worse off. Migrants and hosts may develop negative group interactions, living in a climate of mutual suspicion. Both communities may end up worse off economically, with hosts or migrants excluded from political and social life as second-class citizens. In many cases, internal migration spawns violent conflict, with one or both sides attacking the other. Placing groups directly beside one another can create competition for jobs, resources, and/or political power, leading to intergroup violence. Ideally, states would be able to intervene to establish order and respond to grievances, but in many countries, states either fail to do so or are implicated in the violence. As this chapter has shown, migration has generated a variety of deadly conflicts, costing countless lives. Having demonstrated the many violent outcomes of internal migration, the next step is to explain why state policies so often lead to such disasters.

References

Balcells, Laia, Lesley-Ann Daniels, and Abel Escribà-Folch. 2016. The Determinants of Low-Intensity Intergroup Violence. The Case of Northern Ireland. *Journal of Peace Research* 53 (1): 33–48.

Barter, Shane Joshua. 2020. *Fighting Armed Conflicts in Southeast Asia: Ethnicity and Difference*. Cambridge: Cambridge University Press Elements.

Bass, Daniel. 2013. *Everyday Ethnicity in Sri Lanka: Up-Country Tamil Identity Politics*. London: Routledge.

Bhattacharyya, Harihar, and Jhumpa Mukherjee. 2018. Bodo Ethnic Self-Rule and Persistent Violence in Assam: A Failed Case of Multinational Federalism in India. *Regional & Federal Studies* 28 (4): 469–487.

Brass, Paul R. 1997. *Theft of an Idol: Text and Context in the Representation of Collective Violence*. Princeton: Princeton University Press.

Côté, Isabelle and Limingcui Emma Huang. 2020. Where are the Daughters? Examining the Effects of Gendered Migration on the Dynamics of 'Sons of the Soil' Conflict. *Studies in Conflict and Terrorism* 43 (10): 837–853.

Côté, Isabelle, and Matthew I. Mitchell. 2017. Deciphering 'Sons of the Soil' Conflicts: A Critical Survey of the Literature. *Ethnopolitics* 16 (4): 333–351.

Côté, Isabelle, Matthew I. Mitchell, and Monica Duffy Toft, eds. 2019. *People Changing Places: New Perspectives on Demography, Migration, Conflict, and the State*. London: Routledge.

Davidson, Jamie S. 2003. The Politics of Violence on an Indonesian Periphery. *South East Asia Research* 11 (1): 59–89.

Davidson, Jamie S. 2008. *From Rebellion to Riots: Collective Violence on Indonesian Borneo*. Madison: University of Wisconsin Press.

de Koninck, Rodolphe. 1996. The Peasantry as the Territorial Spearhead of the State in Southeast Asia: The Case of Vietnam. *Sojourn* 11 (2): 231–258.

Fearon, James D., and David D. Laitin. 2011. Sons of the Soil, Migrants, and Civil War. *World Development* 39 (2): 199–211.

Hoefle, Scott William. 2006. Twisting the Knife: Frontier Violence in the Central Amazon of Brazil. *The Journal of Peasant Studies* 33 (3): 445–478.

Horowitz, Donald. 2001. *The Deadly Ethnic Riot*. Berkeley: University of California Press.

Hugo, Graeme John. 2006. Forced Migration in Indonesia: Historical Perspectives. *Asia and Pacific Migration Journal* 15 (1): 53–92.

Human Rights Watch. 1999. Indonesia: The Violence in Ambon.

Jackson, Stephen. 2006. Sons of Which Soil? The Language and Politics of Autochthony in Eastern DR Congo. *African Studies Review* 49 (2): 95–124.

Khairkar, Vijaya P. 2008. Segregation of Migrants Groups in Pune City, India. *Anthropologist* 10(2): 155–161.

Manogaran, Chelvadurai, and Bryan Pfaffenberger, eds. 1994. *The Sri Lankan Tamils: Ethnicity and Identity*. London: Routledge.

McRae, Dave. 2013. *A Few Poorly Organized Men: Interreligious Violence in Poso, Indonesia*. Leiden: Brill Publishers.

Metz, Brent, Lorenzo Mariano, and Julian Lopez Garcia. 2010. The Violence After 'La Violencia' in the Ch'orti Region of Eastern Guatemala. *The Journal of Latin American and Caribbean Anthropology* 15 (1): 16–41.

Montalvo, José G., and Marta Reynal-Querol. 2005. Ethnic Polarization, Potential Conflict and Civil War. *American Economic Review* 95 (3): 796–816.

Reinnoldt, Charlotte. 2019. *Asserting Indigenous Identity to Substantiate Customary Forest Claims: A Case Study of the Dayaks of West Kalimantan, Indonesia*. Claremont CA: Claremont McKenna College.

Rhee, Steve. 2009. The Cultural Politics of Collaboration. In *The Decentralization of Forest Governance: Politics, Economics, and the Fight for Control of Forests in Indonesian Borneo*, eds. Moira Moeliono, Eva Wollenberg, and Godwin Limberg, 43–60. London: Earthscan.

Sen, Rumela. 2019. Competing Mobilization of Tribal and Class Identity: Politics of Internal Migration in North India. In *Internal Migration: Challenges in*

Governance and Integration, eds. Shane Barter and William Ascher, 63–76. New York: Peter Lang.

Tambiah, Stanley J. 1996. *Leveling Crowds*. Berkeley: University of California Press.

Tay, Elaine. 2006. Discursive Violence on the Internet and the May 1998 Riots. In *Violent Conflicts in Indonesia: Analysis, Representation, Resolution*, ed. Charles Coppel, 58–71. London: Routledge.

Thawnghmung, Ardeth. 2016. The Politics of Indigeneity in Myanmar: Competing Narratives in Rakhine State. *Asian Ethnicity* 17 (4): 527–547.

Tigno, Jorge V. 2006. Migration and Violent Conflict in Mindanao. *Population Review* 45 (1): 23–47.

Tuminez, Astrid S. 2007. This Land is Our Land: Moro Ancestral Domain and Its Implications for Peace and Development in the Southern Philippines. *SAIS Review of International Affairs* 27 (2): 77–91.

Vandekerckhove, Nel. 2009. 'We Are Sons of This Soil': The Endless Battle Over Indigenous Homelands in Assam, India. *Critical Asian Studies* 41 (4): 523–548.

Weiner, Myron. 1978. *Sons of the Soil: Migration and Ethnic Conflict in India*. Princeton: Princeton University Press.

Wilkinson, Steven I. 2015. *Army and Nation: The Military and Indian Democracy since Independence*. Harvard University Press.

Yang, Anand A. 1980. Sacred Symbol and Sacred Space in Rural India: Community Mobilization in the 'Anti-Cow Killing' Riot of 1893. *Comparative Studies in Society and History* 22 (4): 576–596.

CHAPTER 12

State Failures

This chapter seeks to identify how state actions may account for the problems of internal migration. As this book emphasizes, the presence of the state, of which migrants and host communities are citizens, largely sets internal migration apart from international migration. Whether population flows are state-initiated, state-managed, or unmanaged, the state is the primary actor shaping internal migration. As a consequence, when internal migration fails, we must look to state accountability and specific failures. Although some states may simply be unable to manage internal migration, we also observe various misguided perceptions and policies, identifying areas that may be remediable.

Some Caveats

One may object that we should not place the blame for migratory failures at the feet of the state, an objection that could be motivated by scorn or sympathy for the state. The most cynical among us may argue that these suspicions, deprivations, and conflicts do not necessarily represent state failures. Although states are expected to secure the well-being of their citizens, leaders may encourage or accept losses to attain some other goal. For instance, officials may manage migration to restive separatist regions to colonize the territory and maintain national borders, accepting

W. Ascher and S. J. Barter, *Moving within Borders*, Politics, Economics, and Inclusive Development,
https://doi.org/10.1007/978-3-031-37549-1_12

ethnic conflict as the price of defeating separatism or avoiding invasion. Authorities may trade off human or economic losses to achieve political ends, or may accept human or political losses to attain economic goals. It is also possible that one level or agency of the state may attain its goals through internal migration, while other parts of the state or the state as a whole see the outcome as unacceptable. States possess several conflicting goals; what may appear as failed internal migration policies may represent success at some level.

Even if we accept that violence, ecological degradation, or underdevelopment may be acceptable to some state actors in the pursuit of other goals, we can still speak of such outcomes as state failures. Although they often fall well short, states are tasked with ensuring the well-being of their citizens and, according to international law, all other residents as well. For internal migration, all involved are residents, meaning that destructive outcomes represent a failure by authorities to uphold their obligations. These may be failures to act (sins of omission) or may be flawed policies (sins of commission). At a minimum, it is likely that the state would like to achieve various goals without sacrificing others.

On the other hand, pointing out state failures could also be seen as misguided if states lack the capacity to do better. States may fail to implement a certain policy, or implement a failed policy, because they do not possess the power to succeed. A long line of scholarship (Huntington 1968; Migdal 1988) rightly points out that even relatively powerful states are sometimes unable to implement their preferred policies. Internal migration is a large, complex phenomenon, with even the strongest of states failing to anticipate its scale, ensuing tensions, and other factors. Citizens may have a right to move to wherever they please and can thus be difficult to impede. Even with state-sponsored migrations, the state is not in complete control; some people slated for sponsorship do not move, while others migrate alongside sponsored families. Many efforts to resettle migrants may work on paper, but implementation falls short because various social forces block or transform them. Landau (2014, 299) elaborates on these limitations in South Africa: "In part because of the inability to control migration practically, the issue of human mobility has become a menace."

Another complicating factor for the state is that different types of internal migrants may flow together or overlap. One result may be that services appropriate for one migrant group such as conflict IDPs may be misplaced or provided to the wrong group even if the state acts in good faith. For example, Reynolds (2014, 2) notes that for IDPs fleeing violence in Mexico: "Given the amount of movement occurring within Mexico and the different factors that push migration north, it may seem difficult to distinguish between those moving for work or family reunification and those who have protection concerns, including individuals and families who are fleeing the consequences of organized criminal groups." It is not uncommon for states to try, but ultimately fail, to navigate the shifting currents of internal migration.

We recognize that many failures to govern migration owe to a lack of capacity, with war-torn or impoverished states unable to manage large-scale migration. That said, incapacity can sometimes serve as a crutch for states to implement policies halfway—a tactic known as "restriction by partial incorporation" (Lasswell and Kaplan 1950, 282–283). States may wish for a limited presence in some regions to maintain plausible deniability and avoid accountability for environmental degradation or the displacement of indigenous communities. Returning to Landau (2014, 299), the quote we provided continues to characterize internal migration in South Africa as "a convenient scapegoat for poor service delivery, crime, and other pathologies." We acknowledge that many of the pathologies identified in this chapter are owed to a lack of state capacity, but some failures are owed to the misuse of resources as well as some common attitudes and perceptions. We hope that recognizing many common failures may serve to heighten state capacity, making better use of scarce resources.

Failures of Planning

Planning represents a core aspect of effective governance and successful policies. Not everything can be planned, especially for a policy area as broad as internal migration, where the numbers involved and mobility of a given community may overwhelm the state. Yet good planning over what can be known and anticipated remains essential to governing internal migration. This is especially so for migration that is initiated and managed by the state, whose ownership of migration policy demands quality planning. Even for unmanaged migration, states may anticipate key factors and plan accordingly.

Failure to Collect Information

Sometimes state agencies fail to collect information, or else the information they do collect is biased toward a certain outcome or group. Decisions involving migration may be rushed, either because of a sudden event such as war or natural disaster, or because planners push a policy through to attain their goals. Failure to collect relevant information about relocation sites, host communities, migrants, and other aspects may then lead to disaster, often at greater cost to the state than initial data collection would have required.

One might assume that state officials would want the most complete information and analysis to maximize their resources and effectiveness. Yet, often there are reasons for the state to neglect the task of collecting and analyzing information on migration flows. Officials may not wish to be held accountable for estimates of migration impacts that prove to be incorrect. Agencies may also want to avoid providing accurate information that contradicts official policy aims. Officials may rush projects to take advantage of political or funding opportunities. For example, the Mahaweli Dam megaproject in Sri Lanka was launched in haste, without researching the site, to help the election prospects of the incumbent government (de Silva 1987). The technical experts capable of assessing the details of migration patterns may be marginalized when political considerations dominate, such as those motivating the Brazilian expansion into the Amazon. Referring to state-managed migration into the Brazilian state of Rondônia, Fearnside (1985, 229–230) observes the "hasty confection of settlement plans…with the various government organs consulted to propose viable agricultural systems for these areas only after the decisions were made to implant the projects." In Indonesia, planners routinely exaggerated the number of official transmigrants to meet state projections and claim further resources, and rarely counted those who returned to Java (Barter and Côté 2015). Finally, expulsions by the military, such as the Turkish army's displacement of Kurds from Anatolia, are typically undertaken in haste and with little consideration for the destinations and well-being of the expelled (Çelik 2005).

One high-profile state failure involving infrastructure-caused displacement was India's Sardar Sarovar Dam Project along the Narmada River. Initially planned in the 1960s, the project moved forward in the 1980s with World Bank funding. In light of the glaring problems of resettlement, the World Bank sent a resettlement specialist into the field, but only after the project was appraised:

> He found that the three participating state governments...did not know the number of people that would be affected, how many of these were tribal peoples, or where they wanted to relocate. There were no feasible plans for their resettlement and rehabilitation and no institutional capacity for implementing the resettlement of 100,000 people from the submergence area and 140,000 people affected by the canal system (World Bank 2006, 33).

After investing significantly in the project, the World Bank withdrew in 1994. India spent far more than expected on the dam, with the government suffering politically as a consortium of tribal IDPs, farmers, environmentalists, and human rights defenders mobilized resistance. In this case, planners failed to collect information on the environmental impact and human displacement caused by the project, and failed to provide information to those affected.

Failure to Provide Information

Even if the state possesses accurate information, officials may fail to share this with those involved, perhaps purposefully withholding it. The likelihood that the state will provide full and honest information to migrants, potential migrants, and host communities is limited by the consideration that virtually every project has problems that critics could cite or that might discourage participants. Officials are unlikely to inform migrant farmers that soil analysis has hardly been done (as in the case of Amazonian land grants) or that migrants will encounter unfamiliar growing conditions. Nor would state officials publicize clashes between migrants and host communities if they wish to fulfill a quota of sponsored migrants.

This is especially the case once migratory processes have begun; perhaps one agency moved too early, recruiting migrants before the state possessed complete information, and now it is too late. Countless examples exist in which state agencies and planners exaggerate the jobs available and infrastructure to be built to pacify populations they know may be adversely affected by the arrival of migrants. When migrants or hosts then discover drastically different conditions and their livelihoods suffer, they may then attribute blame to the other side.

Failure to Plan Resettlement

In cases of state-initiated and managed migration, migrants as well as host communities may be disappointed as programs are poorly designed and benefits do not materialize. When intended economic pursuits prove to be nonviable, heightened competition for resources may deepen tensions between hosts, migrants, and the state. It is difficult for any state to estimate the number of migrants, how many jobs require training, how much physical infrastructure is needed, if further relocations will be necessary, and so on. Maintaining an adequate budget over time, when government revenues are volatile or when new governments come to office, adds to the difficulty. This means that even well-intentioned state projects may fail over time.

Rural, agricultural resettlement presents challenges in understanding the climate, soil conditions, and other aspects of sustainable agriculture, or whether the migrants' agricultural knowledge and customs can be adapted to the resettlement area. Resettlements designed to encourage industrial expansion in the context of initially weak physical infrastructure are problematic if plans adopt the wrong types or magnitudes of facilities. These failures may result from limited research and planning in program development, perhaps reflecting weak analytic capability, indifference, or haste. Richter (2016) identifies the major challenge of Cambodia's Land Allocation for Social and Economic Development Project as identifying suitable farmland, which depended on collaboration among rivalrous government ministries. This challenge was magnified by the threat of losing foreign funding, prompting the government to hastily resettle communities before the feuding ministries could complete adequate studies. Consequently, some of the sites selected for resettlement had poor soils, insufficient irrigation, or poor drainage in the rainy season, leading the program to be regarded as a failure.

Poor resettlement sites may be chosen because policymakers wish to avoid conflict between migrants and hosts, so seek what appear to be "unoccupied" lands. Such sites may be empty for a reason, perhaps being unsuitable for sustained cultivation. Officials may identify seemingly good land, only to discover that it floods during monsoon rains or that soils are exhausted after a handful of harvests. Continuing with the Cambodian example, planners chose degraded forest lands with poor soils as the site for some migrants because they were sparsely inhabited (Richter 2016, 13–17). In China, involuntary resettlement for the Shuikou Hydro-Project avoided adding to already congested areas by moving people to hillside sites, which soon suffered from poor soil and hydrologic vulnerability (Eriksen 1999, 127). In Nepal, many families displaced from the Royal Chitwan National Park were settled on land with insufficient potable water and low soil fertility rather than in more promising areas with larger populations (McLean and Straede 2003, 520). To lower costs and avoid conflicts, states may encourage migration to lands that cannot support settlements, a problem amplified by low support and higher-than-expected numbers of migrants.

Failure to Estimate the Volume of Migration

Even if a suitable resettlement location is found, planners may err in estimating the volume of migration. Sometimes, the actual number of migrants is much lower than anticipated, perhaps because recruits had second thoughts, planners exaggerated the number involved, or migrants do not remain in their new homes. Migration sites, especially those far from host communities, may then lack the populations necessary for a viable community. In response, settlers may move to other areas, without any advance planning, sometimes clashing with new host communities or degrading fragile ecosystems, further diminishing the population of resettlement sites.

At other times, actual migration exceeds predictions, especially as unmanaged migrations of family and friends follow in the wake of official processes. For example, when Brazil and Peru launched resettlement initiatives into the Amazon, "the prospect of free property attracted many more migrants than expected" (Scriven 2010, 21–22). As more settlers arrived and had large families, communities continued their outward expansion into forested areas. In Indonesia, Henley and Davidson (2008, 828) note that "Sometimes the officially supervised settlement was matched or exceeded by an additional inflow of 'spontaneous' (unorganized) transmigrants, especially Madurese in Kalimantan and Bugis throughout eastern Indonesia." In this case, even state-sponsored migration entails immense uncertainty. Larger than anticipated migratory flows may generate unexpected tensions with host communities that would not have happened with smaller numbers. They may also exhaust promised state support for migrants, with infrastructure such as roads, electricity, schools, and hospitals failing to keep up with demand.

Failure to Support Material Well-Being

Arguably, the most obvious state failures relate to the material well-being of migrants and hosts. States may fail to provide economic support to migrants or hosts, to ensure property rights for either group, to work with non-state actors, and to recognize development opportunities stemming from migration. If migrants and hosts do not have their material well-being accounted for, the success of internal migration policies will be limited.

State efforts to relocate its people from one area, perhaps densely-populated centers, to frontier areas are typically accompanied by several promises. Planners may speak of new highways, schools, and more as they seek to convince migrants to take the risk of resettling. When states fail to provide such support, internal migrants may be left high and dry, stranded in remote areas with poor soils, little access to equipment and fertilizers, and few ways to market produce even if their crops are successful. Many state-initiated resettlements fizzle out after a few years, with migrants returning home worse off than when they left or becoming more aggressive toward host communities. This represents great hardship for poor migrants, but also threatens ecological degradation as more sites are cleared with the false hope that they would be viable, and migrants then settle in new areas. Failures also bring serious financial losses for the very states that cannot afford them.

It is possible, though, that officials may send migrants and then be satisfied with a weak state presence so that growth-inhibiting regulations are not enforced. State officials may want to encourage tensions and frontier lawlessness so that settlers can usurp native lands illegally. When this is the case, the result is often lingering, long-term tensions, future, expensive legal battles, and excluded, embittered indigenous communities.

By the same token, urbanizing migrants, often forced into the poorest neighborhoods and peripheral spaces, also find limited state support. Official policies often tie state benefits to the migrants' home areas, providing a means to deny benefits to migrants. China's hukou system is perhaps the most extensive example, although recent reforms have liberalized the opportunities to receive social services away from the migrant's home area. State officials have gotten "away with not paying the 'full bill' for industrialization by…excluding migrants from urban benefits and programs" (Chan 2010, 83). Chan adds that "this cannot be a long-term approach," as poor migrants that are not integrated or supported "are often much more costly in social and political terms in the longer run." Similar systems exist in many countries, with subnational and national governments economizing by refusing support to migrants. In Vietnam, migrants "are by default not eligible for the 'poor list' because they are not official residents" (Thanh et al. 2013, 14–15). Kabeer (2014, 101) adds that migrants among Vietnam's ethnic minorities "earn half as much as those from the Kinh majority, are far less likely to have a work contract, and far less likely to receive help in finding a job." Similarly, in Kyrgyzstan, internal migrants arriving in the capital from the rural south lack legal status, making them subject to official discrimination. Nasritdinov (2008, 118) notes that "The informal nature of migration and migrants' illegal status made them frequent objects of abuse by police, authorities, and employers, and also deprived them of some basic rights." City officials in Brazil withhold services from migrants, forcing them into shanty-towns. Feler and Henderson (2008, 1) note that the "provision of bad living conditions for migrants is a way for existing residents to discourage in-migration to a locality, particularly of low-income migrants."

Denying services is a common tactic for state leaders to exclude internal migrants, often as a mechanism for subnational governments to stifle the flow of internal migration. Even if the leaders of urban areas use local laws and denial of services to limit the flow of internal rural migrants, continued rural poverty may nonetheless compel urban migration, frequently creating a bitter, poor underclass without access to education and health services, even if employment opportunities have benefited other urbanizers. This may limit long-term state policies, as segments of its population are essentially stateless and develop alternative systems of governance, including organized crime.

Of course, informal urban settlements are not marked by a total absence of the state. Urban squatter settlements typically see periods of state invisibility punctuated by extreme moments of enforcing public order, as in military "invasions" of favelas in Rio de Janeiro or the Tondo landfill in Manila.

Failure to Manage Property Rights

Land disputes represent points of contention for migrants and hosts. The failure to respect indigenous property or allow migrants to own land may represent a chronic source of economic insecurity and frustration. To ensure stability and avoid deprivations, states must be able to fairly enforce property rights and mediate disputes.

When relatively wealthy migrants relocate to poorer, peripheral areas, especially with state support, the result is often collusion to obtain indigenous lands. Indigenous peoples with different conceptions of property may lack formal titles or sign lands away, with migrants and businesses familiar with state laws coming to own the most productive lands. Osawa (2005) reports the slowness of the Brazilian government in demarcating indigenous reserves in the face of non-indigenous migrations and the drastic reduction in the areas of existing reserves. When states are slow to demarcate indigenous lands, perhaps intentionally, or simply refuse to recognize communal landholdings, this can sow lasting tensions between migrants and hosts. Even where land and other property could be fairly purchased from host communities if migrants have adequate funds, and the negotiations are uncoerced, enforcing these transactions still burdens the state. Moreover, insofar as the state favors state-sponsored migrants as its clients, this undermines the fairness of legal transactions, as courts may not be neutral venues in the case of disputes.

In other instances, it is the property rights of migrants that are overlooked. IDPs in both rural and urban areas are particularly vulnerable here, as they have no prior claims to land or residential sites in their new area and may be at the mercy of local officials. Newly arrived migrants may have to resort to establishing squatter settlements. In Sudan, authorities forcibly relocated people from development sites, allowing IDPs temporary access to land. Many attempted to settle in, in the hopes of gaining later legal recognition from authorities. However, these squatters have typically been disappointed, as "evictions have intensified…Of the estimated 665,000 IDPs who have had their homes demolished and been forcibly relocated since 1989, more than half have been moved since 2004" (de Geoffroy 2005, 38).

IDPs also may not get recognition for the property losses of their old homes. When IDPs are forcibly relocated by the state, perhaps to encourage development or attain political goals, officials may seek to make their projects more profitable, denying IDPs fair compensation. The property rights of expelled people are violated unless full compensation is provided. Terminski (2013, 38) summarizes a prevalent pattern:

> An often observed practice in the countries of the global south is lack of or very slight compensation received by people who have no legal right to the land they live on (such as tribals, advasi [sic] people and several categories of illegal settlers). Another problem is the inadequacy of compensation for property left behind, in the form either of cash or of prospects for obtaining land in the new area. In the case of many development projects, at least in Latin America, the compensation received cannot even restore, let alone improve, the conditions of displaced and affected people.

Failure to Recognize Development Opportunities

State officials may choose not to manage IDPs, content to have them live in slums and camps. Internal migrants are too often ignored or kept in limbo, rarely assisted with productivity-enhancing opportunities or training. Beyond being a human tragedy, this represents a lost opportunity, exemplifying how states fail to perceive potential benefits from internal migration. International agencies increasingly emphasize migration as a development opportunity (World Bank 2016), but promoting the productivity of migrants, particularly those cramped into IDP camps, imposes greater burdens and risks of accountability for the state.

Therefore, IDPs are rarely approached by authorities as sources of economic productivity and partners in development. Because they are seen as temporary arrangements, even after several decades, IDP camps rarely provide employment opportunities. Officials may both see IDP camps as drains on their resources and fail to enact policies that could make them anything else. Referring to both IDPs and refugees, Harild (2016, 4–5) argues that:

> Policymakers, planners and other actors see displacement as a largely humanitarian issue. They ignore its inevitable longevity, and the typical response therefore stays in a short-term mode… If the policy framework stays in a short-term humanitarian mode during protracted displacement, there is every potential for this to breed exclusion, poverty, degradation, possible radicalisation, and new conflict and violence as well as significant economic and fiscal pressure on host countries…The first step

> towards fundamental change would be for all actors to accept that conflict-induced forced displacement is predominantly a development issue with humanitarian elements – and not the other way around.

A need exists not just for more effective state action, but also for a different mindset, a new lens through which state officials view IDPs and other internal migrants. Such migrants are not just crises to be accommodated with aid, but instead demand long-term developmental strategies.

Political Inclusion and Partnerships

At the heart of many failures to ensure the material well-being of migrants and hosts are some squarely political concerns. States may encourage migration for political reasons, perhaps seeking to project a sense of national unity or protect their borders. In doing so, states often fail to respect the civic rights of migrants or hosts. This failure denies citizens the benefits of citizenship, fostering a sense of exclusion and statelessness. When migrations are politically driven, states may refuse to work with various partners, placing political sensitivities ahead of citizen well-being. The result is that migration intended to foster unity instead sows divisions.

Failure to Recognize Civic Rights

Like international migrants, civic participation among internal migrants is often restricted. This is especially true for IDPs, despite Principle 22 of the UN Guiding Principles on Internal Displacement (UN OCHA 2004) that calls on the state to guarantee IDPs the right "to associate freely and participate equally in community affairs; the right to vote and to participate in governmental and public affairs, including the right to have access to the means necessary to exercise this right." Undocumented, deprived internal migrants are often denied a voice in local politics; as a result, their interests are not fully known to policymakers and they may seek alternative ways to be heard.

Even in democratic countries, internal migrants may be unable to vote in either their former homes or new homes. On the one hand, domicile qualifications are common and reasonable. Typically, a voter must reside in a given district for a specified period, because a total lack of domicile requirements could fuel various forms of political corruption, for instance, trucking in supporters to a contested district. However, at a certain point, barring internal migrants from voting represents political exclusion. Internal migrants are often disenfranchised over long periods, allowing host communities to maintain political dominance. As noted, various subnational governments in India have been known to deny internal migrants the right to vote, maintaining power by stoking nativist fears. As mentioned in Chapter 7, urban governments often withhold ration cards from out-of-state migrants, thus refusing them access to public services, opening a bank account, and voting. In Indonesia, despite a national non-discrimination doctrine, regional discrimination persists. National citizenship laws are often challenged by nativism, with host communities reviving native traditions. This nativism has many cultural benefits, such as promoting local cultural awareness, but it is also used to exclude internal migrants. Jones (2013, 66) clarifies that "the dark side of this revival is the use of tradition to justify excluding migrants from resources or targeting them for discrimination, including monetary payments, and, in some cases, deadly violence." As Indonesia has decentralized authority to its four hundred-plus districts, localized forms of exclusion have become commonplace.

In Côte d'Ivoire, decades of unsponsored northern migration to the more prosperous south have led to the exclusion of internal migrants. McCauley (2013, 159) notes that "generations of Northerners brought to the South by economic opportunity now feel socially disenfranchised according to their ethnicity, religion, or place of origin, and little trust exists between themselves and 'pure' southern Ivoirians." These patterns are understandable because local leaders may lose support if long-standing residents lose benefits and relative power, making it politically expedient to exclude migrants. Therefore, politically vulnerable local government leaders, unless accountable for the fate of state-sponsored migration, often are motivated to keep the migrants from being in a political position to demand more.

When subnational authorities receive support from groups that invoke Sons of the Soil claims, state officials have the incentive to deny participation to groups designated (though often controversially) as "migrants" or even to expel them, even if they have resided in the area for a lengthy period. National governments often do not recognize or do not wish to challenge subnational authorities that contravene national laws for their own benefit. Again, exclusion may represent one of the few ways local governments can slow migration and prevent conflict. But it may also represent self-interest, an effort to maintain power and profit from undocumented underclasses. A system that serves to entrench inequality for the sake of stability may be neither ethical nor sustainable.

However, in many countries, we see efforts to overcome the disenfranchisement of internal migrants through stronger forms of national citizenship. Focusing on Nigeria's violence-prone Jos area, Afolabi (2016, 14) challenges the political marginalization of internal migrants by demanding civic participation for all residents:

> [T]he constitution needs amendment in order to confer citizenship rights and privileges on all Nigerians irrespective of state of origin and place or region of residence. The constitution should be made to tell all contending parties in the Jos North crisis that every person either of the Berom, Afizare, Hausa, Anaguta, Fulani, Yoruba, Igbo or Urhobo origin, is a citizen of Nigeria...The constitution should be made to unequivocally and explicitly state that the home of a Nigerian citizen is the place that he/she has found conducive for residence and livelihood.

Similarly, in assessing the more than half-century aftermath of the involuntary resettlement of 48,000 Egyptian Nubians for the Aswan High Dam, Scudder (2016, 36) reports Nubian complaints about "inadequate opportunities to participate in the development and politics of Aswan Governorate." Removed from their homes, these development IDPs campaigned to reclaim their civic rights.

In general, efforts to exclude migrants indefinitely from civic rights must be resisted by the state. This is especially true since exclusion may plant seeds for intergroup conflict. For many migrants, civic rights may be no less important than economic support, and the denial of a political voice may also jeopardize their economic opportunities.

Failure to Partner with Non-state Actors

Because state failure to support internal migrants may be rooted in incapacity, with weak states unable to extend adequate support, officials may be reluctant to offer support, lest migrants come to expect it. At the same time, states often invest scarce resources in internal migration processes, only to see these funds wasted as projects fail. Such failures are all the more confusing given a common tendency of state leaders to refuse help from non-state actors. States may fail by trying to shoulder too much of the burden, overlooking complementary non-state, societal mechanisms. There is a need not just for allowing such systems, but also for creative collaborations. When violence breaks out, authorities may come to see the creation of peace as the provision of the state agencies alone, the job of security forces or governments. This may be misguided for low-capacity states, especially those whose neutrality is called into question by migrants or hosts. States need to recognize the work of non-state actors. This may include civil society organizations, but may also lay in traditional societal forces.

Localized forms of peacebuilding may be seen as competing with the state's authority to mediate conflicts or may be seen as supporting a particular side. Customs may also seem to be archaic and run against the rational, modern state. James-Allen et al. (2010, 21) point to the clash between the formal, state-directed processes of conflict reconciliation and Liberia's traditional "Palava Hut": "a town or village gathering place where disputes are settled and issues resolved, usually through the mediation of a respected member of the community." They suggest that this local tradition may violate global human rights standards, especially as they involve "trials by ordeal," such as "physical tests to adjudicate guilt or innocence" (James-Allen et al. 2010, 22).

NGOs, whether domestic or international, often exist in precarious relation with the state. In taking over social services that are conventionally provided by the state, state officials may feel threatened. NGOs may serve as vehicles for political opposition to the incumbent government leaders. When NGOs document the deprivations of migrants or host communities, this exposes the weakness or unwillingness of the state to address the problems. Too often, officials would rather not see migratory deprivations recognized or addressed, as they seek to save face, even if this exacerbates problems in the years to come.

State actions to muzzle NGOs can range from demanding some sort of registration to seizing financial assets, expulsion, or violence. The constraints on NGOs can be in effect simply through the risk of such sanctions. The Ethiopian Derg regime expelled Médecins Sans Frontières in 1985; in 2009, international NGOs active in Darfur IDP camps were expelled by the Sudanese government (Young and Maxwell 2009). Zeccola (2011, 315–316) demonstrates that after the 2004 tsunami devastated Aceh, Indonesian authorities allowed NGOs to assist disaster IDPs, but blocked them from assisting conflict IDPs. International NGOs thus faced a dilemma: "ignoring the directives of the Indonesian authorities could also jeopardise access to tsunami-affected areas because the authorities had the power to expel any international agency if it stepped out of line." States may block NGO assistance to conflict IDPs for political reasons and may block aid to state-initiated migrations and disaster IDPs for what essentially comes down to pride. State efforts to manage non-state assistance may even represent an opportunity for states to take partial credit and expand their effectiveness.

Sociocultural Factors

As noted, internal migration has important sociocultural consequences, as either side may come to feel that its traditions are disrespected and its group lesser than others. Cultural factors are important for a group's collective self-worth, interacting closely with economic and political factors. There are several ways in which states fail to take cultural factors into account, undermining the viability of internal migration.

Failure to Consider Compatibility

Resettlement planning may also be blind to the cultural, social, or economic compatibility of migrant and host communities. For instance, planners may seek to resettle migrants in communities with the same faith, but other groups settling with state migrants, secondary migration, or flows that are larger than expected may bring different cultures and faiths into contact with one another. In Indonesia, Javanese migrants integrated more easily into nearby Muslim communities in southern Sumatra, intermarrying and developing shared traditions, than in Christian parts of eastern Indonesia. Meanwhile, disaster relocations due to volcanic activity in Bali led resettlement agencies to send some Hindu Balinese to Central Sulawesi, where communities integrated with animist and Christian groups (Davis 1976), as well as Lampung, where they have stood apart and sometimes clashed with native Muslim communities (Côté 2019).

Compatibility also has important, underrecognized socioeconomic dimensions, especially in terms of class and occupation. When states relocate poor farmers to settle previously less used lands, they may integrate rather easily into local economic systems and patronage networks. Without state coordination, more privileged migrants may then arrive and seek to capture markets, votes, or landholdings, thus clashing with local leaders. Host communities and outside observers may then blame the state, even when it was not state-managed migrants who generated conflict. This is the case for Indonesian transmigration, for which Javanese farmers resettled by the state did not generate tensions with hosts, but unmanaged entrepreneurial migrations did, flows wrongly attributed to state planners (Barter and Côté 2015). Weiner (1978, 91) comes to similar conclusions in Assam, where early migrants to tea plantations "have never been...economic, cultural, or political threats to the Assamese." This is because "the jobs they hold are not those sought by the Assamese," plantation migrants did not become involved in local politics, and they lived in previously uninhabited regions. It was only decades later, when Bengali merchants and bureaucrats arrived, that conflicts erupted between Assamese and migrants. Thus, tensions between migrants and host communities are not inevitable, but can be exacerbated when planners fail to consider various forms of compatibility.

Failure to Respect Migrant/Host Cultures

Cultural deprivations may occur when internal migrants arrive in less developed, remote regions. A numerical imbalance of migrants compared to local people as well as state assimilation efforts may require host communities to adopt the cultural practices and language of the migrants. As mentioned in Chapter 3, host community cultures are often stigmatized when sponsored migration targets areas populated by marginalized people with an implicit or explicit goal of civilizing natives. A parallel problem often occurs when marginal populations migrate to host communities of higher economic status. Kaltman (2014, 75) characterizes a common perception of mainstream Han Chinese of the Uighurs as "a primitive, fierce people. They can't easily be controlled and they have no desire to change. Most Uighur in Shanghai are thieves. Punishing Uighur does no good because most have nothing to lose, or they just don't care." Unless the state can effectively counter such stereotypes, marginal groups may feel compelled to shed some of their cultural practices, including language, to minimize the differences that result in discrimination against them. Others might respond with deeper forms of communal identity, perhaps reifying stereotypes.

Cultural conflicts are especially volatile in terms of religion. When migrants and hosts have different faiths, and the state supports its co-religionists, this may elevate material clashes to spiritual crises. In many parts of the world, highland communities maintain distinctive religious practices from lowland majorities. In Asia, hill communities often resisted the spread of Hinduism, Buddhism, and Islam. Some hill communities maintain animist faiths, while others embraced Christianity from missionaries. As a result, internal migration may be seen by remote minorities as an effort to proselytize, spreading the faith of the majority against remote minorities. In Thailand, internal migrants arriving in the country's northern hill communities, as well as the Muslim south, typically receive state support for creating Buddhist temples, including support for monks by the national Sangha. In the Patani region, conflict has led the state to militarize Buddhist temples, further reinforcing the links between the state and internal migrants in the eyes of local Muslims (Jerryson 2009). From the state's view, this may just be supporting its people. For non-Buddhist natives, such policies may generate existential fears, representing a threat to their cultural identity.

Migratory Insecurity

Poor planning, economic loss, political exclusion, and cultural indignity are often mutually reinforcing. They can generate the sort of conflicts described in Chapter 11. In such situations, states may fail to implement effective responses in numerous ways.

Failure to Provide Order

When the state signals that it is unwilling or unable to take action against those inciting violence, whether by migrants against hosts or hosts against migrants, provocateurs may believe that they can incite with impunity. Failure to provide public order in the face of violence may signal to one or both sides that they are free to act, escalating violence and triggering counter-mobilization.

In remote, rural frontiers, inaction may be rooted in incapacity. Remoteness also allows the state to eschew its responsibilities for indigenous communities, failing to provide security in the face of incursions from migrants. As a result, in locations such as Papua New Guinea, indigenous communities respond to land appropriation and violence by internal migrants with violence. When rural migrants try to settle in protected areas, state officials can reduce their accountability for their security by castigating the migrants as offenders.

Urban ghettoes may also represent a frontier of a sort vis-à-vis the state. Frontline officials such as judges, social workers, inspectors, and police sometimes abandon these neighborhoods as too dangerous to enter. Tranchant (2013, 3) reports that in Nairobi, "the police tend to only enter slums for repressive actions (such as raids to target suspected criminals) and are otherwise absent and feared by the population." In Rio de Janeiro's favelas, the state effectively abandoned one-fifth of the city's population to gangs. This led the urban poor to mobilize militias to challenge gangs and provide security, but it soon became clear that "the ultimate goal of the militias... was economic profit, levying heavy security taxes on inhabitants and business, and charging for services such as electricity, cable, gas, etc." (Magaloni et al. 2015, 8). The state's failure to provide security leads non-state actors to fill the gap, with mafioso and militias providing stop-gap security for internal migrants, but greater long-term insecurity. Authorities may find it easier to intervene early on to provide security than to wait and try to defeat non-state armed groups later on.

Failure to Remain Neutral

As mentioned in Chapter 5, state-initiated and managed migration tends to treat migrants as favored clients. The state may provide greater benefits to migrants and side with the migrants in potential conflicts, disadvantaging host communities. For example, in Indonesia's Central Sulawesi, "transmigrants received state-provided houses and agricultural areas of what natives considered their ancestral land." In this case, "the apparently uniform yet unequally beneficial regulations of the Suharto regime aggravated the Protestants' regional nationalism and nativism as well as the Muslims' willingness to listen to militant rhetoric about their unfulfilled rights to Indonesia's wealth and political supremacy" (Aragon 2013, 165). As a result, the state is not a neutral party in the eyes of host communities, as it actively favors migrant groups.

Real or even perceived favoritism toward migrants also may induce the migrants to take advantage of this support to act aggressively toward the host community. Fearon and Laitin (2011, 203) observe that, in Sri Lanka, "In assuring security to settlers in part through the visibility of the state security apparatus in the region of settlement, the state was giving license to settlers to provoke indigenous Tamils." Knowledge of state support can create a moral hazard among migrants, who then act recklessly knowing that they have a backup.

Of course, the opposite may be the case for poorer urban migrants. City or state governments may favor host communities, perhaps even stoking tensions with migrants to secure votes. As migrants may not possess civil and political rights, governments may work for locals because they alone have a voice at the ballot box. Again, control of the local state, including security forces, may encourage hosts to abuse and provoke migrants, seeking to goad powerless groups into confrontation.

Either way, when migrants or hosts capture the state, and the state openly favors them, the other side is left unrepresented and relatively powerless. States may abuse migrants or hosts to gain favor from their allies, and their allies may abuse migrants or hosts knowing that they will not be held accountable. When one side perceives the state as working for the other, it may then come to perceive all state actions as partial and threatening. They may also perceive actions from the other community to represent state policy. The result can be growing inequality, tensions, and violence.

Conclusions

Although states may behave effectively and in good faith for both migrants and home communities, for every dimension of state obligation, one finds examples of state failures. Some failures reflect pernicious state goals or weak state capacity, the latter including an inability to generate accurate data or enforce policies among subnational authorities. Other shortcomings result from favoritism toward migrants or host communities. States may approach internal migration with various biases, refuse to work with civil society, or suppress accurate information due to policy objectives that are at odds with the well-being of migrant and host communities. A recurrent thread is that state officials often minimize their resource commitments, exposure, and accountability through means ranging from formal to informal. Local authorities are often able to discriminate against migrants and hosts, formally or informally. Another thread is the importance of time horizons, as short-term failures to collect information or limit migratory flows through exclusion can have long-term, more expensive consequences.

This chapter has focused on how state failures to provide adequate governance can turn opportunity into disaster. But we must not limit our focus to failures. Given the overwhelming, uncontrollable nature of migratory flows within countries, one may be tempted to throw up one's hands, seeing this policy area as ungovernable. Such responses are especially unfortunate given the potential for well-governed internal migration to improve the lives of so many people. With this in mind, the next and final section of this book is more optimistic, looking at modest and major successes in governing internal migration.

References

Afolabi, Oladiran. 2016. Migration and Citizenship Question in Nigeria: A Study of the Berom and Hausa/Fulani Conflict in Jos. *African Journal of Political Science and International Relations Review* 10 (2): 8–15.

Aragon, Lorraine V. 2013. Development Strategies, Religious Relations, and Communal Violence in Central Sulawesi, Indonesia: A Cautionary Tale. In *Development Strategies, Identities, and Conflict in Asia*, eds. William Ascher and Natalia Mirovitskaya, 153–182. New York: Palgrave Macmillan.

Barter, Shane, and Isabelle Côté. 2015. Strife of the Soil? Unsettling Transmigrant Conflicts in Indonesia. *Journal of Southeast Asian Studies* 46 (1): 60–85.

Çelik, Ayşe Betül. 2005. 'I Miss My Village!': Forced Kurdish Migrants in Istanbul and their Representation in Associations. *New Perspectives on Turkey* 32: 137–163.

Chan, Kam Wing. 2010. Crossing the 50 Percent Population Rubicon: Can China Urbanize to Prosperity? *Eurasian Geography and Economics* 53 (1): 63–86.

Côté, Isabelle. 2019. 'Adopting Migrants as Brothers and Sisters'—Fictive Kinship as a Mechanism of Conflict Resolution and Conflict Prevention in Lampung, Indonesia. In *Internal Migration: Challenges in Governance and Integration*, eds. Shane Barter and William Ascher, 97–111. New York: Peter Lang.

Davis, Gloria. 1976. *Parigi: A Social History of the Balinese Movement to Central Sulawesi, 1907–1974*. Doctoral Dissertation, Stanford University.

de Geoffroy, Agnes. 2005. IDPs and Urban Planning in Khartoum. *Forced Migration Review* 24: 38–39.

de Silva, Chandra Richard. 1987. *Sri Lanka: A History*. New Delhi: Vikas.

Eriksen, John H. 1999. Comparing the Economic Planning for Voluntary and Involuntary Resettlement. In *The Economics of Involuntary Resettlement: Questions and Challenges*, ed. Michael Cernea, 83–146. Washington, DC: World Bank.
Fearnside, Philip. 1985. Deforestation and Decision-Making in the Development of the Brazilian Amazonia. *Interciencia* 10 (5): 243–247.
Fearon, James D., and David D. Laitin. 2011. Sons of the Soil, Migrants, and Civil War. *World Development* 39 (2): 199–211.
Feler, Leo, and J. Vernon Henderson. 2008. Exclusionary Policies in Urban Development: How Under-Servicing of Migrant Households Affects the Growth and Composition of Brazilian Cities. *National Bureau of Economic Research Working Papers*. No. 14136.
Harild, Niels. 2016. Forced Displacements: A Development Issue with Humanitarian Elements. *Forced Migration Review* 52: 4–7.
Henley, David, and Jamie S. Davidson. 2008. In the Name of Adat: Regional Perspectives on Reform, Tradition, and Democracy in Indonesia. *Modern Asian Studies* 42 (4): 815–852.
Huntington, Samuel P. 1968. *Political Order in Changing Societies*. New Haven: Yale University Press.
James-Allen, Paul, Aaron Weah, and Lizzie Goodfriend. 2010. *Beyond the Truth and Reconciliation Commission: Transitional Justice Options in Liberia*. New York: International Center for Transitional Justice.
Jerryson, Michael. 2009. Appropriating a Space for Violence: State Buddhism in Southern Thailand. *Journal of Southeast Asian Studies* 40 (1): 33–57.
Jones, Peter S.J.. 2013. A Governance Analysis of the Galapagos Marine Reserve. *Marine Policy* 41: 65–71.
Kabeer, Naila. 2014. Social Justice and the Millennium Development Goals: The Challenge of Intersecting Inequalities. *The Equal Rights Review* 13: 91–116.
Kaltman, Blaine. 2014. *Under the Heel of the Dragon: Islam, Racism, Crime, and the Uighur in China*. Ohio University Press.
Landau, Loren. 2014. Religion and the Foundation of Urban Difference: Belief, Transcendence, and Transgression in South Africa and Johannesburg. *Global Networks* 14 (3): 291–305.
Lasswell, Harold D., and Abraham Kaplan. 1950/2017. *Power and Society*. New Haven and New York: Yale University Press and Routledge.
Magaloni, Beatriz, Edgar Franco, and Vanessa Melo. 2015. Killing in the Slums: An Impact Evaluation of Police Reform in Rio de Janeiro. *Working Paper* 556, Center for Democracy, Development and the Rule of Law. Palo Alto, CA: Stanford University.
McCauley, John. 2013. Economic Development Strategy and Conflict: A Comparison of Côte d'Ivoire and Ghana 50 Years after Independence. In

Development Strategies and the Evolution of Violence in Africa, eds. William Ascher and Natalia Mirovitskaya, 141–169. New York: Palgrave Macmillan.
McLean, J., and S. Straede. 2003. Conservation, Relocation, and the Paradigms of Park and People Management—A Case Study of Padampur Villages and the Royal Chitwan National Park, Nepal. *Society and Natural Resources* 16 (6): 509–526.
Migdal, Joel S. 1988. *Strong Societies and Weak States: State-Society Relations and State Capabilities in the Third World*. Princeton, NJ: Princeton University Press.
Nasritdinov, Emil. 2008. Discrimination Against Internal Migrants in Bishkek. In *Kyrgyzstan Today: Policy Briefs on Civil Society, Migration, Islam, Corruption*, ed. John Couper, 114–118. Bishkek: Social Research Center, American University of Central Asia.
Osawa, Mario. 2005. *Foreigners in Our Own Country*. London: Amnesty International.
Reynolds, Sarnata. 2014. *Mexico's Unseen Victims*. Washington, DC: Refugees International.
Richter, Iris. 2016. *Experiences from the Implementation of Social Land Concessions in Cambodia*. Bonn: Deutsche Gesellschaft für Internationale Zusammenarbeit. January.
Scriven, Joel. 2010. Markets & Payments for Ecosystem Services: Engaging REDD+ on Peru's Amazonian Frontier. Diss. Oxford: Oxford University.
Scudder, Thayer. 2016. *Aswan High Dam Resettlement of Egyptian Nubians*. Singapore: Springer.
Terminski, Bogumil. 2013. *Development-Induced Displacement and Resettlement: Theoretical Frameworks and Current Challenges*. Geneva: Ibidem Press.
Thanh, Hoang Xuan, Truong Tuan Anh, and Dinh Thi Thu Phuong. 2013. *Urban Poverty in Vietnam: A View from Complementary Assessments*. London: International Institute for Environment and Development.
Tranchant, Jean-Pierre. 2013. Making the Urban Poor Safer: Lessons from Nairobi and Maharashtra. IDS Policy Briefing 47. Sussex: Institute for Development Studies.
UN OCHA (Office for the Coordination of Humanitarian Affairs). 2004. *Guiding Principles on Internal Displacement*. Geneva: United Nations.
Weiner, Myron. 1978. *Sons of the Soil: Migration and Ethnic Conflict in India*. Princeton: Princeton University Press.
World Bank. 2006. Infrastructure: Lessons from the Last Two Decades of World Bank Engagement. World Bank Infrastructure Network Discussion Paper. http://documents.worldbank.org/curated/en/291191468166484472/pdf/351991 0vol-01.pdf.
World Bank. 2016. Migration and Development. Washington, DC.
Young, Helen, and Daniel Maxwell. 2009. Targeting in Complex Emergencies: Darfur Case Study. Feinstein International Center Report. Medford, MA: Tufts University.

Zeccola, Paul. 2011. Dividing Disasters in Aceh, Indonesia: Separatist Conflict and Tsunami, Human Rights and Humanitarianism. *Disasters* 35 (2): 308–328.

PART III

What to Do About It

The rather depressing diagnoses of deprivations, conflicts, and failures suffered by migrants and host communities are not inevitable. Internal migration offers the potential to better distribute wealth and opportunities while promoting development; its frequent success in achieving these goals is one reason for the expansive volume of internal migration.

State officials, if held accountable, can play a positive role both in resettlement programs and in reacting to issues that arise with unsponsored migration. Because of the difficulties that frequently arise from both forms of migration, and the pressure that state officials face, accountability often presents a threat to these officials. Thus, Chapter 13 focuses on the factors that determine whether officials will embrace or evade accountability.

In Chapter 14, we outline some best practices and state policies that can reduce migratory flows and manage conflicts. As important as the national-level state institutions are, other domestic actors, whether governmental at subnational levels or non-state forces, can help to provide resources and resolve conflicts. Thus, the cases presented in Chapter 15 demonstrate that migrants and host communities can rely on traditional mechanisms to resolve conflicts, with the state playing a facilitative role. The chapter also considers civil society initiatives to assist migrants and host communities. Chapter 16 demonstrates that the international community has much to offer, whether in practices already available, initiatives yet to be brought to fruition, and suggestions original to this book. International organizations, with greater coordination than currently prevails, can do much more through collaboration and conditionality.

Finally, Chapter 17 concludes by laying out important lessons in governing internal migration. Primarily, there is a need to increase attention to internal migration vis-à-vis the preoccupation with international migration, to recognize the centrality of state agencies overseeing migration.

CHAPTER 13

State Accountability: Theory, Evasion, and Potential Remedies

A crucial insight into state behavior is officials' preoccupation with their accountability. Understanding the dynamics of accountability is important for knowing why state actors often fail to adopt the most effective governance of migration and engage in misleading rhetoric that makes it difficult to assess migratory outcomes.

To be "accountable" can simply mean that officials recognize—and therefore hopefully act upon—their responsibility for adverse consequences emerging from migration. This also refers to whether officials, agencies, and leaders are *held* accountable for outcomes. Even the most brazenly authoritarian governments have to worry about losing the confidence and respect of stakeholders. If being held accountable for adverse outcomes is costly, avoiding accountability becomes a high priority for any government. Even if a government clings to power, the costs of maintaining the compliance needed to pursue the regime's goals can escalate when stakeholders hold officials accountable for unacceptable performance. Thus, an essential political question for state officials is how to minimize accountability when it constitutes a threat to the state's standing. To the degree that state leaders worry about accountability for their actions, they have to wrestle with the dilemma of either minimizing their role in the hope that they will therefore not be held responsible, or monopolizing decision-making in the hope of maximizing their control

W. Ascher and S. J. Barter, *Moving within Borders*, Politics, Economics, and Inclusive Development, https://doi.org/10.1007/978-3-031-37549-1_13

over outcomes. Therefore, understanding the dynamics of accountability, and how accountability is evaded, is important for knowing why state actors often fail to effectively govern internal migration.

As a consequence of the state's primacy in initiating, managing, or reacting to internal migration, officials typically bear the greatest potential accountability for migratory outcomes, whether or not initiated or managed by the state. It is widely accepted that the state has a duty of care for its citizens and other residents. Thus, when conflict erupts between migrants and host communities, the state may be criticized for not maintaining order. Additionally, as violence displaces people, the state may be called upon to find a place of refuge for them. In varying circumstances, state officials may be judged by the public, organized domestic groups, international actors, and other elements of the state itself. Officials may gain praise from what are seen as successful management of internal migration, but they also risk accusations ranging from incompetence to corruption, resulting in potentially harsh reactions.

Degrees of Accountability

The dynamics of accountability follow some general patterns as well as specifics for instances of migration. Although it does not hold in all cases, the importance of state accountability typically rises along two gradients. Most obvious is the magnitude of stakes: the number of stakeholders and the severity of the consequences to be caused or averted. The second gradient is the depth of state involvement: from minimal reactions to migrations that bear no state involvement, to assistance for unmanaged migrants, to direct state management of both voluntary and coercive resettlements.

The premise that state oversight is positively associated with the degree of accountability is challenged when unsponsored migrants clash with host communities, resulting in casualties. In the case of the Gedeo-Guji conflicts in Ethiopia cited above, federal officials claimed that 140 fatalities occurred in 1998, in contrast to other claims that 3,000 were killed (Dagne 2013, 223). If it was widely accepted that 3,000 Gedeo and Guji died in the 1998 conflict, the criticisms against state officials' failures to broker a lasting truce would have gained even greater currency. More broadly, the state can be blamed for the problematic constitutional arrangement of ethnically-defined regional states that created boundaries (Dagne 2013; Kinfemichael 2014, 78–79). This arrangement implicitly defines migrants as beyond their rightful territory, creating undocumented internal migrants, who may then be subjected to harassment or expulsion. In short, the Ethiopian state, insofar as it could have been held responsible for the 1991 constitution and its implementation, could be accountable for considerable inter-ethnic violence even though most of the migrations responsible for ethnic inter-mingling occurred long ago, and perhaps the failure to limit migration might have caused more conflict.

Identifying the Reasons and Mechanisms for Evading Accountability

Self-Accountability Obstacles

Often the first step to holding the state accountable is for officials to recognize their own accountability. If they do not recognize their responsibility for problems, they will resist calls for change. Therefore, it is important to understand how and why officials are susceptible to self-delusion about the adverse impacts of their actions.

Attribution theory posits that when things go badly, the unfortunate actions of others tend to be attributed to their traits, whereas one's own actions are attributed to circumstances (Heider 1958). The response to criticism—"under the circumstances we took the best available option"—and attributing negative traits to others involved can reinforce a deeply-held if inaccurate belief that state strategy and actions were appropriate. For example, Indonesian officials could convince themselves that placing roughly 35,000 Madurese conflict IDPs in camps near conflict areas in 1999 was a sound response. When violence recurred, it was not seen as the fault of the state officials' actions, but rather as the combativeness of the Madurese and competition with other groups. Brazilian officials in the National Institute for Colonization and Agrarian Reform could attribute the failures of Amazonian resettlements to budget constraints, law-breaking migrants, and the uncontrollable flood of unsponsored migrants, not shortcomings inherent in their policies.

Cognitive biases in attributing motives and responsibility deepen through the corollary that what might be construed as hostile opposition is attributed to malevolent intent (Dodge 2006). Actions in opposition to state initiatives are attributed to malice rather than straightforward defense of group interests. Therefore, troubles that may emerge from migration might be attributed to the ill-will or other deficiencies of migrants, host community members, or others.

Low Expectations, Low Accountability

In light of likely connections between stated objectives and accountability based on meeting these objectives, we would expect that both resettlement initiatives and treatment of unsponsored migrations could be couched in terms of objectives that are easy to meet. For resettlement initiatives, unambitious goals may simply be the very presence of migrants in a given area. For example, the Thai government has resettled people from the Northeast and the North into the South, with the inducement of government-constructed villages. The very fact that the migrants' presence partly offsets Buddhists' flight from the South due to security threats is, for Thai officials, an accomplishment in itself. To be sure, security forces have had to provide security for the migrants, even mobilizing militias. Nevertheless, placing Thai Buddhists in the south can be regarded as fulfilling a key objective.

Alternatively, the objective may be rhetorically popular, but its accomplishment is difficult to assess. For example, if the stated goal is to "civilize" ostensibly unsophisticated peoples—as with Indonesian officials resettling Javanese in Kalimantan and Papua (Kivimäki 2016, 68) or India resettling Bengalis to tribal areas (Bose 2006, 64)—resettlement places groups from more developed regions in less developed native host communities. Whether "civilizing" occurs, over some unspecified period, is a weak basis for gauging accountability (Duncan 2004).

Another tactic to reduce accountability is to frame objectives in terms of inputs rather than outcomes. The degree of control declines in going from inputs, such as budget or staff, to the output activities that these inputs generate, and even less control typically in the outcomes caused by these activities. Consider the scenario in which the state announces the goal of providing grants to 10,000 prospective migrant families to move and increase the resettlement area's productivity. Officials could simply provide resources for grants and transport. The state has less control over how many families will accept the offer, and even greater uncertainty holds as to whether the arrival of some uncertain number of migrants would increase productivity. Yet, if the resources are spent as planned, this may be claimed by some as a successful policy.

Blaming Others

Although the denial of responsibility may be a cognitive failing, it might also be a conscious tactic involving how the program and the rhetoric are structured to place the blame for adverse outcomes on migrants, hosts, or both. For example, clashes that occur when sponsored migrants are sent to "civilize backward peoples" may be rationalized as the unavoidable reaction of the "primitives" confronted with the need to change. When urban refugees fleeing violence protest the lack of state recognition of their refugee status and their rights to receive state support, as in Colombia, state officials might dispute their claims, arguing that they are merely job-seekers seeking unwarranted benefits (Zea 2019).

Uncertainty of Outcomes

Uncertainty about the probabilities of causal patterns plays a surprisingly large role in blunting accountability judgments. For example, the decision of Ethiopian officials to repatriate displaced Gedeo people has been criticized as premature (Wilson 2019). Yet, state officials could argue that Gedeos' situation away from their homes may put them at greater risk of deprivation. Whether state officials should be held accountable for rushing the return is thus debatable.

An even more straightforward way to reduce accountability is to minimize or ignore information about the impacts of displacement and other forms of migration. The sudden scattering of people, particularly in fleeing violence, creates problems in knowing the magnitude of the migration. This reflects both limited capacities to collect information and ambiguities in defining displacement: if a family goes to live with relatives, is it displacement or a family reunion? And if they continue to live with extended families, for how long should we consider them displaced? Some outcomes are difficult to assess, amplified by official unwillingness to try.

Ambiguity of State Obligations

Accountability judgments rest on comparisons between presumed obligations, in both objectives and conduct, and the degree to which these obligations are met. When obligations are ambiguous, accountability is as well. Obligations regarding objectives are unclear because of uncertainty as to whether objectives improve overall well-being, whether the balance among tradeoffs of objectives is appropriate (e.g., benefiting migrants vs. host communities), and whether the objectives are worth the costs (e.g., conservation vs. deprivations of people displaced from reserves, or economic growth at the expense of suffering coercion). Little definitive guidance exists regarding state obligations concerning the degree and balance of care for migrants and host communities. This ambiguity is rooted in the degree of coercion involved in the migration, vague international norms, and the balance of concern for host communities in relation to migrants.

Ambiguity of the Degree of Coercion

State obligations depend on whether migration is compulsory or voluntary, or more precisely, the degree of coercion involved. To justify coercion, a state takes on the responsibility to ensure that the use of force results in net improvements. In short, the stakes are higher for a state that is more likely to be held accountable because of heavy-handed actions. International standards define the distinctions, but cannot definitively resolve the status of any given initiative. The World Bank's 2004 Operational Policy 4.12 on Involuntary Resettlement defines "involuntary" as "actions that may be taken without the displaced person's informed consent or power of choice." The key ambiguity here is the "power of choice." If regulations undermine livelihoods to the extent that leaving is necessary to maintain the family's livelihood, the residents can be said to lack choice—this is economically involuntary resettlement. Furthermore, "restricted access to resources" is deemed as a form of involuntary displacement even when people are not physically removed. The distinction between "forced" and "impelled" migrations is crucial, because impelled migration implies discretion on the part of people as to whether they must migrate and how, but forced migration puts the state into what ought to be a more accountable status (Petersen 1958).

In addition to clear indications that the locality can no longer sustain sufficient economic gain for some of its residents, local people may find that the "voluntary" agreement to resettle is a less risky choice than refusing to leave, which may result in extreme limitations on extractive activities within the protected area, harassment, denial of benefits, or other adverse consequences. Experiences in Vietnam's Cat Tien National Park exemplify how "distinctions between voluntary and involuntary resettlement from protected areas are not always clear" (Morris-Jung and Roth 2010, 19). Resettlement was complicated by "histories of migration and displacement, uncertain and insecure tenure arrangements, and the social and political disadvantages of poverty and marginalization that typify local communities in protected areas." Within the park, authorities were able to sign agreements with local inhabitants to relocate, but these agreements led to divergent interpretations and troubled implementation, with locals feeling coerced into the relocation process.

Referring to state-sponsored resettlements to clear protected areas, Schmidt-Soltau and Brockington (2007, 2185) argue that, given the many forms of migration and degrees of compulsion, "we also have to be wary of assigning any given migration to one particular category. Consent to movement is not given or withheld simply. Consent is won by diverse mixtures of force, argument, and appeal to self-interest or higher moral values." Because voluntary migration may not be entirely voluntary, and forced migration may not be entirely forced, state responsibilities remain ambiguous.

Ambiguity of International Norms

Ambiguity regarding state obligations to host communities is compounded by the absence of clear international norms or concerns. State officials wishing to comply with international norms may learn that these norms are layered and feature uncertain enforcement. Although internal migrants are often overlooked by international actors, this is even truer for host communities. The result is less pressure on the state to attend to host communities and unclear obligations for those that try. Regarding the treatment of IDPs, the 1998 UN Guiding Principles on Internal Displacement state that IDPs "shall enjoy, in full equality, the same rights and freedoms under international and domestic law as do other persons in their country. They shall not be discriminated against in the enjoyment of any rights and freedoms on the ground that they are internally displaced" (Principle 1.1). Mobility within one's home country is a widely endorsed international doctrine. Chapter 3 notes that the Universal Declaration of Human Rights lists the right to freedom of movement and residence within one's state, along with the right to leave and return to their country. That said, the right to movement may clash with other policies, such as efforts to contain pandemics or to protect the integrity of autonomous regions or indigenous peoples, or simply to reduce the risk of conflict. The Guiding Principles also state that: "National authorities have the primary duty and responsibility to provide protection and humanitarian assistance to internally displaced persons within their jurisdiction" (Principle 3.1, UNHCR 1998). Yet, how much humanitarian assistance is enough? Betts (2010, 377) judges these Guiding Principles as a promising model for the treatment of internal migrants, yet they are non-binding "soft law."

The African Union's 2009 Kampala Convention binds ratifiers not only to proper treatment of IDPs, but also to protect maltreated IDPs in other countries. Yet, roughly half of sub-Saharan nations have not ratified the Convention, and some ratifiers, including countries home to many IDPs such as Nigeria, have yet to implement the Convention. Despite efforts to put IDPs ahead of state sovereignty, the results have not been encouraging. These international issues are examined in greater depth in Chapter 16.

Ambiguous Obligations to Host Communities

Another ambiguity exists as to how far the state ought to go to address the well-being of host populations. For officials fearful of being held accountable for the oversight of resettlement programs, their concern is most likely the well-being of migrants. This is partly because program evaluation is likely to be dominated, in the short run, by the willingness of people to migrate as the resettlement program specifies. Resettlement plans must have sufficient attraction for the population that the state wishes to move. More generally, the state must be concerned about the migrants' asset acquisition, work, and general well-being. If sponsored migrants express disappointment or leave, the resettlement is likely to be regarded as not fulfilling the most prominent rhetorical claim of helping the migrants. Thus, if sponsored migrants are "clients," the host communities are at a disadvantage if the resettlement program wrests assets and opportunities from them. Even when much effort goes into identifying and planning for potential migrants, identifying affected host communities is often difficult, let alone anticipating their economic, political, and social deprivations that call for remediation. As proponents of the resettlement initiative, state leaders may shy away from an intensive examination of the potential deprivations of the host populations and neglect, or even suppress, information about their vulnerabilities. In some cases, the state's stance that resettlement areas are essentially uninhabited (perhaps presumed when the residents are shifting cultivators or nomads) short-circuits the assessment of impacts.

Obligations toward host communities also are complicated by the crucial fact, first raised in Chapter 1, that, whether or not state-managed resettlement is voluntary for the migrants, it is rarely voluntary for the host community. Where the arrival of new communities is a fait accompli, it may be difficult for officials to negotiate with host communities and respond to their grievances. Agencies may see their responsibilities as resettling IDPs, not with long-term integration or support for host communities.

The Temporal Dimension of Accountability

The neglect of long-term thinking in planning state-managed migrations or in coping with unmanaged migrations reflects the declining relevance of future events and circumstances in the accountability of today's officials. Nobel Laureate Herbert Simon (1981, 179–180) observed that:

> The events and prospective events that enter into our value systems are all dated, and the importance we attach to them generally drops off sharply with their distance in time. For the creatures of bounded rationality that we are, this is fortunate. If our decisions depended equally upon their remote and their proximate consequences, we could never act but would be forever lost in thought. By applying a heavy discount factor to events, attenuating them with their remoteness in time and space, we reduce our problems of choice to a size commensurate with our limited computing capabilities.

This means that the attention of those holding the state accountable is likely to be focused on immediate expectations. Equally important, though, is the fact that more temporally distant outcomes are harder to trace to today's actions, as more events, policies, and circumstances intervene between today's actions and outcomes at a more distant future date. The preference for input indicators, as opposed to output or outcome indicators, also has a temporally limited dimension, as outputs and outcomes are later consequences of providing inputs. Officials can claim they are accountable for fulfilling their commitments in providing the promised inputs.

Preempting the State's Evasion of Accountability

What can stakeholders do to reduce the tendency of state officials to evade their accountability in the ways outlined above? It is useful to begin with demanding more attention to the politics of internal migration and the role of the state. If accountability depends on awareness of successes and failures, it is important to be able to counter the information concerning migration impacts that may come from state agencies intent on suppressing or distorting evaluations. By the same token, independent projections of the potential consequences of migrations can counter the rosy rhetoric that often is used to justify migrations. These projections, insofar as they paint the state as poised to engage in reckless resettlements, may be able to halt or delay unsound initiatives. In addition, these projections can be used to assess whether state officials who pursued reckless resettlements could have known better. For example, many voices spoke out against hastily formulated Amazonian resettlement initiatives, correctly predicting the ensuing chaos (Wade 2016). Although the Brazilian government largely ignored these warnings, the fact that they existed but were ignored had a chastening impact on subsequent Brazilian governments. If the government is receiving support from other entities, perhaps they can require particular actions and monitoring of these actions.

The state's support for some migrant groups at the expense of host communities can be countered by credible assessments of impacts in the target areas. The key point here is credibility. It is presumed in many contexts that NGOs dedicated to defending populations facing adverse impacts of migration are biased in favor of host communities. This presumption may be unfair, but to neutralize it, evaluations by organizations seen as more neutral may be necessary.

Spreading Accountability as an Incentive for Co-management

Insofar as state officials are preoccupied with reducing the damage of negative evaluations of problematic migration outcomes, other institutions may be in a position to participate, implicitly spreading accountability while being in a position to both help shape migration policies and monitor their consequences. For example, although the IOM was initially dedicated to technical assistance for international migration programs, it later expanded its reach to internal migration and in 1999 created the Emergency and Post-Conflict Unit to support relief activities. This puts the IOM in a much better position to understand the actions and circumstances of the states with which it participates.

Conclusions

Improved migratory governance, entailing the welfare of migrants and hosts, starts with an improved understanding of state accountability. Officials may not feel accountable to those involved, owed partly to ambiguous norms, complexity, and time horizons. If international actors and domestic groups can encourage state accountability in governing internal migration, the question becomes which policies can best regulate internal migration and support human development, to which we turn our attention in Chapter 14.

References

Betts, Alexander. 2010. Survival Migration: A New Protection Framework. *Global Governance: A Review of Multilateralism and International Organizations* 16 (3): 361–382.

Bose, Pablo. 2006. Dilemmas of Diaspora: Partition, Refugees, and the Politics of 'Home.' *Refuge: Canada's Periodical on Refugees* 23 (1): 58–68.

Dagne, Shibru Abate. 2013. Conflict and Conflict Resolution Mechanisms in Ethiopia: The Case of Gedeo and Guji Ethnic Groups. Master's Thesis: Andhra University.

Dodge, Kenneth A. 2006. Translational Science in Action: Hostile Attributional Style and the Development of Aggressive Behavior Problems. *Development and Psychopathology* 18 (3): 791–814.

Duncan, Christopher, ed. 2004. *Civilizing the Margins: Southeast Asian Government Policies for the Development of Minorities*. Ithaca: Cornell University Press.

Heider, Fritz. 1958. *The Psychology of Interpersonal Relations*. Hillsdale, NJ: Lawrence Erlbaum Associates.

Kinfemichael, Girum. 2014. The Quest for Resolution of Guji-Gedeo Conflicts in Southern Ethiopia: A Review of Mechanisms Employed, Actors and Their Effectiveness. *Ethiopian Journal of the Social Sciences and Humanities* 10 (1): 59–100.

Kivimäki, Timo. 2016. *Can Peace Research Make Peace? Lessons in Academic Diplomacy*. Oxford: Routledge.

Morris-Jung, Jason, and Robin Roth. 2010. The Blurred Boundaries of Voluntary Resettlement: A Case of Cat Tien National Park in Vietnam. *Journal of Sustainable Forestry* 29 (2–4): 202–220.

Petersen, William. 1958. A General Typology of Migration. *American Sociological Review* 23 (3): 256–266.

Schmidt-Soltau, Kai, and Dan Brockington. 2007. Protected Areas and Resettlement: What Scope for Voluntary Relocation? *World Development* 35 (12): 2182–2202.

Simon, Herbert. 1981. *The Sciences of the Artificial*. Cambridge, MA: MIT Press.

UNHCR (United Nations High Commission for Refugees). 1998. UN Guiding Principles on Internal Displacement. Geneva: UNHCR. www.unhcr.org/en-us/protection/idps/43ce1cff2/guiding-principles-internal-displacement.html.

Wade, Robert H. 2016. Boulevard to Broken Dreams, Part 1: The Polonoroeste Road Project in the Brazilian Amazon and the World Bank's Environmental and Indigenous Peoples' Norms. *Brazilian Journal of Political Economy* 36 (1): 214–230.

Wilson, Tom. 2019. Ethnic Violence in Ethiopia has Forced Nearly 3 Million People from Their Homes. *Los Angeles Times*, May 30.

Zea, Juan Esteban. 2019. How IDPs Navigate the Resettlement Process in Bogotá, Colombia. In *Internal Migration: Challenges in Governance and Integration*, eds. Shane Barter and William Ascher, 33–46. New York: Peter Lang.

CHAPTER 14

State Responses and Best Practices

A core message of this book is that the state is the essential actor in understanding internal migration, but not that its role is uniformly negative. Although many state actions covered thus far have provoked conflict, well-governed internal migration can benefit migrants, host communities, and their countries more broadly. In Chapter 5, we showed some sympathy for the state, as internal migration represents a complex policy terrain. In that spirit, this chapter demonstrates how the state can more successfully manage internal migration, reduce conflict, and promote human development.

This book would be incomplete without a discussion of best practices, but it is unclear how to frame this discussion. It is perhaps problematic to discuss "successes," as shortcomings and negative consequences exist in any policy, especially related to internal migration. In addition, ambiguity exists in terms of the appropriate distribution of benefits and burdens. Journalists, scholars, and policymakers have an easier time being pessimistic, highlighting negative practices; those discussing best practices risk being seen as naïve, partisan, or as downplaying the challenges faced by anyone losing out. Further, policy success can entail non-events—the absence of violence, protest, and other signs of failure—which obviously tend to get far less attention. In discussing some best practices in terms of internal migration governance, we do not suggest that any policy is

W. Ascher and S. J. Barter, *Moving within Borders*, Politics, Economics, and Inclusive Development, https://doi.org/10.1007/978-3-031-37549-1_14

without shortcomings. Instead, success means that policymakers avoided some of the problems identified in earlier chapters. Some yardsticks for success include avoiding violent conflict, promoting human development, and encouraging integration between migrant and host communities.

This chapter is organized according to conflict processes (see Moore 2014). First, we discuss state efforts to prevent internal migration. If internal migration can sometimes threaten human security and cause violence, then it makes sense to discuss the sensitive topic of policies that can diminish the volume of internal migration. Second, we discuss ways to prevent conflict after the migration has occurred. If internal migration is occurring, what are some best practices to minimize conflicts? Here, we focus on ways to improve state migration projects and emphasize the importance of balancing privileges among migrants and host communities. Third, we discuss ways to overcome conflict. When large-scale internal migration generates conflict, what policies can help bring groups together and limit further hostilities? Here, we look at policies that encourage separation as well as integration.

Restricting Internal Migration

A delicate balance exists among majority interests, local entitlement, and migrant rights. Deprivations and conflict may occur no matter what, which again speaks to the idea of restricting internal migration to avoid forcing the state to make painful decisions as to whom to favor when migrant-host violence erupts.

Restrictions on internal migration are sometimes explicitly directed to maintain peaceful intergroup relations and avoid ethnoreligious conflicts. Fearon and Laitin (2011, 208) observe that some civil wars result from the "inability of the state to commit to a policy of restricting all future migration into areas claimed by sons of the soil." In Indonesia, as Christian-Muslim violence flared in Maluku, partly the consequence of Muslim migration to Christian strongholds, the government blocked the departure of Muslim groups from Java that threatened to escalate the conflict (Barton 2002, 306). The Maluku conflict, as well as conflicts in Sulawesi, Papua, and East Timor, are often attributed to government transmigration programs. More accurately, they were products of enterprising non-state migrants from Sulawesi (Barter and Côté 2015; Soedirgo 2020). So-called BBM migrants (the Buginese, Butonese, and Makassarese ethnic groups from Sulawesi) had come to dominate the economies of many eastern Indonesian cities, leading to conflict with Christian leaders. As human rights organizations campaigned to stop migration to Christian areas, this amounted to a call to restrict the rights of Muslim migrants, protecting the rights of one group by limiting the rights of another. As mentioned in Chapter 3, the Singaporean government has taken an active role in shaping residency patterns to prevent ethnic conflict, requiring that all Housing Development Boards (HDBs) maintain an ethnic balance roughly equal to national proportions of Chinese, Malays, Indians, and "Others." Singapore inherited ethnic enclaves from British colonizers, which had the effect of limiting intergroup contact, and may have fueled communal riots. Although breaking up enclaves also represents an electoral strategy—avoiding minority voting blocs that could elect opposition candidates—ethnic housing quotas have also encouraged integration (Sim et al. 2003). It is not that members of different ethnic groups cannot relocate within the city-state, but instead, that government regulations prohibit relocating when doing so would lead to ethnic imbalance—an interesting example of restrictions on internal migration to avoid conflict.

Internal migration also may be restricted to protect vulnerable minorities. Countless cases around the world have seen ethnic minorities, often indigenous peoples, inundated by ethnic majority settlers. Often, states encourage internal migration, but a significant portion of settlers tend to be spontaneous migrants, as in the colonization of Mindanao by Catholic Filipinos.

Various governments have limited migration to ethnic minorities and indigenous regions, doing so in a variety of ways. In Finland's Swedish-speaking Åland Islands, domicile laws state that only locals may purchase real estate or create businesses, an effort to preserve the minority's cultural traditions. Many territorial autonomous regions enjoy some capacity to police internal and international migration as a means to preserve their identities. In China, Special Autonomous Regions with distinctive historical identities such as Hong Kong and Macau allow governments to control internal migration, utilizing checkpoints and passports to keep out mainlanders. Migration to Tibet has also been surprisingly limited (unlike migration to Xinjiang), largely owing to early bans on internal migration and more recent discrimination against those outside of their registered place of origin (Hu and Salazar 2008). In Taiwan, ethnic Chinese face restrictions in relocating to aboriginal regions in the island's interior (Selya 2004, 406). In Malaysia, the eastern states of Sabah and Sarawak employ a system of regional citizenship, which limits the ability of peninsular Malaysians to live and work in the Borneo states. As Sadiq (2009, 7) observes, this system of regional citizenship is founded upon "the preservation of a native cultural identity" as well as controlling jobs and resources.

In the 1990s, the Indian government reintroduced migration controls and returned land ownership to local leaders (Reuveny 2008). We also see restricted migration to indigenous regions within Latin America. In 2009, natives of Rapa Nui held a series of protests against Chilean migration to the island, culminating in restrictions to limit settlers. These laws were later struck down by the Chilean Supreme Court because Chilean citizens possess the right to internal migration. Shortly afterward, a referendum in Rapa Nui and local government protest led to new Chilean laws to provide exceptions for indigenous regions (Young 2019).

Internal migration may also be restricted to preserve delicate ecosystems. Although many governments have used environmental protection as a pretext to restrict the movement of indigenous communities for the benefit of forestry and plantation companies, legitimate reasons also exist as to why internal migration might be restricted for the sake of ecology. Sometimes ecological restrictions exist to protect residents. Regions prone to flooding or fires may be declared off-limits to new settlement (Hunter 2005). In other cases, migration may be limited for the sake of protected species or environments. This is a common challenge in sub-Saharan African countries, where wildlife refuges have been threatened by growing populations in dire need of resources, demanding a more nuanced, approach to sustainable nature reserves (Neumann 2001). The Galapagos Islands are subject to stringent residential restrictions by Ecuadorian authorities, deporting thousands of internal migrants from the fragile ecosystem; only those born on the islands or married to locals may reside here (Jones 2013). In China, minority leaders have worked to restrict ethnic Han migration to preserve fragile local ecosystems, as in the grasslands of Inner Mongolia or drought-prone regions further west (Côté 2014, 121).

Another set of restrictions on internal migration involves urbanization. As covered in Chapter 7, urban migration represents a strategy of upward mobility; however, it can also lead to conflicts with natives and other migrants, as well as generate informal settlements such as shantytowns and add to congestion. As a result, many governments limit migration to cities. For some, this may echo colonial or authoritarian practice, with colonizers creating cities and towns as administrative centers, working to keep them free from colonized peoples in the name of 'sanitation' and control. In Papua New Guinea, post-independence leaders have maintained colonial-era controls on urbanization. In blocking urban migration, leaders cite the need to limit conflict and preserve rural Papuan culture. This has been carried out through vagrancy laws, evictions, and repatriation to rural areas (Koczberski et al. 2001).

Returning to China's hukou system, Wallace (2014, 3–4) credits restrictions on urban migration as a factor in maintaining China's stability and prosperity, emphasizing the "political importance of the location of citizens within a territory"; and that "giant improvised communities found at the heart of other cities in developing countries are not to be found in China." Hukou has hardly been a static, entirely oppressive policy, shifting to an incentive-based system of permits and fines, and concentrating on limiting migration to unstable cities while allowing it in more stable, high-growth areas (Wallace 2014, 143). China has also tried to reduce the need to migrate by lowering rural taxes and investing in rural infrastructure. Thus, although controversial, restricting rural poor and protecting urban areas, hukou-related migration restrictions in China from the late 1990s onward can be seen as successfully avoiding many problems associated with mass urban migration.

Instead of restricting migration through legal impediments and denying social services, other policies can diminish the need for large-scale urban migration. One reason for mass urban migration in developing countries is that governments tend to prioritize economic development in major cities and neglect rural development. To reduce urban migration, one approach is to promote rural development; bringing education, jobs, investment, and modernity to rural communities. This is hardly a novel idea and is no easy task, but the importance of rural development is clear (Richardson 1987; Limpanonda 2015; Lucas 2021, 406). Although this is not the place to discuss the many approaches to rural development, rural economic specialization is promising in some contexts. Many countries have taken inspiration from Japanese programs to stem urbanization such as "One Village, One Product." In Thailand, leaders created the "One Tambon, One Product" policy to encourage local production of handicrafts and exports (Natsuda et al. 2012). Another means to stem urbanization is to upgrade the living standards in rural areas through better healthcare and education. In Thailand and Indonesia in the 2000s, rural healthcare played an especially important role in making rural regions livable. Again, this is an important feature of China's hukou reforms, reducing the government's "urban bias" by transferring resources to rural provinces, opening up schools and clinics, and "cutting the fiscal burden placed on the rural population" (Wallace 2014, 127).

A related strategy to avoid some of the problems inherent in urbanization, also reprised in Chapter 7, is to promote secondary urban centers or satellite cities to absorb rural migrants. Many developing countries feature a single primary city, leaving few options for prospective urban migrants. Creating secondary cities can help mitigate some of these problems, deconcentrating wealth through regional capitals and new cities (Rondinelli et al. 1983). Migrants might prefer nearby cities to more distant metropolises, remaining closer to kinship and support networks. Just as many international migrants begin as internal migrants, Long (2008) finds that in Peru, many migrants to metropolitan Lima initially began by migrating to nearby regional capitals, traveling further only after it became clear that opportunities were limited. Zimmer et al. (2020) find that secondary urban areas are growing across southern African countries, bringing more diffuse economic growth. That said, secondary cities may flounder if not provided with sufficient administrative power or funding, with countries such as Kenya needing to devolve power if secondary cities are to relieve the strain from capitals (Otiso 2005).

Less coercive policies to reduce urban migration through reinvesting resources can present challenges, especially if the growth or rural areas and smaller cities alters power dynamics within a given country. There is a relationship between the concentration of power and the concentration of people, and as a result, the dispersion of people will be connected to a dispersion of power. In response, an alternative to geographically separate new cities is to develop satellite cities at the edges of metropolises, easing the burden of urban cores while containing power near it. Either way, the global trend toward decentralization and the creation of alternative centers helps ensure that power is less concentrated in metropolitan capitals, thus limiting the most severe population congestion.

In summary, despite such policies violating important freedoms, many countries prevent internal migration to some extent. Restrictions on urbanization have achieved some success in preventing problems associated with urbanization. We do not advocate for restricting internal migration in general, but instead suggest that measures be considered in specific circumstances for specific goals, such as preserving minority rights, protecting sensitive ecosystems, or preventing conflict. However, such policies may antagonize people who believe that their opportunities are unfairly limited. These problems call for shifting the focus from preventing internal migration to preventing problems arising from internal migration.

Preventing Conflicts

What can be done to prevent destructive conflict, especially if state leaders are unwilling or unable to channel or limit internal migration? This section surveys policies that can reduce conflict, improve state-led migration, and prioritize the rights of native host communities.

Reforming State-led Migration

After being heralded by development experts in the 1960s and 70s, extensive state-led resettlement became the target of widespread criticism, seen as a form of social engineering that generated conflict, corruption, ecological damage, and cultural loss. However, criticisms of state-led migration may have gone too far, misattributing blame for a variety of problems on state resettlement and failing to differentiate between state-sponsored migrants from spontaneous migrants (Barter and Côté 2015). Although not all states will seek to redistribute people from densely to sparsely populated areas as a matter of policy, many states have to relocate their people following conflicts or disasters. State-led migration is controversial, but sometimes necessary, demanding consideration of site selection, migrant selection, and support systems. As Lujala et al. (2020) argue, continued climate change will increase the need for states to relocate communities from at-risk or infertile areas, suggesting that state-managed migration may become even more pressing in the coming years, necessitating accurate lessons from previous experiences.

Selecting appropriate sites for state-led migration or resettlement is an important first step. In Indonesia, critics have asserted that transmigration sent migrants to rebellious regions to colonize and prevent separatism. Some observers have asserted that Indonesian transmigration programs targeted "problematic regions such as Aceh, erstwhile East Timor, Papua, as well as regions with international borders" (Tanasaldy 2012, 39–40). As noted, the vast majority of transmigrants were sent to parts of Sumatra that lacked widespread conflict, such as North Sumatra, South Sumatra, and Lampung. Even in Kalimantan, Sulawesi, and Papua, which received transmigrants in the 1980s and later witnessed violent migratory conflicts, it was mostly spontaneous migrants who were targeted, not state transmigrants. Part of the reason for this, as mentioned earlier, is that spontaneous migrants went to towns, clashing with local leaders for political and economic power, while state-sponsored transmigrants tended to be relocated to rural areas. In Central Kalimantan and Papua, Javanese were sent to reclaimed wetlands and floodplains that were previously sparsely inhabited (Hardjono 1986). Central Kalimantan experienced widespread Javanese transmigration, now 20 percent of the provincial population, but despite violent conflicts, Javanese were not targeted, as they are more remote and their agricultural work in marginal lands tends to be seen as beneficial to native groups.

One lesson from Indonesian *transmigrasi* is that state planners can usefully focus on relocations to rural areas. Of course, moving people to sparsely inhabited, peripheral regions represents a major undertaking, demanding infrastructure and long-term support. Remote sites with low population densities require the construction of roads and other infrastructure to support migrants, services that must also help native residents. Early studies of colonial state-led resettlement in Sumatra suggest that poor planning can determine success or failure of resettlement projects. The Dutch colonial government did not fully consider irrigation, health care, roads, or schools, and wrongly assumed that a Javanese farmer skilled at cultivating rice paddies would also possess the skills to transform new lands into rice fields; this led to the earliest migration sites facing high mortality rates and desertion (Pelzer 1945, 194). Pelzer emphasizes the importance of relocating farmers to areas with similar soils and ecological conditions. In a more recent study, Bazzi et al. (2016) find that agroclimatic similarity between out- and in-migration sites has a strong effect on long-term agricultural yields. Peripheral regions often have poor soils, sometimes producing single harvests and then becoming exhausted. As a result, officials must research agricultural prospects before relocation, begin migration processes slowly, and provide long-term support, which may include productivity-enhancing inputs such as fertilizer and improved or varied crops.

Another challenge relates to selecting potential migrants for government migration programs. Pelzer (1945, 193) notes that initial transmigration programs placed recruitment in the hands of district officials, who tended to use programs as opportunities to rid their areas of undesirables that were ill-suited to agricultural work. Recruitment systems were necessary to make new settlements work, bringing in young farmers and their families, taking into account the traits of both individuals as well as ethnic groups.

Historical examples allow us to understand the long-term importance of ethnoreligious compatibility between migrants and hosts. Lampung, at the southern tip of Sumatra, has received a larger share of transmigrants than any other Indonesian province. This was selected by Dutch colonial authorities as the first transmigration site for Javanese migrants in 1911. After decades of failed projects due to poor planning and recruitment, large-scale migration commenced in 1932, with 60,000 migrants resettled by 1941 (Pelzer 1945, 214). With independence, Indonesian planners continued to send Javanese migrants to Lampung, with Javanese soon comprising two-thirds of the provincial population. There have been no major conflicts between native Lampungese and Javanese transmigrants, groups that are increasingly integrated. However, there have been conflicts between Lampungese and Balinese transmigrants (Côté 2019). This can be explained by two factors. First, Javanese transmigrants and native Lampungese are Muslim, making it easier for migrants to intermarry with locals and integrate into the host society. Meanwhile Hindu Balinese, with different kindship structures and marriage rites, have been slower to integrate. A second factor is that the *transmigrasi* scattered Javanese peasant farmers throughout rural areas, including in Lampung, motivating them to integrate into local society. In contrast, Balinese were disaster IDPs, arriving in Lampung as entire villages, maintaining a sense of collective identity and their own leaders. Across Indonesia, migratory conflicts tended to involve unsponsored migrants in urban areas or disaster IDPs arriving as entire villages with different religious identities, as in native Muslim-Balinese Hindu clashes in Lampung and native Christian-Makianese Muslim conflicts in North Maluku. Consideration of cultural and vocational compatibilities often are central for integration and the avoidance of conflict.

In addition to selecting sustainable rural sites and disadvantaged classes that share a religion with host communities, states may restrict spontaneous migration that tends to follow state-led transmigration, especially when this involves migrant co-ethnics bound for urban areas. We have seen that although Indonesia's transmigration rightly has many critics and ecological shortcomings (Fearnside 1997), state transmigrants, namely ethnic Javanese peasants, have generally not been involved in migratory conflicts. Instead, spontaneous migration, either to specific transmigration sites or nearby towns, can be the most problematic. In colonial Mindanao, Pelzer (1945, 139) suggests that the arrival of spontaneous migrants to relocation sites, groups that then demanded state support, made effective management "difficult if not impossible." Unmanaged Christian settlers were encouraged by presidential decrees, but upon arrival, faced uncertainty. These additional migrants would draw funds from state migration programs, compete with official migrants, and contribute to ethnic violence as those lacking state land occupied Muslim lands. Abinales (2004) suggests that migrant-settler relations were initially amicable, with native Moros and Lumad welcoming investment that came with state migration projects. This changed with the growth of spontaneous migration, with these arrivals clashing with both natives and state migrants. Classified as squatters, many resorted to land-grabbing and/or joined local militias, a shift which forever damaged migrant-host community relations (Abinales 2004, 101). Although limiting the right of domestic migration is controversial, it may be less so if restrictions are limited to specific areas developed by the state, barring non-state migrants to make for more effective state-led resettlement projects.

Once a new community has been settled by migrants, planners must work to ensure its long-term economic viability. In several Southeast Asian countries, Pelzer (1945, 193) finds that early sites provided support that was too generous, namely grants and free equipment, attracting profit-seekers with short-term interests and leading migrants to waste funds on drinking. Later, more successful policies provided long-term support in terms of markets, and many partnered with major firms to ensure their purchase of crops such as coffee, rubber, palm oil, and more.

One largely successful, but rarely discussed case of state-led migration is Malaysia's Federal Land Development Authority (FELDA). Established in 1956 to resettle landless Malays from Pahang, FELDA oversaw the creation of an estimated 441 communities. Seen by some as "one of the most successful land resettlement initiatives" of the Cold War Era (Barau and Said 2016, 423; see also Sutton 1989), FELDA is considered successful largely because of its integrated approach. The agency was part of larger state-wide development plans, providing continued farming and business education for settlers as well as linking FELDA communities to large agribusinesses. FELDA operates its own schools, offering scholarships for pioneer children to study abroad. The system has evolved its roles over time, to the point that by the late 1990s, it became more of a rural development agency than a migration body and previous settlers are now farm managers hiring seasonal/foreign labor. FELDA communities can gain grants related to using new technology and social sustainability methods (Barau and Said 2016, 425). FELDA is open to important ecological critiques, as these smallholder settlements are primary producers of the country's palm oil exports. Yet, the integrated, long-term FELDA model must be regarded as a successful case of state-managed internal migration.

Rewarding Host Communities

It should be clear that long-term state support is crucial to the success of migrant communities. However, if migrant-host conflicts are typically the result of deprivations and insecurity among host communities, then it stands to reason that states can reduce conflict by supporting those already residing in target regions.

Supporting host communities to avoid conflict can be accomplished by supporting elites as well as ordinary people. One could cynically perceive this as paying off or coopting locals, but this can represent an important conflict-avoidance mechanism. As Fearon and Laitin (2011, 208) observe, avoiding migratory conflicts can involve "buying off violent opposition." Many Sons of the Soil conflicts involve elite competition over resources and electoral support. We know that sustained violence involves conflict entrepreneurs, persons who frame grievances and mobilize armed groups. There is something to be said for providing incentives for host elites to desist from instigating conflict, although this strategy cannot be pursued in isolation from wider policies to provide assurances to host communities (Brass 1991, 25–30). Reserving some power for host leaders can reassure the host community as a whole, as well as limit the creation of potential conflict entrepreneurs. In the Patani region of southern Thailand, years of assimilation, migration, and armed conflict were ameliorated in the 1980s by a concerted strategy of coopting Malay elites. Thai leaders provided off-budget revenue for Malay elites and brought them into political networks, with the Muslim Wadah faction becoming part of national political parties. The cornerstone of this policy was the Southern Border Provinces Administration Center, which provided venues and funding for ethnic Malay leaders. It is no coincidence that the Patani conflict reignited shortly after Prime Minister Thaksin Shinawatra, believing that he could not control it, disbanded the Center and marginalized local elites (Wheeler 2010).

Similarly, in the southern Philippines, the national government has long worked to coopt Muslim elites, with some of the strongest state support coming from Muslim politicians. Before Philippine independence, American colonizers overcame initial Moro resistance by providing funding opportunities for various datus (Abinales 2004, 57). Moro secessionism began as the Philippines dismantled these systems and migrant Christian elites mounted successful electoral competition against Muslim leaders (McKenna 1998). Muslim elites rebelled because they were marginalized, with Marcos responding by supporting Muslim elites to diminish the conflict, coopting Muslim elites one by one. This strategy was only partially successful, as the state aligned with corrupt Muslim politicians just as a new group of Islamic leaders ascended in Moro society, leaders who became the core of the rebel movement. Subsequent peace agreements with Moro separatists essentially recognized these new Moro elites, providing rebel leaders with control over local governments and resource revenue. Many peace agreements essentially involve rewarding and coopting rebel leaders, promising them the power to overcome rebellion.

Another case of elite cooptation can be found in Tibet, where the Chinese government shifted policies in the 1980s to reduce the number of Han government leaders and cultivate a class of pliable Tibetan provincial leaders. Tibet and other ethnic minority regions, such as Inner Mongolia, have some of the country's highest levels of party membership and public-sector employment, as China has worked to create a loyal class of minority elites (Ang 2016).

Another way to satisfy the elites of host communities is to recognize and perhaps strengthen systems of informal power. Encouraging migration among poorer communities, and discouraging it among more powerful actors, helps ensure that internal migration serves poverty-alleviation roles as well as avoids inter-elite conflicts. This requires eschewing the strategy of sending in higher-status migrants to "civilize" local people—a strategy that is problematic in any event. If anything, states should encourage migrants to adapt to host communities. Although state support for local elites who can incorporate migrants within their networks can be criticized as strengthening local elites, this can provide host communities respect and reassurance in the face of migration.

The effectiveness of rewarding local elites could be enhanced by pairing it with benefits for local communities as a whole. This may come in the form of development projects or cash transfers, or perhaps extending special benefits and protection for local people. To avoid deprivations to migrant groups, it is useful to provide additional support for hosts. In many countries, disadvantaged native communities may receive tax breaks, special welfare payments, or special titles to land ownership. It may be useful to open new schools and clinics that may benefit host communities, but also make clear that these new services have been established alongside the arrival of migrant groups. Studying refugee settlements in Tanzania, Whitaker (2002) shows how the early reduction of access to schools, clinics, fresh water, and food caused tensions with hosts, but as international actors worked with the government to provide new services, these tensions were reduced. Here, policies "reflected a deliberate donor decision to compensate Tanzanians collectively for the burden of hosting refugees" (Whitaker 2002, 343). A UNHCR study highlights the importance of recognizing and rewarding host societies to counteract potential tensions with IDPs, noting successes in donors building drop-in communities and legal aid centers that can be used by hosts as well as IDPs (Davies 2012, 14, 34). It is also useful for those overseeing resettlement camps to work with local businesses, generating new opportunities for farmers, drivers, restaurants, and other businesses within the nearby host community.

Various global organizations have lobbied for special indigenous rights, especially the ILO and UN, whose 2007 Declaration on the Rights of Indigenous Peoples asserts a right for indigenous peoples to self-govern and manage their affairs. In the past decade, several Latin American countries have recognized special indigenous rights. Bolivia was one of the first such countries, to respond to indigenous poverty and activism by recognizing ancestral lands and providing natives special tenure rights. Similar provisions have also been enacted in Brazil, Colombia, Costa Rica, Panama, Paraguay, and Peru (Roldán-Ortega 2004). In Ghana, Côté and Mitchell (2015, 664) attribute the absence of conflict in agricultural regions, despite extensive migration, to the fact that "indigenes continue to wield economic and political power over migrants." Here, natives control customary land-tenure regimes that force migrants to adapt to local norms. The authors conclude that conflict can be avoided where native communities maintain power, or at least migrants are not able to dominate native groups.

A related set of policies involves encouraging migrant integration with host communities, specifically through language and education. In regions with distinctive identities, especially those enjoying political autonomy, the state can encourage migrants to learn local languages, culture, and history. Research on international migration finds that integration depends in large part on providing opportunities to learn about the host society and its language, and evidence suggests that this is equally true subnationally (Goodman 2010). Well-managed state migration involves pre-departure and continued education for migrant groups, not only about agriculture, but also about host societies. Seymour and Brzezinski (2019) have shown that, when it is politically expedient, even weak states can provide a range of programs and incentives to encourage integration (and when it is not expedient, can block integration). Integration policies must support native culture, providing hosts with security and respect in the face of migration.

Resolving Conflicts

Once large-scale migration has occurred, and conflict has unfolded between migrant and host communities, what are the means to overcome conflict and avoid future clashes? This section discusses policy options in terms of separating migrants and natives, thus promoting short-term stability by promoting separation or integration, depending on the context. These options of course may be pursued alongside the abovementioned prevention efforts; for example, if there is a conflict, then emergency restrictions on migration may help slow its spread.

Separation

For host communities, one of the first reactions to large-scale internal migration may be to demand that migrants return to their places of origin, through voluntary or, in extreme situations, forced repatriation. This is sometimes a possibility, especially if migrants have not resided in their new homes for very long, have moved because of temporary conditions (e.g., natural disasters), and have somewhere viable to return. Many internal migrants, including rural-to-urban migrants, or persons moving to a country's periphery for work, do return home in times of unrest. Especially for more mobile, wealth-seeking migrants, return represents an important strategy in the face of conflict. For poorer migrants relocating in larger groups, this option is more limited. Poor migrants may have little to return to, especially IDPs whose homes have been destroyed by war, disasters, or development. It may even be the case that migrants have left their homes due to the migration of other groups. For instance, Moros in the southern Philippines have moved into indigenous Lumad territories, having been squeezed out of their home territory by Catholic migration, so that Moros would not have a place to return if Lumads demanded it.

Many migrant communities develop local roots. Even though hosts might perceive groups as alien, and observers may label them as such, migrants may possess strong ties to their new communities. This is especially true of the children of migrants. It is telling that in cases such as the southern Philippines or Indonesia, many observers refer to Christians or Javanese as "migrants," even though most are locally born, many descended from colonial-era migrants. We should not overlook the possibility of repatriating migrants in response to conflict, but this is often not an appropriate or even feasible response.

Separation may be advisable when migrant groups relocate to new regions, either spontaneously or with state support. When internal migration does not work out, migrants often continue onward in search of a better home. For example, many migrants to the Brazilian Amazon moved from one site to another as their farming failed. Here, the state can play a role in planning new relocation sites and managing migration. Spontaneous, unplanned migration can be problematic, as migrants may relocate to peripheral lands or to regions where problems recur. State relocation programs may be less controversial, managing an existing uprooted community instead of being responsible for uprooting them in the first place. State roles could include maintaining temporary IDP camps, seeking suitable relocation sites, overseeing relocation, and then supporting migrants in their new homes. To reiterate the points made in the previous section, states must support new host communities to ensure that tensions and insecurities do not cause new conflicts. State-managed internal migration thus represents a potential solution to the conflict, not simply a cause.

Sometimes state-led resettlement can be local; instead of searching for new settlement sites in other provinces, governments may seek to separate groups into neighboring districts. Administrative separation may be perceived as a potential conflict-prevention mechanism. In most cases, however, local administrative separation should be a last resort, as it limits integration among groups that may have continued interactions in settings other than a residence, without the opportunities to share experiences (Brown and Hewstone 2005). Further, host communities may be unlikely to agree to have any territory set aside. For groups that have experienced conflict, locals may see this as necessary; administrative separation may help to avoid intergroup competition, provide elites with secure administrative posts, and allow groups to self-govern.

Administrative separation may involve truncating native lands, demanding that natives recognize the permanent occupation of some of their territory. As a result, this strategy only can work in cases where natives and migrants are territorially concentrated and tensions are long-standing. In Indonesia, decentralization has brought with it rapid growth in administrative regions, with the number of districts/cities swelling from 300 in 2001 to over 500 by 2017. Known locally as *pemekaran* (blossoming), this administrative mitosis has been driven by competition over access to state resources, but has also served to diminish ethnic tensions, including native-migrant divisions (Kimura 2010). In the Indian state of Andhra Pradesh, conflicts between indigenous Telanganas and migrant Andhras were defused when the national government brokered a deal that would reserve jobs and provide autonomy for native peoples. The Indian Supreme Court struck down these laws as unconstitutional, but subsequent decrees and reforms provided natives with their own administrative units and special funding for their governments. Telangana attained statehood in 2014, helping to overcome a long-standing Sons of the Soil conflict (Benbabaali 2016). Separating migrant and local groups is not ideal, but in the face of sustained conflict, represents an important way to manage ethnic tensions.

Integration

Compared to separation, a more advisable response—and in some cases the only plausible option—is to attempt to overcome tensions and build a sense of shared community. This involves integration, a key mechanism for conflict prevention and resolution. Of course, integration is not easy. It involves a fundamental question: Integration to what? It is likely that if migrants represent the dominant national culture, states, and migrants will champion integration into that culture, while host communities will demand integration on their own terms. Once conflict has flared, both sides must compromise, integrating into some spheres but perhaps preserving distinction in others. In some contexts, host community interests should be prioritized, as migrants should be convinced to accept some local cultural practices.

In the wake of migratory conflicts, it is important to encourage integration through peace processes of some sort. Unlike cases of interstate conflict or conflict between organized rebels and state forces, we should not expect formal peace negotiations between two groups to be effective. Most migrant-host conflicts are not fought by hierarchical, cohesive armed groups, but instead by collections of youths, gangs, sports clubs, and more, with violence flaring sporadically (McRae 2013). Because Sons of the Soil conflicts involve members of broader communities, there is a need to pursue more symbolic, joint ceremonies involving trusted community leaders—elders, religious leaders, and other such figures—to show goodwill and build intergroup trust.

One potential model is the Malino Accords in Indonesia. The 2001 Malino Declaration took place in Poso, Central Sulawesi, where violence between indigenous Christians and migrant Muslims left over one thousand dead. The Indonesian government encouraged both sides to select 25 community leaders for intergroup talks. The talks led to a mutual declaration of forgiveness, the creation of community-led disarmament and resettlement commissions, and a series of religious ceremonies. Religious leaders made public statements focusing on common values and scriptural teachings, such as Muslim veneration for Isa (Jesus), while also working to educate each other on religious differences through interfaith organizations (al Qurtuby 2013). With funds from the central government, the Malino process was steeped in ritual, with both sides taking part in communal feasts and several loosely related village ceremonies (Lowry and Littlejohn 2006). The process revived a traditional practice called *pela*, in which village clan and vocational alliances were revived to connect previously warring villages (Bräuchler 2015). The Malino process was surprisingly successful, inspiring the 2002 Malino II Accords in a different migrant conflict in Maluku. International agencies have since recommended this model elsewhere, including for Buddhist-Muslim violence in Myanmar (Della-Giacoma 2012).

Various institutions can encourage intergroup cooperation. Many sites of migrant-native conflict feature elements of localized consociationalism, restricting electoral competition by reserving positions to ethnic groups to provide guarantees to minority groups. Several ethnically divided societies have evolved systems in which political candidates partner with politicians from different ethnic groups. In Nigeria, candidates select running mates from different regions to win votes, with the party chairperson typically chosen from ethnic groups not represented by these candidates to broaden their appeal (Reilly 2006). Less formally, in major world cities such as Jakarta, Manila, and Mexico City, it is common for mayoral candidates to select rural migrants as running mates, an effort to appeal to important voters, while bringing groups together. Tomsa (2009) notes that across Indonesia, especially in regions home to migrant-native conflicts, subnational elections have been contested by candidate pairs across ethnoreligious divides. In Maluku, which suffered from migration-based Christian-Muslim violence, all gubernatorial candidate pairs in the 2008 election were mixed religious tickets. Similarly, in Riau and Lampung provinces, it is standard practice for parties to ensure a native-migrant pairing in local elections (Côté and Mitchell 2016, 666). Similar patterns are also found in Kalimantan and Lombok (Aspinall 2011, 303).

Along with executive selection, electoral systems can also be engineered to diminish ethnic tensions. Proportional representation typically features coalition governments and fragmented party systems, limiting efficiency but providing broad representation. Reilly (2006) shows how proportional representation can go even further in divided societies, with laws dictating the ethnic composition of party lists and the creation of aggregative parties. Ranked-list systems have been credited with encouraging peace in systems as disparate as Ireland and Papua New Guinea, allowing voters of each group to rank their ethnic parties highest, but then rank more liberal parties from other groups higher than radical rival groups. If all communities vote in this way, it effectively pushes out extremists, leading to more moderate governments. Although electoral competition may stoke migrant-host tensions, some institutional modifications can help bring groups together, integrating migrants and natives into a shared political community (Wilkinson 2004).

Conclusions

Although earlier chapters emphasized what goes wrong, this chapter has discussed relatively successful cases and policies in governing internal migration. It has emphasized best practices, even if no policy can ever be seen as unproblematic or fully successful. Several mechanisms exist to avoid or overcome tensions generated by large-scale migratory flows. The state plays a key role in promoting the rights of native peoples, avoiding the colonization of host communities while protecting migrant rights. The state may be able to provide aid, relocate people, promote economic growth and employment opportunities, change administrative borders, and enact language policies that can help quell tensions. Even so, states in developing countries may struggle to perform these roles. Developing states need help, including non-state domestic actors (Chapter 15) and international actors (Chapter 16).

References

Abinales, Patricio N. 2004. *Making Mindanao: Cotabato and Davao in the Formation of the Philippine Nation-State*. Manila: Ateneo de Manila University Press.

Al Qurtuby, Sumanto. 2013. Peacebuilding in Indonesia: Christian–Muslim Alliances in Ambon Island. *Islam and Christian–Muslim Relations* 24.3: 349–367.

Ang, Yuen Y. 2016. Co-optation and Clientelism: Nested Distributive Politics in China's Single-Party Dictatorship. *Studies in Comparative International Development* 51 (3): 235–256.

Aspinall, Edwards. 2011. Democratization and Ethnic Politics in Indonesia: Nine Theses. *Journal of East Asian Studies* 11 (2): 289–319.

Barau, Aliyu Salisu, and Ismail Said. 2016. From Goodwill to Good Deals: FELDA Land Resettlement Scheme and the Ascendancy of the Landless Poor in Malaysia. *Land Use Policy* 54: 423–431.

Barter, Shane, and Isabelle Côté. 2015. Strife of the Soil? Unsettling Transmigrant Conflicts in Indonesia. *Journal of Southeast Asian Studies* 46 (1): 60–85.

Barter, Shane Joshua. 2015. 'Second-Order' Ethnic Minorities in Asian Secessionist Conflicts: Problems and Prospects. *Asian Ethnicity* 16 (2): 123–135.

Barton, Greg. 2002. *Abdurrahman Wahid: Muslim Democrat, Indonesian President: A View from the Inside*. Honolulu: University of Hawaii Press.

Bazzi, Samuel, Arya Gaduh, Alexander D. Rothenberg, and Maisy Wong. 2016. Skill Transferability, Migration, and Development: Evidence from Population Resettlement in Indonesia. *American Economic Review* 106 (9): 2658–2698.

Benbabaali, Dalel. 2016. From the Peasant Armed Struggle to the Telangana State: Changes and Continuities in a South Indian Region's Uprisings. *Contemporary South Asia* 24 (2): 184–196.

Brass, Paul R. 1991. *Ethnicity and Nationalism*. London: Sage.

Bräuchler, Birgit. 2015. *The Cultural Dimension of Peace: Decentralization and Reconciliation in Indonesia*. London: Springer.

Brown, Rupert, and Miles Hewstone. 2005. An Integrative Theory of Intergroup Contact. *Advances in Experimental Social Psychology* 37: 255–343.
Côté, Isabelle, and Matthew I. Mitchell. 2015. Elections and 'Sons of the Soil' Conflict Dynamics in Africa and Asia. *Democratization* 23 (4): 657–677.
Côté, Isabelle. 2014. Internal Migration and the Politics of Place: A Comparative Analysis of China and Indonesia. *Asian Ethnicity* 15 (1): 111–129.
Côté, Isabelle. 2019. 'Adopting Migrants as Brothers and Sisters'—Fictive Kinship as a Mechanism of Conflict Resolution and Conflict Prevention in Lampung, Indonesia. In *Internal Migration: Challenges in Governance and Integration*, eds. Shane Barter and William Ascher, 97–111. New York: Peter Lang.
Davies, Anne. 2012. *IDPs in Host Families and Host Communities: Assistance for Hosting Arrangements*. Geneva: UNHCR.
Della-Giacoma, Jim. 2012. *What Could Myanmar Learn from Indonesia? The Malino Accord*. Zürich: ETH Zürich.
Fearnside, Philip. 1997. Transmigration in Indonesia: Lessons from Its Environmental and Social Impacts. *Environmental Management* 21 (4): 553–570.
Fearon, James D., and David D. Laitin. 2011. Sons of the Soil, Migrants, and Civil War. *World Development* 39 (2): 199–211.
Goodman, Sara Wallace. 2010. Integration Requirements for Integration's Sake? Identifying, Categorising and Comparing Civic Integration Policies. *Journal of Ethnic and Migration Studies* 36 (5): 753–772.
Hardjono, Joan. 1986. "Transmigration: Looking to the Future." *Bulletin of Indonesian Economic Studies* 22 (2): 28–53.
Hu, Xiaojiang, and Miguel A. Salazar. 2008. Ethnicity, Rurality and Status: Hukou and the Institutional and Cultural Determinants of Social Status in Tibet. *The China Journal* 60: 1–21.
Hunter, Lori M. 2005. Migration and Environmental Hazards. *Population and Environment*. 26 (4): 273–302.
Jones, Peter S.J.. 2013. A Governance Analysis of the Galapagos Marine Reserve. *Marine Policy* 41: 65–71.
Keating, Michael. 1996. *Nations against the State: The New Politics of Nationalism in Quebec, Catalonia and Scotland*. London: Palgrave Macmillan.
Kimura, Ehito. 2010. Proliferating Provinces: Territorial Politics in Post-Suharto Indonesia. *South East Asia Research* 18 (3): 415–449.
Koczberski, Gina, George N. Curry, and John Connell. 2001. Full Circle or Spiralling Out of Control? State Violence and the Control of Urbanisation in Papua New Guinea. *Urban Studies* 38 (11): 2017–2036.
Limpanonda, Suphannada. 2015. Provincial Disparities, Convergence and Effects on Poverty in Thailand. *The Singapore Economic Review* 60 (2): 1–21.
Long, Norman. 2008. Translocal Livelihoods, Networks of Family and Community, and Remittances in Central Peru. In *Migration and Development Within*

and Across Borders: Research and Policy Perspectives on Internal and International Migration, eds. Josh DeWind and Jennifer Holdaway, 39–70. Geneva: IOM.

Lowry, C.S, and S.W. Littlejohn. 2006. Dialogue and the Discourse of Peacebuilding in Maluku, Indonesia. *Conflict Resolution Quarterly*. 23: 409–426.

Lucas, Robert E.B.. 2021. *Crossing the Divide: Rural to Urban Migration in Developing Countries*. Oxford: Oxford University Press and KNOWMAD.

Lujala, Päivi., Sosina Bezu, Ivar Kolstad, Minhaj Mahmud, and Arne Wiig. 2020. How do Host-Migrant Proximities Shape Attitudes toward Internal Climate Migrants. *Global Environmental Change* 65: 1–15.

McKenna, Thomas M. 1998. *Muslim Rulers and Rebels: Everyday Politics and Armed Separatism in the Southern Philippines*. Berkeley, CA: University of California Press.

McRae, Dave. 2013. *A Few Poorly Organized Men: Interreligious Violence in Poso, Indonesia*. Leiden: Brill Publishers.

Moore, Christopher W. 2014. *The Mediation Process: Practical Strategies for Resolving Conflict*. San Francisco: Wiley and Sons, Fourth Edition.

Natsuda, Kaoru, Kunio Igusa, Aree Wiboonpongse, and John Thoburn. 2012. One Village One Product-Rural Development Strategy in Asia: The Case of OTOP in Thailand. *Canadian Journal of Development Studies/revue Canadienne D'études Du Développement* 33 (3): 369–385.

Neumann, Roderick P. 2001. Africa's 'Last Wilderness': Reordering Space for Political and Economic Control in Colonial Tanzania. *Africa* 71 (4): 641–665.

Otiso, Kefa M. 2005. Kenya's Secondary Cities Growth Strategy at a Crossroads: Which Way Forward? *GeoJournal* 62 (1): 117–128.

Pelzer, Karl J. 1945. *Pioneer Settlement in the Asiatic Tropics*. New York: American Geographical Society Special Publication No. 29.

Reilly, Benjamin. 2006. Political Parties and Political Engineering in Divided Societies. *Democratization* 13 (5): 811–827.

Reuveny, Rafael. 2008. Ecomigration and Violent Conflict: Case Studies and Public Policy Implications. *Human Ecology* 36 (1): 1–13.

Richardson, Harry W. 1987. Whither National Urban Policy in Developing Countries? *Urban Studies* 24 (3): 227–244.

Roldán-Ortega, Roque. 2004. *Models for Recognizing Indigenous Land Rights in Latin America*. Washington, DC: World Bank.

Rondinelli, Dennis, John R. Nellis, and G. Shabbir Cheema. 1983. *Decentralization in Developing Countries: A Review of Recent Experience*. Washington, DC: World Bank.

Sadiq, Kamal. 2009. When Being 'Native' is Not Enough: Citizens as Foreigners in Malaysia. *Asian Perspective* 33 (1): 5–32.

Selya, Roger Mark. 2004. *Development and Demographic Change in Taiwan*. Singapore: World Scientific.

Seymour, Lee, and Marek Brzezinski. 2019. Unsettled States: Displacement, Governance, and Integration in the Southern Caucasus. In *Internal Migration: Challenges in Governance and Integration*, eds. Shane Barter and William Ascher, 47–62. New York: Peter Lang.

Sim, Loo Lee, Shi Mang Yu, and Sun Sheng Han. 2003. "Public Housing and Ethnic Integration in Singapore." *Habitat International* 27 (2): 293–307.

Soedirgo, Jessica. 2020. Quotidian Institutions and Identity Formation: Explaining Patterns of Identity Salience in Maluku, Indonesia. *Asian Politics and Policy* 13 (1): 56–71.

Sutton, Keith. 1989. Malaysia's FELDA Land Settlement Model in Time and Space. *Geoforum* 20 (3): 339–354.

Tanasaldy, Taufiq. 2012. *Regime Change and Ethnic Politics in Indonesia*. Leiden: KITLV Press.

Tomsa, Dirk. 2009. Local Elections and Party Politics in a Post-Conflict Area: The Pilkada in Maluku. Indonesian Studies Working Papers Sidney: University of Sidney.

Wallace, Jeremy W. 2014. *Cities and Stability: Urbanization, Redistribution, & Regime Survival in China*. Oxford: Oxford University Press.

Wheeler, Matt. 2010. People's Patron or Patronizing the people? The Southern Border Provinces Administrative Centre in perspective. *Contemporary Southeast Asia* 32 (2): 208–233.

Whitaker, Beth Elise. 2002. Refugees in Western Tanzania: The Distribution of Burdens and Benefits Among Local Hosts. *Journal of Refugee Studies* 15 (4): 339–358.

Wilkinson, Steven I. 2004. *Votes and Violence: Electoral Competition and Ethnic Riots in India*. Cambridge: Cambridge University Press.

Young, Forrest Wade. 2019. Rapa Nui. *The Contemporary Pacific* 31 (1): 225–234.

Zimmer, Andrew, Zack Guido Tuholske, Alex Pakalnksis, Sara Lopus, Kelly Caylor, and Tom Evans. 2020. Dynamics of Population Growth in Secondary Cities across Southern Africa. *Landscape Ecology* 35 (11): 2501–2516.

CHAPTER 15

Societal Responses

In Chapter 12, we noted that one important state failure in governing internal migration occurs when authorities refuse to accept help. States may jealously guard their roles, not wanting to face criticism or appear weak. As a result, IDPs and other vulnerable migrants do not obtain needed assistance because of what amounts to pride or the demand for control. Low-capacity states may be better off accepting their limitations and welcoming help, provided that they still oversee non-state actors, serving as partners instead of the extremes of monopolizing or abandoning governance roles. This help may come from above, provided by international actors, the focus of the next chapter. This chapter looks below the state, to the domestic realm.

Governing internal migration, especially ensuring that assistance is provided to victims, demands recognizing and working with non-state, domestic actors. This could include private firms managing and planning displacement sites, even if some businesses also represent a source of displacement. One area where private businesses can be especially helpful to internal migrants relates to remittances, where banks and new non-banking alternatives (such as mobile phone accounts) can help urban migrants send money to their home communities with little overhead (Biggs 2016). While businesses have the potential to help internal migrants, our focus is on the roles of religious organizations, civil society,

W. Ascher and S. J. Barter, *Moving within Borders*, Politics, Economics, and Inclusive Development, https://doi.org/10.1007/978-3-031-37549-1_15

and traditional leaders in providing shelter and assistance to vulnerable internal migrants and host communities.

Just as we approached the state critically but also with sympathy, we must see societal actors in a balanced light. When speaking about civil society and traditional leaders, observers tend to have rose-colored glasses (this is less the case for religious actors, whose potential may be underappreciated). This echoes policy research related to democratization in the 1990s, where civil society was often seen as a "magic bullet"; if NGOs and human rights defenders could be supported, they could produce a groundswell of liberal activism and topple dictatorships. This view of civil society has been criticized on several fronts, as it underestimates authoritarian resilience and romanticizes civil society. Civil society may be corrupt, unaccountable, exclusionary, and illiberal. Indeed, some have even suggested that "civil society" and similar buzzwords "should be stricken from the agenda" of policymakers (Kendzior 2012). This goes too far, in our opinion, as civil society organizations can be valuable allies in achieving numerous goals, even in authoritarian contexts. Religious groups, civil society, and traditional leaders can help manage the deprivations of internal migrants and avoid violent conflict. They may also be partial, self-interested, patriarchal, or exclusionary, requiring state oversight.

Give Me Shelter: Religion in Internal Migration

When people are forced from their homes, many immediately turn to churches, mosques, or temples for help. Religious buildings often serve as community centers, with faith-based organizations providing charity and counseling. In migratory conflicts, religious buildings may be seen as sacred, so are sometimes spared from violence. In natural disasters, religious buildings, often built more sturdily than dwellings, may be some of the few structures left standing, providing shelter and a place for food, volunteers, and counseling. For some migrants arriving in new areas, especially cities, faith-based organizations can provide sorely needed food and medicine, as well as a sense of community. Religion can thus provide crucial resources to mitigate migratory crises.

Conflict IDPs

In violent conflicts, religion is sometimes a source of intolerance, difference, and extremism, seen as fueling violence. While sometimes true, religion may also provide examples of peace and charity, serving as an alternative to violence. Religious groups often provide shelter, aid, and counseling to those fleeing war. In Southeast Asian separatist conflicts, Barter (2014, 60) finds that "those who lost their homes often fled to mosques and schools." Interviewees described their instinctual turn in the face of danger to the mosque, which offered physical and spiritual security. Armed groups may respect religious leaders and perceive religious buildings as off-limits, meaning that these were some of the few buildings spared in areas of intense fighting. Persons seeking shelter within them were often left unharmed, as religious buildings serving as sanctuaries is part of many faiths, allowing religious leaders to help those facing adversity even if they are not co-religionists. Research on localized "peace zones" in conflict areas often observes their religious dimensions. Mitchell (2007, 11) describes traditions across numerous faiths as "divinely sanctioned, inviolable spaces where refuge could be afforded to miscreants and security to noncombatants." Peace zones in the Philippines have important religious dimensions, organized by Catholic bishops and, in the south, Islamic leaders. However, in southern Thailand, where violence led Buddhist migrants to seek shelter in temples, over time this led to the militarization of the temples, which housed local police and military forces as well (Jerryson 2009). In Sri Lanka, the Catholic Church represented "a place of refuge and sanctuary for Tamils displaced from their villages," with even non-Christians generally respecting churches (Hancock and Iyer 2007, 43).

Religious buildings can also provide sites for distributing humanitarian aid to IDPs. Humanitarian assistance in war has deep religious roots, evident in groups such as the Red Cross and Red Crescent (Benthall 1997). They may be part of transnational networks, bringing foreign aid and advocacy from co-religionists abroad. In Islam, the concept of a transnational community of believers (the *ummah*) has driven global donations to distressed Palestinians and Rohingya, (de Cordier 2009). In Mindanao, mosques were able to help IDPs in part due to aid received from Arab charities and other donors, even if this aid was not intended to be spent on provisions (Barter 2014). Christianity also provides networks through which co-religionists can channel aid through faith-based organizations to assist IDPs. In northern Myanmar, faith-based organizations have proven to be some of the most important sources of aid for IDPs, benefiting from local volunteers, organizational strength, and transnational donors (Benson and Jaquet 2014). Orji (2011) notes that a considerable portion of aid to IDPs in northern Nigeria has been delivered through Catholic, Protestant, and Muslim organizations, with co-religionists from around the world sending money to help. Cohen and Deng (2012, 46) emphasize the importance of religious groups helping IDPs in Sierra Leone, where churches distributed food, operated camps, opened clinics, provided loan programs and career training, and more. Duncan (2005, 32) explains how after conflicts in Sulawesi, the state failed to provide much aid to IDPs, who instead found support through churches, mosques, and community associations. In Colombia, religious leaders have provided lifelines to IDPs, seen by some as "by far the most important institution assisting IDPs...[and] frequently the preferred channel for international aid" (Sanford 2003, 113).

Faith-based organizations, though they often arouse antagonism against people of other religions, sometimes provide a sense of hope, emotional support, and reconciliation in times of intergroup conflict. Parsitau (2011) examines church aid to IDPs in the aftermath of the 2007 electoral violence in Kenya. Churches operated alongside secular agencies, benefiting from international assistance from Western churches. Church grounds served as IDP camps and shared resources with camps operated by secular agencies. Not only did churches provide shelter and channel international aid, but church leaders also provided IDPs with spiritual and psychological support "to overcome challenges compounded by displacement" (Parsitau 2011, 494). Churches provided trauma counseling, reaching vulnerable groups such as elders that were skeptical of foreign agencies. Aid provided to vulnerable IDPs had spiritual significance, providing compassion for those pushed from their homes.

Disaster IDPs

A similar story exists for disaster IDPs, with faith-based organizations providing shelter, assistance, transnational links, and counseling. While a sense of sanctity may spare religious buildings in war, religious buildings may also be spared from natural disasters. The reasons that temples, churches, and mosques survive disasters may vary in the eyes of outside observers and local peoples. Religious buildings are typically constructed using better materials than other structures, as they benefit from donors and are less prone to corrupt contractors. As a result, when a disaster occurs, religious buildings may be more likely to be left standing, enabling them to serve the needs of disaster IDPs. For the engineer, this is a product of better construction. For the faithful, this may signify divinity, with buildings protected by cosmological forces.

Clear examples of this phenomenon came in the aftermath of the 2004 Indian Ocean tsunami. In the Indonesian province of Aceh, years of conflict resulted in widespread underdevelopment. The massive earthquake and tsunami destroyed entire coastal towns and cities, flattening the landscape and leaving hundreds of thousands of casualties. Several accounts note that the only buildings left standing were mosques, whose open-air design, elevated foundations, and quality materials enabled them to stand while the areas around them were flattened. Aceh's mosques were "less likely to be cheated by corrupt contractors who use lower quality materials in houses and ordinary buildings to cut costs," and their design allowed waters that would destroy flat walls to flow through (Jatmiko 2014). For survivors, the durability of mosques was seen as a sign from God. This led to a religious revival in the province, with some seeing the tsunami as divine punishment for sinful ways and years of civil war. The post-disaster religion was also fueled by the activities of Islamic NGOs, with both international and domestic Islamic groups providing crucial assistance to IDPs in Aceh (Benthall 2016).

The activities of faith-based organizations in helping disaster IDPs can have important political consequences. One famous case was the 1992 Cairo Earthquake, which left hundreds dead and tens of thousands displaced. In the face of inept state responses, the Muslim Brotherhood assisted, thus bolstering its popularity. The well-organized Brotherhood dispatched engineers to construct emergency shelters, using its resources to provide water and food, as well as distributing cash to displaced families (Walsh 2003). Similar situations unfolded in the 1999 earthquake in Turkey, the 2007 drought in Turkey, and the 2005 earthquake in Pakistan. In these cases, authoritarian governments were embarrassed by the effectiveness of faith-based assistance for disaster IDPs. Officials undermined their standing further by cracking down on Islamists by providing aid instead of working with them, indirectly fueling the growth of Islamic parties (Cheema et al. 2014).

Shortcomings of Faith-Based Migratory Aid

As much as faith might energize people to share their resources and provide support, it can also bring problems. For one, faith-based organizations may help migrants in hopes of proselytizing. In non-Christian countries, the practice or perception of aid encouraging conversion can generate controversy and violence. International agencies such as World Vision, Jesuit Refugee Service, Catholic Relief Service, Samaritan's Purse, and Christian Aid have faced criticism from Muslim, Hindu, and Buddhist governments for influencing vulnerable IDPs. Samuels (2015) shows how rumors of Christians delivering aid and placing Muslim orphans into Christian homes led to protests and tensions in post-tsunami Aceh. In Sri Lanka, the government banned some Christian NGOs from helping disaster IDPs upon suspicion that they were distributing bibles (Chen 2015). The practice of helping migrants to gain coverts not only threatens to generate conflict, but it may also jeopardize the work of other humanitarian groups (Miller 2014).

If faith-based groups do not seek to help IDPs of different faiths for fear of appearing to proselytize, they may alternatively help only co-religionists. Numerous reports suggest that the problem with faith-based aid to migrants is the absence of efforts to help those of other religions. Benson and Jaquet (2014) suggest that, in Myanmar, different Christian sects are perceived as helping only their congregations, so IDPs, in turn, self-select, only approaching groups from their particular church. In Nigeria, Orji (2011, 486) finds that religious organizations adopt what he calls a faith-centric approach, "providing support to members of their own faith community first, or, at times, exclusively." This could be a result of not wanting to appear to be seeking converts, or else it could represent bias, with groups wanting to help only their own. This could still fuel conversion, showing the benefits of membership. Either way, faith-based assistance to internal migrants encounters issues related to bias and exclusion, demanding oversight.

Making Migration Work: Civil Society Advocacy and Assistance

Civil society organizations can play similar roles as faith-based organizations. By some definitions, faith-based organizations are parts of civil society, if we see civil society as the space between the family and the state.

For others, "organized religion" represents an alternative to civil society, "not a part of it," especially if membership is involuntary (Putnam 1994, 107).

We should not always assume that civil society will help to resolve tensions; groups may be highly partisan, perhaps reinforcing differences by bonding groups instead of bridging different communities. Civil society and religious actors play similar roles in helping IDPs and poor migrants, especially in terms of providing aid. However, NGOs and social movements also take part in protests and forms of advocacy for internal migrants that are not always evident in terms of religion. Civil society support is also hopefully less biased and open to all in need.

Domestic NGOs often provide crucial humanitarian assistance to IDPs and other migrants. This may involve partnerships with transnational organizations such as the IOM or Red Cross, or NGOs may provide aid directly, drawing funding from domestic and international donors. Some domestic NGOs are dedicated to helping internal migrants, such as Ethiopia's Action for the Needy or India's Migration and Asylum Project. However, it is more common that internal migrants are supported by either broader domestic human rights organizations or else by NGOs focusing on health or refugees. The Red Cross is especially interesting, as it is organized both as an international organization (the International Committee of the Red Cross, ICRC) as well as a network (the International Red Cross and Red Crescent Movement, IFRC) of over 190 national Red Cross/Red Crescent organizations. Unlike many global organizations, the Red Cross is decentralized and rooted in various countries, making it both a domestic and global NGO that can help displaced peoples around the world.

Aid provision can be especially effective when international NGOs partner with domestic groups. As in other Latin American countries, conflict, landlessness, and drought have led to large-scale urban migration in Peru. Urban migrants suffer many hardships, especially in terms of water and sanitation, as Lima is located in a high desert with limited rainfall. Years of frustration in providing help to urban migrants led local NGOs to develop a larger consortium, the Institute for Local Democracy, and to partner with Save the Children. In addition to assisting urban migrants, they pressured the city government to cooperate, drawing up urban planning surveys that rethought existing state programs (Dawson 1992). Stepputat and Sørensen (2001) observe how church and domestic NGOs provided extensive support for IDPs throughout Peru, especially in secondary cities such as Huancayo. They suggest that local understanding of IDPs changed over time, and that NGO preferences may clash with those of aid recipients.

Previous chapters emphasized that internal migrants may be excluded; unable to access public services, vote, or own property; and made second-class citizens by host communities and subnational governments. In other contexts, it is host communities whose rights are denied, with traditional property systems not recognized by the state or settlers. Either way, some of the most important, under-recognized civil society groups to regulate internal migration are legal aid foundations. Around the world, activist lawyers have offered their services to marginalized peoples, with legal aid helping to ensure that citizenship rights are enjoyed equally (Waldrauch and Hofinger 1997). In Bangladesh, NGOs such as Ain o Salish Kendra (ASK) provide legal aid for urban migrants, while others such as Nari Udyog Kendra (NUK) provide housing assistance. In China, Guangzhou's Panyu Center provides legal aid to rural migrants who are unable to access services or defend themselves in courts against employers. Established in 1998, Panyu has helped thousands of migrants, although it has often faced legal challenges from the Chinese state, which has revoked the Center's operation permit. That said, Panyu continued its work, inspiring the creation of other groups to help rural migrants in Chinese cities, such as the Shenzhen Labor Disputes Center (Fu 2018, 45).

Civil society groups can help migrants by publicizing their plight to the media, international agencies, and the government. This often involves efforts to help organize migrants, playing a supporting role in social movements. In Colombia, Zea (2019) notes how government agencies would routinely deny government aid to IDPs in urban areas. Migrants would then utilize "collective agency," resisting officials and organizing protests with the help of NGO networks. Large, city-wide marches were organized by a consortium known as *Coordinación Nacional de Desplazados* (CND, National Coordination of Displaced People). CND marches were crucial in calling out state inaction and publicizing the plight of IDPs.

Another example is found in India, where Yadav (2019) finds that development IDPs with civil society allies have been able to pressure governments to recognize their rights and gain compensation, whereas IDPs lacking civil society connections have failed to press their demands. In response to displacement caused by one SEZ, locals led protests alongside community organizations, which then gained the attention of national NGOs, in turn elevating their struggle. That said, Yadav argues that national NGOs had different goals than the displaced people, as they were "more invested in reversing the SEZ" and opposing neoliberalism than with "negotiating an effective and fair implementation" of SEZ promises (Yadav 2019, 88). This shows that civil society may not speak with one voice, and NGOs may have different goals than the IDPs they seek to support.

A further illustration is the case of conflict IDPs in the southern Philippines. Here, violence from communist rebels, Muslim separatists, private armies, and state security forces led to repeated displacement for many communities. Eventually, IDPs became frustrated, meeting with NGOs to organize resistance and publicize their plight. The resulting movement was known as Bakwit (Evacuee) Power, echoing the national People Power Movement. Canuday (2009) documents how Bakwit worked with NGOs to occupy roadways and pressure armed groups, demanding ceasefires, humanitarian aid, and compensation. In 2003, evacuees, religious leaders, and NGOs formed a kilometer-long line, taking over a major highway. The protest ended with government and rebel officials acknowledging the Bakwit Power manifesto, moving toward a ceasefire and allowing international NGOs to deliver aid.

Come Together: Traditional Leaders and Social Integration

While faith-based organizations may provide shelter and aid, and civil society organizations may bring aid and advocacy, informally organized, traditional leaders may contribute something very different in terms of managing internal migration. An important aspect of managing conflicts between migrants and hosts is some level of integration. This need not entail assimilation, but rather developing community partnerships, complementary economic relationships, and shared traditions. In a sense, it is about migrants no longer being considered migrants, becoming recognized as legitimate residents.

Integration can sometimes be encouraged by the state and civil society. For states, programs may be available to internal migrants that are not unlike those available to international migrants in Western countries. Migrants may be sponsored by host families or assigned aid workers, or perhaps state-sponsored programs provide education, training, or career counseling. NGOs may organize joint workshops between hosts and natives, especially but not necessarily in post-conflict environments. In African cities, people from various ethnic groups live side by side as strangers, leading to various civil society initiatives to encourage the development of social capital among diverse urban migrants (Madhavan and Landau 2011). In Rwanda, NGOs have led peace education efforts, challenging extreme views of one or the other side as invaders by showing a long history of mixed communities and criticizing colonial constructions of group differences (Freedman et al. 2008, 675). In Sri Lanka, Malholtra and Liyanage (2005) find that participation in workshops involving conflicting parties results in increased long-term empathy and cooperation. Sen (2019) shows that in remote Indian states, labor organizations diminished tensions by bringing together poor and working-class people from local and migrant communities, helping them to see common challenges. This class lens was not able to overcome migratory divisions, but it reduced them by emphasizing cross-cutting cleavages. This serves as a reminder that the migrant/host cleavage may not necessarily represent the dominant divide, as class, ideological, religious, and other differences may remain more salient.

Formal organizations play important roles in integrating migrant and host communities. However, some of the most important integration efforts take place within communities. Here, everyday people and traditional leaders have brought communities together, helping to avoid and resolve conflicts and make internal migration work. Below, we provide further details of three traditional, micro-level efforts to help integrate migrants and hosts in Indonesia.

In the southern corner of Sumatra in Indonesia, native Lampungese have become minorities in the face of decades of internal migration, mostly from Java. The 2010 census recorded that the province is now two-thirds Javanese, with only about 14 percent native Lampungese. In a sense, Lampung should represent a prime candidate for Sons of the Soil conflict, if not now, then in preceding decades. However, conflict has not occurred, as Javanese and Lampungese have maintained cordial relations. Côté (2019) attributes this partly to the fact that Javanese transmigrants were uneducated farmers, so did not challenge native elites, demonstrating socioeconomic complementarity. Another reason for a lack of conflict is cultural traditions in which Javanese symbolically become Lampungese, paying symbolic respect to native culture. The *mawori/angkat saudara* custom involves Javanese being "adopted" into Lampungese clans and taking on a Lampung name. It undergirds some marriages, business partnerships, political campaigns, and conflict resolution. This "adoptive kinship" recognizes Lampungese as the original culture, "thereby granting Lampungese a certain degree of cultural authority and legitimacy over other groups," which provides an avenue for migrant integration (Côté 2019, 101). The practice of mawori has helped to transform migrants into *putra daerah* (sons of the soil). It must be noted, though, that the Javanese share Islamic beliefs with the Lampungese.

On the other end of Sumatra, Islamic leaders adapted a traditional ceremony called the *peusijuek* (cooling off) to help integrate various migrants. The *peusijuek* is an Acehnese ceremony used to integrate those returning from long absences, such as the pilgrimage to Mecca or work abroad, helping them as the person they have become. The ceremony can vary in scale and format, but generally involves communal prayers, the sprinkling of holy water, speeches, and communal feasts. The *peusijuek* is explained as a way to make difficult social changes smoother, recognizing changes and affirming village solidarity (Bräuchler 2017). After the separatist conflict and devastating 2004 tsunami, the ceremony was adopted by traditional Islamic leaders, without formal coordination, to welcome back former fighters and conflict IDPs, as well as integrate disaster IDPs into new villages and formalize the creation of new villages (Barter 2019). The *peusijuek* was held for former rebel leaders, praying alongside conflict victims and conflict IDPs, with smaller ceremonies held for rebel rank and file. Along the west coast, the ceremony was used to bless new communities of tsunami survivors, focusing on recognizing shared losses and getting to know new community members.

Despite being an excellent example of a community-led integration ceremony for IDPs, the *peusijuek* also had shortcomings in terms of inclusion. Just as mawori was not open to Lampung's Balinese, many felt that the *peusijuek* should not be performed for non-Acehnese, especially ethnic Javanese, who were also targeted by the rebels during the conflict (Noviana 2018).

Traditional institutions might be able to promote the integration of migrants and displaced peoples, but the role of the state in such cases is unclear. Traditions may work because they are non-state processes, under the radar of high-level politics and lacking resources that might attract corruption. Yet, if these processes help calm tensions, perhaps the state should promote them. And if they exclude some groups, some state oversight may be necessary. In Aceh, the IOM recognized the importance of the *peusijuek*, providing small stipends to notable Islamic leaders for food and travel. Years later, international agencies provided limited support for Acehnese leaders to visit other regional conflict areas, sharing their traditions with another region home to IDPs and violence (Barter 2019). The important point is that instead of taking over the ceremony, outside actors have provided quiet support for it.

Another Indonesian case, discussed in previous chapters, exemplifies the intersection of traditional leaders and the state. In the late 1990s and early 2000s, Sulawesi and Maluku saw similar migratory conflicts, with Christian natives clashing with Muslim migrants, the latter including both Javanese farmers settled by the state as well as the unmanaged migration of Muslim traders from nearby areas. Conflicts in Poso (Sulawesi) and Ambon (Maluku) left thousands dead and tens of thousands displaced. The state struggled to calm violence, as local officials and security forces supported one or the other side. Especially damaging were police forces helping Christians while the army helped Muslims and allowed the arrival of militants from other parts of the country. As violence simmered, Muslim and Christian leaders worked together to build peace. This included recognizing Muslim migrants as residents while opposing the arrival of Muslim militants. Indonesian government officials, most notably Jusuf Kalla, a Sulawesi native, stepped in to support and formalize traditional responses, leading to the 2001 Malino Accord. The agreement was a hybrid of traditional and state approaches, including inter-communal prayer and feasting (Bräuchler 2015), as well as formal commissions tasked with disarming both sides, repatriating IDPs, and monitoring violence. Point Six of the Accord emphasizes that all Indonesian citizens have a right to migrate to Poso and become residents, but also that migrants must respect local customs. The agreement was imperfect, with funds evaporating through corruption and debates over the meaning of returning IDPs to "their respective places of origin" (Aragon 2013, 171). Yet despite its limitations, the Malino Accord is widely seen as helping to overcome migratory violence and integrate the communities (Trihartono and Viartasiwi 2015). The model was soon adopted in Maluku, with the 2002 Malino II Accords helping to diminish violence and integrate migrant and host communities.

Conclusions

When states, especially those with limited capacity, confront the many challenges associated with internal migration, they sometimes need help. Authorities may be loath to admit they need support in integrating host and migrant groups, providing humanitarian aid and development assistance, counseling victims, and reconciling warring communities, so may be unwilling to partner with other actors. This chapter has provided a cursory glance at the many domestic, societal forces that can help govern internal migration, avoiding the sort of deprivations, conflicts, and policy failures described in earlier chapters. We focused on faith-based organizations, civil society, and traditional leaders, all with an eye to how and why the state should remain involved in overseeing their operations.

Where the state does accept and encourage non-state domestic actors to help migrant and host communities, authorities may be tempted to step back and let them do the work, especially if this saves scarce resources and blurs accountability. But societal forces may also be corrupt, limit state capacity down the road, exclude some groups, and otherwise harm those involved in migration. Generally, states should not reject help from non-state actors, nor should they simply let such groups take over. State officials may want to take over, capturing resources or taking credit for non-state work. Religious groups may be more trusted than the state, or local ceremonies may succeed because they lack corruptible resources, so state interference may jeopardize the successes of non-state processes. States may best see themselves as partners, overseeing non-state groups and developing capacity through them.

This chapter has looked within countries, even though at times we discussed connections to international groups. When discussing the importance of actors beyond the state in governing internal migration, international actors play important roles, as discussed in Chapter 16.

References

Aragon, Lorraine V. 2013. Development Strategies, Religious Relations, and Communal Violence in Central Sulawesi, Indonesia: A Cautionary Tale. In *Development Strategies, Identities, and Conflict in Asia*, eds. William Ascher and Natalia Mirovitskaya, 153–182. New York: Palgrave Macmillan.

Barter, Shane Joshua. 2014. *Civilian Strategy in Civil War: Insights from Indonesia, Thailand, and the Philippines*. New York: Palgrave Macmillan.

Barter, Shane Joshua. 2019. Displacement and Reintegration in Aceh, Indonesia. In *Internal Migration: Challenges in Governance and Integration*, ed. Shane Barter and William Ascher, 113–128. New York: Peter Lang.

Benson, Edward, and Carine Jaquet. 2014. Faith-Based Humanitarianism in Northern Myanmar. *Forced Migration Review* 48: 48–50.

Benthall, Jonathan. 1997. The Red Cross and Red Crescent Movement and Islamic Societies, with Special Reference to Jordan. *British Journal of Middle Eastern Studies* 24 (2): 157–177.

Benthall, Jonathan. 2016. *Islamic Charities and Islamic Humanism in Troubled Times*. Manchester: University of Manchester.

Biggs, Diana C. 2016. How Non-Banks are Boosting Financial Inclusion and Remittance. In *Banking Beyond Banks and Money*, eds. Paolo Tasca, Tomaso Aste, Loriana Pelizzon, and Nicolas Perony, 181–196. Springer.

Bräuchler, Birgit. 2015. *The Cultural Dimension of Peace: Decentralization and Reconciliation in Indonesia*. London: Springer.

Bräuchler, Birgit. 2017. Social Engineering the Local for Peace. *Social Anthropology* 25 (4): 437–453.

Canuday, Jose Jowel. 2009. *Bakwit: The Power of the Displaced*. Manila: Ateneo de Manila University Press.

Cheema, Abdur Rehman, Regina Scheyvens, Bruce Glavovic, and Muhammad Imran. 2014. Unnoticed but Important: Revealing the Hidden Contribution of Community-Based Religious Institution of the Mosque in Disasters. *Natural Hazards* 71 (3): 2207–2229.

Chen, Ted Yu Shen. 2015. Habitat for Humanity's Post-Tsunami Housing Reconstruction Approaches in Sri Lanka. *International Journal of Mass Emergencies and Disasters* 33 (1): 96–117.

Cohen, Roberta, and Francis Deng. 1998. *Masses in Flight: The Global Crisis of Internal Displacement*. Washington: Brookings Institution Press.

de Cordier, Bruno. 2009. Faith-Based Aid, Globalisation, and the Humanitarian Frontline: An Analysis of Western-Based Muslim Aid Organisations. *Disasters* 33 (4): 608–628.

Côté, Isabelle. 2019. 'Adopting Migrants as Brothers and Sisters'—Fictive Kinship as a Mechanism of Conflict Resolution and Conflict Prevention in Lampung, Indonesia. In *Internal Migration: Challenges in Governance and Integration*, eds. Shane Barter and William Ascher, 97–111. New York: Peter Lang.

Dawson, Elsa. 1992. District Planning with Community Participation in Peru: The Work of the Institute for Local Democracy IPADEL. *Environment and Urbanization* 4 (2): 90–100.

Duncan, Christopher. 2005. Unwelcome Guests: Relations between Internally Displaced Persons and their Hosts in North Sulawesi, Indonesia. *Journal of Refugee Studies* 18 (1): 25–46.

Freedman, Sarah Warshauer, Harvey K. Weinstein, Karen Murphy, and Timothy Longman. 2008. Teaching History After Identity-Based Conflicts: The Rwanda Experience. *Comparative Education Review* 52 (4): 663–690.

Fu, Diana. 2018. *Mobilizing Without the Masses: Control and Contention in China*. Cambridge University Press.

Hancock, Landon E. and Pushpa Iyer. 2007. The Nature, Structure, and Variety of Peace Zones. In *Zones of Peace*, eds. Landon E. Hancock and Christopher Mitchell, 29–50. Kumarian Press.

Jatmiko, Andi. 2014. *How Indonesian Mosques Survived the Tsunami*. Associated Press, December 23.

Jerryson, Michael. 2009. Appropriating a Space for Violence: State Buddhism in Southern Thailand. *Journal of Southeast Asian Studies* 40 (1): 33–57.

Kendzior, Sarah. 2012. Stop Talking about Civil Society: Using Terms like 'Civil Society' Is a Distraction from the Real Problems in Authoritarian Countries. *Foreign Policy*, December 02.

Madhavan, Sangeetha, and Loren B. Landau. 2011. Bridges to Nowhere: Hosts, Migrants, and the Chimera of Social Capital in Three African Cities. *Population and Development Review* 37 (3): 473–497.

Manirakiza, Vincent. 2014. Promoting Inclusive Approaches to Address Urbanisation Challenges in Kigali. *African Review of Economics and Finance* 6 (1): 161–180.

Miller, Sarah Ann, and Deardorff. 2014. Faith-Based Organizations and International Responses to Forced Migration. In *The Changing World Religion Map*, ed. Stanley Brunn, 3115–3133. London: Springer.

Mitchell, Christopher. 2007. The Theory and Practice of Sanctuary: From Asylia to Local Zones of Peace. In *Zones of Peace*, eds. Landon E. Hancock and Christopher Mitchell, 1–28. London: Kumarian Press.

Noviana, Nana. 2018. Integritas Kearifan Lokal Budaya Masyarakat Aceh dalam Tradisi Peusijuk. *Deskovi: Art and Design Journal* 1 (1): 29–34.

Orji, Nkwachukwu. 2011. Faith-Based Aid to People Affected by Conflict in Jos, Nigeria: An Analysis of the Role of Christian and Muslim Organizations. *Journal of Refugee Studies* 24 (3): 473–492.

Parsitau, Damaris Seleina. 2011. The Role of Faith and Faith-Based Organizations among Internally Displaced Persons in Kenya. *Journal of Refugee Studies* 24 (3): 493–512.

Putnam, Robert D. 1994. *Making Democracy Work: Civic Traditions in Modern Italy*. Princeton: Princeton University Press.

Samuels, Annemarie. 2015. Narratives of Uncertainty: The Affective Force of Child-Trafficking Rumors in Postdisaster Aceh, Indonesia. *American Anthropologist* 117 (2): 229–241.

Sanford, Victoria. 2003. Eyewitness: Peacebuilding in a War Zone: The Case of Colombian Peace Communities. *International Peacekeeping* 10 (2): 107–118.

Sen, Rumela. 2019. Competing Mobilization of Tribal and Class Identity: Politics of Internal Migration in North India. In *Internal Migration: Challenges in Governance and Integration*, eds. Shane Barter and William Ascher, 63–76. New York: Peter Lang.

Stepputat, Finn, and Ninna Nyberg Sørensen. 2001. The Rise and Fall of 'Internally Displaced People' in the Central Peruvian Andes. *Development and Change* 32 (4): 769–791.

Trihartono, Agus, and Nino Viartasiwi. 2015. Engaging the Quiet Mission: Civil Society in Breaking the Cycle of Violence in the Post-Conflict Poso, Indonesia. *Procedia Environmental Science* 28: 115–123.

Waldrauch, Harald, and Christoph Hofinger. 1997. An Index to Measure the Legal Obstacles to Integration of Migrants. *Journal of Ethnic and Migration Studies* 23 (2): 271–285.

Walsh, John. 2003. Egypt's Muslim Brotherhood: Understanding Centrist Islam. *Harvard International Review* 24 (4): 32–36.

Yadav, Vineeta. 2019. The Political Economy of Special Economic Zones and Internal Displacement in India. In *Internal Migration: Challenges in Governance and Integration*, eds. Shane Barter and William Ascher, 77–95. New York: Peter Lang.

Zea, Juan Esteban. 2019. How IDPs Navigate the Resettlement Process in Bogotá, Colombia. In *Internal Migration: Challenges in Governance and Integration*, eds. Shane Barter and William Ascher, 33–46. New York: Peter Lang.

CHAPTER 16

The International Community: A Brief for International Involvement

The international community can make significant contributions to enhancing the positive impacts of internal migrations within developing countries. Several multilateral organizations, most prominently the ILO, the UN Food and Agriculture Organization (FAO), and World Bank have recognized that voluntary migration can enhance productivity. A 2012 report sponsored by the FAO and the British Department for International Development affirmed that: "The increasing importance of intra-state migration suggests that migration is becoming a common aspect of livelihood strategies for rural inhabitants of developing countries" (Deshingkar et al. 2012, 9). However, far from simply becoming merely "common," internal migration has long been a strategy for those seeking a better life.

Contributing to the potential for constructive internal migration is in the interest of the international community in several respects; the opportunities and challenges associated with internal migration in developing countries are indeed shared, global concerns. First, developing countries that have prospered through increased productivity due to urbanization and remittance-funded rural improvements have increased the demands for goods and services of developed countries. Improved livelihoods in developing countries may then lead to less need for development assistance and more opportunity for trade.

W. Ascher and S. J. Barter, *Moving within Borders*, Politics, Economics, and Inclusive Development,
https://doi.org/10.1007/978-3-031-37549-1_16

Second, international support to keep internal migrants from further migrations to other countries can reduce the political burden of accommodating immigrants, many of whom may be deemed unwanted. Hugo (2016, 665) notes that "internal migration as a precursor to international migration in Asia is the movement of workers from largely rural hinterland areas to transit zones which are the launching points for international labour migration." Urbanizing young migrants who are unable to achieve their desired success often continue to cities in other countries. Although it is difficult to determine how much to attribute two-stage migration to poor conditions following initial, internal migrations, clearly some fraction of international migration reflects insufficient incomes or personal insecurity following internal migration. Ferri and Borsato (2018, 9) note:

> Africa as a continent experienced the unusual phenomenon of urbanization without growth…In addition, the social mobility of the slum residents had been even lower than the economic one which implied that the slums were poverty traps rather than places of hope as was predicted by the modernization hypothesis… In turn, the condition of African slums may be a further push factor for the rural people who moved there to try to continue their journey abroad. Whatever improvements in African cities for rural-to-urban migrants that international support can provide may be able to reduce the tragedies of African drowning when their boats capsize on the way to Europe.

Third, when foreign assistance eases conflicts in resource-stressed migration sites to reduce internal displacement, the need for even more assistance to support IDP camps and international peacekeepers is diminished. The IDMC (2023) estimates that, in 2022, some 28.3 million persons were displaced by conflict and violence. It is difficult to estimate the magnitude of international funding for IDPs, as it may be entangled with aid for refugees. Based on OECD data, Ferris (2014, 32) estimates that US $143 billion of development assistance went to projects focusing on IDPs, with US $1.7 billion earmarked for projects mentioning IDPs along with other beneficiaries.

Fourth, international support aimed at better internal migration governance can serve the preemptive function of reducing the spillover of conflict to neighboring countries. It may do so indirectly, by reducing the number of conflicts involving migrants, or more directly, by managing conflict IDPs. For example, in a precursor to the 1994 Rwandan genocide, migration contributed to hostility due to the killing of Tutsis in an area that had experienced in-migration. Verwimp (2013, 132) reports "the killing of several hundred Tutsi in Bugesera, a region located to the south of Kigali where Hutu…recently migrated and settled." In the aftermath of the genocide, many Tutsis fled to Uganda and Kenya, burdening those countries economically and exacerbating ethnic tensions.

What the International Community can do

In light of the combination of concern for migrants and host communities, and the risks to the international community if migrants or host communities do not prosper, it is imperative to evaluate and act on the potential contributions that the international community can make to improve the outcomes of internal migrations. These potential contributions include:

- increase the overall support for displaced persons
- direct international financial resources to reduce the economic stress on migrants and hosts in low-income rural areas or small towns
- cooperate with governments to reform national and subnational laws, regulations, and practices that deprive migrants of income-earning opportunities and reasonable degrees of free movement
- support programs to reduce technical barriers to work and social assistance
- support physical infrastructure development to minimize the displacement and socioeconomic distress of affected people
- facilitate income-generating opportunities for IDPs confined to camps.

Increase Support for IDPs

International funding has both a direct impact and, insofar as it is combined with state funds, can have a multiplier effect. Because of humanitarian concerns, the dominant direct focus of funding from the international community addresses IDPs, especially conflict-induced displacement. For example, between 2000 and 2018, the World Bank Group funded projects targeting conflict-induced IDPs in 21 countries, including 14 in sub-Saharan Africa and 6 in eastern Europe (World Bank 2019). Programs directly targeting IDPs require state personnel to focus on the displaced population and the host communities, and the co-financing by the governments, likely in all but the poorest countries, magnifies the effort.

The most visible international efforts regarding intra-state migrants relate to IDP camps operated by the United Nations High Commissioner for Refugees (UNHCR), often with the cooperation of the IOM. However, the proportion of IDPs in UNHCR camps is less than one percent of the total IDP population worldwide. In sub-Saharan Africa, only half of the IDPs reside in officially recognized camps (World Bank 2017a, 26–27). Therefore, the international community cannot depend on the UNHCR, which was established in 1950 to address international refugees and only in 1993 expanded its mandate to address IDPs. This role is explicitly subsidiary to the mission of sheltering international refugees, as stated in an internal evaluation of the UNHCR:

> The General Assembly affirmed its support for UNHCR to provide humanitarian assistance and protection to [IDPs] …It also set out criteria for such efforts, including that they 'should not undermine the refugee mandate of the Office and the institution of asylum.' (UN Office of Internal Oversight Services 2017, 7)

The UNHCR's limited emphasis on IDPs is reflected in its funding allocations; the 2021 expenditure of US $785 million was only 16% of the total expenditures, compared to $3.859 billion, or 78.5% going to international refugees (UNHCR 2021, 21) Moreover, because of the UNHCR's insecure resources, for 2021 only 56% of the total budgeted amount was forthcoming (UNHCR 2021, 21). There is a clear need for dedicated programs led by international organizations that focus on the specific challenges.

Direct Financial Resources to Low-Income Rural Areas or Small Towns

It is important to not lose sight of the potential for the international community to contribute in situations that do not involve IDPs, but rather the less visible rural-to-rural migrations that add resource stresses with the potential to improve lives but also to create conflict. While considerable attention on internal migration is dedicated to the 60.9 million people displaced in 2022, the total annual number of internal migrations is in the range of 240 million. Because a fifth of migrations are urban-to-urban, and 30% are rural-to-urban, roughly 120 million people migrate each year to rural sites, far more than the total number of IDPs. Insofar as bilateral assistance agencies and international financial institutions have discretion in channeling resources to different locations within countries, targeting migration areas that present fairly clear risks of destructive conflict can address economic distress and therefore can contribute to reducing conflict.

However, this strategy may be controversial, because these areas may not be the poorest in the country. Governments may resist a focus on the migration sites if they are committed to targeting the poorest areas, or if their political calculations call for different allocations. If diverting assistance funds from the poorest areas requires explicit justification, it can be pointed out that some areas experiencing migration run a serious risk of greater poverty because of stress on resources and the potential for disruptive conflict. Yet, the risks of future deprivation and conflict are particularly uncertain, as poor information about the volume of migration and the socioeconomic impacts of migrations that are not state-initiated. Therefore, channeling requires the capacity to track migration patterns and assess risks.

Cooperate with Governments to Reform Laws, Regulations, and Practices

International organizations can encourage national policy reforms to reduce restrictions on employment and social services for internal migrants. In many countries, laws and even constitutional provisions require equal treatment for citizens regardless of their area of origin, but discrimination against migrants from other jurisdictions remains common. In India, Borhade (2011, 219) finds that laws in place to protect the rights of migrant workers, such as the Inter-State Migrant Workmen Act, "are widely disregarded by employers and intermediaries because of a lack of political will to implement them." Intergovernmental agencies and international organizations can publicize these violations and press for compliance. The ILO's 1958 C111 Discrimination (Employment and Occupation) Convention has been ratified by 175 countries (ILO 2021). For forced displacement, the UN's Guiding Principles were published in 2004 by the UN Office for the Coordination of Humanitarian Affairs (UNOCHA 2004), with the result that "more than 190 states adopted the World Summit Outcome document, which specifically recognized the Guiding Principles as an important international framework for the protection of IDPs" (Cohen and Deng 2008, 5).

Regarding more direct access to private-sector hiring, in 2006 the World Bank Group's private lending facility, the International Finance Corporation, adopted the Policy and Performance Standards on Environmental and Social Sustainability, which includes the requirement to "promote the fair treatment, non-discrimination and equal opportunity of workers..." (International Finance Corporation 2012, 267–268).

Support Programs to Reduce Technical Barriers to Work and Social Assistance

International organizations can support programs that provide individual identity documentation so that migrants can access social assistance and employment opportunities. This can address the pervasive problem that individuals who may be well-known in their home villages or towns may be unable to prove their identity in the new site. For example, the World Bank's Identification for Development (ID4D) Program is promoting an anonymous biometric identification system, designed to cover all citizens within a country (World Bank 2021). In case employers seek to retain such identification, or if it is simply lost in transit, it is also imperative to encourage systems in which migrants may receive new copies of their identification documentation.

Support Infrastructure Development to Minimize Displacement and Socioeconomic Distress

The international community can help to finance infrastructure so that sitie selection and design minimize displacement. The alternatives that could mitigate these harms frequently reduce revenues and increase costs. Lower revenues result from lower power generation due to departing from the generation-maximizing dam site, height, design, and turbine type to reduce displacement and ecological damage. Higher costs are often due to the need for ecological considerations, truly adequate compensation for affected people, and responsible resettlement. Therefore, relatively benign dams are less likely to be intrinsically profitable. However, if international funds are provided to subsidize these dams, whether from development agencies or any of the variety of climate funds and carbon-offset mechanisms, governments may approve the benign designs rendered profitable by the subsidies (Patel et al. 2020). For example, Pakistan's Gulpur Dam project explicitly accommodated both social and environmental impacts, supported by subsidies from the Asian Development Bank, the Australian government's technical assistance, and loan guarantees granted by the World Bank Group's Multilateral Insurance Guarantee Agency (Brown et al. 2019).

Facilitate Income-generating Opportunities for IDPs Confined to Camps

The primary thrust of assistance to IDPs has been through humanitarian aid focusing on basic needs. For example, the World Bank funded 33 IDP-focused projects in 2005–18 (World Bank 2016, 2017a, 2017b). Of these, 14 projects were in countries where IDPs outnumbered refugees. The projects entailed various combinations of support for health and nutrition, education, social protection, and water security (World Bank 2017b). While aid is essential, it has largely neglected approaches to increase economic productivity that would reduce the dependence of the IDPs. This is not for lack of developing doctrines to focus on productivity:

> For development actors, the 'point' of engagement is not about where people live—it is about whether they still need dedicated development support. The rationale for providing such assistance dissipates when the forcibly displaced have overcome their vulnerabilities and can take full advantage of broader poverty reduction programs. This socioeconomic approach complements the traditional framework of rights and legal protection. It also acknowledges the importance of both economic rights and effective access to opportunities... For example, development actors can best contribute by helping address the socioeconomic dimensions of the forced displacement crisis as part of their broader poverty reduction mandate. This is partly distinct from some of the elements of a traditional refugee or IDP protection agenda, but it is an integral part of the search for comprehensive solutions. World Bank (2017a, 10, 33-34)

Yet, even the World Bank, a leader in addressing development opportunities for IDPs, has been slow to incorporate these approaches. The World Bank Group's Independent Evaluation Group (2019, 12) noted: "For 33 countries with large forcibly displaced populations, there is limited or no reference to forced displacement in country strategy documentation."

It may be that this absence reflects the concern that addressing the development of IDPs directly would antagonize local communities, insofar as the host community may fear job competition from the newcomers. Based on research in Sri Lanka, Brun (2003, 23) highlights the increasingly rigid dichotomy between migrants and host communities when appeals for international assistance invoke the plight of migrants alone. In Indonesia, Duncan (2005, 36–37) reports jealousy of both host communities and IDPs outside official camps in Sulawesi because of the relatively generous benefits coming to in-camp IDPs. Therefore, it is "critical to create economic opportunities for both the forcibly displaced and host communities" (World Bank Group 2017a, 10–1).

Managing Difficult Relations with the State

In recognition of the pervasive role of the state in instigating, limiting, or otherwise influencing internal migration, the international community's contributions depend heavily on interactions with the state. Many relations with state officials are cordial and constructive, as summarized above, yet the international community needs to address potentially contentious issues for the benefit of migrants and host communities.

Press for Greater Acknowledgment and Support of IDPs

The international community may still be concerned with the sufficiency of IDP support provided by the state, although their ability to act on these concerns may confront state sovereignty. For example, the conditions of IDP camps administered by international institutions such as the UNHCR are constrained by whatever limits the government places on camp officials, including the capacity to guard residents when they venture out of the camp (Luedke 2019). It is essential to get the host state on board with efforts to assist internal migrants and host communities, whose well-being represents a shared challenge.

The pressure on governments to provide care for IDPs beyond the reach of the UNHCR can be found in multinational agreements, especially those drafted by regional organizations that have the potential to establish stronger standards for the treatment of IDPs. The most relevant effort to this point is the African Union Convention for the Protection and Assistance of Internally Displaced Persons in Africa (Kampala

Convention), adopted in 2009 and ratified by roughly half of AU members.

The Kampala Convention calls for governments to prohibit and prevent arbitrary displacement, exclusion, marginalization, and human rights violations. Linking to other international doctrines, it demands that governments "respect and ensure respect for international humanitarian law regarding the protection of internally displaced persons." The Convention requires member states to meet IDPs' "basic needs" and facilitate "rapid and unimpeded access by humanitarian organizations." Governments are required to protect and assist IDPs, and this must be done "without prejudice to receiving international support." Ferris (2014, 6) emphasizes the treaty's distinctiveness as "the first instrument intended to legally bind an entire region on matters related to preventing situations of mass displacement and to addressing the vulnerabilities and needs of those who have been displaced." The Kampala Convention is also notable in that unlike many pronouncements on state responsibilities in the face of forced displacement, it addresses the interests of the host communities. It also requires governments to adopt "other measures as appropriate, including strategies and policies on internal displacement at national and local levels, taking into account the needs of host communities."

Despite the promise of the Kampala Declaration, its implementation has thus far been very limited. Kälin and Schrepfer (2013, 12) observe major discrepancies "between having a national instrument and implementing it in a displacement situation." In 2006, the Nigerian government began creating a policy to protect IDPs, but after subsequent revisions, it remains in draft form. Further, the "Kampala Convention has not been domesticated making the legal application of its provisions within the national legal system" (Adeola 2016). Addaney et al. (2017, 22) note that the failure to adopt laws to implement the Convention "has a grave impact on the recognition and realisation of the rights of IDPs in Nigeria, particularly the extent to which the courts can be used to hold the state accountable." The ambiguity is whether Nigeria, not having implemented the Convention regarding its own IDPs, has an obligation as a signatory to help enforce it. While it is doubtful that the Kampala Convention's obligation for international intervention in the case of the egregious state abuse of IDPs will ever be invoked, it does put governments on notice of the possibility of international opprobrium.

Defend Just Compensation for Infrastructure IDPs

Although many governments have formally acknowledged the doctrine of adequate compensation for families displaced by physical infrastructure development, the international community must be alert to two incentives for the state to shirk this obligation. First, state-financed projects are more likely to be profitable if IDPs are under-compensated, reducing pressures on the state budget and bringing opportunities for rents. Second, state officials have an incentive to permit private firms to shirk state compensation by encouraging private-sector participation. Many case studies demonstrate that compensation often falls woefully short (Cernea 2008; Zaman et al. 2020). Following through on just compensation depends on the capacity to monitor compliance and willingness to withhold resources if the doctrine is not followed. Cawley (2019, 1347) notes that:

> The governments of developing countries often restrict access to or outright ban parties from investigating project impacts, especially when those investigations aim to undermine a project's development...Compelling host governments to allow such investigation would thus require the backing of IFIs, who could then put pressure on host governments to permit independent review of projects by lending project funds contingent upon their compliance with the Monitoring Function.

Pressure from the international community to encourage states to follow through on proper compensation for IDPs not only supports vulnerable peoples, but it may bring long-term benefits, making such groups more economically active and avoiding future unrest.

Offsett Biases in Favor of Migrants

When voluntary state-managed resettlements create contentious encounters with host communities, state-sponsored migrants typically have the political advantage of being "clients" of the state (see Chapter 6). International actors, insofar as they are called upon to help finance resettlement, may have some leverage regarding the conduct of the resettlement and the allocation of resources, property rights, and so on. The capacity of international actors to monitor interactions among migrants, host communities, and the state is a prerequisite if a bias can be recognized and addressed.

Protect Against Problematic Displacements

As discussed, in some instances the state intentionally displaces some people for problematic reasons, such as changing political balances, weakening or punishing groups seen as antagonistic to the state, or populating an area for geopolitical reasons at the expense of the migrants and host communities. In these cases, the international community has an especially important role in responding to strategic involuntary relocations. The justifications for diplomatic efforts and the limited use of conditionality for loans or grant to be approved are compelling in such cases, as there is a need to call out states that use internal migration for inappropriate strategic ends.

Encourage Recognition of IDP Status

Because official recognition of formal IDP status is often necessary to maximize the assistance from both national and international sources, international actors ought to press governments to overcome reluctance to recognize this status. Koch (2020, 7) reports that: "many governments deny that internal displacement occurs on their territory because they fear international sanctions or a loss of reputation." When physical infrastructure entails the displacement of low-income families, those lacking clear property rights are often expelled without formal designation as IDPs. Conflicts and natural disasters that disperse people beyond camps also are frequently undercounted and not officially recognized. For example, despite over fifty years of conflict displacement in Colombia, the formal recognition of IDP status occurred only in 1997 (Lopez et al. 2011, 9). In addition to people displaced by violence, physical infrastructure development, or obvious natural disasters, many migrants are compelled to leave because of the deteriorating productivity of their home areas. The deterioration of economic security in such areas frequently contributes to intergroup conflict over shrinking resources (Black et al. 2011). International actors may be able to provide a combination of incentives and pressure for governments to recognize and address this broader range of IDPs.

Pressure for Reforms

Although opportunities exist for the international community to partner with governments to enact reforms for the welfare of migrants and host communities, as outlined above, officials are frequently resistant. Although economic pressure to induce these reforms is inevitably controversial, its selective use is warranted if policy reforms could overcome egregious discrimination against migrants.

The potential for inducing national governments to devote the resources, and possibly endure political opposition, to anti-discrimination measures exists through trade agreements. Garcia (2009, 43, 110) notes that the North American Agreement on Labor Cooperation (NAALC), a component of the North American Free Trade Agreement, requires nondiscrimination in employment, and violations are open to trade sanctions. As of 2016, the United States has regional trade agreements with Canada, Colombia, Mexico, Panama, and South Korea that require observance of ILO guidelines; Canadian agreements with the same requirement exist with Colombia, Jordan, Mexico, Peru, and the United States (Siroën and Andrade 2016).

International and bilateral development agencies often can require that loans and grants to national and subnational governments ensure nondiscriminatory hiring and contracting for the funded programs. Mwakagali (2018) documents many IFI initiatives to build anti-discrimination provisions into loan and grant agreements. The European Union has utilized conditionality with nearby countries for humanitarian ends, including stipulations that Balkan countries protect and return IDPs as a condition for aid and membership talks (Keane 2005, 254). Donors may select recipients willing to comply with donor objectives, or the donor may have the option of devoting the resources elsewhere (Stokke 2013). The aforementioned endorsement of anti-discrimination principles provides legitimacy to direct foreign assistance where these principles are observed in practice. Even if these efforts face constraints of limited monitoring capacity and government invocation of sovereignty principles, they exert pressure on national governments and can strengthen the national government's capacity to insist on anti-discrimination practices by subnational governments.

Finally, international NGOs may be of assistance in supporting domestic NGOs in mobilizing migrants and assisting in court challenges against discriminatory policies or practices. In addition, regional human rights courts may provide opportunities for international NGOs to press for migrants' rights to employment as well as government services. Because the African Human Rights Court does not require that claims of discrimination against indigenous people be filed by citizens of the relevant country, international NGOs such as Amnesty International have been able to contest such violations (Zips-Mairitsch 2013, 109).

Overcome State Restrictions on Information

Many of the above challenges are exacerbated by the limitations on information, not only because of the intrinsic difficulty of tracking migration, but also because of restrictions imposed by state actors. In developing sound approaches, the international community may have to address information restrictions that may be motivated to evade accountability (see Chapter 13), as reflected by government denials of displacement. Therefore, international actors must be concerned with how to engage in adequate assessments and monitoring. This capacity may have to be independent of the government, insofar as government leaders are unwilling to gather or share information about migration patterns. In recognition of this need, intergovernmental agencies have expanded their presence in many developing countries; for example, the UN Food and Agriculture Organization (FAO) has offices in more than 130 developing countries. NGOs also may be useful to enhance this capacity, as long as their potential limitations are taken into account.

Addressing the Challenges to Effective International Contributions

Several distinct challenges face the international community in enacting the approaches outlined above.

Uncertainty Regarding Future Conflict

For migrations that are not engineered by the state, the migrants' arrival, deprivations, and conflict may be difficult to identify, and problems serious enough to warrant international concern and action are unlikely to be recognized until they emerge. Often the information asymmetry in favor of national authorities vis-à-vis international actors is even greater than the asymmetry advantage local authorities have over their national authorities.

The same ambiguity as to whether migration is voluntary or forced makes it difficult for the international community to assess the degree of responsibility deemed appropriate for the state as well as for itself. Insofar as responsibility for care is considered less compelling for voluntary migration than for forced migration, international actors face a quandary of knowing how much obligation is warranted. One way to overcome the uncertainty of migrants' motives and circumstances is to commission fine-grained surveys. As noted in a 2017 World Bank assessment, to understand instances of forced displacement, "aggregate data often need to be complemented by microlevel studies…to determine the factors that may cause people to move, to assess their socioeconomic situation, or to evaluate their economic impact on host communities" (World Bank 2017a, 28–29). NGOs are a potential source of information, as long as policymakers are aware of potential shortcomings. Thus, another rationale for supporting NGOs beyond their good works is their potential to assist international policymakers.

Collective Action Weaknesses

Because conflicts arising from migration are predominantly within lower-income countries, wealthier states are unlikely to view problems associated with internal migration as a priority. Multilateral assistance agencies such as the World Bank, regional development banks, and several UN bodies addressing forced displacement and migration currently do not muster enough financial resources to address the problems adequately. There is a need for concerted action to tackle problems associated with internal migration, but it is difficult to convince individual international actors to act alone. Three options are worth considering.

First, donor governments could address the collective action problem through the establishment of a World Bank-administered "Global Internal Migration Assistance Facility," akin to the Global Environment Facility (2015), to raise the costs to a government that fails to meet its commitments. Such facilities could secure funding through a quota-based replenishment formula, with replenishments scheduled after a predetermined number of years. The political economy logic of replenishment-based funding mechanisms, pioneered by the World Bank's International Development Association soft lending and granting facility, is that any government that balks at paying its allotment runs the risk that others will gain greater influence, whether through formal voting shares or informal influence in the allocation of the funds and any conditions associated with the funding.

Another risk, common to collective action agreements in general, is that reneging by one participant could lead to reneging by others, leaving desirable actions unsupported. Given the World Bank's coordinating initiatives such as the Global Program on Forced Displacement (GPFD) and the growing emphasis on addressing the intra-state migration issue as a development challenge, it makes sense for the World Bank to administer the Facility. Its focus should be on localities experiencing substantial internal migration, rather than limiting its focus to IDPs.

A second option is to elevate the importance of migration as a priority in the international community. One way to do this would be to strengthen organizations such as the IOM. Although the IOM has long included assistance in situations of internal migration as part of its mandate (Angenendt and Koch 2017), this has been confined to IDPs, with budgetary concerns limiting its approach to coordination and technical cooperation. In June 2007, at the 94th Session of IOM Member States, the "IOM Strategy" document declared: "The primary goal of IOM is to facilitate the orderly and humane management of international migration" (IOM 2007, 3). Of the 12 functions listed to carry out the IOM strategy, none explicitly referred to internal migration. Yet, by 2019, the IOM declared that it possesses "the widest reach with respect to internally displaced populations, in terms of both operational scope and financial resources. People may be displaced for a broad range of reasons, notably conflict, but also environmental disasters such as floods and droughts" (IOM 2019, 11).

To expand its role and place greater priority on internal migration, whether or not migration is forced, the IOM funding mechanism ought to substitute the current project-by-project funding formula with a quota formula as with most other international organizations. According to the 2022 budget, the IOM's contribution quotas for the 174-member governments cover only the administrative budget of roughly US$54 million, with an operating budget of just under US$1.2 billion (IOM 2022). Project-by-project funding secures support from governments, generally the foreign assistance agencies, interested in specific cases, without reciprocal obligations to fund the organization beyond its administrative needs. As it is, the dependence on discretionary funding by governments means that the IOM still has a quite limited role overall; "IOM is primarily a service provider for its donor countries, which it supports in pursuing their own migration interests" (Angenendt and Koch 2017, 15). Many foreign assistance agencies would allocate assistance to that country regardless of the participation of the IOM. Therefore, requiring quota-based support by governments for operations and administrative functions would provide the IOM the same funding status as other international organizations such as the UN Food and Agriculture Organization. The fact that the IOM became a UN affiliate in 2016 makes this more viable, as does the currently acute crisis of international migration; obviously, the hope would be that a greater and more secure IOM budget would increase its capacity to address migration.

Third, donor states can do more to anchor multinational funding efforts, while also assisting in coordination. For example, the World Bank Group hosts the GPFD, supported by Denmark, Norway, and Switzerland. The GPFD is designed to foster cooperation among bilateral as well as multilateral assistance agencies. It also collaborates with several international organizations, including the UN Development Programme, the UNHCR, the UN OCHA, the AU, and more, as well as NGOs such as the Danish Refugee Council, the IDMC, the International Rescue Committee, the Joint IDP Profiling Service, and the Norwegian Refugee Council (World Bank GPFD 2015, i). While such efforts may be confined to analysis and efforts at coordination, they draw attention to the challenges of IDPs even without imposing funding quotas.

Despite distrust of the World Bank in some quarters, it is the most appropriate institution to oversee these initiatives. Observing the World Bank's leadership in linking human rights risks to development IDPs, Vanclay (2017, 5) reports that international financial institutions (IFIs) generally share the same disposition toward the effects of their projects, including resettlement. Similarly, Price (2015, 128), though acknowledging that IFIs provide a small fraction of the private-sector capital investment for displacement-prone infrastructure projects, emphasizes both the convergence of World Bank-initiated standards and the adoption of these standards by private investors:

> The World Bank's original involuntary resettlement policy principles have transformed into a global benchmark utilized in multilateral, bilateral and state formulations...private sector entities must generally engage with international safeguard policy standards if they are doing business directly or indirectly with an IFI – in this way leveraging extends the IFIs' policy coverage to associated project components that they do not directly finance.

Cooperation Among International Organizations

International efforts to address humanitarian crises facing IDPs and others affected by internal migration face serious coordination challenges, exacerbated by the operations of bilateral as well as multilateral institutions, and the common occurrence of IDPs and international refugees in the same country. A UNHCR-commissioned evaluation of its coordination with other agencies (Collinson and Schenkenberg 2019, 6) concluded:

> There is considerable confusion in the interface and interactions between the multitude of (UN-led) international coordination mechanisms. Refugee responses may overlap significantly with other humanitarian, development, human rights, and protection and peace/stabilization systems, some of which UNHCR may also be involved in directly (e.g., IDP assistance, responses to mixed flows, or development programmes benefiting populations of concern to UNHCR, and host communities). Especially in mixed flows, which see refugees together with IDPs, migrants and/or affected resident communities, there has been confusion and, at times, tension around how the multiple coordination platforms...can co-exist.

With the IOM, the UN Office for the Coordination of Humanitarian Affairs (whose coordination role was resisted by UNHCR when it was created in 1998), and myriad other UN and non-UN agencies involved with IDPs and refugees, responsibilities, and accountability are murky and inconsistent; "The UNHCR Representative at the country level remains accountable for leading and coordinating the refugee response, while the Humanitarian Coordinator, as the most senior UN official in the country, is overseeing the entire humanitarian response" (Collinson and Schenkenberg 2019, 6). It should be possible at least to resolve the ambiguity of authority among the UN-related agencies, let alone unrelated groups.

Concern over the Permanence of Resettlement

Some international actors may be concerned that assisting migrants, in particular IDPs, will discourage return. The 2015 World Bank GPFD progress report (2015, 67) notes that: "The political sensitivity of forced displacement can still limit the willingness of policymakers to discuss the issue from a development perspective, as this might signal an acceptance of long-term, protracted displacement." While this pertains more to international migration than intra-state migration, such concerns may encompass both international and domestic settlements.

This is exemplified in the Caucasus, where the conflicts over Nagorno-Karabakh, Abkhazia, and South Ossetia have prompted the governments of Azerbaijan and Georgia to hinder the socioeconomic integration of displaced populations (Seymour and Brzezinski 2019). In such cases, international advocacy and the implicit threat of donors withholding assistance are potential approaches to leveraging policy change. For instance, the Georgian government's reversal of the earlier stand of impeding integration of Georgians displaced from Abkhazia and South Ossetia—areas claimed by Georgian leaders as their territory—reflected pressure by UN agencies, the multilateral Organization for Security and Co-operation in Europe (OCSE), and NGOs. Seymour and Brzezinski (2019, 53) note several visits and statements by UN agencies criticizing the government's response, recommending "a shift toward an approach to IDPs which considered 'durable solutions' beyond return."

Conclusions: Challenges of Coordination

As is common across a range of foreign assistance efforts, coordination among multilateral, bilateral, and nongovernmental assistance agencies is a challenge for addressing migration. While several entities have been set up to try to coordinate the analytic and delivery efforts, such as the aforementioned GPFD, the challenge remains.

Part of the coordination problem lies in the overlap of migration-focused international agencies and bilateral-donor initiatives, which not only raises issues of competition for jurisdiction and funding, but also of consistent responses. Responses to challenges associated with internal migration operate "within a multitude of parallel and overlapping institutions and consultative forums...this structure encourages 'venue-shopping' in the sense that states are free to choose the institutional context that offers the best prospects of achieving one's own political objectives" (Angenendt and Koch 2017, 23). One consequence of weak coordination among donors is the reduced leverage that any particular international actor has to induce the government of a country experiencing migratory crises to adhere to appropriate standards of care and governance. Perhaps the most prominent and long-standing example of this weakness is the possibility of receiving bilateral funding for hydroelectric dams without committing to the multilateral banks' requirement that displaced people be left no worse off than they were before the displacement.

However, the recent spate of coordination efforts and recommendations for stronger institutional foci on migration bode well for improved coordination. The need for more coordination is indicated by the creation of new consultative fora: The IDMC, GPFD, Global Forum on Migration and Development, the Global Knowledge Partnership on Migration and Development, the Global Migration Group, and the International Centre for Migration Policy, as well as a multitude of regional entities. If a "Global Internal Migration Assistance Facility" or a beefed-up IOM were to become major channels of quota-based nation-state contributions with sufficient focus on intra-state migration, donor states could assist in migration contexts in a more coordinated way, leaving their geopolitical or trade objectives to other aspects of their bilateral foreign assistance.

References

Addaney, Michael, Elsabe Boshoff, and Bamisaye Olutola. 2017. The Climate Change and Human Rights Nexus in Africa. *Amsterdam Law Forum* 9 (3): 5–28.

Adeola, Romola. 2016. Kampala Convention and Protection of IDPs in Nigeria. *Punch*. Available at http://punchng.com/kampala-convention-protection-idps-nigeria/.

Angenendt, Steffen, and Anne Koch. 2017. Global Migration Governance and Mixed Flows: Implications for Development-Centred Policies. SWP Research Paper 8. Berlin: Stiftung Wissenschaft und Politik.

Black, Richard, W. Neil Adger, Nigel W. Arnell, Stefan Dercon, Andrew Geddes, and David Thomas. 2011. The Effect of Environmental Change on Human Migration. *Global Environmental Change* 21: S3–S11.

Borhade, Anjali. 2011. Migrants'(Denied) Access to Health Care in India. *Human Development in India*. New Delhi: UNESCO.

Brown, Cate, Vaqar Zakaria, Alison Joubert, Muhammad Rafique, Jahanzeb Murad, Jackie King, Jessica Hughes, Pablo Cardinale, and Leeanne Alonzo. 2019. Achieving an Environmentally Sustainable Outcome for the Gulpur Hydropower Project in the Poonch River Mahaseer National Park, Pakistan. *Sustainable Water Resources Management* 5 (2): 611–628.

Brun, Cathrine. 2003. Local Citizens or Internally Displaced Persons? Dilemmas of Long Term Displacement in Sri Lanka. *Journal of Refugee Studies* 16 (4): 376–397.

Cawley, Brian P. 2019. Damning the Mekong: Project Finance's Inability to Cure the Steep Costs of Hydropower Development in the Mekong River Basin. *Wisconsin Law Review* 2019 (5): 1309–1350.

Cernea, Michael M. 2008. Compensation and Benefit Sharing: Why Resettlement Policies and Practices Must be Reformed. *Water Science and Engineering* 1 (1): 89–120.

Cohen, Roberta and Francis Deng. 2008. The Genesis and the Challenges: Ten Years of the Guiding Principles on Internal Displacement. *Forced Migration Review* 4–5.

Collinson, Sarah, and Ed Schenkenberg. 2019. *UNHCR's Leadership and Coordination Role in Refugee Response Settings December*. Geneva: UNHCR Evaluation Service.

Deshingkar, Priya, Jon Sward, and Elisenda Estruch-Puertas. 2012. Decent Work Country Programmes and Human Mobility. Migrating out of Poverty Research Programme Consortium Working Paper 5. Sussex: University of Sussex.

Duncan, Christopher. 2005. Unwelcome Guests: Relations between Internally Displaced Persons and their Hosts in North Sulawesi. *Indonesia. Journal of Refugee Studies* 18 (1): 25–46.

Ferri, Giovanni and Roshan Borsato. 2018. *Urbanization and International Migration from Africa*. Rome: LUMSA University. https://repec.lumsa.it/wp/wpC29.pdf.

Ferris, Elizabeth. 2014. *Ten Years After Humanitarian Reform: How Have IDPs Fared?* Washington, DC: Brookings-LSE: Project on Internal Displacement.

Garcia, Kimberly A. Nolan. 2009. Transnational Advocacy and Labor Rights Conditionality in the International Trading Order. PhD dissertation. Albuquerque: The University of New Mexico.

Global Environment Facility. 2015. *Instrument for the Establishment of the Restructured Global Environment Facility*. Washington, DC.

Hugo, Graeme John. 2016. Internal and International Migration in East and Southeast Asia: Exploring the Linkages. *Population, Space and Place* 22 (7): 651–668.

IDMC (Internal Displacement Monitoring Center). 2023. IDMC Data Base. https://www.internal-displacement.org/database/displacement-data.

ILO (International Labour Organization). 2021. Ratifications of C111—Discrimination (Employment and Occupation) Convention, 1958 (No. 111).

ILO (International Labour Organization). 2020. Road Map for Developing a Policy Framework for the Inclusion of Internal Migrant Workers in India.

International Finance Corporation. 2012. *Policy and Performance Standards on Environmental and Social Sustainability*. Washington, DC: World Bank Group.

IOM (International Organization for Migration). 2007. *IOM Strategy, 94th Session of IOM Member States, June*. Geneva: IOM.

IOM (International Organization for Migration). 2019. *IOM Strategic Vision 2019–2023: Setting a Course for IOM*. Geneva: IOM.

IOM (International Organization for Migration). 2022. COUNCIL 112th Session Resolution No. 1395, Programme and Budget for 2022.

Kälin, Walter, and Nina Schrepfer. 2013. *Internal Displacement and the Kampala Convention: An Opportunity for Development Actors*. Geneva: IDMC.

Keane, Roy. 2005. The Partnership-Conditionality Binary in the Western Balkans: Promoting Local Ownership for Sustainable Democratic Transition. *Cambridge Review of International Affairs* 18 (2): 246–257.

Koch, Anne. 2020. On the Run in their Own Country: Political and Institutional Challenges in the Context of Internal Displacement. Berlin: Stiftung Wissenschaft und Politik -SWP- Deutsches Institut für Internationale Politik und Sicherheit.

Lopez R., C. Arredondo, and J. Salcedo. 2011. *The Effects of Internal Displacement on Host Communities. A Case Study of Suba and Ciudad Bolívar Localities in Bogotá, Colombia*. Washington, DC: Brookings Institution.

Luedke, Alicia. 2019. Preventing and Responding to Sexual and Gender-Based Violence in and Around South Sudan's Protection of Civilian (POC) Sites. In *Internal Migration: Challenges in Governance and Integration*, eds. Shane Barter and William Ascher, 19–31. New York: Peter Lang.

Mwakagali, Mpoki. 2018. International Financial Institutions and Labour Standards: A Legal Study of the Role of These Institutions in the Promotion and Implementation of Freedom of Association and Collective Bargaining. PhD dissertation. Stockholm: Stockholm University.

Patel, Sejal, Clare Shakya, and Neha Rai. 2020. *Climate Finance for Hydropower: Incentivising the Low-Carbon Transition*. London: International Institute for Environment and Development.

Price, Susanna. 2015. Is There a Global Safeguard for Development Displacement? In *Development Induced Displacement and Resettlement: New Perspectives on Persisting Problems*, eds. Irge Satiroglu and Narae Choi, 127–141. Abingdon: Routledge.

Seymour, Lee, and Marek Brzezinski. 2019. Unsettled States: Displacement, Governance, and Integration in the Southern Caucasus. In *Internal Migration: Challenges in Governance and Integration*, ed. Shane Barter and William Ascher, 47–62. New York: Peter Lang.

Siroën, Jean-Marc., and David Andrade. 2016. *Regional Trade Agreements and Diffusion of International Labour Standards*. Paris: Université Paris-Dauphine.

Stokke, Olav. 2013. *Aid and Political Conditionality*. London: Routledge.

UN Office of Internal Oversight Services. 2017. Evaluation of the Office of the United Nations High Commissioner for Refugees. Economic and Social Council, 12 January 2017.

UN OCHA (Office for the Coordination of Humanitarian Affairs). 2004. *Guiding Principles on Internal Displacement*. Geneva: United Nations

UNHCR (United Nations High Commission for Refugees). 1998. UN Guiding Principles on Internal Displacement. Geneva: UNHCR. www.unhcr.org/en-us/protection/idps/43ce1cff2/guiding-principles-internal-displacement.html.

UNHCR (United Nations High Commission for Refugees). 2021. UNHCR Global Report. Geneva: UNHCR. https://reporting.unhcr.org/globalreport2021/pdf.

Vanclay, Frank. 2017. Project-Induced Displacement and Resettlement: From Impoverishment Risks to an Opportunity for Development? *Impact Assessment and Project Appraisal* 35 (1): 3–21.

Verwimp, Philip. 2013. *Peasants in Power: The Political Economy of Development and Genocide in Rwanda*. London: Springer.

World Bank GPFD (Global Program on Forced Displacement). 2015. *Annual Progress Report*.

World Bank. 2016. *Migration and Development*. Washington, DC.

World Bank. 2017a. *Forcibly Displaced: Toward a Development Approach Supporting Refugees, the Internally Displaced, and their Hosts*. Washington, DC.

World Bank. 2017b. *Approach Paper: An Evaluation of World Bank Group Support in Conflict Induced Situations of Forced Displacement*. Washington, DC.

World Bank. 2019. *World Bank Group Support in Situations Involving Conflict-Induced Displacement: An Independent Evaluation*. Washington DC: Independent Evaluation Group.

World Bank. 2021. https://id4d.worldbank.org/. Date accessed 22 November 2023.

Zaman, Mohammad, Reshmy Nair, and Shi Guoqing, eds. 2020. *Resettlement in Asian Countries: Legislation, Administration and Struggles for Rights*. Oxford: Routledge.

Zips-Mairitsch, Manuela. 2013. *Lost Lands? (Land) Rights of the San in Botswana and the Legal Concept of Indigeneity in Africa*. Münster: LIT Verlag.

CHAPTER 17

Lessons in Safeguarding the Benefits of Internal Migration

Drawing from examples from a wide variety of countries, this book has made a case for greater attention to internal migration as a subject of advocacy, policy, and research. This echoes what the IOM repeatedly calls for as its first policy recommendation—the urgent need to "take into account internal migration in developing planning and sectoral and inter-sectoral policies" (IOM 2018, x). This book has explained the many challenges, dilemmas, failures, and successes faced by all involved. By way of conclusion, we identify 16 major lessons in governing internal migration, lessons that mirror the progression of this book. Perhaps the broadest lesson is that internal migration matters. Migrating within a country's borders comes with underappreciated human consequences, developmental challenges alongside benefits, and important connections to international migration.

Lesson One: Internal Migration can Benefit All

If appropriately managed by state and other actors, there is cause for optimism about large-scale internal migration and its potential to improve people's lives. Although the problems that arise from internal migrations often attract the most attention, many migrations benefit all concerned,

W. Ascher and S. J. Barter, *Moving within Borders*, Politics, Economics, and Inclusive Development, https://doi.org/10.1007/978-3-031-37549-1_17

even if they occur with less fanfare and even if it is challenging to identify unmitigated successes.

First, truly voluntary migration involves people who have some basis to believe that they will be better off in a new location. They bring their labor to areas—especially cities—where they believe they can be more productive as well as happier. Of course, the migrants that do not willingly leave their home areas are less likely to be prepared to enhance their own productivity and that of others. Therefore, the assessment of the prospects for a positive outcome depends on judging the "push or pull" balance.

Second, migrants can enhance the prosperity for all in the target area. This may involve entrepreneurial migrants bringing goods and services to the host communities. Here, efforts to promote good information on local needs could preempt migrations that would be disappointing because of a mismatch between migrant resources and host community needs. More broadly, migrants may help to exploit under-used resources. This would have to be exploited with due recognition of the user rights of host communities, and awareness that local actors may aspire at some point to exploit these resources.

Third, internal migration may bring sustained benefits to the regions sending their sons and daughters to new homes. For highly congested areas, reducing population can relieve the pressure on resources, and often can reduce the potential for conflict. The opening of the Brazilian Amazon to voluntary migrants, though resulting in significant problems, has reduced the risk of conflict between the landless and the landowners in the South. In Indonesia, continued population growth led critics to suggest that transmigration failed to relieve pressures in Java, an assessment that overlooks how much more crowded the island would have been if not for internal migration. Of course, migrants do not simply leave—they may return, thus connecting their old homes with their new ones. The remittances that many migrants send back to their home areas can strengthen the economies and provide a safety net for emergencies among the people who remain in the home area. The section on migrant-origin communities in Chapter 9 highlights the common phenomenon of hometown associations maintaining economic and social links between migrants and their birthplace.

Fourth, internal migration can benefit the state in numerous ways. This may include reducing congestion and spreading development, improving public welfare, and economic activity expanding the tax base and attracting foreign investment. Insofar as state officials stand to benefit from resettlement programs that can provide them credit for bringing greater prosperity with minimal conflict to the targeted areas, they have the incentive to devote adequate resources to the program. In the positive cases, accountability can be desired rather than evaded.

Lesson Two: What can go Wrong

One of the most striking lessons of this book is that although migration is intended to make those involved better off, the result is often greater poverty, environmental degradation, violent conflict, and various policy failures. Internal migration is a high-stakes policy area. Migration may leave migrants and hosts worse off, suffering from various deprivations while costing precious resources from the states that can least afford it.

Ambiguous property rights, unequal access to state support, disrespect, and various other factors can then lead to destructive intergroup conflicts. Although it is difficult to assess the volume of violence and resulting loss of life, it is clear that migratory conflicts are immensely costly, with a large proportion of civil wars involving internal migrants at some level. We analyzed different forms of migratory violence, including nativist Sons of the Soil as well as settler violence. As groups feel threatened and perceive that one side enjoys state support, they may mobilize for violence. Such violence is indeed difficult to overcome, as migrants and hosts often continue to live alongside one another, or else one group becomes IDPs, arriving in new areas where the process begins anew, especially as IDPs bear the scars of mistrust. In some instances, states may accept human losses in pursuit of some policy goal. That said, such conflicts can also undo state policies, leading to the failure of state-managed migration or development projects.

Lesson Three: The Primacy of the State

A chief lesson arising from the study of internal migration is the primacy of the state. Research on international migration tends to look to international organizations, NGOs, and foreign governments because there is no sovereign body overseeing those crossing borders. For internal migration, the state claims jurisdiction of the people and territory in question. In some ways, this makes it easier to provide assistance, as officials may implement policies to govern migration and support all parties. But when states represent the cause of migration, levels of government diverge in terms of helping migrants, or when states are unable to act, sovereignty can serve to block other actors from assisting migrants as well as hosts. As a result, IDPs can be among the most vulnerable communities in the world.

It is not simply that the state provides or blocks assistance from reaching beleaguered migrants. Official policies may serve as the drivers of internal migration, or at least shape its direction and scale. Many forms of internal migration are initiated by states seeking to secure borders, promote development, assimilate minorities, or a host of other goals. Even the weakest of states is intimately involved in internal migration at some level. This may involve encouraging internal migration, perhaps building roads or opening forested lands, but also limiting internal migration by excluding migrants and protecting host communities.

Even where states seek to plan and support internal migration, they may fail to maintain support over time. Sometimes, states promise support to migrants and host communities that never materializes. Officials may want people out of a given area or to a target area, but then cut them loose once they arrive. In such instances, host communities may be resentful of the state and migrants, but migrants themselves have been misled by the state. Migrants may then be difficult to manage; they may move beyond settlement areas and expand their economic activities. Even when officials sincerely want to provide support, the scale of migration or budgetary limitations may scuttle their efforts. Aid may fail to reach migrants due to corruption, or terminate after initial disbursements, even though migrant settlements may require long-term investment in agriculture and infrastructure.

The host state—with its many agencies, levels of government, and officials—casts a long shadow over internal migration, inhabiting a central position not found in international migration. Working with the state is essential in any effort to improve the lives of migrants, even in situations where the state itself threatens migrant well-being.

Lesson Four: Governing Internal Migration

The potentials for success as well as for catastrophic failure, alongside the primacy of the state, lead to the conclusion that internal migration demands governance. There is a need for policies that can increase efficiency and avoid disaster, as good long-term planning is essential to making internal migration work. Many of the best practices discussed in this book relate to coordination, compensation, seeing development opportunities in internal migration, and thinking long-term. It may also involve controversial measures, such as limiting internal migration.

One area in which internal migration can be governed more successfully is in coordination within the national government. Because the state may be fragmented across horizontal lines, an important principle for successful internal migration is communication and cooperation among state agencies. Horizontally, this means creating committees, task forces, and agencies that can bring together stakeholders. For example, development, welfare, and environmental ministries require formal or informal coordination to understand the many factors associated with a given population displacement. Initiatives by state agencies that have no mandate regarding the management of migration may have major impacts on the volume and directions of unsponsored migration; changes in mining regulations or highway construction (Davidson 2015). Too often, vital coordination among agencies is lacking. Even with infrastructure-development displacement involving compensation, the agencies involved in estimating and providing compensation may not be involved in determining, or even knowing, where displaced people will go. Coordination problems are often exacerbated by bureaucratic rivalries. It is not uncommon for resettlement agencies, environmental agencies, and agricultural ministries to battle over jurisdiction. Across different state agencies, there is a clear need for horizontal coordination.

Despite a real need for coordination within the state and with non-state actors, it is rare to see specialized offices related to internal migration. Indonesia had a Department for Transmigration, one that was folded into other offices since the 1990s. In Ukraine and Georgia, we see agencies focusing on IDPs. It is sometimes difficult to know which offices might be responsible for internal migration in a given country, and whether the issue is seen as one of development, employment, human rights, the environment, indigenous issues, or more. In countries where internal migration is high politics, this is perhaps surprising. There seems to be a need for specialized offices focusing on migratory issues, if not a ministry or department, then an office coordinating stakeholders and publishing information. In India, this has been an ongoing recommendation from international organizations, suggesting that the Ministry of Labour and Employment develop a "nodal agency" tasked with "ensuring the inclusion and welfare of migrants across various domains" through coordinating policies and gathering systematic data (ILO 2020, 30).

Another important policy area in successfully governing internal migration relates to how the state perceives it. Too often, authorities respond to displacement and urbanization as short-term problems. There is real need to understand that many forms of migration are long-term or even permanent. Doing so will lead governments and other organizations away from only providing assistance and toward potential pathways to development. For instance, conflict IDPs are, hopefully, provided with emergency aid. Thinking long-term involves policies such as investment in education, training, and seeding productive activities. Indeed, there is a danger that seeing development opportunities in internal migration may lead some groups not to return to their former homes when it is appropriate, or perhaps supplant locals from their jobs and property. While these are valid concerns, it is also true that displacement typically endures much longer than anticipated, with some IDP settlements existing for decades. When it is safe to return, conflicts, floods, droughts, and other push factors in displacement may recur. In many cases, providing vocational training and jobs for displaced people may be among the best ways to help them return to normal lives, conserve state resources consumed by long-term dependency, restore dignity, and encourage integration.

All the potential costs and complexities of internal migration suggest that states should think long and hard before initiating migration programs, though internal migration is not always a choice for the state, especially with disaster IDPs or urban migrants. Yet when it is a choice, such as when states seek to develop migration policies or displace communities for development projects, states must be aware of the tremendous costs involved. The toll of internal migration may even suggest that states might restrict internal migration in some way. Restricting migration conflicts with the principle of freedom of movement, but we are forced to conclude that in some instances the state is justified in limiting freedom of movement to avoid conflict or environmental degradation, especially when migration sites are ecologically at risk or home to indigenous communities. And while we want to avoid the sort of political exclusion that is found when subnational governments seek to limit internal migration by denying the rights of internal migrants, some degree of clear domicile requirements are common as well as sensible (i.e., to avoid short-term residents skewing elections or taking advantage of different tax policies). Restricting internal migration is illiberal, but may sometimes serve liberal ends and avoid various deprivations.

Lesson Five: Vertical Coordination

Perhaps the most important disjuncture within the state relates to coordination upwards and downward, across administrative tiers. In many cases, subnational governments are captured by host communities and work to exclude migrants. While national governments may provide legal guarantees to internal migrants, the reality may be very different in provinces and cities, where governments deny services and civic rights to migrants. In India, the federal government guarantees the right of internal migration and sometimes pays lip service to this, but in reality, subnational governments routinely erect barriers to citizenship rights for migrants. Many Indian states treat internal migrants as if they were undocumented international migrants and deny them legal benefits, perhaps to limit the flow of migration, maintain local power, or simply keep migrants poor so that local elites can exploit them more easily. In Colombia, national policies recognizing IDPs fall short in major cities, where officials refuse to recognize IDPs as anything but regular urban migrants. In rural areas, some subnational governments aligned with settlers may exclude indigenous groups, as in the southern Philippines or northern Thailand. Although subnational governments can exclude migrants or hosts in opposition to national policies, the inverse can also be true; national governments could restrict immigration, but subnational governments, in need of labor or facing unemployment, may then find ways around national laws. In the Malaysian states of Sabah and Sarawak, Indonesians and Filipinos have been brought in to work the oil palm plantations, crowding out some of the indigenous people.

Challenges related to the various tiers of the state can be magnified by the overall positive trend toward decentralization. Enthusiasm toward governmental decentralization that enables more participatory democracy and states that are more responsive to local conditions can also have adverse effects for migrants. Subnational governments may act in the interests of established residents, using newfound powers to ban or harass migrants from other jurisdictions, and to limit their rights. Urban migrants, in particular, have faced resistance from city or provincial/state governments in response to the dissatisfaction of established city residents, even if the national government recognizes the overall productivity gains that typically go along with urbanization. The harassment and denial of rights of Biharis in Maharashtra State and the "beautification programs" that eject migrants from Vietnamese cities are counterproductive for the country as well as for the urbanizers. Despite some clear gains from decentralization, large-scale internal migration demands central government oversight to ensure the well-being of citizens across subnational borders.

Lesson Six: State Officials Evade Accountability

State officials should be held accountable for how both state-managed and unsponsored migrations impact all citizens. Yet, we must also recognize that the risk of negative accountability assessments can drive state officials to actions—or inaction—that harm migrants, host communities, or both. This may occur in four ways. First, officials may neglect to oversee unsponsored migration out of fear that taking responsibility would damage their standing. Such shirking may involve failures to monitor known unsponsored migrations, to intervene when problems are known, to resolve intra-governmental conflicts, or to prevent lower-level governments from abandoning responsibility for resettlement programs once migrants have arrived. Refusing to govern migration is especially common if the fate of unsponsored migrants or the host communities is not expected to reach broad awareness.

Second, if a program's success is assessed in terms of the sustainability of the resettlement and their prosperity, officials may side with migrants if there are clashes with the host communities. For state-sponsored resettlement programs, migrants abandoning the target area because of the antagonism of the host community (e.g., Buddhists fleeing Thailand's southern provinces because of Muslim resistance; the risks faced by Han in Xinjiang because of Uighur resistance) signals a policy failure for the host state, often prompting repression against the host community. Less extreme cases hold in land disputes and appointments of leaders (e.g., Javanese governors of West Kalimantan).

Third, shirking may mean devolving responsibility to subnational governments. National leaders frequently foist the burden onto under-resourced or potentially biased subnational institutions, leaving "outsider" migrants at risk. It is crucial that national governments maintain responsibility for internal migration, especially given that migration connects multiple sites across a given country.

Fourth, by not resolving painful inter-agency rivalries at any given governmental level, shirking often results in hasty resettlements that one agency undertakes to claim jurisdiction over the resettlement area. This may undermine the success and sustainability of government programs, potentially excluding important bodies that may then resist playing roles to help migrants.

Overall, if the state oversees internal migration, a key lesson is that officials may duck accountability of costly outcomes, an evasion with important human consequences. Domestic and international actors should anticipate this, insisting on and motivating accountability through rewards to state officials when managing the consequences of migration is relatively successful.

Lesson Seven: The Overlapping Forms of Internal Migration

International migration tends to take place among the prosperous and the poor, with the former seeking education and employment in another country, while the latter arrive as refugees. Without meaning to downplay the diversity of international migrants, this book has emphasized the far greater diversity of internal migrants. Urban and entrepreneurial migrants, as well as conflict IDPs, appear in many ways to be the internal equivalents of international labor migrants and refugees. Other types of internal migrants, including disaster IDPs, development IDPs, and state-managed transmigrants, lack clear international equivalents. Several implications flow from this diversity, including the limited utility of concepts derived from international migration.

The many forms of internal migration have led scholars and policymakers to approach various types separately. To be sure, an urbanizing migrant who relocates voluntarily in search of work will have different challenges than a migrant forcibly relocated by an authoritarian government. As such, it makes sense that the scholarly literature is typically specialized, focusing on one type of internal migrant. In contrast, this book has been premised on the idea that, while specialization has some benefits, there is also a need to approach internal migration as a broad subject. Different forms of internal migration feature common challenges and factors, such as the role of the state.

Most importantly, many individuals fall into multiple migratory categories, such as violence-fleer, employment-seeker, and entrepreneur. This can be true sequentially, with urbanizers becoming development IDPs when relocated from informal settlements. It can also occur simultaneously, with many urbanizers also being in conflict or some other form of IDP. In this case, the location and conditions of urban migration will be relevant, but the inability to return and the trauma endured by migrants will demand approaches derived from experiences with conflict IDPs. In Indonesia, many urban communities have long histories of conflict displacement (Hugo 2016). A person in Java may have been pushed by historical conflicts to inhabit marginal spaces, then become a disaster IDP, then migrate to informal urban settlements only to be removed for urban "development." Specialized subfields of different types of internal migration are useful, but there is a need to approach internal migration holistically.

Lesson Eight: The Centrality of Ambiguity

It is important to recognize the role of ambiguity in the difficulties of managing the challenges of migrations. Ambiguity exists when there is an overlap between "push"- and "pull"-based motivations, leaving state officials to decide whether migrants deserve support because they are truly forced to leave their home areas. Although sudden events such as earthquakes make it clear that migration is forced, gradual natural disasters such as drought or seawater incursion leave doubt as to the appropriate state action. Similarly, planning for the future of displaced populations who fled violence or natural disasters is made far more difficult when uncertainty exists as to whether and when return is possible and attractive to the migrants. Effective planning and execution are also more difficult when ambiguity exists in responsibilities among different agencies within a given governmental level or between different levels of government.

No matter how precisely a state resettlement program specifies the target number of families to be involved, state officials and other actors must be prepared for a very different volume of total migration, perhaps lower but often much higher. The same is true for state-instigated migrations, such as building a road into an area that previously was less accessible. Chapter 12 cites the surprisingly large volume of migrants into the Brazilian and Peruvian Amazon, and the unsponsored migrants joining formal *transmigrasi* resettlement in Indonesia. Resettlement initiatives need to develop contingency plans to cope with unexpected migrants, perhaps including policies to control the influx of unofficial migrants.

Ambiguity is also intrinsic in rights doctrines. The civic rights of people migrating from one Indian state to another frequently are limited by state governments, despite national constitutional provisions. The ambiguity of property rights is often used to justify restricting people from using the land on which they had traditionally depended for their livelihoods. Insofar as people's rights obligate the state, the officials may be tempted to take advantage of the ambiguity of the doctrines to shirk accountability.

Meanwhile, in the interactions among migrants, host communities, and the state, the frequent ambiguity of autochthony claims can raise conflict levels, as groups reject one another's claims and the state is caught in the middle. "Sons of the Soil" arguments favoring particular groups are often based on questionable and contested historical claims.

On the international level, the uncertainty as to whether resettlements possibly entail a degree of coercion often makes it difficult for international actors to take a position of support or condemnation. In addition, ambiguity is widespread in terms of the obligations of international actors to intervene when displaced persons are suffering grievous harm. The Kampala Convention is the only explicit international treaty that establishes the obligation to intervene, and yet even this convention has never been invoked.

Lesson Nine: Fair Compensation for the Displaced

Economic development initiatives that require involuntary displacement give rise to the dilemma that full compensation to displaced people might undermine a project's economic viability. For leaders under pressure to undertake ambitious infrastructure projects, the temptation to under-compensate IDPs may be strong, especially since what constitutes "adequate" compensation is uncertain. Yet inaction often carries greater long-term costs, leaving uncompensated groups impoverished, economically unproductive, and potentially disruptive.

A related dilemma of involuntary development displacement is how to ensure fair compensation in light of the fact that IDPs may not be in a position to invest in the long run. Providing one-off compensation payments may be easier, but if IDPs lack investment opportunities, compensation may not achieve its long-term goals. Promising approaches to increase economic sustainability based on extended compensation, such as treating IDPs as perpetual owners entitled to rents on the expropriated land, require early formulation. Of course, efforts to ensure the sustainability of the livelihoods of displaced people may well require the state to maintain an ongoing commitment, which in turn binds future state officials.

Lesson Ten: Avoid "Warehousing" IDPs

IDP camps often limit opportunities for camp residents to be productive, either because of the lack of resources brought into the camps, or the restrictions on leaving the camps to seek employment. IDP sites are often seen as temporary, even long after it becomes clear that relocation is a distant option. Although it is understandable that some local officials are concerned with protecting local employment opportunities, continued economic dependency of camp dwellers can increase the duration and costs of the camps, as well as reduce opportunities for integration.

Lesson Eleven: Attention to Host Communities

Just as internal migrants vary considerably in their composition, goals, and welfare, so do host communities. The success of internal migration—the ability of migrants to integrate, avoid conflict, and improve their welfare—hinges a great deal on the host community. In studies of international migration, host communities are not exactly ignored, but their importance is vastly outweighed by the attention to refugees. For internal migration, inattention to the characteristics of the host community and its potential incompatibility with characteristics of migrants can lead to disaster.

In some instances, states initiate internal migration in order to undermine host communities, seeking to capture their resources, dilute rebellion, or assimilate them. Such cases, where internal migration is used strategically against host communities, have few parallels with international migration.

We have emphasized that host communities may stand as victims of internal migration, especially when states and migrants are aligned. Yet, host communities may also represent sources of abuse and exploitation of internal migrants, as in many cities. In many ways, what matters is which side enjoys state support. When migrants dominate hosts, they often do so in tandem with the state, and when hosts dominate migrants, they typically do so through subnational governments.

State support for migrants also must be available to host communities, perhaps with forms of assistance crafted to their needs or provided with explicit reference to in-migration. Especially important is a sense of complementarity between hosts and migrants, with shared cultural traits such as a common faith or else compatible economic roles. Studies in

Bangladesh emphasize that a key factor in host communities supporting disaster IDPs is social and psychological distance, with hosts more committed to supporting those with shared values and shared experiences (Lujala et al. 2020). In Indonesia, Javanese transmigrants were mostly poor farmers, so they did not challenge local elites and have integrated fairly successfully across the country, despite the immense scale of *transmigrasi*. Relocating migrants of a different faith or overlapping economic interests would be more problematic.

Earlier, we emphasized the importance of compensating the displaced in cases of state-led, development displacement. At times, host communities also may be deserving of some form of compensation. This is most apparent when authorities initiate internal migration, sending significant numbers of people to remote areas. In such circumstances, avoiding tensions and ensuring the success of migration projects demands that host communities are also provided with resources, including agricultural tools, training, and other development opportunities. Crucially, the form of compensation demands dialogue with host communities, especially since the assimilationist aims of many migration projects could be amplified with state-defined development opportunities for minority groups.

Foreign assistance could be more effective in bringing out the best of internal migration if the location of areas expected to experience in-migration could be given special attention. It is rare that migration target areas are incorporated in the criteria of foreign assistance planning. Of course, such planning requires the capacity to anticipate where unsponsored migrants will go and the resource constraints they will face.

Lesson Twelve: Do Not Overlook Sending Communities

As mentioned in Lesson One, the maintenance of connections between migrants and their home communities can be a strength. Most clearly, there may be real economic benefits in remittances and future migration, either to the same site or back to the home community. Sustaining connections between migratory sites may also reduce feelings of isolation, enabling migrants to maintain social and spiritual ties to ancestral homes while encouraging host communities to create ties to their neighbors' homelands. Connections between communities sending and receiving migrants could therefore be enhanced through actions by the state or NGOs. Improving media links, reducing the costs of transmitting remittances, and supporting cultural activities ought to be explored.

Lesson Thirteen: The State is Not Alone

Though the primary actor overseeing internal migration, the state is not alone in governance. Some of the above suggestions, such as proper planning and compensation, demand resources that may be scarce. Although state officials may not want other actors involved in some forms of migration, especially for state-initiated and sponsored migration, governing migration demands that officials cooperate with non-state actors.

In some cases, the state should partner with domestic non-state actors. We described the importance of faith-based organizations, NGOs, and traditional authorities in providing assistance, advocacy, and integration for internal migrants. That said, we noted some shortcomings as well. The state should thus not abandon governing internal migration to these actors, but instead oversee them and develop partnerships to extend the capacity to govern.

The international community has the potential to exert much more influence to enhance the positive outcomes and mitigate the problems of internal migration. Many problems arising from internal migration can result in international migration being deemed problematic by states and organizations, but the difficulty in judging the importance of this connection has held back the impetus for stronger action. The international community has recourse to doctrines and resources to play a more constructive role but has fallen short in many instances, such as the aforementioned neglect of the Kampala Convention. The IOM has expanded its role vis-à-vis internal migration, but it is underfunded, especially for internal migration. The UNHCR, also dependent on sometimes fickle voluntary contributions, has been hobbled by rules that limit its operations within IDP camps. The potential for development assistance organizations to pressure aid recipients to adhere to sound migratory governance has not been fulfilled. In an interconnected world, problems associated with internal migration stand as both regional and global challenges. Today's IDPs may be tomorrow's refugees. Underdevelopment, exclusion, and conflict impact immediate neighbors and beyond.

The argument that sovereignty limits external pressure, let alone direct intervention, can be countered by international norms and current practice. Human rights conventions and the general doctrine of care are strong counters to this sovereignty claim. Moreover, forms of conditionality on the grounds of development effectiveness and poverty alleviation have a long history that can be invoked to reward leaders who provide adequate care for migrants and hosts, and deny assistance where the well-being of stakeholders is ignored or sacrificed for political purposes. Development assistance can be targeted more effectively to areas experiencing migration, to offset the common concerns that the arrival of migrants may reduce local income-earning capacities, displace them from their occupations, and strain pre-existing social services.

We have found that the international community itself needs greater coordination in addressing issues of internal migration. Recent initiatives to provide greater cooperation and coordination are as much a symptom of a greater need for constructive collaboration. Just as state agencies are sometimes prone to jurisdictional rivalries, so too are bilateral and multilateral assistance agencies and other international organizations. These agencies need to work together to establish doctrines and work with governments to avert the problems identified in this book.

Lesson Fourteen: Bring Critics In

State policies to resettle or instigate migrations are typically launched with the optimism that the initiatives have been well formulated, with the implication that critics are simply naysayers. However, while some initiatives indeed are quite successful, no initiative is without problems. Even as state officials promote initiatives to gain support and credit, they need to avoid stifling valid criticisms. For instance, it was very important that the World Bank's sensitivity to the situations of both displaced people and host communities was informed by anthropologists, even if they continually criticize the World Bank's efforts as insufficient (Cernea 2008).

Lesson Fifteen: Targeted Conditionality

The long-established practice of international organizations to require foreign assistance recipients to comply with "conditionalities" (policies the state is required to adopt to receive assistance) can more explicitly seek to protect migrants and host communities. Beyond insisting that aid focus on in-migration areas and commitments of fair compensation for infrastructure IDPs, conditionality ought to focus on adequate and continued state support for migrants and host communities, and avoidance of coercion in resettlement programs.

Lesson Sixteen: Migration is Only the Beginning

Planning resettlement programs or responding to unsponsored migration requires understanding not just the first phase of migration, but also subsequent migrations and the evolution of areas subject to migration. Migrants may deliberately use their first new location as a jumping off point for other migrations, as in the case of Moroccans relocating from the mountains to cities so as to prepare to migrate to Western Europe. Others simply find that the first location is not satisfactory and feel compelled to migrate further, as in the case of Brazilians moving from one Amazonian location to another as their first farms fail. Host communities may be supplanted and become migrants themselves, as many Uighurs have been displaced by the influx of ethnic Han Chinese. Because of these later changes, the categories of the migrants can change over time—Ethiopia's Gedeos began as entrepreneurial voluntary migrants, but then became IDPs.

Equally important, the conditions of the migrants and home communities may change significantly even if further migrations do not occur. The initial conditions of the migrants or host community may change—for better or for worse. Migrant shantytowns can become more substantial neighborhoods if the local government does not bulldoze them down. Migrants and host communities may be at odds initially, but then acclimate to one another. In other cases, such as the Ethiopian Gedeos and Gujis, early cooperation, based on symbiotic economic relations, falls apart when both groups began to compete over land. Migration involves highly variable long-term relationships that endure long after the initial movement of persons.

Migration is a long-term process rather than a single event. The possibility of temporal shifts calls not only for efforts to forecast potential changes as an essential part of planning, but also continual monitoring. There is a risk that state officials, always facing new challenges, will neglect the longer-term opportunities and risks of past migrations.

Final Thoughts

This book has attempted to better understand how states and other actors shape large-scale internal migration. It has endeavored to shine a light on internal migration as a distinct but broad phenomenon. Internal migration is clearly more common and affects more people than international migration, therefore requiring more attention and action than it has received thus far. This book calls for a holistic approach to internal migration, hopefully encouraging more research and policy work. On behalf of groups that find themselves on the move for one reason or another, we hope to have laid out how to make the best of the complex opportunities and challenges of internal migration.

References

Cernea, Michael M. 2008. Compensation and Benefit Sharing: Why Resettlement Policies and Practices Must be Reformed. *Water Science and Engineering* 1 (1): 89–120.

Davidson, Jamie S. 2015. *Indonesia's Changing Political Economy: Governing the Roads*. Cambridge: Cambridge University Press.

Hugo, Graeme John. 2016. Internal and International Migration in East and Southeast Asia: Exploring the Linkages. *Population, Space and Place* 22 (7): 651–668.

ILO (International Labour Organization). 2020. Road Map for Developing a Policy Framework for the Inclusion of Internal Migrant Workers in India.

IOM (International Organization for Migration). 2018. *Mongolia: Internal Migration Study*. New York: United Nations.

Lujala, Päivi., Sosina Bezu, Ivar Kolstad, Minhaj Mahmud, and Arne Wiig. 2020. How do Host-Migrant Proximities Shape Attitudes toward Internal Climate Migrants. *Global Environmental Change* 65: 1–15.

References

Abinales, Patricio N. 2004. *Making Mindanao: Cotabato and Davao in the Formation of the Philippine Nation-State*. Manila: Ateneo de Manila University Press.

Abubakar, Ismaila Rimi, and Petra Leisenring Doan. 2017. Building New Capital Cities in Africa: Lessons for New Satellite Towns in Developing Countries. *African Studies* 76 (4): 1–20.

Acharya, Avidit, David D. Laitin, and Anna Zhang. 2018. 'Sons of the Soil': A Model of Assimilation and Population Control. *Journal of Theoretical Politics* 30 (2): 184–223.

Addaney, Michael, Elsabe Boshoff, and Bamisaye Olutola. 2017. The Climate Change and Human Rights Nexus in Africa. *Amsterdam Law Forum* 9 (3): 5–28.

Adeola, Romola. 2016. Kampala Convention and Protection of IDPs in Nigeria. *Punch*. Available at http://punchng.com/kampala-convention-protection-idps-nigeria/.

Adepoju, Aderanti. 1998. Linkages between Internal and International Migration: The African Situation. *International Social Science Journal* 50 (157): 387–395.

Adewale, J. Gbemiga. 2005. Socio-Economic Factors Associated with Urban-Rural Migration in Nigeria: A Case Study of Oyo State, Nigeria. *Journal of Human Ecology* 17 (1): 13–16.

Afolabi, Oladiran. 2016. Migration and Citizenship Question in Nigeria: A Study of the Berom and Hausa/Fulani Conflict in Jos. *African Journal of Political Science and International Relations Review* 10 (2): 8–15.

W. Ascher and S. J. Barter, *Moving within Borders*, Politics, Economics, and Inclusive Development,
https://doi.org/10.1007/978-3-031-37549-1

African Union. 2009. Convention for the Protection and Assistance of Internally Displaced Persons in Africa. https://au.int/en/treaties/african-union-convention-protection-and-assistance-internally-displaced-persons-africa..

Agbese, Pita Ogaba. 1996. Ethnic Conflicts and Hometown Associations: An Analysis of the Experience of the Agila Development Association. *Africa Today* 43 (2): 139–156.

Aguilar, Soledad, and Elisa Morgera. 2009. Wildlife Law and the Empowerment of the Poor in Latin America. FAO Legal Papers Online 80. Rome: UN Food and Agriculture Organization.

Agunbiade, Muyiwa E, Oluwafemi A. Olajide, and Hakeem Bishi. 2015. The Limit of Land Regularisation as Poverty Alleviation Strategy in Informal Settlements: Empirical Evidence from Lagos, Nigeria. *Journal of Construction Project Management and Innovation* 5 (1): 1045–1063.

Ahmad, Junaid, Shantayanan Devarajan, Stuti Khemani, and Shekhar Shahet. 2005. Decentralization and Service Delivery. World Bank Policy Research Working Paper 3603. World Bank, Washington, DC.

Ahram, Ariel I. 2015. Development, Counterinsurgency, and the Destruction of the Iraqi Marshes. *International Journal of Middle East Studies* 47 (3): 447–466.

Ahsan, Syed Aziz-al, and Bhumitra Chakma. 1989. Problems of National Integration in Bangladesh: The Chittagong Hill Tracts. *Asian Survey* 29 (10): 959–970.

Alexander, Peter, and Anita Chan. 2004. Does China Have an Apartheid Pass System? *Journal of Ethnic and Migration Studies* 30 (4): 609–629.

Alzate, Maria. 2006. *La Estratificación Socioeconómica para el Cobro de los Servicios Públicos Domiciliarios en Colombia: ¿Solidaridad o Focalización?* Bogotá: CEPAL.

Ammarell, Gene. 2002. Bugis Migration and Modes of Adaptation to Local Situations. *Ethnology* 41 (1): 51–67.

Amrith, Sunil S. 2011. *Migration and Diaspora in Modern Asia*. Cambridge: Cambridge University Press.

Anderson, George. 2009. *Fiscal Federalism: A Comparative Introduction*. Oxford: Oxford University Press.

Ang, Yuen Y. 2016. Co-optation and Clientelism: Nested Distributive Politics in China's Single-Party Dictatorship. *Studies in Comparative International Development* 51 (3): 235–256.

Angenendt, Steffen, and Anne Koch. 2017. Global Migration Governance and Mixed Flows: Implications for Development-Centred Policies. SWP Research Paper 8. Berlin: Stiftung Wissenschaft und Politik.

Anh, Dang Nguyen, Gabriel Demombynes, and Linh Hoang Vu. 2016. Reforming Vietnam's Household Registration System. World Bank & Vietnam Academy of Social Sciences (VASS).

Aragon, Lorraine V. 2013. Development Strategies, Religious Relations, and Communal Violence in Central Sulawesi, Indonesia: A Cautionary Tale. In *Development Strategies, Identities, and Conflict in Asia*, eds. William Ascher and Natalia Mirovitskaya, 153–182. New York: Palgrave Macmillan.

Arifin, Bustanul. 2010. Global Sustainability Regulation and Coffee Supply Chains in Lampung Province, Indonesia. *Asian Journal of Agriculture and Development* 7 (2): 67–89.

Arnall, Alex. 2019. Resettlement as Climate Change Adaptation: What Can be Learned from State-Led Relocation in Rural Africa and Asia? *Climate and Development* 11 (3): 253–263.

Aspinall, Edwards. 2011. Democratization and Ethnic Politics in Indonesia: Nine Theses. *Journal of East Asian Studies* 11 (2): 289–319.

Asthana, Vandana. 2012. Forced Displacement: A Gendered Analysis of the Tehri Dam Project. *Economic and Political Weekly* 47 (48): 96–102.

Balcells, Laia, Lesley-Ann Daniels, and Abel Escribà-Folch. 2016. The Determinants of Low-Intensity Intergroup Violence. The Case of Northern Ireland. *Journal of Peace Research* 53 (1): 33–48.

Balueva, Olga, and Elena Chuprina. 2018. Strategic Processes for the Internal Migration Processes Regulation in Ukraine. *Baltic Journal of Economic Studies* 4 (1): 16–24.

Barau, Aliyu Salisu, and Ismail Said. 2016. From Goodwill to Good Deals: FELDA Land Resettlement Scheme and the Ascendancy of the Landless Poor in Malaysia. *Land Use Policy* 54: 423–431.

Barkan, Joel D, Michael L. McNulty, and M.A.O. Ayeni. 1991. 'Hometown' Voluntary Associations, Local Development, and the Emergence of Civil society in Western Nigeria. *Journal of Modern African Studies* 29 (3): 457–480.

Barker, Jonathan. 2019. The Debate on Rural Socialism in Tanzania. In *Towards Socialism in Tanzania*, ed. Bismarck Mwansasu and Cranford Pratt, 95–124. Toronto: University of Toronto Press.

Bar-Tal, Daniel, Lily Chernyak-Hai, Noa Schori, and Ayelet Gundar. 2009. A Sense of Self-Perceived Collective Victimhood in Intractable Conflicts. *International Review of the Red Cross* 91 (874): 229–258.

Barter, Shane, and Isabelle Côté. 2015. Strife of the Soil? Unsettling Transmigrant Conflicts in Indonesia. *Journal of Southeast Asian Studies* 46 (1): 60–85.

Barter, Shane Joshua, and William Ascher, eds. 2019. *Internal Migration: Challenges in Governance and Integration*. New York: Peter Lang.

Barter, Shane Joshua. 2014. *Civilian Strategy in Civil War: Insights from Indonesia, Thailand, and the Philippines*. New York: Palgrave Macmillan.

Barter, Shane Joshua. 2015. 'Second-Order' Ethnic Minorities in Asian Secessionist Conflicts: Problems and Prospects. *Asian Ethnicity* 16 (2): 123–135.

Barter, Shane Joshua. 2018. Rethinking Territorial Autonomy. *Regional Studies* 52 (2): 298–309.

Barter, Shane Joshua. 2019. Displacement and Reintegration in Aceh, Indonesia. In *Internal Migration: Challenges in Governance and Integration*, eds. Shane Barter and William Ascher, 113–128. New York: Peter Lang.

Barter, Shane Joshua. 2020. *Fighting Armed Conflicts in Southeast Asia: Ethnicity and Difference*. Cambridge: Cambridge University Press Elements.

Barton, Greg. 2002. *Abdurrahman Wahid: Muslim Democrat, Indonesian President: A View from the Inside*. Honolulu: University of Hawaii Press.

Baruah, Sanjib. 1986. Immigration, Ethnic Conflict, and Political Turmoil—Assam, 1979–1985. *Asian Survey* 26 (11): 1184–1206.

Barutciski, Michael. 1998. Tensions between the Refugee Concept and the IDP Debate. *Forced Migration Review* 3: 11–14.

Bass, Daniel. 2013. *Everyday Ethnicity in Sri Lanka: Up-Country Tamil Identity Politics*. London: Routledge.

Bazzi, Samuel, Arya Gaduh, Alexander D. Rothenberg, and Maisy Wong. 2016. Skill Transferability, Migration, and Development: Evidence from Population Resettlement in Indonesia. *American Economic Review* 106 (9): 2658–2698.

Becquelin, Nicolas. 2000. Xinjiang in the Nineties. *The China Journal* 44: 65–90.

Bell, Martin, Elin Charles-Edwards Philipp Ueffing, John Stillwell, Marek Kupiszewski, and Dorota Kupiszewska. 2015. *Internal Migration and Development: Comparing Migration Intensities around the World*. Population Council.

Benbabaali, Dalel. 2016. From the Peasant Armed Struggle to the Telangana State: Changes and Continuities in a South Indian Region's Uprisings. *Contemporary South Asia* 24 (2): 184–196.

Benson, Edward, and Carine Jaquet. 2014. Faith-Based Humanitarianism in Northern Myanmar. *Forced Migration Review* 48: 48–50.

Benthall, Jonathan. 1997. The Red Cross and Red Crescent Movement and Islamic Societies, with Special Reference to Jordan. *British Journal of Middle Eastern Studies* 24 (2): 157–177.

Benthall, Jonathan. 2016. *Islamic Charities and Islamic Humanism in Troubled Times*. Manchester: University of Manchester.

Betts, Alexander. 2009. *Forced Migration and Global Politics*. London: Wiley-Blackwell.

Betts, Alexander. 2010. Survival Migration: A New Protection Framework. *Global Governance: A Review of Multilateralism and International Organizations* 16 (3): 361–382.

Bhagat, Ram. 2010. Internal Migration in India: Are the Underprivileged Migrating More? *Asia-Pacific Population Journal* 25 (1): 27–45.

Bhagat, Ram. 2011. Migrants' (denied) right to the city. In *Urban Policies and the Right to the City in India: Rights, Responsibilities and Citizenship*. Faetanini Marina, ed. 86–99, New Delhi: UNESCO.

Bhattacharyya, Harihar, and Jhumpa Mukherjee. 2018. Bodo Ethnic Self-Rule and Persistent Violence in Assam: A Failed Case of Multinational Federalism in India. *Regional & Federal Studies* 28 (4): 469–487.

Biggs, Diana C. 2016. How Non-Banks are Boosting Financial Inclusion and Remittance. In *Banking Beyond Banks and Money*, eds. Paolo Tasca, Tomaso Aste, Loriana Pelizzon, and Nicolas Perony, 181–196. Springer.

Binswanger-Mkhize, Hans, and Klaus Deininger. 2009. History of Land Concentration and Redistributive Land Reforms. In *Agricultural Land Redistribution: Toward Greater Consensus*, eds. Hans Binswanger-Mkhize, Camille Bourguignon, and Rogier van den Brink, 45–86. Washington, DC: World Bank.

Bird, Kate. 2009. 'Voluntary' Migration in Lao People's Democratic Republic. Overseas Development Institute Policy Brief 3.

Black, Richard, W. Neil Adger, Nigel W. Arnell, Stefan Dercon, Andrew Geddes, and David Thomas. 2011. The Effect of Environmental Change on Human Migration. *Global Environmental Change* 21: S3–S11.

Bock, P.G, and Irene Fraser Rothenberg. 1979. *Internal Migration Policy and New Towns*. Champaign: University of Illinois Press.

Bonilla, Jaime, Denis López, and Carlos E. Sepúlveda. 2014. Estratificación Socioeconómica en Colombia: Contexto General y Diagnóstico. In *Los límites de la Estratificación: En Busca de Alternativas*, eds. Carlos E. Sepúlveda, Denis López, and J. Gallego, 23–40. Bogotá Editorial Universidad del Rosario.

Boone, Catherine, and Dennis Kwame Duku. 2012. Ethnic Land Rights in Western Ghana: Landlord-Stranger Relations in the Democratic Era. *Development and Change* 43 (3): 671–693.

Borhade, Anjali. 2011. Migrants'(Denied) Access to Health Care in India. *Human Development in India*. New Delhi: UNESCO.

Borras, Saturnino M, Jr. 2009. Land Redistribution in the Philippines. In *Agricultural Land Redistribution: Toward Greater Consensus*, eds. Hans Binswanger-Mkhize, Camille Bourguignon, and Rogier van den Brink, 215–240. Washington, DC: World Bank.

Bosankić, Nina, Enisa Mešić, and Bojan Šošić. 2019. The Floating Pumpkin Syndrome: Forced Migration, Humanitarian Aid, and the Culture of Learned Helplessness. *Journal of Balkan and near Eastern Studies* 21 (1): 61–73.

Bose, Pablo. 2006. Dilemmas of Diaspora: Partition, Refugees, and the Politics of 'Home.' *Refuge: Canada's Periodical on Refugees* 23 (1): 58–68.

Brass, Paul R. 1991. *Ethnicity and Nationalism*. London: Sage.

Brass, Paul R. 1997. *Theft of an Idol: Text and Context in the Representation of Collective Violence*. Princeton: Princeton University Press.

Bräuchler, Birgit. 2015. *The Cultural Dimension of Peace: Decentralization and Reconciliation in Indonesia*. London: Springer.
Bräuchler, Birgit. 2017. Social Engineering the Local for Peace. *Social Anthropology* 25 (4): 437–453.
Bredenoord, Jan, and Paul van Lindert. 2010. Pro-Poor Housing Policies: Rethinking the Potential of Assisted Self-Help Housing. *Habitat International* 34 (3): 278–287.
Brown, Cate, Vaqar Zakaria, Alison Joubert, Muhammad Rafique, Jahanzeb Murad, Jackie King, Jessica Hughes, Pablo Cardinale, and Leeanne Alonzo. 2019. Achieving an Environmentally Sustainable Outcome for the Gulpur Hydropower Project in the Poonch River Mahaseer National Park, Pakistan. *Sustainable Water Resources Management* 5 (2): 611–628.
Brown, Graham K. 2008. Horizontal Inequalities and Separatism in Southeast Asia: A Comparative Perspective. *Horizontal Inequalities and Conflict: Understanding Group Violence in Multiethnic Societies*, ed. Frances Stewart, 252–281. London: Palgrave Macmillan.
Brown, Rupert, and Miles Hewstone. 2005. An Integrative Theory of Intergroup Contact. *Advances in Experimental Social Psychology* 37: 255–343.
Brun, Cathrine. 2003. Local Citizens or Internally Displaced Persons? Dilemmas of Long Term Displacement in Sri Lanka. *Journal of Refugee Studies* 16 (4): 376–397.
Bullock, Noah. 2017. Towards a Response: Addressing Forced Displacement by Violence in El Salvador. *Humanitarian Exchange* 69: 9–12.
Cai, Qian. 2003. Migrant Remittances and Family Ties: A Case Study in China. *International Journal of Population Geography* 9 (6): 471–483.
Calderón-Mejía, Valentina, and Ana María Ibáñez. 2016. Labour Market Effects of Migration-Related Supply Shocks: Evidence from Internal Refugees in Colombia. *Journal of Economic Geography* 16 (3): 695–713.
Cambon, Laurent, Vincent Yzerbyt, and Sonya Yakimova. 2015. Compensation in Intergroup Relations: An Investigation of Its Structural and Strategic Foundations. *British Journal of Social Psychology* 54 (1): 140–158.
Campbell, Donald T. 1965. Ethnocentrism and Other Altruistic Motives. *Nebraska Symposium on Motivation*, vol. 13, 283–311. Lincoln: University of Nebraska Press.
Canuday, Jose Jowel. 2009. *Bakwit: The Power of the Displaced*. Manila: Ateneo de Manila University Press.
Cattaneo, Andrea, and Sherman Robinson. 2020. Multiple Moves and Return Migration within Developing Countries: A Comparative Analysis. *Population, Space and Place* 26 (7): 1–21.
Cawley, Brian P. 2019. Damning the Mekong: Project Finance's Inability to Cure the Steep Costs of Hydropower Development in the Mekong River Basin. *Wisconsin Law Review* 2019 (5): 1309–1350.

Çelik, Ayşe Betül. 2005. 'I Miss My Village!': Forced Kurdish Migrants in Istanbul and their Representation in Associations. *New Perspectives on Turkey* 32: 137–163.

Cernea, Michael. 2006. Development-Induced and Conflict-Induced IDPs: Bridging the Research Divide. *Forced Migration Review* 261: 25–27.

Cernea, Michael M. 2008. Compensation and Benefit Sharing: Why Resettlement Policies and Practices Must be Reformed. *Water Science and Engineering* 1 (1): 89–120.

Cernea, Michael, and Kai Schmidt-Soltau. 2006. Poverty Risks and National Parks: Policy Issues in Conservation and Resettlement. *World Development* 34 (10): 1808–1830.

Chadha, Vikram, and Ishu Chadda. 2018. Policies and Performance of Social Sector in India since Independence: A Critical Evaluation. *International Journal of Social Science and Development Policy* 4 (2): 64–90.

Chakma, Nikhil, and Mathilde Maitrot. 2016. How Ethnic Minorities Became Poor and Stay Poor in Bangladesh: A Qualitative Enquiry. *EEP/Shiree.*

Chakrabarti, Anuradha, Reena Tiwari, and Haimanti Banerji. 2021. Migrants' Narratives on Urban Governance: A Case from Kolkata, a City of the Global South. *Sustainability* 13 (2): 1009–1025.

Chan, Kam Wing. 2010. Crossing the 50 Percent Population Rubicon: Can China Urbanize to Prosperity? *Eurasian Geography and Economics* 53 (1): 63–86.

Chandrasekhar, S. 2018. *Mobility of Workers in Rural India: Estimates, Implications, and Knowledge Gaps, Background Paper for The State of Food and Agriculture 2018.* Rome. Italy: Food and Agriculture Organization of the United Nations.

Cheema, Abdur Rehman, Regina Scheyvens, Bruce Glavovic, and Muhammad Imran. 2014. Unnoticed but Important: Revealing the Hidden Contribution of Community-Based Religious Institution of the Mosque in Disasters. *Natural Hazards* 71 (3): 2207–2229.

Chen, Ted Yu Shen. 2015. Habitat for Humanity's Post-Tsunami Housing Reconstruction Approaches in Sri Lanka. *International Journal of Mass Emergencies and Disasters* 33 (1): 96–117.

Cohen, Roberta. 2006. Developing an International System for Internally Displaced Persons. *International Studies Perspectives* 7 (2): 87–101.

Cohen, Roberta and Francis Deng. 2008. The Genesis and the Challenges: Ten Years of the Guiding Principles on Internal Displacement. *Forced Migration Review* 4–5.

Cohen, Roberta, and Francis Deng. 1998. *Masses in Flight: The Global Crisis of Internal Displacement*. Washington: Brookings Institution Press.

Collinson, Sarah, and Ed Schenkenberg. 2019. *UNHCR's Leadership and Coordination Role in Refugee Response Settings December*. Geneva: UNHCR Evaluation Service.

Combes, Pierre-Philippe, Sylvie Démurger, Shi Li, and Jianguo Wang. 2020. Unequal Migration and Urbanisation Gains in China. *Journal of Development Economics* 142: 1–17.

Confino, Alon. 2005. Remembering the Second World War, 1945–1965: Narratives of Victimhood and Genocide. *Cultural Analysis* 4: 46–75.

Costello, Michael A. 1987. Slums and Squatter Areas as Entrepots for Rural-Urban Migrants in a Less Developed Society. *Social Forces* 66 (2): 427–445.

Côté, Isabelle. 2019a. 'Adopting Migrants as Brothers and Sisters'—Fictive Kinship as a Mechanism of Conflict Resolution and Conflict Prevention in Lampung, Indonesia. In *Internal Migration: Challenges in Governance and Integration*, eds. Shane Barter and William Ascher, 97–111. New York: Peter Lang.

Côté, Isabelle. 2019b. Internal Migration, Political Liberalization, and Violent Conflict in Authoritarian China. In *People Changing Places: New Perspectives on Demography, Migration, Conflict, and the State,* eds. Isabelle Côté, Matthew I Mitchell, and Monica Duffy Toft, 86–103. London: Routledge.

Côté, Isabelle, and Limingcui Emma Huang. 2020. Where are the Daughters? Examining the Effects of Gendered Migration on the Dynamics of 'Sons of the Soil' Conflict. *Studies in Conflict and Terrorism* 43 (10): 837–853.

Côté, Isabelle. 2014. Internal Migration and the Politics of Place: A Comparative Analysis of China and Indonesia. *Asian Ethnicity* 15 (1): 111–129.

Côté, Isabelle, and Matthew I. Mitchell. 2015. Elections and 'Sons of the Soil' Conflict Dynamics in Africa and Asia. *Democratization* 23 (4): 657–677.

Côté, Isabelle, and Matthew I. Mitchell. 2017. Deciphering 'Sons of the Soil' Conflicts: A Critical Survey of the Literature. *Ethnopolitics* 16 (4): 333–351.

Côté, Isabelle, Matthew I. Mitchell, and Monica Duffy Toft, eds. 2019. *People Changing Places: New Perspectives on Demography, Migration, Conflict, and the State*. London: Routledge.

Cravino, Maria. 2002. Las Transformaciones en la Identidad Villera...la Conflictiva Construcción de Sentidos. *Cuadernos de Antropología Social* 15: 29–47.

Crisp, Jeff, Tim Morris, and Hilde Refstie. 2012. Displacement in Urban Areas: New Challenges, New Partnerships. *Disasters* 36 (S1): S23–S42.

Dagne, Shibru Abate. 2013. Conflict and Conflict Resolution Mechanisms in Ethiopia: The Case of Gedeo and Guji Ethnic Groups. Master's Thesis: Andhra University.

Datta, Ayona. 2012. *The Illegal City: Space, Law and Gender in a Delhi Squatter Settlement*. Burlington, VT: Ashgate.

Davidson, Jamie S. 2003. The Politics of Violence on an Indonesian Periphery. *South East Asia Research* 11 (1): 59–89.

Davidson, Jamie S. 2008. *From Rebellion to Riots: Collective Violence on Indonesian Borneo*. Madison: University of Wisconsin Press.
Davidson, Jamie S. 2015. *Indonesia's Changing Political Economy: Governing the Roads*. Cambridge: Cambridge University Press.
Davies, Anne. 2012. *IDPs in Host Families and Host Communities: Assistance for Hosting Arrangements*. Geneva: UNHCR.
Davis, Gloria. 1976. Parigi: A Social History of the Balinese Movement to Central Sulawesi, 1907–1974. Doctoral Dissertation, Stanford University.
Dawson, Elsa. 1992. District Planning with Community Participation in Peru: The Work of the Institute for Local Democracy IPADEL. *Environment and Urbanization* 4 (2): 90–100.
de Cordier, Bruno. 2009. Faith-Based Aid, Globalisation, and the Humanitarian Frontline: An Analysis of Western-Based Muslim Aid Organisations. *Disasters* 33 (4): 608–628.
de Geoffroy, Agnes. 2005. IDPs and Urban Planning in Khartoum. *Forced Migration Review* 24: 38–39.
de Haas, Hein. 2005. Morocco's Migration Transition: Trends, Determinants, and Future Scenarios. *Global Migration Perspectives* 28. Global Commission on International Migration, Nijmegen, The Netherlands.
de Haas, Hein. 2006. Migration, Remittances, and Regional Development in Southern Morocco. *Geoforum* 37 (4): 565–580.
de Jonge, Huub, and Gerben Nooteboom. 2006. Why the Madurese? Ethnic Conflicts in West and East Kalimantan Compared. *Asian Journal of Social Science* 34 (3): 456–474.
de Koninck, Rodolphe. 1996. The Peasantry as the Territorial Spearhead of the State in Southeast Asia: The Case of Vietnam. *Sojourn* 11 (2): 231–258.
de Silva, Chandra Richard. 1987. *Sri Lanka: A History*. New Delhi: Vikas.
Debelo, Asebe Regassa. 2007. Ethnicity and inter-ethnic relations. The 'Ethiopian experiment' and the case of the Guji and Gedeo. Master's thesis, Universitetet i Tromsø.
Delang, Claudio O. 2002. Deforestation in Northern Thailand: The Result of Hmong Farming Practices or Thai Development Strategies? *Society & Natural Resources* 15 (6): 483–501.
Della-Giacoma, Jim. 2012. *What Could Myanmar Learn from Indonesia? The Malino Accord*. Zürich: ETH Zürich.
Deshingkar, Pryia, and Sven Grimm. 2005. *Internal Migration and Development: A Global Perspective*. New York: International Organization for Migration.
Deshingkar, Priya, Jon Sward, and Elisenda Estruch-Puertas. 2012. Decent Work Country Programmes and Human Mobility. Migrating out of Poverty Research Programme Consortium Working Paper 5. Sussex: University of Sussex.

Deshingkar, Priya, Sushil Kumar, Harendra Kumar Chobey, and Dhananjay Kumar. 2006. *The Role of Migration and Remittances in Promoting Livelihoods in Bihar*. London: Overseas Development Institute, December.

Dodge, Kenneth A. 2006. Translational Science in Action: Hostile Attributional Style and the Development of Aggressive Behavior Problems. *Development and Psychopathology* 18 (3): 791–814.

Doshi, Sapana. 2011. *The Right to the Slum? Redevelopment, Rule, and the Politics of Difference in Mumbai*. Diss. Berkeley, CA: University of California.

Douglass, Mike, and Liling Huang. 2007. Globalizing the City in Southeast Asia: Utopia on the Urban Edge–the Case of Phu My Hung, Saigon. *International Journal of Asia Pacific Studies* 3 (2): 1–42.

Duncan, Christopher, ed. 2004. *Civilizing the Margins: Southeast Asian Government Policies for the Development of Minorities*. Ithaca: Cornell University Press.

Duncan, Christopher. 2005. Unwelcome Guests: Relations between Internally Displaced Persons and their Hosts in North Sulawesi. *Indonesia. Journal of Refugee Studies* 18 (1): 25–46.

Elling, Rasmus. 2013. *Minorities in Iran: Nationalism and Ethnicity After Khomeini*. New York: Palgrave Macmillan.

England, Vaudine. 2001. Indonesia's Greatest Failure. *South China Morning Post*. 18 July.

Eriksen, John H. 1999. Comparing the Economic Planning for Voluntary and Involuntary Resettlement. In *The Economics of Involuntary Resettlement: Questions and Challenges*, ed. Michael Cernea, 83–146. Washington, DC: World Bank.

Erik, Harms. 2012. Beauty as Control in the New Saigon: Eviction, New Urban Zones, and Atomized Dissent in a Southeast Asian City. *American Ethnologist* 39 (4): 735–750.

Erik, Harms. 2013. Eviction Time in the New Saigon: Temporalities of Displacement in the Rubble of Development. *Cultural Anthropology* 28 (2): 344–368.

Evans, Martin. 2010. Primary Patriotism, Shifting Identity: Hometown Associations in Manyu Division, South-West Cameroon. *Africa* 80 (3): 397–425.

Evrard, Olivier, and Yves Goudineau. 2004. Planned Resettlement, Unexpected Migrations and Cultural Trauma in Laos. *Development and Change* 35 (5): 937–962.

Falla, Jonathan. 1991. *True Love and Bartholomew. Rebels on the Burmese Border*. Cambridge: Cambridge University Press.

Fan, C. Cindy. 2008. Migration, Hukou, and the Chinese City. In *China Urbanizes: Consequences, Strategies, and Policies*, eds. Shahid Yusuf and Tony Saich, 65–89. Washington, DC: World Bank.

Farrell, Kyle. 2017. The Rapid Urban Growth Triad: A New Conceptual Framework for Examining the Urban Transition in Developing Countries. *Sustainability* 9 (8): 1407.

Fearnside, Philip. 1985. Deforestation and Decision-Making in the Development of the Brazilian Amazonia. *Interciencia* 10 (5): 243–247.

Fearnside, Philip. 1997. Transmigration in Indonesia: Lessons from Its Environmental and Social Impacts. *Environmental Management* 21 (4): 553–570.

Fearon, James D. and David D. Laitin. 2011. Sons of the Soil, Migrants, and Civil War. *World Development* 39 (2): 199–211.

Feler, Leo, and J. Vernon Henderson. 2008. Exclusionary Policies in Urban Development: How Under-Servicing of Migrant Households Affects the Growth and Composition of Brazilian Cities. National Bureau of Economic Research Working Papers. No. 14136.

Fernandes, Walter. 2017. Internally Displaced Persons and Northern India. *International Studies* 50 (4): 1–19.

Ferri, Giovanni and Roshan Borsato. 2018. *Urbanization and International Migration from Africa*. Rome: LUMSA University. https://repec.lumsa.it/wp/wpC29.pdf.

Ferris, Elizabeth. 2014. *Ten Years After Humanitarian Reform: How Have IDPs Fared?* Washington, DC: Brookings-LSE: Project on Internal Displacement.

Fields, Gary S. 1975. Rural-Urban Migration, Urban Unemployment and Underemployment, and Job-Search Activity in LDCs. *Journal of Developmental Economics* 2 (2): 165–187.

Fitzgerald, David. 2008. Colonies of the Little Motherland: Membership, Space, and Time in Mexican Migrant Hometown Associations. *Comparative Studies in Society and History* 50 (1): 145–169.

Flyvbjerg, Bent, Massimo Garbuio, and Dan Lovallo. 2009. Delusion and Deception in Large Infrastructure Projects: Two Models for Explaining and Preventing Executive Disaster. *California Management Review* 51 (2): 170–193.

Fox, Sean. 2017. Neglected Drivers of Urbanisation in Africa. *International Growth Centre.*

Fox, Sean, and Tom Goodfellow. 2016. *Cities and development*, 2nd ed. Abington, UK: Routledge.

Freedman, Sarah Warshauer, Harvey K. Weinstein, Karen Murphy, and Timothy Longman. 2008. Teaching History After Identity-Based Conflicts: The Rwanda Experience. *Comparative Education Review* 52 (4): 663–690.

Fu, Diana. 2018. *Mobilizing Without the Masses: Control and Contention in China*. Cambridge University Press.

Gaikwad, Nikhar, and Gareth Nellis. 2017. The Majority-Minority Divide in Attitudes toward Internal Migration: Evidence from Mumbai. *American Journal of Political Science* 61 (2): 456–472.

Galvin, Marc, and Tobias Haller, eds. 2008. *People, Protected Areas, and Global Change: Participatory Conservation in Latin America, Africa, Asia, and Europe*. Bern: Geographica Bernensia.

Garcia, Kimberly A. Nolan. 2009. Transnational Advocacy and Labor Rights Conditionality in the International Trading Order. PhD dissertation. Albuquerque: The University of New Mexico.

Gardner, Tom. 2019. Shadow Falls Over Ethiopia Reforms as Warnings of Crisis Go Unheeded, *The Guardian*. March 14.

Gebre, Yntiso. 2003. Resettlement and the Unnoticed Losers: Impoverishment Disasters among the Gumz in Ethiopia. *Human Organization* 62 (1): 50–61.

Gengo, Tieti G, Rahul C. Oka, Varalakshmi Vemuru, Mark Golitko, and Lee T. Gettler. 2018. Positive Effects of Refugee Presence on Host Community Nutritional Status in Turkana County, Kenya. *American Journal of Human Biology* 30 (1): 1–14.

Ghai, Yash. 2000. Ethnicity and Autonomy: A framework for Analysis. In *Autonomy and Ethnicity: Negotiating Competing Claims in Multi-Ethnic States*, 1–27. Yash Ghai. Cambridge: Cambridge University Press.

Ghai, Yash. 2001. *Public Participation and Minorities*, vol. 1. London: Minority Rights Group.

Global Environment Facility. 2015. *Instrument for the Establishment of the Restructured Global Environment Facility*. Washington, DC.

Gonese, Francis T. and Charles M. Mukora. 2003. Beneficiary Selection, Infrastructure Provision and Beneficiary Support. In *Delivering Land and Securing Rural Livelihoods: Post-Independence Land Reform and Resettlement in Zimbabwe*, eds. Michael Roth and Francis Gonese, 205–235. Centre for Applied Sciences, University of Zimbabwe, and Land Tenure Center, University of Wisconsin-Madison.

Goodman, Sara Wallace. 2010. Integration Requirements for Integration's Sake? Identifying, Categorising and Comparing Civic Integration Policies. *Journal of Ethnic and Migration Studies* 36 (5): 753–772.

Gosnell, H, and J. Abrams. 2011. Amenity Migration: Diverse Conceptualizations of Drivers, Socioeconomic Dimensions, and Emerging Challenges. *GeoJournal* 76 (4): 303–322.

Goulding, Michael, Nigel J.H Smith, and Dennis J. Mahar. 1996. *Floods of Fortune: Ecology and Economy Along the Amazon*. Columbia University Press.

Government of Ghana, Ministry of the Interior. 2016. *National Migration Policy for Ghana*. Accra, Ghana.

Greenlees, Don. 1999. Unwanted Arrivals. *The Weekend Australian*. March 27.

Grundy-Warr, Carl, and Elaine Wong Siew. Yin. 2002. Geographies of Displacement: The Karenni and the Shan across the Myanmar-Thailand Border. *Singapore Journal of Tropical Geography* 23 (1): 93–122.

Guha, Ramachandra. 2007. Adivasis, Naxalites and Indian Democracy. *Economic and Political Weekly*. 3305–3312.

Gullette, Gregory. 2019. Constrained Urban Aspirations: Development, Structural Precarity, and Inequalities within Thai Migration. *Asian and Pacific Migration Journal* 28 (3): 300–323.

Gurr, Ted. 1970. *Why Men Rebel*. Princeton University Press.

Haase, Dagmar, Burak Güneralp, Bharat Dahiya, Xuemei Bai, and Thomas Elmqvist. 2018. Global Urbanization. In *The Urban Planet: Knowledge Towards Sustainable Cities*, ed. Thomas Elmqvist, et al., 19–44. Cambridge: Cambridge University Press.

Hagendoorn, Louk, Edwin Poppe, and Anca Minescu. 2008. Support for Separatism in Ethnic Republics of the Russian Federation. *Europe-Asia Studies* 60 (3): 353–373.

Hamnett, Chris. 2020. Is Chinese Urbanisation Unique? *Urban Studies* 57 (3): 690–700.

Hancock, Landon E. and Pushpa Iyer. 2007. The Nature, Structure, and Variety of Peace Zones. In *Zones of Peace*, eds. Landon E. Hancock and Christopher Mitchell, 29–50. Bloomington, CT: Kumarian Press.

Hardjono, Joan. 1986. Transmigration: Looking to the Future. *Bulletin of Indonesian Economic Studies* 22 (2): 28–53.

Hardoy, Jorge E, and David Satterthwaite. 2014. *Squatter Citizen: Life in the Urban Third World*. Routledge.

Harild, Niels. 2016. Forced Displacements: A Development Issue with Humanitarian Elements. *Forced Migration Review* 52: 4–7.

Harms, Erik. 2016. Urban Space and Exclusion in Asia. *Annual Review of Anthropology* 45: 45–61.

Hasija, Namrata. 2012. Migrant Unrest in China. New Delhi: Institute of Peace and Conflict Studies China Research Programme. www.ipcs.org/issue_briefs/issue_brief_pdf/SR119-CRP-MigrantUnrestinChina.pdf.

Hatcher, Craig, and Susan Thieme. 2016. Institutional Transition: Internal Migration, the Propiska, and Post-Socialist Urban Change in Bishkek, Kyrgyzstan. *Urban Studies* 53 (10): 2175–2191.

Havrylchyk, Olena, and Nadiya Ukrayinchuk. 2016. *Living in Limbo: Economic and Social Costs for Refugees*. Lille: University of Lille.

Hedman, Eva Lotta, ed. 2008. *Conflict, Violence, and Displacement in Indonesia*. Ithaca: Southeast Asia Programme Publications, Cornell University.

Heider, Fritz. 1958. *The Psychology of Interpersonal Relations*. Hillsdale, NJ: Lawrence Erlbaum Associates.

Heming, Li, Paul Waley, and Phil Rees. 2001. Reservoir Resettlement in China: Past Experience and the Three Gorges Dam. *Geographical Journal* 167 (3): 195–212.

Henley, David, and Jamie S. Davidson. 2008. In the Name of Adat: Regional Perspectives on Reform, Tradition, and Democracy in Indonesia. *Modern Asian Studies* 42 (4): 815–852.

Hnatkovska, Viktoria, and Amartya Lahiri. 2015. Rural and Urban Migrants in India: 1983–2008. *The World Bank Economic Review* 29 (1): S257–S270.

Hoefle, Scott William. 2006. Twisting the Knife: Frontier Violence in the Central Amazon of Brazil. *The Journal of Peasant Studies* 33 (3): 445–478.

Homewood, Katherine, Ernestina Coast, and Michael Thompson. 2004. In-Migrants and Exclusion in East African Rangelands: Access, Tenure, and Conflict. *Africa* 74 (4): 567–610.

Horowitz, Dan. 1982. Dual Authority Politics. *Comparative Politics* 14 (3): 329–349.

Horowitz, Donald. 2001. *The Deadly Ethnic Riot*. Berkeley, CA: University of California Press.

Hu, Xiaojiang, and Miguel A. Salazar. 2008. Ethnicity, Rurality and Status: Hukou and the Institutional and Cultural Determinants of Social Status in Tibet. *The China Journal* 60: 1–21.

Hugo, Graeme John. 2006. Forced Migration in Indonesia: Historical Perspectives. *Asia and Pacific Migration Journal* 15 (1): 53–92.

Hugo, Graeme John. 2016. Internal and International Migration in East and Southeast Asia: Exploring the Linkages. *Population, Space and Place* 22 (7): 651–668.

Human Rights Watch. 1999. Indonesia: The Violence in Ambon.

Hunter, Lori M. 2005. Migration and Environmental Hazards. *Population and Environment.* 26 (4): 273–302.

Huntington, Samuel P. 1968. *Political Order in Changing Societies*. New Haven: Yale University Press.

ICCPR (International Covenant on Civil and Political Rights) 1966.

IDMC (Internal Displacement Monitoring Centre). 2017. Dam Displacement.

IDMC (Internal Displacement Monitoring Centre). 2018. *Global Report on Internal Displacement 2018.* Geneva.

IDMC (Internal Displacement Monitoring Centre). 2019. *Global Report on Internal Displacement 2019.* Geneva.

IDMC (Internal Displacement Monitoring Centre). 2020. *Global Report on Internal Displacement 2020.* Geneva.

IDMC (Internal Displacement Monitoring Center). 2021. *Global Report on Internal Displacement 2021: Internal Displacement in a Changing Climate.* Geneva.

IDMC (Internal Displacement Monitoring Center). 2022. *Global Report on Internal Displacement 2022: Internal Displacement in a Changing Climate.* Geneva.

IDMC (Internal Displacement Monitoring Center). 2023. IDMC Data Base. https://www.internal-displacement.org/database/displacement-data.
ILO (International Labour Organization). 2020. Road Map for Developing a Policy Framework for the Inclusion of Internal Migrant Workers in India.
ILO (International Labour Organization). 2021. Ratifications of C111—Discrimination (Employment and Occupation) Convention, 1958 (No. 111).
International Commission on Large Dams. 2021. World Register of Dams. https://www.icold-cigb.org/GB/publications/world_register_of_dams.asp.
International Finance Corporation. 2012. *Policy and Performance Standards on Environmental and Social Sustainability*. Washington, DC: World Bank Group.
IOM (International Organization for Migration). 2015. *Program Budget for 2016, Council 106th Session*. Geneva: IOM.
IOM (International Organization for Migration). 2007. *IOM Strategy, 94th Session of IOM Member States, June*. Geneva: IOM.
IOM (International Organization for Migration). 2018a. *World Migration Report 2018*. New York: United Nations.
IOM (International Organization for Migration). 2018b. *Mongolia: Internal Migration Study*. New York: United Nations.
IOM (International Organization for Migration). 2019. *IOM Strategic Vision 2019–2023: Setting a Course for IOM*. Geneva: IOM.
IOM (International Organization for Migration). 2020. *World Migration Report*. New York: United Nations.
IOM (International Organization for Migration). 2022. COUNCIL 112th Session Resolution No. 1395, Programme and Budget for 2022.
IOM (International Organization for Migration). 2023. Ukraine Internal Displacement Report: General Population Survey Round 12.
Jackson, Stephen. 2006. Sons of Which Soil? The Language and Politics of Autochthony in Eastern DR Congo. *African Studies Review* 49 (2): 95–124.
James-Allen, Paul, Aaron Weah, and Lizzie Goodfriend. 2010. *Beyond the Truth and Reconciliation Commission: Transitional Justice Options in Liberia*. New York: International Center for Transitional Justice.
Jatmiko, Andi. 2014. *How Indonesian Mosques Survived the Tsunami*. Associated Press, December 23.
Jerryson, Michael. 2009. Appropriating a Space for Violence: State Buddhism in Southern Thailand. *Journal of Southeast Asian Studies* 40 (1): 33–57.
Jessel, Ella. 2017. 'If I'm Stratum 3, that's who I am': Inside Bogotá's Social Stratification System. *Guardian,* November 9.
Jones, Gavin W, and Hazel V. Richter. 1982. Introduction. In *Resettlement Programs in Southeast Asia,* eds. Gavin W. Jones and Hazel V. Richter. Canberra: Australian National University.

Jones, Peter S.J. 2013. A Governance Analysis of the Galapagos Marine Reserve. *Marine Policy* 41: 65–71.

Jory, Patrick. 2011. *Muslim Merit-Making in Thailand's Far South*. London: Springer.

Joshi, Bhagwati. 2018. Recent Trends of Rural Out-Migration and Its Socio-economic and Environmental Impacts in Uttarakhand Himalaya. *Journal of Urban and Regional Studies on Contemporary India* 4 (2): 1–14.

Joshi, Kirti Kusum, and Tatsuhito Kono. 2009. Optimization of Floor Area Ratio Regulation in a Growing City. *Regional Science and Urban Economics* 39 (4): 502–511.

Juliawan, Benny Hari. 2010. Extracting Labor from Its Owner: Private Employment Agencies and Labor Market Flexibility in Indonesia. *Critical Asian Studies* 42 (1): 25–52.

Kadalayil, Chitrabhanu. 2021. Is India's Federalism Facing Needless Stress Tests? The National, April 5. https://www.thenationalnews.com/opinion/comment/is-india-s-federalism-facing-needless-stress-tests-1.1196245.

Kabeer, Naila. 2014. Social Justice and the Millennium Development Goals: The Challenge of Intersecting Inequalities. *The Equal Rights Review* 13: 91–116.

Kälin, Walter, and Nina Schrepfer. 2013. *Internal Displacement and the Kampala Convention: An Opportunity for Development Actors*. Geneva: IDMC.

Kaltman, Blaine. 2014. *Under the Heel of the Dragon: Islam, Racism, Crime, and the Uighur in China*. Ohio University Press.

Keane, Roy. 2005. The Partnership-Conditionality Binary in the Western Balkans: Promoting Local Ownership for Sustainable Democratic Transition. *Cambridge Review of International Affairs* 18 (2): 246–257.

Keating, Michael. 1996. *Nations against the State: The New Politics of Nationalism in Quebec, Catalonia and Scotland*. London: Macmillan.

Keller, Edmond J. 1985. State, Party, and Revolution in Ethiopia. *African Studies Review* 28 (1): 1–17.

Kendzior, Sarah. 2012. Stop Talking about Civil Society: Using Terms like 'Civil Society' Is a Distraction from the Real Problems in Authoritarian Countries. *Foreign Policy*, December 02.

Kerkvliet, Benedict J. 1971. *The Huk Rebellion: A Study of Peasant Revolt in the Philippines*. Berkeley: University of California Press.

Khairkar, Vijaya P. 2008. Segregation of Migrants Groups in Pune City, India. *Anthropologist* 10 (2): 155–161.

Kimura, Ehito. 2010. Proliferating Provinces: Territorial Politics in Post-Suharto Indonesia. *South East Asia Research* 18 (3): 415–449.

Kinfemichael, Girum. 2014. The Quest for Resolution of Guji-Gedeo Conflicts in Southern Ethiopia: A Review of Mechanisms Employed, Actors and Their Effectiveness. *Ethiopian Journal of the Social Sciences and Humanities* 10 (1): 59–100.

Kivimäki, Timo. 2016. *Can Peace Research Make Peace? Lessons in Academic Diplomacy*. Oxford: Routledge.

Koch, Anne. 2020. On the Run in their Own Country: Political and Institutional Challenges in the Context of Internal Displacement. Berlin: Stiftung Wissenschaft und Politik -SWP- Deutsches Institut für Internationale Politik und Sicherheit.

Koczberski, Gina, and George N. Curry. 2004. Divided Communities and Contested Landscapes: Mobility, Development, and Shifting Identities in Migrant Destination Sites in Papua New Guinea. *Asia Pacific Viewpoint* 45 (3): 357–371.

Koczberski, Gina, George N. Curry, and John Connell. 2001. Full Circle or Spiralling Out of Control? State Violence and the Control of Urbanisation in Papua New Guinea. *Urban Studies* 38 (11): 2017–2036.

Kolstø, Pål. 2019. The Concept of 'Rootedness' in the Struggle for Political Power in the Former Soviet Union in the 1990s. In *People Changing Places: New Perspectives on Demography, Migration, Conflict, and the State*, eds. Isabelle Côté, Matthew I Mitchell, and Monica Duffy Toft, 107–127. London: Routledge.

Kone, Zovanga L, Maggie Y. Liu, Aaditya Mattoo, Çağlar Özden, Siddharth Sharma. 2017. Internal Borders and Migration in India. World Bank Policy Research Working Paper 8244. Washington, DC: World Bank.

König, Anika. 2013. Smelling the Difference: The Senses in Ethnic Conflict in West Kalimantan, Indonesia. In *Senses and Citizenships: Embodying Political Life*, eds. Susanna Trnka, Christine Dureau, and Julie Park, 120–135. New York: Routledge.

Kosiński, Leszek A, and R. Mansell Prothero. 1975. Data and Measures in Migration Research. In *People on the Move: Studies on Internal Migration*, eds. Leszek Kosiński and R. Mansell Prothero, 1–17. New York: Taylor & Francis.

Kubát, Daniel, and Anthony H. Richmond. 1976. Introduction. In *Internal Migration: The New World and the Third World vol. 4*, eds. Daniel Kubát and Anthony H. Richmond. Beverly Hills, CA: Sage Publications.

Landau, Loren. 2014. Religion and the Foundation of Urban Difference: Belief, Transcendence, and Transgression in South Africa and Johannesburg. *Global Networks* 14 (3): 291–305.

Lasswell, Harold D, and Abraham Kaplan. 1950/2017. *Power and Society*. New Haven: Yale University Press; New York: Routledge.

Lecamwasam, Menaka. 2014. The Internally Displaced in South Asia: Lessons from Kampala. *Asia-Pacific Journal on Human Rights and the Law* 15 (1–2): 147–173.

Lee, Everett S. 1966. A Theory of Migration. *Demography* 3 (1): 47–57.

Lewis, Nathaniel M. 2012. Remapping Disclosure: Gay Men's Segmented Journeys of Moving Out and Coming Out. *Social & Cultural Geography* 13 (3): 211–231.

Limpanonda, Suphannada. 2015. Provincial Disparities, Convergence and Effects on Poverty in Thailand. *The Singapore Economic Review* 60 (2): 1–21.

Lipset, Seymour Martin, and Stein Rokkan, eds. 1967. *Party Systems and Voter Alignments: Cross National Perspectives*. New York: Free Press.

Litvack, Jennie, Junaid Ahmad, and Richard Bird. 1998. *Rethinking Decentralization in Developing Countries*. Washington, DC: World Bank.

Liu, Yongzheng, Jorge Martinez-Vazquez, and Alfred M. Wu. 2017. Fiscal Decentralization, Equalization, and Intra-Provincial Inequality in China. *International Tax and Public Finance* 24 (2): 248–281.

Lo, Kevin, and Mark Wang. 2018. How Voluntary is Poverty Alleviation Resettlement in China? *Habitat International* 73: 34–42.

Lofchie, Michael F. 2014. *The Political Economy of Tanzania: Decline and Recovery*. Philadelphia: University of Pennsylvania Press.

Long, Norman. 2008. Translocal Livelihoods, Networks of Family and Community, and Remittances in Central Peru. In *Migration and Development Within and Across Borders: Research and Policy Perspectives on Internal and International Migration*, eds. Josh DeWind and Jennifer Holdaway, 39–70. Geneva: IOM.

Lopez R, C. Arredondo, and J. Salcedo. 2011. *The Effects of Internal Displacement on Host Communities. A Case Study of Suba and Ciudad Bolívar Localities in Bogotá, Colombia*. Washington, DC: Brookings Institution.

Lowry, C.S, and S.W. Littlejohn. 2006. Dialogue and the Discourse of Peacebuilding in Maluku, Indonesia. *Conflict Resolution Quarterly*. 23: 409–426.

Lucas, Robert E.B.. 2021. *Crossing the Divide: Rural to Urban Migration in Developing Countries*. Oxford: Oxford University Press and KNOWMAD.

Luedke, Alicia. 2019. Preventing and Responding to Sexual and Gender-Based Violence in and Around South Sudan's Protection of Civilian (POC) Sites. In *Internal Migration: Challenges in Governance and Integration*, eds. Shane Barter and William Ascher, 19–31. New York: Peter Lang.

Lujala, Päivi, Sosina Bezu, Ivar Kolstad, Minhaj Mahmud, and Arne Wiig. 2020. How do Host-Migrant Proximities Shape Attitudes toward Internal Climate Migrants. *Global Environmental Change* 65: 1–15.

MacMillan, Gordon. 1995. *At the End of the Rainbow? Gold, Land, and People in the Brazilian Amazon*. New York: Columbia University Press.

Madhavan, Sangeetha, and Loren B. Landau. 2011. Bridges to Nowhere: Hosts, Migrants, and the Chimera of Social Capital in Three African Cities. *Population and Development Review* 37 (3): 473–497.

Magaloni, Beatriz, Edgar Franco, and Vanessa Melo. 2015. Killing in the Slums: An Impact Evaluation of Police Reform in Rio de Janeiro. Working Paper

556, Center for Democracy, Development and the Rule of Law. Palo Alto, CA: Stanford University.

Mahaphonh, Nouphanh, Pheuiphanh Ngaosrivathana, Meena Phimphachanh, Sysaweui Chittasupha, Serntai Pasay, and Peter Jones. 2007. Study on Land Conflicts and Conflict Resolution in Lao PDR. Vientiane: Lao-German Land Policy Development Project Land Policy Study 9.

Malesky, Edmund J, and Francis E. Hutchinson. 2016. Varieties of Disappointment: Why has Decentralization not Delivered on Its Promises in Southeast Asia? *Journal of Southeast Asian Economies* 33 (2): 125–138.

Malholtra, Depark, and Sumanasiri Liyange. 2005. Long-Term Effects of Peace Workshops in Protracted Conflicts. *Journal of Conflict Resolution* 49 (6): 908–924.

Manirakiza, Vincent. 2014. Promoting Inclusive Approaches to Address Urbanisation Challenges in Kigali. *African Review of Economics and Finance* 6 (1): 161–180.

Manogaran, Chelvadurai, and Bryan Pfaffenberger, eds. 1994. *The Sri Lankan Tamils: Ethnicity and Identity*. London: Routledge.

Manouchehri, Bahar, Masoumeh Tork, and Hossein Vahidi. 2015. Motivations for Settlement in New Towns in a Developing Country: A Case Study of Andisheh New Town, Iran. *International Journal of Development and Sustainability* 4 (4): 461–478.

Martin, Susan F. 2014. *International Migration: Evolving Trends from the Early Twentieth Century to the Present*. New York: Cambridge University Press.

Martin, Susan F, Patricia Weiss Fagen, Kari M. Jorgensen, Andrew Schoenholtz, and Lydia Mann-Bondat. 2005. *The Uprooted: Improving Humanitarian Responses to Forced Migration*. Lanham, MD: Lexington Books.

Martin, Terry. 1998. The Origins of Soviet Ethnic Cleansing. *Journal of Modern History* 70 (4): 813–861.

Martinez Portilla, Isabel, Corona Aguilar, Antonia, and Ianez Dominguez, Antonio. 2011. Mujeres Desplazadas y Estrategias de Vida: Experiencias de Jefas de Hogar Asentadas en Medellín, Colombia. Departamento de Antropologia Social, Universidad de Sevilla.

Martínez-Vázquez, Jorge, Santiago Lago-Peñas, and Agnese Sacchi. 2017. The Impact of Fiscal Decentralization: A Survey. *Journal of Economic Surveys* 31 (4): 1095–1129.

Mason, Elisa. 2018. Internally Displaced Persons: Guide to Legal Information Resources on the Web. Forced Migration Current Awareness. https://fmcab.blogspot.com/p/idps.html.

Maybank, J, B. Bonsai, K. Jones, R. Lawford, E.G. O'Brien, E.A. Ripley, and E. Wheaton. 1995. Drought as a Natural Disaster. *Atmosphere-Ocean* 33 (2): 195–222.

McCargo, Duncan, and Krisadawan Hongladarom. 2004. Contesting Isan-ness: Discourses of Politics and Identity in Northeast Thailand. *Asian Ethnicity* 5 (2): 219–234.

McCauley, John. 2013. Economic Development Strategy and Conflict: A Comparison of Côte d'Ivoire and Ghana 50 Years After Independence. In *Development Strategies and the Evolution of Violence in Africa*, eds. William Ascher and Natalia Mirovitskaya, 141–169. New York: Palgrave Macmillan.

McConahay, John. 1986. Modern Racism, Ambivalence, and the Modern Racism Scale. In *Prejudice, Discrimination, and Racism*, eds. John Dovidio and Samuel Gaertner, 91–125. Orlando, FL: Academic Press.

McGhee, Derek. 2006. Getting 'Host' Communities on Board: Finding the Balance between 'Managed Migration' and 'Managed Settlement' in Community Cohesion Strategies. *Journal of Ethnic and Migration Studies* 32 (1): 111–127.

McGibbon, Rodd. 2004. Plural Society in Peril: Migration, Economic Change, and the Papua Conflict. *East-West Center Policy Studies* 13.

McKenna, Thomas M. 1998. *Muslim Rulers and Rebels: Everyday Politics and Armed Separatism in the Southern Philippines*. Berkeley, CA: University of California Press.

McLean, J, and S. Straede. 2003. Conservation, Relocation, and the Paradigms of Park and People Management- A Case Study of Padampur Villages and the Royal Chitwan National Park, Nepal. *Society and Natural Resources* 16 (6): 509–526.

McRae, Dave. 2013. *A Few Poorly Organized Men: Interreligious Violence in Poso, Indonesia*. Leiden: Brill Publishers.

Metz, Brent, Lorenzo Mariano, and Julian Lopez Garcia. 2010. The Violence After 'La Violencia' in the Ch'orti Region of Eastern Guatemala. *The Journal of Latin American and Caribbean Anthropology* 15 (1): 16–41.

Migdal, Joel S. 1988. *Strong Societies and Weak States: State-Society Relations and State Capabilities in the Third World*. Princeton, NJ: Princeton University Press.

Miller, Sarah Ann, and Deardorff. 2014. Faith-Based Organizations and International Responses to Forced Migration. In *The Changing World Religion Map*, ed. Stanley Brunn, 3115–3133. London: Springer.

Mills, Mary Beth. 2012. Thai Mobilities and Cultural Citizenship. *Critical Asian Studies* 44 (1): 85–112.

Mitchell, Christopher. 2007. The Theory and Practice of Sanctuary: From Asylia to Local Zones of Peace. In *Zones of Peace*, eds. Landon E. Hancock and Christopher Mitchell, 1–28. London: Kumarian Press.

Montalvo, José G, and Marta Reynal-Querol. 2005. Ethnic Polarization, Potential Conflict and Civil War. *American Economic Review* 95 (3): 796–816.

Mooney, Erin. 2005. The Concept of Internal Displacement and the Case for Internally Displaced Persons as a Category of Concern. *Refugee Survey Quarterly* 24 (3): 9–26.

Moore, Christopher W. 2014. *The Mediation Process: Practical Strategies for Resolving Conflict*. San Francisco: Wiley and Sons, Fourth Edition.

Moore, Will H, and Stephen M. Shellman. 2006. Refugee or Internally Displaced Person? To Where Should One Flee? *Comparative Political Studies* 39 (5): 599–622.

Moradi, Sanan. 2014. Mellat and Qowm: A Political Geography of 'Nation' and 'Ethnicity' in Iran. PhD dissertation. Oxford, OH: Miami University of Ohio.

Morris-Jung, Jason, and Robin Roth. 2010. The Blurred Boundaries of Voluntary Resettlement: A Case of Cat Tien National Park in Vietnam. *Journal of Sustainable Forestry* 29 (2–4): 202–220.

Mueller, Valerie, and Abusaleh Shariff. 2011. Preliminary Evidence on Internal Migration, Remittances, and Teen Schooling in India. *Contemporary Economic Policy* 29 (2): 207–217.

Muggah, H.C.R. 2000. Conflict-Induced Displacement and Involuntary Resettlement in Colombia: Putting Cernea's IRLR Model to the Test. *Disasters* 24 (3): 198–216.

Muggah, Robert. 2008. *Relocation Failures in Sri Lanka: A Short History of Internal Displacement and Resettlement*. London: Zed Books.

Mwakagali, Mpoki. 2018. International Financial Institutions and Labour Standards: A Legal Study of the Role of These Institutions in the Promotion and Implementation of Freedom of Association and Collective Bargaining. PhD dissertation. Stockholm: Stockholm University.

Myers, Daniel J. 2000. The Diffusion of Collective Violence: Infectiousness, Susceptibility, and Mass Media Networks. *American Journal of Sociology* 106 (1): 173–208.

Nasritdinov, Emil. 2008. Discrimination Against Internal Migrants in Bishkek. In *Kyrgyzstan Today: Policy Briefs on Civil Society, Migration, Islam, Corruption*, ed. John Couper, 114–118. Bishkek: Social Research Center, American University of Central Asia.

Natsuda, Kaoru, Kunio Igusa, Aree Wiboonpongse, and John Thoburn. 2012. One Village One Product-Rural Development Strategy in Asia: The Case of OTOP in Thailand. *Canadian Journal of Development Studies/revue Canadienne D'études Du Développement* 33 (3): 369–385.

Navarro, Zander. 2009. Expropriating Land in Brazil. In *Agricultural Land Redistribution: Toward Greater Consensus*, eds. Hans Binswanger-Mkhize, Camille Bourguignon, and Rogier van den Brink, 267–290. Washington, DC: World Bank.

Neumann, Roderick P. 2001. Africa's 'Last Wilderness': Reordering Space for Political and Economic Control in Colonial Tanzania. *Africa* 71 (4): 641–665.

Nielsen, Ingrid, and Russell Smyth. 2006. Rural Migrants and Public Security. In *Economic Growth, Transition, and Globalization in China*, ed. Yu Yanrui, 121–152. Cheltenham: Edward Elgar.

Norris, Jacob. 2013. Exporting the Holy Land: Artisans and Merchant Migrants in Ottoman-era Bethlehem. *Mashriq & Mahjar: Journal of Middle East and North African Migration Studies* 1 (2): 14–40.

Noveria, Mita. 2002. *Internal Migration and Heterogeneous Ethnic Groups: Conflict Among Ethnic Groups (A Case Study on Migrant Receiving Areas in the North Sulawesi Province)*. Jakarta: Research Centre for Population-Indonesian Institute of Sciences.

Noviana, Nana. 2018. Integritas Kearifan Lokal Budaya Masyarakat Aceh dalam Tradisi Peusijuk. *Deskovi: Art and Design Journal* 1 (1): 29–34.

Oberai, A.S. 1983. *An Overview of Migration-Influencing Policies and Programmes*. New York: St. Martins Press.

Ofcansky, Thomas and LaVerle Berry, eds. 1991. *Ethiopia: A Country Study*. Washington: GPO for the Library of Congress. Resettlement and Villagization, http://countrystudies.us/ethiopia/.

Olthof, Douglas Allan. 2016. Compounding Fractures: State-Society Relations and Inter-Ethnic Estrangement in Thailand's 'Deep South'. PhD dissertation, Simon Fraser University. Burnaby, BC.

Orji, Nkwachukwu. 2011. Faith-Based Aid to People Affected by Conflict in Jos, Nigeria: An Analysis of the Role of Christian and Muslim Organizations. *Journal of Refugee Studies* 24 (3): 473–492.

Osawa, Mario. 2005. *Foreigners in Our Own Country*. London: Amnesty International.

Otiso, Kefa M. 2005. Kenya's Secondary Cities Growth Strategy at a Crossroads: Which Way Forward? *GeoJournal* 62 (1): 117–128.

Parreñas, Rhacel Salazar. 2005. *Children of Global Migration: Transnational Families and Gendered Woes*. Stanford: Stanford University Press.

Parsitau, Damaris Seleina. 2011. The Role of Faith and Faith-Based Organizations among Internally Displaced Persons in Kenya. *Journal of Refugee Studies* 24 (3): 493–512.

Patel, Sejal, Clare Shakya, and Neha Rai. 2020. *Climate Finance for Hydropower: Incentivising the Low-Carbon Transition*. London: International Institute for Environment and Development.

Pelzer, Karl J. 1945. *Pioneer Settlement in the Asiatic Tropics*. New York: American Geographical Society Special Publication No. 29.

Perz, Stephen G, Flavia Leite, Cynthia Simmons, Robert Walker, Stephen Aldrich, and Marcellus Caldas. 2010. Intraregional Migration, Direct Action

Land Reform, and New Land Settlements in the Brazilian Amazon. *Bulletin of Latin American Research* 29 (4): 459–476.
Petersen, William. 1958. A General Typology of Migration. *American Sociological Review* 23 (3): 256–266.
Petras, James. 1998. The Political and Social Basis of Regional Variation in Land Occupations in Brazil. *The Journal of Peasant Studies* 25 (4): 124–133.
Pol, Megha. 2020. We Didn't Know our Home was Illegal: Diva Residents. *Hindustan Times*, January 9.
Polian, Pavel. 2004. *Against their Will: The History and Geography of Forced Migrations in the USSR*. Budapest: Central European University Press.
Porter, Matthew, and Nick Haslam. 2005. Predisplacement and Postdisplacement Factors Associated with Mental Health of Refugees and Internally Displaced Persons: A Meta-Analysis. *Journal of the American Medical Association* 294 (5): 602–612.
Poston, David. 1990. The Development of Rural Manufacturing Industry in Central Africa: With Special Reference to Metalworking. PhD dissertation, University of Warwick. Warwick, UK.
Price, Susanna. 2015. Is There a Global Safeguard for Development Displacement? In *Development Induced Displacement and Resettlement: New Perspectives on Persisting Problems*, eds. Irge Satiroglu and Narae Choi, 127–141. Abingdon: Routledge.
Priyadarshini, Anamika and Sonamani Chaudhury. 2020. The Return of Bihari Migrants After the COVID-19 Lockdown. In *Borders of an Epidemic: Covid-19 and Migrant Workers*, ed. Ranabir Samaddar, 66–75. Kolkata: Calcutta Research Group.
Prothero, Mansell. 1994. Forced Movements of Population and Health Hazards in Tropical Africa. *International Journal of Epidemiology* 23 (4): 657–654.
Prud'homme, Remy. 1995. The Dangers of Decentralization. *World Bank Research Observer* 10 (2): 201–220.
Putnam, Robert D. 1994. *Making Democracy Work: Civic Traditions in Modern Italy*. Princeton: Princeton University Press.
Quang, Binh Bui, Thi Thu, Nguyen, and Chuong Ong Nguyen. 2016. Internal Migration in the Context of Trade Liberalisation in Vietnam. *Malaysian Journal of Economic Studies* 53 (2): 195–209.
Ramakrishnan, Kavita. 2014. Cosmopolitan Imaginaries on the Margins: Negotiating Difference and Belonging in a Delhi Resettlement Colony. *Contemporary South Asia* 22 (1): 67–81.
Ravenstein, Ernst G. 1885. The Laws of Migration. *Journal of the Statistical Society of London* 48 (2): 167–235.
Reddy, I.U.B, and Smrithi Talwar. 2014. *How Fair is 'Fair Compensation' under India's New Land Acquisition Act? World Bank End Poverty in South Asia Blog*. Washington, DC: World Bank.

Rees, Philip, M. Bell, Martin Bell, Marek Kupiszewski, Dorota Kupiszewska, Philipp Ueffing, Bernard Aude, Elin Charles-Edwards, and John Stillwell. 2017. The Impact of Internal Migration on Population Redistribution: An International Comparison. *Population, Space and Place* 23 (6): 20–36.

Refstie, Hilde, Chris Dolan, and Moses Chrispus Okello. 2010. Urban IDPs in Uganda: Victims of Institutional Convenience. *Forced Migration Review* 34: 32–33.

Reilly, Benjamin. 2006. Political Parties and Political Engineering in Divided Societies. *Democratization* 13 (5): 811–827.

Reimer, Tanya. 2010. Brazil's Landless Movement (MST) and the Changing Culture of Property. *On Politics* 2 (1): 1–41.

Reinnoldt, Charlotte. 2019. *Asserting Indigenous Identity to Substantiate Customary Forest Claims: A Case Study of the Dayaks of West Kalimantan, Indonesia*. Thesis: Claremont McKenna College.

Requia, Weeberb J, Henrique Llacer Roig, Petros Koutrakis, and Maria Silvia Rossi. 2016. Mapping Alternatives for Public Policy Decision Making Related to Human Exposures from Air Pollution Sources in the Federal District, Brazil. *Land Use Policy* 59: 375–385.

Reuveny, Rafael. 2008. Ecomigration and Violent Conflict: Case Studies and Public Policy Implications. *Human Ecology* 36 (1): 1–13.

Reynolds, Sarnata. 2014. *Mexico's Unseen Victims*. Washington, DC: Refugees International.

Rhee, Steve. 2009. The Cultural Politics of Collaboration. In *The Decentralization of Forest Governance: Politics, Economics, and the Fight for Control of Forests in Indonesian Borneo*, eds. Moira Moeliono, Eva Wollenberg, and Godwin Limberg, 43–60. London: Earthscan.

Richardson, Harry W. 1987. Whither National Urban Policy in Developing Countries? *Urban Studies* 24 (3): 227–244.

Richter, Iris. 2016. Experiences from the Implementation of Social Land Concessions in Cambodia. Bonn: Deutsche Gesellschaft für Internationale Zusammenarbeit. January.

Roberts, Bryan R. 2020. *The Making of Citizens: Cities of Peasants Revisited*. New York: Routledge.

Rodriguez, Robyn Magalit. 2010. *Migrants for Export: How the Philippine State Brokers Labor to the World*. Minneapolis: University of Minnesota Press.

Roldán-Ortega, Roque. 2004. *Models for Recognizing Indigenous Land Rights in Latin America*. Washington, DC: World Bank.

Rondinelli, Dennis, John R. Nellis, and G. Shabbir Cheema. 1983. *Decentralization in Developing Countries: A Review of Recent Experience*. Washington, DC: World Bank.

Rondinelli, Dennis. 2006. Government Decentralization and Economic Development: The Evolution of Concepts and Practices. *Research in Public Policy Analysis and Management* 15: 433–445.

Roquet, Vincent, Luciano Bornholdt, Karen Sirker, and Jelena Lukic. 2015. *Urban Land Acquisition and Involuntary Resettlement: Linking Innovation and Local Benefits*. World Bank, 2015.

Roy, Rajkumari Chandra Kalindi. 2000. *Land Fights of the Indigenous Peoples of the Chittagong Hill Tracts, Bangladesh*. Document No. 99. Copenhagen: International Work Group for Indigenous Affairs.

King, Russell and Ronald Skeldon. 2010. 'Mind the Gap!' Integrating Approaches to Internal and International Migration. *Journal of Ethnic and Migration Studies* 36 (10): 1619–1646.

Sadiq, Kamal. 2009. When Being 'Native' is Not Enough: Citizens as Foreigners in Malaysia. *Asian Perspective* 33 (1): 5–32.

Samaddar, Arghadip, Ravisekhar Gadepalli, Vijaya Lakshmi Nag, and Sanjeev Misra. 2020. The Enigma of Low COVID-19 Fatality Rate in India. *Frontiers in Genetics* 11 (854): 1–9.

Samuels, Annemarie. 2015. Narratives of Uncertainty: The Affective Force of Child-Trafficking Rumors in Postdisaster Aceh, Indonesia. *American Anthropologist* 117 (2): 229–241.

Sánchez, Luis. 2007. Splitting the Country: The Case of the Atlantic Coast of Nicaragua. *Journal of Latin American Geography* 6 (1): 7–23.

Sanford, Victoria. 2003. Eyewitness: Peacebuilding in a War Zone: The Case of Colombian Peace Communities. *International Peacekeeping* 10 (2): 107–118.

Sante, Delli, and Angela. 1996. *Nightmare or Reality: Guatemala in the 1980s*. Amsterdam: Thela.

Sasse, Gwendolyn. 2020. War and Displacement: The Case of Ukraine. *Europe-Asia Studies* 72 (3): 347–353.

Savage, Michael. 1986. The Imposition of Pass Laws on the African Population in South Africa 1916–1984. *African Affairs* 85 (339): 181–205.

Schewel, Kerilyn and Asmamaw Legass Bahir. 2019. Migration and Social Transformation in Ethiopia. International Migration Institute Working Papers Series No. 152. Oxford: IMI.

Schmidt-Soltau, Kai, and Dan Brockington. 2007. Protected Areas and Resettlement: What Scope for Voluntary Relocation? *World Development* 35 (12): 2182–2202.

Schneider, Aaron. 2003. Decentralization: Conceptualization and Measurement. *Studies in Comparative International Development* 38 (3): 32–56.

Schneider, Leander. 2004. Freedom and Rural Development: Julius Nyerere, Ujaama Vijijini, and Villagization. *Canadian Journal of African Affairs* 38 (2): 344–392.

Scriven, Joel. 2010. *Markets & Payments for Ecosystem Services: Engaging REDD+ on Peru's Amazonian Frontier*. Diss. Oxford: Oxford University.

Scudder, Thayer. 2016. *Aswan High Dam Resettlement of Egyptian Nubians*. Singapore: Springer.

Selway, Joel Sawat. 2011. The Measurement of Cross-cutting Cleavages and Other Multidimensional Cleavage Structures. *Political Analysis* 19 (1): 48–65.

Selya, Roger Mark. 2004. *Development and Demographic Change in Taiwan*. Singapore: World Scientific.

Sen, Rumela. 2019. Competing Mobilization of Tribal and Class Identity: Politics of Internal Migration in North India. In *Internal Migration: Challenges in Governance and Integration*, eds. Shane Barter and William Ascher, 63–76. New York: Peter Lang.

Seymour, Lee, and Marek Brzezinski. 2019. Unsettled States: Displacement, Governance, and Integration in the Southern Caucasus. In *Internal Migration: Challenges in Governance and Integration*, ed. Shane Barter and William Ascher, 47–62. New York: Peter Lang.

Shaojun, Chen. 2006. A Study of Poverty Risks Based on Involuntary Migration of Chinese Village Dwellers. *Chinese Sociology & Anthropology* 38 (3): 19–39.

Shaw, William H. 2003. They Stole Our Land: Debating the Expropriation of White Farms on Zimbabwe. *Journal of Modern African Studies* 41 (1): 75–89.

Sherif, Muzafer, ed. 1962. *Intergroup Relations and Leadership*. New York: Wiley.

Sim, Loo Lee, Shi Mang Yu, and Sun Sheng Han. 2003. Public Housing and Ethnic Integration in Singapore. *Habitat International* 27 (2): 293–307.

Simmons, C.S, R.T. Walker, E.Y. Arima, S.P. Aldrich, and M.M. Caldas. 2007. The Amazon Land War in the South of Pará. *Annals of the Association of American Geographers* 97 (3): 567–592.

Simon, Herbert. 1981. *The Sciences of the Artificial*. Cambridge, MA: MIT Press.

Simpson, Brad. 2021. Indonesian Transmigration and the Crisis of Development, 1968–1985. *Diplomatic History* 45 (2): 268–284.

Sina, Dantje, Alice Chang-Richards, Suzanne Wilkinson, and Regan Potangaroa. 2019. A Conceptual Framework for Measuring Livelihood Resilience: Relocation Experience from Aceh, Indonesia. *World Development* 117: 253–265.

Siroën, Jean-Marc, and David Andrade. 2016. *Regional Trade Agreements and Diffusion of International Labour Standards*. Paris: Université Paris-Dauphine.

Siroky, David, and Michael Hechter. 2016. Ethnicity, Class, and Civil War: The Role of Hierarchy, Segmentation, and Cross-Cutting Cleavages. *Civil Wars* 18 (1): 91–107.

Skeldon, Ronald. 1990. *Population Mobility in Developing Countries: A Reinterpretation*. London: Belhaven.

Skeldon, Ronald. 2008. International Migration as a Tool in Development Policy: A Passing Phase? *Population and Development Review* 34 (1): 1–18.

Skeldon, Ronald. 2009. *International Migration, Internal Migration, Mobility, and Urbanization: Towards More Integrated Approaches*. Geneva: IOM Publications.

Skeldon, Ronald. 2018. International Migration, Internal Migration, Mobility and Urbanization: Towards More Integrated Approaches. IOM Migration Research Series 53.

Soedirgo, Jessica. 2020. Quotidian Institutions and Identity Formation: Explaining Patterns of Identity Salience in Maluku, Indonesia. *Asian Politics and Policy* 13 (1): 56–71.

Srur, Muradu. 2013. Rural Commons and the Ethiopian State. *Law, Social Justice & Global Development* 2 (1): 1–47.

Stahl, Charles W. 1995. Theories of International Labor Migration: An Overview. *Asian and Pacific Migration Journal* 4 (2–3): 211–232.

Stark, Oded, and David Bloom. 1985. The New Economics of Labor Migration. *American Economic Review*, 75 (2): 173–178.

Stecklov, G. 2008. *The Components of Urban Growth in Developing Countries*. Unpublished manuscript. New York: United Nations.

Stepputat, Finn, and Ninna Nyberg Sørensen. 2001. The Rise and Fall of 'Internally Displaced People' in the Central Peruvian Andes. *Development and Change* 32 (4): 769–791.

Stocks, Gabriela. 2014. *Assessing the Long-Term Effects of Development-Forced Displacement and Resettlement: The Case of Nuevo Arenal, Costa Rica*. Doctoral Dissertation, University of Florida. Gainesville, FL.

Stokke, Olav. 2013. *Aid and Political Conditionality*. London: Routledge.

Straits Times. 2018. Rohingya Crisis Could Pose Security Risk to Region, Najib Warns. March 18.

Sutton, Keith. 1989. Malaysia's FELDA Land Settlement Model in Time and Space. *Geoforum* 20 (3): 339–354.

Tadjoeddin, M. Zulfan, and Anis Chowdhury. 2009. Socioeconomic Perspectives on Violent Conflict in Indonesia. *The Economics of Peace and Security Journal* 4 (1): 39–47.

Tambiah, Stanley J. 1996. *Leveling Crowds*. Berkeley: University of California Press.

Taghados, Mostafa Javaheri, Mahin Nastaran, Esfandiar Zebardast, and Maysam Basirat. 2021. A Future Study on the Role of New Towns in Establishing Balance in the Spatial-Physical Structure of the Metropolitan Regions Based on the National Spatial Planning Approaches and Policies. *Quarterly Journal of the Macro and Strategic Policies* 8 (4): 772–794.

Tanasaldy, Taufiq. 2012. *Regime Change and Ethnic Politics in Indonesia*. Leiden: KITLV Press.

Tanzi, Vito. 2001. Pitfalls on the road to fiscal decentralization. Working Paper No. 19. Carnegie Endowment for International Peace, Washington DC. April. http://www.carnegieendowment.org/files/19Tanzi.pdf.

Tay, Elaine. 2006. Discursive Violence on the Internet and the May 1998 Riots. In *Violent Conflicts in Indonesia: Analysis, Representation, Resolution*, ed. Charles Coppel, 58–71. London: Routledge.

Taylor, Lewis. 1998. Counter-Insurgency Strategy, the PCP-Sendero Luminoso, and the Civil War in Peru, 1980–1996. *Bulletin of Latin American Research* 17 (1): 35–58.

Techakesari, Pirathat, Fiona Kate Barlow, Matthew J. Hornsey, Billy Sung, Michael Thai, and Jocelyn LY. Chak. 2015. An Investigation of Positive and Negative Contact as Predictors of Intergroup Attitudes in the United States, Hong Kong, and Thailand. *Journal of Cross-Cultural Psychology* 46 (3): 454–468.

Terminski, Bogumil. 2013. *Development-Induced Displacement and Resettlement: Theoretical Frameworks and Current Challenges*. Geneva: Ibidem Press.

Thanh, Hoang Xuan, Truong Tuan Anh, and Dinh Thi Thu. Phuong. 2013. *Urban Poverty in Vietnam: A View from Complementary Assessments*. London: International Institute for Environment and Development.

Thawnghmung, Ardeth. 2016. The Politics of Indigeneity in Myanmar: Competing Narratives in Rakhine State. *Asian Ethnicity* 17 (4): 527–547.

Thede, Nancy. 2009. Decentralization, Democracy, and Human Rights: A Human Rights-Based Analysis of the Impact of Local Democratic Reforms on Development. *Journal of Human Development and Capabilities* 10 (1): 103–123.

Tigno, Jorge V. 2006. Migration and Violent Conflict in Mindanao. *Population Review* 45 (1): 23–47.

Todaro, Michael P. 1976. *Migration and Economic Development: A Review of Theory, Evidence, Methodology and Research Priorities*. Nairobi: University of Nairobi.

Tomsa, Dirk. 2009. Local Elections and Party Politics in a Post-Conflict Area: The Pilkada in Maluku. Indonesian Studies Working Papers Sidney: University of Sidney.

Tostensen, Arne, Inge Tvedten, and Mariken Vaa, eds. 2001. *Associational Life in African Cities: Popular Responses to the Urban Crisis*. Stockholm: Nordiska Afrikainstitutet.

Tranchant, Jean-Pierre. 2013. Making the Urban Poor Safer: Lessons from Nairobi and Maharashtra. IDS Policy Briefing 47. Sussex: Institute for Development Studies.

Trihartono, Agus, and Nino Viartasiwi. 2015. Engaging the Quiet Mission: Civil Society in Breaking the Cycle of Violence in the Post-Conflict Poso, Indonesia. *Procedia Environmental Science* 28: 115–123.

Tsui, Amy O, Tod A. Ragsdale, and Aden I. Shirwa. 1991. The Settlement of Somali Nomads. *Genus* 47: 131–152.

Tuminez, Astrid S. 2007. This Land is Our Land: Moro Ancestral Domain and Its Implications for Peace and Development in the Southern Philippines. *SAIS Review of International Affairs* 27 (2): 77–91.

Turton, David. 2003. Conceptualising Forced Migration. RSC Working Paper No. 12: Working Paper Series. Oxford: University of Oxford.

UDHR (Universal Declaration of Human Rights) 1948.

Uehling, Greta L. 2004. *Beyond Memory: The Crimean Tatars' Deportation and Return*. London: Springer.

UN FAO. 2016. Migration, Agriculture, and Rural Development. Rome.

UN General Assembly. 1948. *Universal Declaration of Human Rights*. New York: United Nations.

UN Habitat. 2016. *World Cities Report 2016: Urbanization and Development; Emerging Futures, United Nations Human Settlements Programme*. Nairobi: UN-Habitat.

UN Habitat. 2020. *World Cities Report 2020*. Nairobi: UN Habitat.

UN OCHA (Office for the Coordination of Humanitarian Affairs). 2004. *Guiding Principles on Internal Displacement*. Geneva: United Nations

UN Office of Internal Oversight Services. 2017. Evaluation of the Office of the United Nations High Commissioner for Refugees. Economic and Social Council, 12 January 2017.

UN Population Division. 2018. *World Urbanization Prospects: The 2018 Revision*. New York: United Nations.

UNESCO. 2018. Policy Briefs on Internal Migration. Bangkok.

UNHCR (United Nations High Commissioner for Refugees). 1998. UN Guiding Principles on Internal Displacement. Geneva: UNHCR. www.unhcr.org/en-us/protection/idps/43ce1cff2/guiding-principles-internal-displacement.html.

UNHCR (United Nations High Commissioner for Refugees). 2019. What is a Refugee? Available at www.unrefugees.org/refugee-facts/what-is-a-refugee/.

UNHCR (United Nations High Commissioner for Refugees). 2021. UNHCR Global Report. Geneva: UNHCR. https://reporting.unhcr.org/globalreport2021/pdf.

Uribe-Mallarino, Consuelo. 2008. Estratificación Social en Bogotá: De la Política Pública a la Dinámica de la Segregación Social. *Universitas Humanística* 65: 139–171.

Van Der Wijst, Ton. 1985. Transmigration in Indonesia: An Evaluation of a Population Redistribution Policy. *Population Research and Policy Review* 4 (1): 1–30.

Van Luong, Hy, and Jonathan Unger. 1998. Wealth, Power, and Poverty in the Transition to Market Economies: The Process of Socio-Economic Differentiation in Rural China and Northern Vietnam. *The China Journal* 40: 61–93.

Vanclay, Frank. 2017. Project-Induced Displacement and Resettlement: From Impoverishment Risks to an Opportunity for Development? *Impact Assessment and Project Appraisal* 35 (1): 3–21.

Vandekerckhove, Nel. 2009. We Are Sons of This Soil': The Endless Battle Over Indigenous Homelands in Assam, India. *Critical Asian Studies* 41 (4): 523–548.

Varshney, Ashutosh, Mohammad Zulfan Tadjoeddin, and Rizal Panggabean. 2004. *Patterns of Collective Violence in Indonesia, 1990–2003*. Jakarta: United Nations Support Facility for Indonesian Recovery.

Verwimp, Philip. 2013. *Peasants in Power: The Political Economy of Development and Genocide in Rwanda*. London: Springer.

Villema, Sietze, Saturnino M. Borras Jr, and Francisco Lara Jr. 2011. The Agrarian Roots of Contemporary Violent Conflict in Mindanao, Southern Philippines. *Journal of Agrarian Change* 11 (3): 298–320.

Wade, Robert H. 2016. Boulevard to Broken Dreams, Part 1: The Polonoroeste Road Project in the Brazilian Amazon and the World Bank's Environmental and Indigenous Peoples' Norms. *Brazilian Journal of Political Economy* 36 (1): 214–230.

Waldrauch, Harald, and Christoph Hofinger. 1997. An Index to Measure the Legal Obstacles to Integration of Migrants. *Journal of Ethnic and Migration Studies* 23 (2): 271–285.

Wallace, Jeremy W. 2014. *Cities and Stability: Urbanization, Redistribution, & Regime Survival in China*. Oxford: Oxford University Press.

Walsh, John. 2003. Egypt's Muslim Brotherhood: Understanding Centrist Islam. *Harvard International Review* 24 (4): 32–36.

Wang, Lan, Ratoola Kundu, and Xiangming Chen. 2010. Building for What and Whom? New Town Development as Planned Suburbanization in China and India. *Suburbanization in Global Society* 10: 319–345.

Weiner, Myron. 1978. *Sons of the Soil: Migration and Ethnic Conflict in India*. Princeton: Princeton University Press.

Weiner, Myron. 1983. The Political Demography of Assam's Anti-Immigrant Movement. *Population and Development Review* 9 (2): 279–292.

Wenban-Smith, Hugh. 2015. *Population Growth, Internal Migration and Urbanisation in Tanzania, 1967–2012: Phase 2 (Final Report)*. London: International Growth Centre.

Wheeler, Matt. 2010. People's Patron or Patronizing the people? The Southern Border Provinces Administrative Centre in perspective. *Contemporary Southeast Asia* 32 (2): 208–233.

Whitaker, Beth Elise. 2002. Refugees in Western Tanzania: The Distribution of Burdens and Benefits Among Local Hosts. *Journal of Refugee Studies* 15 (4): 339–358.

Wilkinson, Steven I. 2004. *Votes and Violence: Electoral Competition and Ethnic Riots in India*. Cambridge: Cambridge University Press.

Wilkinson, Steven I. 2015. *Army and Nation: The Military and Indian Democracy since Independence*. Harvard University Press.

Wilson, Tom. 2019. Ethnic Violence in Ethiopia has Forced Nearly 3 Million People from their Homes. *Los Angeles Times,* May 30.

Wood, Charles H. 2002. Introduction: Land Use and Deforestation in the Amazon. In *Deforestation and Land Use in the Amazon,* eds. Charles H. Wood and Roberto Porro, 1–40. University of Florida Press.

World Bank. 1994. *Resettlement and Development: The Bankwide Review of Projects Involving Involuntary Resettlement 1986–1993*. Washington, DC.

World Bank. 2004 *Operational Policy 4.12 on Involuntary Resettlement*.

World Bank. 2006. *Infrastructure: Lessons from the Last Two Decades of World Bank Engagement*. World Bank Infrastructure Network Discussion Paper. http://documents.worldbank.org/curated/en/291191468166484472/pdf/351991 0vol-01.pdf.

World Bank, 2009. *World Development Report*. Washington, DC.

World Bank. 2001. *What, Why, and Where*. Washington, DC.

World Bank. 2016. *Migration and Development*. Washington, DC.

World Bank. 2017a. *Forcibly Displaced: Toward a Development Approach Supporting Refugees, the Internally Displaced, and their Hosts*. Washington, DC.

World Bank. 2017b. *Approach Paper: An Evaluation of World Bank Group Support in Conflict Induced Situations of Forced Displacement*. Washington, DC.

World Bank. 2019. *World Bank Group Support in Situations Involving Conflict-Induced Displacement: An Independent Evaluation*. Washington DC: Independent Evaluation Group.

World Bank GPFD (Global Program on Forced Displacement). 2015. *Annual Progress Report*.

World Commission on Dams. 2000. *Dams and Development: A New Framework for Decision-Making: Final Report of the World Commission on Dams*. London: Earthscan.

Yadav, Vineeta. 2019. The Political Economy of Special Economic Zones and Internal Displacement in India. In *Internal Migration: Challenges in Governance and Integration*, eds. Shane Barter and William Ascher, 77–95. New York: Peter Lang.

Yang, Anand A. 1980. Sacred Symbol and Sacred Space in Rural India: Community Mobilization in the 'Anti-Cow Killing' Riot of 1893. *Comparative Studies in Society and History* 22 (4): 576–596.
Young, Forrest Wade. 2019. Rapa Nui. *The Contemporary Pacific* 31 (1): 225–234.
Young, Helen and Daniel Maxwell. 2009. *Targeting in Complex Emergencies: Darfur Case Study*. Feinstein International Center Report. Medford MA: Tufts University.
Zaman, Mohammad, Reshmy Nair, and Shi Guoqing, eds. 2020. *Resettlement in Asian Countries: Legislation, Administration and Struggles for Rights*. Oxford: Routledge.
Zea, Juan Esteban. 2019. How IDPs Navigate the Resettlement Process in Bogotá, Colombia. In *Internal Migration: Challenges in Governance and Integration*, eds. Shane Barter and William Ascher, 33–46. New York: Peter Lang.
Zeccola, Paul. 2011. Dividing Disasters in Aceh, Indonesia: Separatist Conflict and Tsunami, Human rights and Humanitarianism. *Disasters* 35 (2): 308–328.
Zezza, Alberto, and Luca Tasciotti. 2010. Urban Agriculture, Poverty, and Food Security: Empirical Evidence from a Sample of Developing Countries. *Food Policy* 35 (4): 265–273.
Zhang, Dong, and Yongjiao Yang. 2022. Internal Migrants' Charitable Giving to Hometowns in China: The Effect of Community Embeddedness. *Population, Space, and Place* 28 (2): e2491.
Zhang, Heather X, P. Mick Kelly, Catherine Locke, Alexandra Winkels, and W. Neil Adger. 2006. Migration in a Transitional Economy: Beyond the Planned and Spontaneous Dichotomy in Vietnam. *Geoforum* 37 (6): 1066–1081.
Zimmer, Andrew, Zack Guido Tuholske, Alex Pakalnksis, Sara Lopus, Kelly Caylor, and Tom Evans. 2020. Dynamics of Population Growth in Secondary Cities across Southern Africa. *Landscape Ecology* 35 (11): 2501–2516.
Zips-Mairitsch, Manuela. 2013. *Lost Lands? (Land) Rights of the San in Botswana and the Legal Concept of Indigeneity in Africa*. Münster: LIT Verlag.

Index

A
Abinales, Patricio, 238, 240
Abkhazia, 284
Abuja (Nigeria), 120
Accommodation of illegal settlements, 81
Accountability
  evasion of, 226
  self-accountability, 219
  state accountability, 117, 191, 218, 227
Accountability evasion of officials, 226
Aceh (Indonesia), 1, 21, 22, 40, 46, 62, 181, 205, 235, 255, 256, 261
Acharya, Avidit, 167
Action for the Needy (Ethiopia), 257
Addaney, Michael, 275
Adeola, Romola, 275
Adepoju, Aderanti, 25
Adewale, J. Gbemiga, 102
Adivisi (India), 111
administrative decentralization, 63, 64
Afizare (Nigeria), 204
Afolabi, Oladiran, 204
Africa. *See also* individual countries
  African Human Rights Court, 279
  African Union (AU), 2, 224, 275, 282
  Central Africa, 50, 163
  hometown associations in, 146, 147
  West Africa, 146
African Human Rights Court, 279
African Union (AU), xii, 2, 224, 275, 282
Afro-Argentines, 152
Afro-Colombians, 152
Agbese, Pita, 146
Aguilar, Soledad, 82
Agunbiade, Muyiwa, 113
Ahmad, Junaid, 63
Ahram, Ariel, 88
Ahsan, Syed, 45
Ain o Salish Kendra (ASK) (Bangladesh), 258
Airports, 47, 129
Åland Islands (Finland), 231
Alexander, Peter, 3

W. Ascher and S. J. Barter, *Moving within Borders*, Politics, Economics, and Inclusive Development, https://doi.org/10.1007/978-3-031-37549-1

Al Qurtuby, Sumanto, 245
Alzate, Maria, 116
Amazonia
  resettlement (Brazil), 48, 219, 226
  Transamazon Highway, 36
Ambiguity, 90, 100, 135, 136, 168, 221, 222, 224, 229, 275, 280, 284, 300, 301
  of international doctrine, 223
  of state obligations, 222, 223
Ambon Island (Indonesia), 1
Amerindians (Argentina), 152
Ammarell, Gene, 105
Amnesty International, 279
Amrith, Sunil, 45
Anaguta (Nigeria), 204
Anatolia (Turkey), 45, 86, 194
Andaman Islands (India), 49
Anderson, George, 60
Andhra Pradesh (India), 49, 140, 163, 244
Andisheh (Iran), 118
Andrade, David, 278
Angenendt, Steffen, 281, 282, 285
Anglophones (Quebec), 62
Ang, Yuen, 240
Anh, Dang, 20, 113, 199
Animists, 39, 206, 208
Arabs, xi, 46, 52, 88, 167
  charities, 253
  in Iran, xi, 167
Aragon, Lorraine, 209, 262
Arenales Hydroelectric Project (Costa Rica), 68
Argentina
  Afro-Argentines, 152
  Amerindians, 152
  Buenos Aires, 43, 152
  federal system in, 59
  slum removal, 43
  Villero identity, 152
Arifin, Bustanul, 103
Armenian merchants, 104
Arnall, Alex, 90, 138
Arredondo, C., 277
Ascher, William, vii
Asian Development Bank, 273
Assam (India), 49, 74, 175, 179, 180, 207
Asthana, Vandana, 130
Aswan High Dam (Egypt), 204
Australia, 273
  technical assistance on migration issues, 163, 226
Autochthony, 178, 180, 301
Avars (Russian Federation), 61
Azerbaijan
  Conflicts with Georgia, 284
  Nagorno-Karabakh, 284
  South Ossetia, 284

B

Bahir, Asmamaw, 101
Bakwit (Evacuee) Power (Philippines), 259
Balcells, Laia, 176
Bali (Indonesia), 17, 21, 206
Balkans
  European Union pressures to return IDPs, 278
Balochs (Iran), 167
Balueva, Olga, 19
Banerji, Haimanti, 120
Bangkok (Thailand), 7, 16, 44, 145, 172
Bangladesh
  Ain o Salish Kendra (ASK), 258
  Chittagong Hill Tracts, 45
  Nari Udyog Kendra (NUK), 258
  Rahman, President Ziaur, 45
  Rohingya refugees, vii
Barau, Aliyu, 238, 239
Barkan, Joel, 121
Bar-Tal, Daniel, 88

Barter, Shane, 1, 22, 40, 46, 62, 161, 185, 194, 207, 230, 235, 253, 261, 262
Barton, Greg, 230
Baruah, Sanjib, 74
Barutciski, Michael, 26, 27
Bashkirs (Russian Federation), 61
Basque region (Spain), 62
Bass, Daniel, 180
Bastar district (India), 170
Bawana resettlement colony (India), 119
Bazzi, Samuel, 236
Becquelin, Nicholas, 46
Bell, Martin, 3
Bengalis
  bureaucrats, 164, 207
  Hindus, 47, 180, 185
  migrants, 49, 179
  Muslims, 47, 185
Benson, Edward, 254, 256
Benthall, Jonathan, 253, 255
Berom (Nigeria), 204
Betawi Brotherhood (Indonesia), 165
Betts, Alexander, 27, 128, 224
Bhagat, Ram, 110, 113
Bhattacharyya, Harihar, 175
Biafra (Nigeria), 181
Biggs, Diana, 251
Bihar State (India), 16, 109
Bilateral aid agencies, 40
Bird, Kate, 90
Bishi, Hakeem, 113
BJP party (India), 114
Black, Richard, 277
Bloom, David, 23
Bock, P.G., 23
Bodoland Territorial Region (India), 175
Bodos (India), 175
Boer War (South Africa), 88
Bogotá (Colombia), 116
Bolivia
  El Alto, 16, 118
  La Paz, 118
  native rights, 241
  peripheral settlements, 119
Boone, Catherine, 60
Border areas, 6, 36
Borneo. *See also* Central Kalimantan Province, East Kalimantan Province, Kalimantan, North Kalimantan Province, Sabah State, Sarawak State, South Kalimantan Province, West Kalimantan Province
  Indonesian, x
  Malaysian, 21, 232
Borras, Saturnino, 95
Borsato, Roshan, 268
Bosankić, Nina, 139
Bose, Pablo, 49, 170, 220
Boshoff, Elsabe, 275
Botswana
  Gaborone, 120
Bougainville (Indonesia), 181
Brass, Paul, 184, 239
Bräuchler, Birgit, 245, 261, 262
Brazil
  agriculture, 35, 103
  Amazon, xi, 16, 35, 47, 48, 72, 94, 95, 103, 166, 182, 194, 197, 243, 292, 300
  Amazonian resettlement, 219, 226
  Brazilian-Paraguayan Itaipu Dam, 129
  conservation, 39
  favelas (shantytowns), 199
  forests, 49, 103
  Manaus, 16
  military, 35, 36, 47
  Movimento dos Trabalhadores Rurais Sem Terra, 48

National Institute for Colonization and Agrarian Reform, 219
Polonoroeste Program, 94
resettlement, 44, 48, 166, 197, 300
Rondonia State, 194
taxation by Rio de Janeiro militias, 199
Transpacific Highway, 151
Bredenoord, Jan, 118
British (rule in India), 39, 231
Brockington, Dan, 223
Brown, Cate, 273
Brown, Graham, 46
Brun, Catherine, 274
Brzezinski, Marek, 47, 242, 284
Buddhists
in India, 39
in Thailand, 16, 52, 169, 208, 220, 253, 298
militarization, 253
temples, 208, 253
Buenos Aires, Argentina, 43, 152
Bugesera region (Rwanda), 269
Buginese (Indonesia), 230
Bullock, Noah, 92
Bumiputera (Malaysia), 21
Bureau of Lands (Philippines), 162
Burmans (Myanmar), 179
Butonese (Indonesia), 39, 230

C
Cai, Qian, 145
Cairo earthquake (Egypt), 255
Calderón-Mejía, Valentina, 112
Cambodia
clinics, 95
forests, 197
Land Allocation for Social and Economic Development Project, 196
Shuikou Hydro-Project, 197
Social Land Concession program, 95
Cambon, Laurent, 140
Cameroon
mutualism in, 146
nature reserves in, 50
remittances, 146
Campbell, Donald, 143
Canuday, José Jowel, 259
Carbon credits, 50
Carrying capacity, 47, 144, 161, 166, 167
Catalonia (Spain), 62
Catholic bishops, 253
Catholic Relief Service, 256
Cattaneo, Andrea, 26
Cát Tiên National Park (Vietnam), 222
Caucasus, 47, 61, 284
Cawley, Brian, 276
Çelik, Ayşe, 45, 86, 194
Central Africa, 50, 163
lack of national policies on ecological IDPs, 51
Central African Republic, 51
nature reserves, 50
Central Americans
migration to the United States, ix
Central Asia, 88
Central Kalimantan (Indonesia), 236
Central Sulawesi (Indonesia), 206, 209, 245
Cernea, Michael, 26, 50, 276, 305
Chadda, Ishu, 110, 116, 140
Chadha, Vikram, 110, 116, 140
Chaga merchants (Tanzania), 104
Chain migration, 145
Chakma, Bhumitra, 45
Chakma, Nikhil, 39
Chakrabarti, Anuradha, 120
Chaldean (Nestorian) merchants, 104
Chan, Anita, 3

Chan, Kam, 20, 112, 199
Chaudhury, Sonamani, 65
Chechens (Russian Federation), 61
Cheema, Shabbir, 234
Chen, Ted, 256
Chen, Xiangming, 119
Chettyar moneylenders (India), 104
Chile, 59
  decentralization, 59
  Rapa Nui, 232
China
  civilizing demand in, 3, 207
  corruption, 80
  dams in, 17
  drought, 232
  Han, 3, 46, 180, 207, 232, 240, 298, 306
  Hukou regulations, 3, 20, 233
  Inner Mongolia, 232, 240
  Panyu Center, 258
  peripheral settlements, 119
  remittances, 23, 111, 145
  resettlement, viii, xi, 79, 197, 298, 306
  residency requirements, 3, 101
  Shanghai, 119, 207
  Shenzhen Labor Disputes Center, 258
  slum removal, 43, 101
  Sons of the Soil conflicts, 179
  Special Autonomous Regions, 231
  tax incentives to keep people in rural areas, 40
  Three Gorges Dam, 129
  Uighurs, 207, 306
  Xinjiang region, 46, 181, 231, 298
Chinese (ethnic), 104, 231
  in Indonesia, 40, 104, 105, 171, 181
  in Thailand, 94, 171
Chittagong Hill Tracts (Bangladesh), 45
Chowdhury, Anis, 39
Christian Aid, 256
Christians
  in Indonesia, 1, 148, 184, 187, 243, 245, 262
  in Myanmar, 254, 256
  in the Philippines, 148, 162, 183, 243, 253
  missionaries in Asia, 208
Chuprina, Elena, 19
Citizenship laws
  India, 203
Citizenship rights
  in India, 297
  in Nigeria, 204
Civilizing demand
  in China, viii, 3, 207
  in India, viii, 3, 170, 220
  in Indonesia, 49
Civil rights, 187
Civil society advocacy, 256
Civil society organizations. *See under* specific organizations
Climate change, 138, 235
Clinics
  in Cambodia, 95
  in China, 233
  in Tanzania, 241
Coast, Ernestina, 102
Coerced migration, 85, 86, 96
Coffee, 238
  in Ethiopia, 77
  in Indonesia, 103
Cohen, Roberta, 24, 25, 27, 254, 272
Collective action weakness, within the international community, 280
Colombia
  Afro-Colombians, 152
  Bogotá, 16, 116
  Coordinación Nacional de Desplazados (CND, National

Coordination of Displaced People), 258
Medellin, 151
native rights, 241, 254, 258, 278
trade agreements observing ILO guidelines, 278
Colonialism and colonization, x, 36, 45, 93, 95, 162, 182, 231, 247
Combes, Pierre-Philippe, 165
Commodification of land, 162
Communal violence, 129
Compensation for expulsion
doctrine of, 130, 276
in Costa Rica, 48
in India in the Philippines, 186
in Rhodesia, 43
Complexity of the state, 54
Conceptualizing Internal Migration, 20
Conditionalities, 277, 278, 305
Confino, Alon, 88
Conflict IDPs, 5, 20–22, 24, 25, 27, 40, 129, 133, 135, 136, 138, 192, 205, 206, 219, 259, 261, 268, 296, 299, 300
Conflict resolution, 76, 261
Congestion, 153, 234, 292
in cities, 48, 49, 86, 232
in Indonesia's Inner Islands, 17
Congo, Democratic Republic of
Sons of the Soil conflicts, 178
Congo, Republic of
nature reserves in, 51
Connell, John, 233
Conservation. *See also* nature reserves
green urbanism, 115
in Brazil, 39
in India, 39
in Peru, 39
in South Asia, 115
in Thailand, 51
Coordinación Nacional de Desplazados (CND, National Coordination of Displaced People) (Colombia), 258
Corruption
in China, 80
in India, 42, 203
in Indonesia, 203, 235, 261, 262
in the Philippines, 261, 262
of contractors, 255
political, 203
Costa Rica
agriculture, 47
Arenales Hydroelectric Project, 68
forests, 48
Instituto Costarricense de Electricidad (ICE), 68
Instituto de Desarrollo Agrario (Agrarian Development Institute), 48, 79
native rights, 48, 241
resettlement, 48, 68, 79
Costello, Michael, 81
Côte d'Ivoire
exclusion of northern migrants, 203
Côté, Isabelle, 1, 3, 46, 161, 170, 176, 177, 179, 182, 183, 186, 194, 206, 207, 230, 232, 235, 237, 241, 260, 261
COVID pandemic, 65, 101
Cravino, Maria, 152
Crime, vii, 101, 112, 116, 135, 136, 152, 186, 193, 199
Crimea (Ukraine), 66
Crisp, Jeff, 21, 24
Cross-cutting cleavages, 148, 260
Cultural compatibility, 73
Cultural deprivations, 171, 207
Cultural symbols, 171
Curry, George, 171, 233
Curses in ceremonies, 78
Customary rights, 162

Cyclone Nargis (Myanmar), 138

D

Dagestan (Russian Federation), 61
Dagne, Shibru, 37, 73, 77, 78, 218
Dams
  Brazilian-Paraguayan Itaipu Dam, 129
  expulsion due to, 130
  in China, 17, 129
  in Egypt, 204
  in India, 130, 132
  in Pakistan, 273
Dandakaranya Resettlement Program (India), 170
Daniels, Lesley-Ann, 176
Danish Refugee Council, 282
Darfur (Sudan), 40, 205
Darul Islam Rebellion (Indonesia), 45
Datta, Ayona, 20
Davidson, Jamie, 49, 151, 171, 180, 185, 197, 295
Davies, Anne, 241
Dawson, Elsa, 257
Dayaks (Indonesia), 49, 150, 171, 180, 184, 185
Debelo, Asebe, 73, 77, 78
Decentralization
  in Chile, 59
  in Ghana, 60
  in Indonesia, 59, 244
  in Thailand, 44
  in the Philippines, 59, 297
  in Uganda, 59
Declaration on the Rights of Indigenous Peoples, 241
de Cordier, Bruno, 253
Dedicated (government) offices, 65
de Geoffrey, Agnes, 200
de Haas, Hein, ix, 145
De Jong, Huub, 317
de Koninck, Rodolphe, 182
Delang, Claudio, 51
Delli Sante, Angela, 88
Demombynes, Gabriel, 20, 113
Deng, Francis, 24, 25, 254, 272
Denmark
  Danish Refugee Council, 282
  support of the Global Program on Forced Displacement, 281
Department for Transmigration (Indonesia), 295
Dependency syndrome of migrants, 139
Derg regime (Ethiopia), 205
Deshingkar, Priya, 109, 110, 159, 267
Development IDPs, 17, 26, 86, 128, 129, 135, 136, 204, 258, 282, 299
Disaster IDPs, 17, 22, 40, 92, 129, 133, 135, 136, 138, 160, 161, 205, 206, 237, 254–256, 261, 296, 299, 303
Discrimination (Employment and Occupation) Convention (ILO), 271
Displacement compensation. *See* compensation for expulsion
Doan, Petra, 120
Dodge, Kenneth, 74, 219
Dodoma (Tanzania), 120
Dolan, Chris, 21
Donbas (Ukraine), 66
Doshi, Sapana, 20, 50
Douglass, Mike, 117
Drought
  difficulty in defining, 257, 296
  in China, 232
  in Ethiopia, 43, 45, 89
  in Turkey, 255
Duku, Dennis, 60
Duncan, Christopher, 49, 220, 254, 274

Dutch East Indies colonial rule, 177

E
Earthquakes
in Cairo, Egypt, 255
in Pakistan, 255
in Turkey, 255
East Kalimantan Province (Indonesia), 178
East Timor, 235
conflicts attributed to transmigration, 230
Ecological degradation and disasters, 8, 128, 140, 192, 198
Ecological IDPs, 51
Ecologically sensitive areas, 9, 89
Ecological motives, 49
Economic development, ix, 7, 19, 153, 159, 233, 301
Ecuador
Galapagos Islands, 232
Education, 2, 94, 95, 104, 109, 110, 114, 144–146, 150, 153, 163, 166, 168, 169, 179, 199, 233, 238, 242, 259, 260, 273, 296, 299
Egypt
Aswan High Dam, 204
Cairo earthquake, 255
Iraqi refugees in, vii
Nubians, 204
El Alto (Bolivia), 16, 118
Elling, Rasmus, 52, 167
El Salvador, 92
fear of the state, 92
England, Vaudine, 1
Entrepreneurial migrants, 103, 104, 150, 292, 299
Environmental IDPs, 27
Equatorial Guinea, 51
nature reserves, 51
Eriksen, John, 197
Escribà-Folch, Abel, 176
Ethiopia
Action for the Needy program, 257
agriculture, 43
Derg regime, 205
drought, 43, 45, 89
forced villagization, 151
Gedeos, 15, 73, 221, 306
gondoro ritual, 78
Gujis, 15, 73, 77, 306
ILO activities in, 267
military, 43
Oromos, 45, 77
villagization, 45, 151
Ethnic cleansing, 19, 176
European Union
use of conditionality for humanitarian ends, 278
Euskadi language (Spain), 62
Evans, Martin, 146, 147
Evrard, Olivier, 87
Exchange perspectives between migrants and host communities, 149
Expulsion of host communities, 16, 40, 53
Expulsion of recent migrants, 112
Expulsion of urbanizers, 111, 113
External (foreign) assistance, 6
Extractive industries, 101, 103

F
Faith-based organizations, 252, 254–256, 259, 263, 304
Faith-centric approach, 256
Falla, Jonathan, 88
Fan, C. Cindy, 20
Farm consolidation, 48
Farm shrinkage, 128
Farrell, Kyle, 109

Favelas (Brazil), 199, 209
Fearnside, Philip, 66, 94, 144, 194, 237
Fearon, James, 45, 176, 177, 180, 181, 209, 230, 239
Federal Land Development Authority (FELDA) (Malaysia), 238
Feelings of superiority, 53
Feler, Leo, 199
Fernandes, Walter, 132
Ferri, Giovanni, 268
Ferris, Elizabeth, 2, 268, 275
Fiji, 3
  nativist violence, 181
  Sons of the Soil conflicts, 181
Finland, 231
  domicile laws (Åland), 231
Fiscal decentralization, 63
Fishers, 92, 150
  and hydroelectric dams, 132
Fitzgerald, David, 14, 121, 147
Floods, 129, 136, 138, 196, 281, 296
Fluidity of migration categories, 21
Flyvbjerg, Bent, 163
Forced migration, 18, 42, 222, 223, 280
Forests
  in Brazil, 16, 49, 94, 103
  in Cambodia, 197
  in Costa Rica, 48
  in Laos, 90
Fox, Sean, Sarah, 111
Franco, Edgar, 209
Freedman, Sarah, 260
Frontier areas, 8, 72, 74, 75, 198
Front-line administrators, 52
Fu, Diana, 258
Fulani (Nigeria), 204

G
Gabon
  nature reserves in, 51
Gaborone (Botswana), 120
Gaikwad, Nikhar, 110, 168
Galapagos Islands (Ecuador), 232
Galvin, Marc, 50
Garbuio, Massimo, 163
Garcia, Kimberly, 182, 278
Gardner, Tom, 78
Gayo (Indonesia), 181
Gedeos (Ethiopia), 15, 73, 221, 306
Gengo, Tieti, 149
Geopolitical strategy, 47
Georgia, 66, 284, 295
  Nagorno-Karabakh conflict with Azerbaijan, 284
  South Ossetia conflict with Azerbaijan and Russia, 284
Germany
  alleged WWII link with Tatars, 88
Ghai, Yash, 62
Ghana, 66, 67, 241
  decentralization, 60
  indigenous power, 241
Global Environment Facility, 280
Global Forum on Migration and Development, 285
Global Internal Migration Assistance Facility, 280, 285
Global Knowledge Partnership on Migration and Development, 285
Global Migration Group, 285
Global Program on Forced Displacement (GPFD), 281
Global warming, 35
Gondoro ritual (Ethiopia), 78
Gonese, Francis, 67
Goodfellow, Tom, 111
Goodfriend, Lizzie, 205
Goodman, Sara, 242
Gosnell, H., 101
Goulding, Michael, 166
Greenlees, Don, 1

Green urbanism, 115
Grimm, Sven, 159
Grundy-Warr, Carl, 88
Guadalajara (Mexico), 121, 147
Guatemala, 82, 88
  Mayan people, 182
  military, viii
Guha, Ramachandra, 74
Gujarati migrants (India), 140, 175
Gujis (Ethiopia), 15, 73, 77, 306
Gullette, Gregory, 145
Gulpur Dam (Pakistan), 273
Guoqing, Shi, 276
Gurr, Ted, 164

H

Haase, Dagmar, 105
Hagendoorn, Louk, 61
Haller, Tobias, 50
Hamnett, Chris, 5
Han Chinese, 3, 46, 180, 207, 232, 240, 298, 306
Hancock, Landon, 253
Hanoi (Vietnam), 39
Han, Sun, 40, 231
Hardjono, 18, 236
Hardoy, Jorge, 43
Harild, Niels, 201
Harms, Erik, 113–115, 117
Haryana State (India), 114
Hasija, Namrata, 80
Haslam, Nick, 139
Hatcher, Craig, 114
Hausa (Nigeria), 204
Havrylchyk, Olena, 139
Healthcare
  in Indonesia, 233
  in Thailand, 233
  role of the World Bank, x, 233
Hechter, Michael, 148
Hedman, Eva, 1
Heider, Fritz, 219
Henderson, J. Vernon, 199
Henley, David, 197
Herders, 77, 101, 139
Highland communities, 51, 208
Highways
  in Brazil, 16, 44
  in Peru, 151
  in the Philippines, 162, 259
Hill Tracts Manual (India), 39
Hill tribes
  in India, 20
Hindu Balinese, 161, 170, 206, 237
Hnatkovska, Viktoria, 100
Ho Chi Minh City (Vietnam), 16, 39, 114, 117
Hoefle, Scott, 182
Hofinger, Christoph, 258
Ho khau (Vietnam), 20, 113
Hometown associations
  in Africa, 147
  in Indonesia, 147, 292
  in Latin America, 147
  in Mexico, 147
  in Turkey, 147
  in West Africa, 146
Homewood, Katherine, 102
Hong Kong, 231
Hongladarom, Krisadawan, 171
Horizontal inequality, 148
Horowitz, Dan, 148
Horowitz, Donald, 184
Host cleavages, 147
Host community perspectives, 143
Housing Development Boards (Singapore), 231
Huancayo (Peru), 258
Huang, Liling, 117
Huang, Limingcui, 177
Hugo, Graeme, ix, 7, 181, 268, 300
Hukou (China), 3, 20, 39, 80, 113, 198, 233, 234

Huk Rebellion (Philippines), 45
Humanitarian assistance, 26, 133, 224, 253, 257, 270
Hunter-gatherers, 101, 139
Hunter, Lori, 232
Huntington, Samuel, 192
Hurricanes, 136
Hussein, Saddam, President (Iraq), 46, 88
Hutchinson, Francis, 59
Hutus (Rwanda), 269
Hu, Xiaojiang, 231
Hydroelectric dams, 42, 47, 129, 130, 132, 285

I
Ibáñez, Ana, 112
Identifications and attributions, 51
Identity documentation, 168, 272
IDP camps, 15, 17, 22, 25, 40, 77, 100, 135, 139, 201, 205, 243, 254, 268, 270, 274, 304
  income generation in, 135
  "warehousing" in, x, 302
IFC Policy and Performance Standards on Environmental and Social Sustainability, 272
Igbo (Nigeria), 204
Illiberal policy, 9
India
  Adivasi, 111
  Andhras, 244
  agriculture, 44
  Andaman Islands, 49
  Andhra Pradesh State, 49, 140, 163, 244
  Assam, 49, 74, 175, 179, 180, 207
  Bastar District, 170
  Bawana resettlement colony, 119
  Bengali Hindus, 180
  Bengali Muslims, 39, 180
  Bengalis, 49, 179, 180
  Bihar State, 16, 109
  BJP party, 114
  Bodos, 175
  British rule, 39, 179, 231
  Buddhists, 16, 39
  Chettyar moneylenders, 104
  citizenship laws, 203
  citizenship rights, 297
  civilizing demand, viii, 3, 170, 220
  conservation, 39
  corruption, 42, 203
  dams, 130
  Dandakaranya resettlement program, 170
  Gujarati migrants, 116, 140, 175
  Haryana State, 114
  Hill Tracts Manual, 39
  hill tribes, 20
  Indian Administrative Service, 52
  India-Pakistan partition, 49
  Inner Line Permit, 20
  Inter-State Migrant Workmen Act, 271
  Kashmir, 47
  Kolkata, 119, 120
  Maharashtra state, 2, 65, 109, 114, 151, 175, 297
  Marathis, 16, 114
  Mawris, 179
  Migration and Asylum Project, 257
  military, 47, 194
  Mumbai, viii, 16, 50, 65, 109, 116, 140, 148, 151, 168
  Muslims, 16, 47, 148, 179
  Narmada River, 194
  Naxalite Belt, 74
  Odisha State, 49
  Prime Minister Rehabilitation Plan 2008, 47
  Rajasthani migrants, 140
  residency requirements, 2

riots in, 179, 185, 231
Shiv Sena party, 114
slum removal, viii
Sons of the Soil conflicts, 179–181, 186, 244
special economic zones (SEZs), 42, 163, 258
Supreme Court, 232, 244
Tehri Dam, 130
Telangana, 244
Tribal areas, 160, 179, 220
Tripura, 49
Uttarakhand State, 144
Uttar Pradesh State, 65, 175
Vadodara-Ahmedabad Expressway, 132
Indonesia
Aceh, 1, 21, 22, 40, 46, 62, 181, 205, 255, 256, 261
agriculture, 44, 105
Ambon Island, 1
Bali, 17, 21, 206, 237
Betawi Brotherhood, 165
Bougainville, 181
Buginese people, 231
Butonese people, 39, 230
Christians, 1, 46, 148, 187, 206, 230, 231, 245, 262
civilizing demand, 49
congestion in the Inner Islands, 1
corruption, 42, 203, 235
Darul Islam Rebellion, 45
Dayaks, 49, 150
decentralization, 59, 244
department of migration, 295
Dutch era, 21
East Kalimantan Province, 178
Gayo people, 181
healthcare, 233
hometown associations in, 147
Java, viii, 2, 21, 206, 236, 237, 243, 261, 292, 303
Kalimantan, 1, 151, 178, 181, 184, 185, 197, 220, 235
Kalla, Jusuf, 262
Kenya people, 178, 234
Lampung, 170, 235, 237, 246, 260, 261
Madurese, 15, 150, 180, 184, 197, 219
Makassarese, 39
Malino Accords, 245, 262
Maluko, 184, 185, 230, 237, 246, 262
Mawori/angkat saudara adoption custom, 260
Merap, 178
Ministry of Transmigration, 66
nationalism, 22, 181, 209
nativist violence, 181
North Sulawesi, 165
Papua (Indonesia), 1
Pemekaran (administrative unit expansion), 244
Peusijuek (cooling off) ceremony, 261
Pontianak, 151
Poso, 185, 245, 262
protestants, 209, 254
riots in, 1, 74, 184, 185
rubber plantations in, 22
Sons of the Soil conflicts, 177, 181, 245
Suharto, President, 1, 46, 209
Sulawesi, 103, 207, 209, 262
Sumatra, viii, 21, 46, 206, 236, 237, 260, 261
Tangerang, 147
Timor, 1, 46, 230
transmigrants, 1, 21, 22, 39, 46, 161, 165, 194, 209, 235–237, 260, 303

Transmigration program (*Transmigrasi*), 7, 17, 230, 236
West Kalimantan, 15, 49, 180, 181
Industrial zones, 44
Informal settlements, 14, 24, 42, 49, 50, 86, 101, 115, 120, 232, 299
Infrastructure IDPs, 7, 130, 132, 276, 305
Inner Line Permit (India), 20
Inner Mongolia (China), 232, 240
Institute for Local Democracy (Peru), 257
Instituto de Desarrollo Agrario (Costa Rica), 48, 79
Inter-agency cooperation, 79
Intermarriage, 21
Internal passports, 39
International agencies, 17, 78, 201, 245, 256, 258, 262, 284
International Centre for Migration Policy, 285
International Committee of the Red Cross (ICRC), 257
International community roles, xii, 6, 9, 27, 28
International coordination challenges, 283
International Covenant on Civil and Political Rights (ICCPR), 80
International Displacement Monitoring Centre (IDMC), 4, 129, 133, 135, 268, 282, 285
International financial institutions (IFIs), 271, 276, 282, 283
International Labour Organization (ILO), 2, 24, 241, 267, 271, 295
advocating indigenous rights, 9
in Ethiopia, 267
International law, 6, 25–27, 192
International migration, vii–x, 3, 5–7, 13–15, 23–26, 54, 66, 88, 110, 144, 145, 191, 226, 231, 242, 268, 281, 282, 284, 291, 293, 294, 299, 302, 304, 307
International Migration (journal), 24, 25
International Migration Review (journal), 24
International norms, 222, 223, 304
International Organization for Migration (IMO), viii, x, 3, 24, 114, 127, 135, 136, 226, 227, 257, 261, 270, 281–283, 285, 291, 304
International organizations, xii, 6, 24, 138, 270–272, 281, 282, 293, 295, 305
International Red Cross and Red Crescent Movement, IFRC, 257
International Rescue Committee, 282
Inter-State Migrant Workmen Act (India), 271
IOM Emergency and Post-Conflict Unit, 227
Iran
Andisheh, 118
Baloch in, 167
Khuzestan, xi, 46, 52
new cities, viii
Persians, xi, 46, 167, 169, 170
Sistan-Baluchistan Province, 167
Sunni in, 167
Iraq, 88
Kurds expelled in, xi, 88
Refugees in Egypt and Jordan, vii
Iraqw people (Tanzania), 102
Isan region (Thailand), 171
Islamic NGOs, 255
Israel/Palestine, 253
Muslims in, 254
Iyer, Pushpa, 253

J
Jackson, Stephen, 21, 178
James-Allen, Paul, 205
Japan, 233
  One Village, One Product Program, 233
Jaquet, Carine, 254, 256
Jatmiko, Andi, 255
Java (Indonesia), viii, 1, 17, 21, 237, 260
Jerryson, Michael, 208, 253
Jessel, Ella, 116
Jesuit Refugee Service, 256
Jewish merchants, 104
Joint IDP Profiling Service, 282
Jones, Gavin, 23, 203
Jones, Peter, 232
Jordan
  Iraqi refugees in, vii
  trade agreements observing ILO guidelines, 278
Jory, Patrick, 169
Joshi, Bhagwati, 144
Joshi, Kirti, 115
Journal of Refugees Studies (journal), 24
Juliawan, Benny, 147

K
Kabeer, Naila, 199
Kadalayil, Chitrabhanu, 114
Kalimantan (Indonesia), 1, 15, 49, 151, 178, 180, 197, 220
Kälin, Walter, 275
Kalla, Jusuf (Indonesia), 262
Kaltman, Blaine, 207
Kampala Convention, xii, 2, 224, 275, 301, 304
Kaplan, Abraham, 169, 193
Karens (Myanmar), 86
Kashmir (India), 47
Keane, Roy, 278
Keating, Michael, 62
Keller, Edmund, 45
Kendzior, Sarah, 252
Kenya
  Nairobi, 209
  nativist violence, 181
  Sons of the Soil conflicts, 177
  strategic hamlets, 88
  Turkana people, 149
  Tutsi refugees, 269
Kenya people (Indonesia), 178
Kerkvliet, Benedict, 46
Khairkar, Vijaya, 114, 116, 175
Khuzestan Province (Iran), xi, 167
Kiev (Ukraine), 135
Kigali (Rwanda), 115, 269
  exclusion of the poor, 115
Kimura, Ehito, 244
Kinfemichael, Girum, 78, 218
King, Russell, 13
Kinh ethnicity (Vietnamese), 182
Kin networks, 146
Kirkuk (Iraq), 46
Kivimäki, Timo, 220
Koch, Anne, 277, 281, 282, 285
Koczberski, Gina, 171, 233
Kolkata (India), 119, 120
Kolsto, Pål, 61
Kone, Zovanga, 114
König, Anika, 150
Kono, Tatsuhito, 115
Kosinski, Leszek, 14
Kubát, Daniel, 14
Kumyks (Russian Federation), 61
Kundu, Ratoola, 119
Kurds, xi, 17, 45, 46, 52, 86, 194
  expulsion in Iraq, 46
  expulsion in Turkey, xi, 45, 86, 194
Kyrgyzstan, 113, 199
  internal registration, 113, 199

L

Labor shortages, 7, 149
Lagos (Nigeria), 121
Lahiri, Amartya, 100
Laitin, David, 45, 176, 177, 180, 181, 209, 230, 239
Lampung (Indonesia), 161, 206, 235, 237, 260
Land Allocation for Social and Economic Development Project (Cambodia), 196
Landau, Loran, 21, 148, 192, 193, 260
Land banks, 48
Land grabs, 50, 186
Land-hungry migrants, 101–103
Landlessness, 47–49, 99, 100, 257
Landslides, 129
Land titling, 36, 94, 113, 132
Laos
  forced villagization, 151
  forests in, 90
  resettlement, 79
La Paz (Bolivia), 118
Lara Jr., Francisco, 95
Lasswell, Harold D., 169, 193
Latin America
  forced resettlements, 88
  hometown associations, 147
  urbanization-discouraging policies, 111
Lebanese merchants, 104
Lecamwasam, Menaka, 2
Lee, Everett, 22
Lewis, Nathaniel, 109
LGBTQI individuals, 109
Liberia, 205
  Palava Hut, 205
Life cycle of migration, 25
Lilongwe (Malawi), 120
Lima (Peru), 234, 257
Limpanonda, Suphannada, 233
Lipset, Seymour, 148
Littlejohn, S.W., 245
Litvack, Jennie, 63
Liu, Alfred, 64
Liu, Yongzheng, 64
Liyanage, Sumanasiri, 260
Local government, 22, 42, 43, 50, 60, 62, 117, 167, 179, 203, 204, 232, 240, 306
Lofchie, Michael, 44
Long, Norman, 21, 145, 234
Lopez, R., 277
Lovallo, Dan, 163
Lowry, C.S., 245
Lucas, Robert, ix, 13, 15, 24, 72, 101, 106, 121, 145, 146, 233
Luedke, Alicia, 2, 40, 274
Lujala, Päivi, 235, 303
Lumad Christians (Philippines), 148, 183
Luzon (Philippines), 183

M

Maasai (Tanzania), 102
Macau (China), 231
MacMillan, Gordon, 94
Madhavan, Sangeetha, 21, 148, 260
Madurese (Indonesia), 15, 150, 171, 180, 184, 185, 197
Magaloni, Beatriz, 209
Mahaphonh, Nouphanh, 79
Maharashtra State (India), 2, 109, 151
Mahar, Dennis, 166
Mahaweli Dam project (Sri Lanka), 194
Maitrot, Mathilde, 39
Makassarese (Indonesia), 39, 230
Malay Muslims (Thailand), 169
Malaysia
  Borneo, 21, 232
  Federal Land Development Authority (FELDA), 238

Javanese refugees in, 22
nativist violence, 177, 181
regional citizenship, 231, 232
resettlement, 88
Sabah State, 231
Sarawak State, 231
Sons of the Soil conflicts, 181
strategic hamlets, 88
Malays (Malaysia), 21, 185, 231, 238
Malesky, Edmund, 59
Malholtra, Depak, 260
Manaus (Brazil), 16
Manirakiza, Vincent, 115
Manogaran, Chelvadurai, 180
Manouchehri, Bahar, 118
Marathis (India), 16, 114
Mariano, Lorenzo, 182
Martinez Portilla, Isabel, 152
Martínez-Vázquez, Jorge, 64
Martin, Susan, 15
Martin, Terry, 15, 46
Mason, Elisa, 27
Mawori/angkat saudara adoption custom (Indonesia), 260
Mawris (India), 179
Maxwell, Daniel, 205
Mayan people (Guatemala), 182
Maybank, J., 136
Mbulu traders (Tanzania), 102
McCargo, Duncan, 171
McCauley, John, 203
McConahay, Jon, 152
McGhee, Derek, 18
McGibbon, Rodd, 17
McKenna, Thomas, 52, 240
McLean, J., 197
McRae, Dave, 185, 245
Mecca pilgrimage, 261
Medan, 22
Médecins Sans Frontières, 205
Medellin (Colombia), 151
Melo, Vanessa, 209
Merap (Indonesia), 178
Merchant migrants, 104, 105
Mešić, Enisa, 139
Metz, Brent, 182
Mexico
decentralization in, 59
hometown associations in, 146, 147
IDPs in, 193
Mexico City, 23, 246
new towns in, 23
trade agreements observing ILO guidelines, 278
Migdal, Joel, 192
Migrant-origin communities, 144, 292
Migration agencies, 65, 79
Migration and Asylum Project (India), 257
Migration restrictions, 233
Migratory insecurity, 208
Militarization of Buddhist temples (Thailand), 253
Military
in Brazil, 35, 36, 47, 199
in Ethiopia, 43
in Guatemala, viii
in Indonesia, 187
in Myanmar, vii
in Peru, 47
in Thailand, 253
in Turkey, 45
Miller, Sarah, 256
Mills, Mary, 44
Mindanao (Philippines), 45, 52, 95, 148, 162, 183
Mineral prospecting, 95
Ministry of Transmigration (Indonesia), 66
Mitchell, Christopher, 253
Mitchell, Matthew, 176, 177, 179, 182, 183, 186, 241, 246
Moneylenders, 104

Mongolia, 114, 232, 240
Mongols, 175
Ulaanbaatar, 114
Mongols, 175
Montalvo, José, 176
Mooney, Erin, 24, 129
Moore, Christopher, 230
Moore, Will, 26
Moradi, Sanan, 169, 170
Morgerea, Elisa, 82
Morocco, ix, 145
remittances, 145
Moro Islamic Liberation Front, 183
Moro Muslims (Philippines), 148
Moro secession (Philippines), 240
Morris-Jung, Jason, 223
Morris, Tim, 21, 24
Moskito Coast (Nicaragua), 62
Mosques, 185, 252–255
Movimento dos Trabalhadores Rurais Sem Terra (Brazil), 48
Mueller, Valerie, 110
Mugabe, President Robert (Zimbabwe), 43
Muggah, H.C.R., 27
Muggah, Robert, 67
Mukherjee, Jhumpa, 175
Mukora, Charles, 67
Multilateral aid agencies, 40. *See also* Regional development banks, World Bank Group
Multiple migrations, 15, 178
Mumbai (India), 16, 109, 140, 148, 151, 168
Muslim Brotherhood, 255
in Egypt, 255
Muslims
Bengali, 39
in India, 16
in Indonesia, 1, 46, 148, 184, 185, 187, 209, 230, 245, 262
in Israel/Palestine, 254
in Myanmar, 179, 245
in southern Thailand, 169, 239
in the Philippines, 45, 148, 162, 183, 240, 259
Mutualism, 146
in Cameroon, 146
Mwakagali, Mpoki, 278
Myanmar
Buddhists, 179, 245
Burmans, 179
Christians, 246, 256
Cyclone Nargis, 138
Karens, 86
military, 254
Muslims, vii, 179
nativist violence, 179
Rakhine State, 179
Rohingya Muslims, vii, 179
Shan State, 86
Sons of the Soil conflicts, 179
Myers, Daniel, 74

N

Nagorno-Karabakh, 284
Azerbaijan-Georgian conflict, 284
Nairobi (Kenya), 209
Nair, Reshmy, 276
Nari Udyog Kendra (NUK) (Bangladesh), 258
Narmada River (India), 194
Nasritdinov, Emil, 199
National Institute for Colonization and Agrarian Reform (Brazil), 219
Nationalism, 22, 61, 181, 209
in Aceh (Indonesia), 1, 21, 22
in Russia, 61
National Land Settlement Association (NLSA) (Philippines), 95
Nation-building, 19, 46, 62, 167–169
in Thailand, 168, 169

Native rights
in Bolivia, 241
in Colombia, 254, 258, 278
in Costa Rica, 48, 241
in Paraguay, 241
in Peru, 21
nativist violence, 181
Natsuda,Kaoru, 233
Natural disasters, xi, 8, 15, 19, 72, 85, 91, 99, 127, 136, 138, 141, 186, 194, 242, 252, 254, 277, 300
Nature reserves
in Cameroon, 50, 51
in Equatorial Guinea, 51
in Gabon, 51
in Nigeria, 51
in the Central African Republic, 50
in the Republic of Congo, 51
Navarro, Zander, 87
Naxalite Belt (India), 74
Nellis, Gareth, 110, 168
Nellis John, 234
Nepal, 197
discrimination against southern migrants, 152
Royal Chitwan National Park, 197
Neumann, Roderick, 232
New Economics of Labor Migration, 23
Nguyen, Chuong, 20, 40
Nguyen, Thi, 20, 40
Nicaragua, 62
Moskito Coast, 62
Nielsen, Ingrid, 171
Nigeria
Abuja, 120
Afizare, 204
agriculture, 102
Anaguta, 204
Berom, 204
Biafra, 181
citizenship rights, 204
Fulani, 204
Hausa, 204
Igbo, 204
Lagos, 113, 121
nature reserves in, 51
remittances, 121
Urhobo, 204
Yoruba, 204
Nogai (Russian Federation), 61
Non-governmental organizations (NGOs), 10, 40, 51, 91, 92, 151, 205, 226, 252, 255–259, 278–280, 282, 284, 293, 304
Nooteboom, Gerben, 311
Norris, Jacob, 104
North American Agreement on Labor Cooperation (NAALC), 278
North American Free Trade Agreement, 278
North Sulawesi (Indonesia), 165
Norway, 282
Norwegian Refugee Council, 282
support of the Global Program on Forced Displacement, 281
Noveria, Mita, 165
Noviana, Nana, 261
Nubians (Egypt), 204
Nyerere, President Julius (Tanzania), 44, 90

O
Oberai, A.S., 23
Odisha (India), 49
Ofcansky, Thomas, 44
Olajide, Oluwafemi, 113
Olthof, Douglas, 94
Olutola, Bamisaye, 275
One Tambon, One Product program (Thailand), 233
One Village, One Product program (Japan), 233

Orang Asli (Malaysia), 21
Organization for Security and Co-operation in Europe (OCSE), 284
Orji, Nkwachukwu, 254, 256
Oromos (Ethiopia), 45, 77
Otiso, Kefa, 234
Ottoman Empire, 104
  migrant networks, 104, 147
Overlapping cleavages, 303
Overlapping nature of migration forms, 7
Özdemir, G., 147

P
Pahang (Malaysia), 238
Palava Hut (Liberia), 205
Palestinians, 253
  global donations to, 253
Panama, 4, 241, 278
  native rights, 4
  trade agreements observing ILO guidelines, 278
Pandemics, 3, 65, 101, 145, 223
Pandits (Kashmir), 47
Panggabean, Rizal, 75
Panyu Center (China), 258
Papua (Indonesia), 1, 17, 39, 220, 230, 235, 236
  Sons of the Soil conflicts, 181
Papua New Guinea, 171, 208, 233, 246
Paraguay, 241
  Itaipu Dam, 129
Parreñas, Rachel, 144
Parsitau, Damaris, 254
Pass system (South Africa), 39
Patani Province (Thailand), 208, 239
Patel, Sejal, 273
Peace zones (Philippines), 253
Pelzer, Karl, 25, 95, 236–238
Pemekaran (administrative districts expansion) (Indonesia), 244
People Power Movement (Philippines), 259
Peripheral settlements
  in Bolivia, 119
  in China, 119
  in India, 119
  in Indonesia, 119
  in Peru, 119
  in Vietnam, 119
Peru
  conservation, 39
  Huancayo, 258
  Institute for Local Democracy, 257
  Lima, 234, 257
  military, 47
  native rights, 21
  remittances, 145
  trade agreements observing ILO guidelines, 278
  Transpacific Highway, 151
Perz, Stephen, 35
Petersen, William, 18, 222
Petras, James, 48
Peusijuek (cooling off) ceremony (Indonesia), 261, 262
Pfaffenberger, Bryan, 180
Philippines
  Bakwit (Evacuee) Power, 259
  Bureau of Lands, 162
  Christians, 148, 162, 183, 240, 243
  corruption, 261, 262
  decentralization, 59, 297
  highways, 162
  Huk Rebellion, 45
  Lumad, 148, 181, 183, 243
  Luzon, 183
  Manila, 199
  Mindanao, 45, 95, 148, 162, 181, 183
  Moro Muslims, 148

Moro secession, 240
National Land Settlement Association, 95
peace zones, 253
People Power Movement, 259
Sons of the Soil conflicts, 181, 186
Tondo area, Manila, 200
Visayas, 183
Phuong, Dinh, 199
Planning failures, xi, xii, 193
Polian, Pavel, 46
Police, viii, 42, 46, 74, 187, 199, 209, 231, 253, 262
Political decentralization, 60, 61
Political deprivations, 167, 168
Political IDPs, 88, 128
Pol, Megha, 115
Polonoroeste Program (Brazil), 94
Pontianak (Indonesia), 151
Population congestion and control, 48, 234
Porter, Matthew, 139
Poso (Indonesia), 185, 245, 262
Post-colonial transitions, 43
Poston, David, 163
Primacy of the state, 5, 7, 293, 294
Property rights, 42, 47, 61, 161, 162, 198, 200, 201, 276, 277, 293, 300
Propiska (Soviet Union), 39
Protestants (Indonesia), 209
Prothero, Mansell, 14, 89, 90
Prud'homme, Remy, 63
Pune (Maharashtra), 116
Push and pull factors, 22, 25
Putnam, Robert, 257

Q
Quang, Binh, 20, 40

R
Rahman, President Ziaur (Bangladesh), 45
Rai, Neha, 273
Rajasthani migrants, 140
Rakhine State (Myanmar), 179
Ramakrishnan, Kavita, 119
Rapa Nui (Chile), 232
Rape (in civil wars), 185
Ration cards, 113, 168, 203
Ravenstein, Ernst, 22
Realistic group conflict theory, 143
Reconciliation rituals, 37, 63, 78, 205, 254
Red Crescent, 253, 257
Red Cross, 253, 257
Reddy, I.U.B., 76
Redistribution demands, 48
Rees, Philip, 26, 101
Refstie, Hilde, 21, 24
Refugee studies, 26
Regional development banks, 280
Reilly, Benjamin, 246
Reimer, Tanya, 48
Reinnoldt, Charlotte, 178
Religion, 81, 148, 203, 208, 237, 252–257
Remittances
in Cameroon, 146
in China, 23, 111, 145
in India, 304
in Mexico, 23, 121
in Morocco, 145
in Nigeria, 121
in Peru, 145
in Thailand, 7, 145
Rent-seeking, 119
Requia, Weeberb, 20
Resettlement programs
Amazonian, 94, 95, 166
in Brazil, 15, 37, 300
in China, 298

in Egypt, 104
in India, 48, 170
in Indonesia, 300
in Iran, 46, 52
in Malaysia, 88
in Nepal, 197
in Papua New Guinea, 171, 181
in Peru, 300
in South Africa, 88
in Tanzania, 44, 90
in Thailand, 298
in Vietnam, 19
World Bank doctrine on, 94
Residency requirements
in China, 3, 101
in India, 168
in the Soviet Union, 39
Resource extractors, 103
Restricting internal migration, viii
Restriction by partial incorporation, 193
Reuveny, Rafael, 232
Reynal-Querol, Marta, 176
Reynolds, Sarnata, 193
Rhee, Steve, 178
Rhodesia, 43. *See also* Zimbabwe
expulsion of white landowners, 67
Richardson, Harry, 233
Richmond, Anthony, 14
Richter, Iris, 23, 95, 196, 197
Right to migrate, 187, 262
Rio de Janeiro (Brazil), 199, 209
Riots
in India, 179, 185
in Indonesia, 1, 185
in Singapore, 185, 231
Road-building, 35
Roberts, Bryan, 112
Robinson, Sherman, 26
Rodriguez, Robyn, 66
Rohingya Muslims (Myanmar), 179
Refugees in Bangladesh, vii
Rokkan, Stein, 148
Roldán-Ortega, Roque, 241
Rondinelli, Dennis, 60, 234
Rondonia State (Brazil), 194
Roquet, Vincent, 68
Roth, Michael, 223
Rothenberg, Irene, 23
Royal Chitwan National Park (Nepal), 197
Roy, Rajkumari, 45
Rubber plantations, 22
in Indonesia, 22
Rural-to-rural migration, 14, 15, 270
Rural-to-urban migration, ix, 16, 20, 105, 106, 109, 112
Russian Federation, 61
Russian migrants, 61
Russians, ix, 61, 66
Russians (in Siberia), 61
Rwanda
genocide, 268
Hutus, 269
Kigali exclusion of the poor, 115
NGOs' peace education programs, 260
Tutsis, 268

S

Sabah State (Malaysia), 231
Sacchi, Agnese, 63
Sadiq, Kamal, 232
Said, Ismail, 238, 239
Salazar, Miguel, 231
Salcedo, J., 277
Samaddar, Arghadip, 101
Samaritan's Purse, 256
Samuels, Annemarie, 256
Sánchez, Luis, 62
Sanford, Victoria, 254
Sangha (Thailand), 208
Sarawak State (Malaysia), 231

Sasse, Gwendolyn, viii, ix, 127
Satellite cities, 24, 48, 116–118, 120, 234
Satterthwaite, David, 43
Save the Children, 257
Schenkenberg, 283, 284
Schewel, Kerilyn, 101
Schmidt-Soltau, Kai, 50, 223
Schneider, Aaron, 60
Schneider, Leander, 90
Schrepfer, Nina, 275
Scriven, Joel, 39, 197
Scudder, Thayer, 204
Seaports, 129
Secondary cities, 49, 112, 234, 258
Security deprivations, 183
Self-Accountability, 219
Self-governance, 60
Selway, Joel, 148
Sending communities, 8, 147, 153
Separation strategy, 242
Separatist conflicts, 21, 183, 253, 261
Seymour, Lee, 47, 242, 284
Shakya, Clare, 273
Shanghai (China), 119, 207
Shan State (Myanmar), 86
Shantytowns, 128, 152, 199, 232, 306
Shaojun, Chen, 171
Shariff, Abusaleh, 110
Shellman, Stephen, 26
Shenzhen Labor Disputes Center (China), 258
Sherif, Muzafer, 143
Shifting cultivators, 101, 139, 225
Shinawatra, President Thaksin (Thailand), 239
Shiv Sena party (India), 114
Shopping complexes, 129
Shuikou Hydro-Project (Cambodia), 197
Siberians (Russian Federation), 182
  exploited by Russian settlers, 182
Sierra Leone, 254
  IDPs aided by religious groups, 254
Sim, Loo, 40, 231
Simmons, C.S., 95
Simon, Herbert, 225
Sina, Dantje, 92
Singapore
  Chinese in, 40, 231
  Indians in, 231
  Javanese refugees in, 22
  Malays in, 22, 231
  riots in, 185
Siroën, Jean-Marc, 278
Siroky, David, 148
Sistan-Baluchistan Province (Iran), 167
Skeldon, Ronald, ix, 5, 7, 13, 15
Slum Improvement Program (Mumbai), 50
Slum removal
  in Argentina, 43
  in China, 43
  in India, viii
  in South Asia, 115
  in Vietnam, 117
Smith, Nigel, 166
Smyth, Russell, 171
Social engineering, 78, 79, 235
Social Land Concession program (Cambodia), 95
Social psychology, 143
Societal responses, 251
Soedirgo, Jessica, 230
Solar arrays, 129
Somalia, 151
  forced villagization, 44, 151
Sons of the soil conflicts
  in China, 179
  in the Democratic Republic of the Congo, 178
  in Fiji, 181

in Indonesia, 181, 244, 260
in Kenya, 181
in Malaysia, 181
in Myanmar, 179
in Nigeria, 181
in Papua, 181
in the Philippines, 186
in Sri Lanka, 180
in Tanzania, 181
in Uganda, 181
in Zimbabwe, 181
Sørensen, Ninna, 257
Šošić, Bojan, 139
South Africa
Boer War, 88
pass system, 39
slum removal, 43
South Asia, 129
strategic hamlets, 88
Southern Border Provinces Administration Center (Thailand), 239
South Ossetia, 284
Conflict between Azerbaijan and Georgia, 284
South Sudan, viii, 2, 40
IDP camps, viii, 40
limits on UNHCR activities, 40
Soviet Union, 39, 61
propiska residency restrictions, 39
Stalin, 88
Special Autonomous Regions (China), 231
Special economic zones (SEZs), 25, 42, 163, 164
displacement from, 42, 163, 258
in India, 42
Spontaneous migration, xi, 161, 237, 238
Sri Lanka
Mahaweli Dam project, 194
nativism, 209
Sons of the Soil conflicts, 180
Tamils, 67, 180, 253
Srur, Muradu, 44
Stahl, Charles, 23
Stalin, Joseph, 46, 88
Stark, Oded, 23
State accountability, 117, 191, 218, 227
State failures, 9, 178, 191, 192, 194, 198, 204, 210, 211, 251
State-initiated migrations, xii, 8, 19, 72, 79, 81, 127, 170, 177, 206
State-instigated migrations, 300
Statelessness, 202
State levels, 114
State-managed migrations, 1, 8, 23, 44, 45, 91, 181, 194, 225, 235, 293
State motives, xi, 36, 41
Stecklov, G., 109
Stepputat, Finn, 257
Stereotyping, 52, 53, 140
Stocks, Gabriella, 68
Stokke, Olav, 278
Straede, S., 197
Strategic hamlets
Kenya, 88
Malaysia, 88
South Africa, 88
Vietnam, 88
Subnational governments, x, 2, 6, 8, 17, 41, 63–65, 114, 176, 179, 183, 186, 187, 199, 203, 258, 278, 296–298, 302
Sub-Saharan Africa
IDPs living outside of camps, 270
limited space for ecological migrants, 5
weakness of urban preparedness, 163

weak support of the Kampala Convention, xii, 2, 275, 301, 304
World Bank Group funding, 269
Suburbanization, 44
Sudan, viii, 200
expulsion of IDPs, 88, 128, 135, 205
expulsion of NGOs from IDP camps, 206
Suharto, President (Indonesia), 1, 46, 209
Sulawesi (Indonesia), 1, 103, 165, 206, 209, 230, 235, 245, 254, 262, 274
Sumatra (Indonesia), viii, x, 21, 46, 103, 177, 206, 235–237, 260, 261
Sutton, Keith, 238
Sward, Jon, 267
Switzerland, 282
support of the Global Program on Forced Displacement, 281
Symbiotic relationships, 306
Symbolic gestures, 46
Syria, viii, 133
IDPs, viii, 133
migrants to Europe, ix

T

Tadjoeddin, Mohammad, 39, 75
Taghados, Mostafa, 118
Taiwan, 231
residency restrictions, 231
Talwar, Smrithi, 76
Tambiah, Stanley, 181
Tamil migrants (in Maharashtra), 180
Tamils (Sri Lanka), 67, 180
Tanasaldy, Taufiq, 235
Tangerang (Indonesia), 147
Tanzania
agriculture, 44
Chaga merchants, 104
clinics in, 241
Dodoma, 120
ILO in, 267
Iraqw people, 102
Maasai people, 102
Mbulu traders, 102
nativist violence, 181
Nyerere, President Julius, 44, 90
Sons of the Soil conflicts, 181
Ujamaa, 90
Tanzi, Vito, 63
Tasciotti, Luca, 102
Tatars (Russian Federation), 61, 88
Taxation. *See also* fiscal decentralization
by Rio de Janeiro militias, 199
incentives to attract migrants, 44
incentives to keep Chinese in rural areas, 40
tax-base increases from internal migration, 292
Tay, Elaine, 185
Taylor, Lewis, 88
Techakesari, Pirathat, 170
Tehran (Iran), 118
Tehri Dam (India), 130
Telangana State (India), 244
Temples
militarization in Thailand, 253
Terminski, Bogumil, 201
Thaification, 169
Thailand
agriculture, 51
Bangkok, 7
Buddhist temples, 208
conservation in, 51
decentralization in, 44
healthcare, 233
Isan region, 171
Malay Muslims, 93

Military, 253
Militarization of Buddhist temples, 253
One Tambon, One Product program, 233
Patani Province, 208, 239
remittances, 7
Sangha, 208
Shinawatra, President Thaksin, 239
Southern Border Provinces Administration Center, 239
temples, 208, 253
Thai ethnicity, 94
Thaification, 169
Thanh, Hoang, 199
Thawnghmung, Ardeth, 179
Thede, Nancy, 60
Thieme, Susan, 114
Thompson, Michael, 102
Three Gorges Dam (China), 129
Thu Thiem New Urban Zone (Vietnam), 117
Tibet, 181, 231, 240
Tigno, Jorge, 183
Timor (Indonesia), 1, 46, 230, 235
Titulars (Russian Federation), 61
Tiwari, Reena, 120
Todaro migration model, 22
Toft, Monica, 176
Tomsa, Dirk, 246
Tondo area, Manila (Philippines), 199
Tork, Masoumeh, 118
Tostensen, Arne, 147
Trade agreements, 278
requiring ILO guideline observance, 278
Trading routes, 132
Traditional conflict resolution mechanisms, 76
Tranchant, Jean-Pierre, 209
Transamazon Highway, 36
Transmigrants (Indonesia), 1, 21, 22, 39, 46, 161, 165, 170, 194, 197, 209, 235–237, 260, 299, 303
Transmigration program (*Transmigrasi*) (Indonesia), 7, 15, 17, 230, 235, 236
Transpacific Highway (Brazil, Peru), 151
Tribal areas (India), 160, 179, 220
Trihartono, Agus, 262
Trinidad, 181
Tripura (India), 49
Tuminez, Astrid, 162, 186
Turkana people (Kenya), 149
Turkey
Anatolia, 45, 194
army, 86, 194
drought, 255
Earthquake, 255
hometown associations in, 147
Kurds in, xi, 45, 86
military, 45
Turton, David, 18
Tutsis (Rwanda), 268
Tvedten, Inge, 147

U

Uehling, Greta, 88
Uganda
conflict IDPs, 21
decentralization in, 59
nativist violence, 181
Sons of the Soil conflicts, 181
Tutsi refugees, 268, 269
Uighurs (China), 207, 306
Ujamaa (Tanzania), 90
Ukraine
Crimea, 66
government offices for IDPs, ix, 19, 66, 133, 135, 295
war with Russia, vii

Ukrayinchuk, Nadiya, 139
Ulaanbaatar (Mongolia), 114
Ummah (Islamic transnationalism), 253
UN 2007 Declaration on the Rights of Indigenous Peoples, 241
UN agencies, 284
Uncertainty of migration outcomes, 221
UN Education, Social, and Cultural Organization (UNESCO), 144
Unger, Jonathan, 165
UN Guiding Principles on Internal Displacement, 202, 223
UN Habitat, 5
United Kingdom Department for International Development, 267
United Nations. *See under* specific UN agencies
United Nations High Commissioner for Refugees (UNHCR), 15, 25, 40, 224, 241, 270, 274, 282, 283, 304
United Nations (UN), 4, 111, 241, 271, 280, 282–284
United States, vii, ix, 74, 278
  trade agreements observing ILO guidelines, 278
Universal Declaration of Human Rights (UDHR), 39, 80, 223
UN Office for the Coordination of Humanitarian Affairs (UNOCHA), 271, 283
Unsponsored migrants, 16, 17, 39, 60, 72, 94, 99, 121, 218, 219, 237, 298, 300, 303
Urbanization, ix, 4, 5, 7, 8, 15, 16, 23, 48, 49, 72, 81, 100, 101, 105, 106, 111–113, 116, 120, 151, 165, 232–234, 267, 268, 296, 297
Urbanization-discouraging policies, 111
  in Latin America, 111
Urban-to-rural migration, 101
Urban-to-urban migration, 34, 271
Urhobo (Nigeria), 204
Uribe-Mallarino, Consuelo, 116
User rights, 35, 47, 50, 162, 292
Uttarakhand State (India), 144
Uttar Pradesh State (India), 65, 175
Uyghurs (China), xi, 179

V

Vaa, Mariken, 147
Vadodara-Ahmedabad Expressway (India), 132
Vahidi, Hossein, 118
Vanclay, Frank, 282
Vandekerckhove, Nel, 180
Van Der Wijst, Ton, 18
Van Lindert, Paul, 118
Van, Luong, 165
Varshney, Ashutosh, 75
Varshney, Rizal, 75
Venezuela, 4
  refugees in Colombia, vii
Vertical coordination of state institutions, 297
Vertical inequality, 148
Verry, LaVerle, 44
Verwimp, Philip, 269
Viartasiwi, Nino, 262
Vientiane (Laos), 16
Vietnam
  Cat Tien National Park, 222
  Hanoi, 39
  ho khau regulations, 20, 113
  Kinh ethnicity, 182
  nativist violence, 181
  peripheral settlements, 119
  slum removal, 43

strategic hamlets, 88
Thu Thiem New Urban Zone, 117
Villagization
in Ethiopia, 45, 151
in Laos, 151
in Somalia, 151
in Tanzania, 44, 90
Villema, Sietze, 95
Villero identity (Argentina), 152
Visayas (Philippines), 183
Voluntary state-managed migration, 92
Voter ID cards, 168
Vu, Linh, 20, 113
Vulnerability of state officials, 74

W

Wade, Robert, 226
Waldrauch, Harald, 258
Wallace, Jeremy, 3, 20, 101, 112, 113, 233, 234
Walsh, John, 255
Wang, Lan, 119
Weah, Aaron, 205
Weiner, Myron, 176, 177, 179, 180, 183, 187, 207
Wenban-Smith, Hugh, 90
West Africa, 146
hometown associations, 146
Western Europe, 306
migration from Morocco, 306
West Kalimantan (Indonesia), 15, 49, 151, 180
Wheeler, Matt, 240
Whitaker, Beth, 241
Wilkinson, Steven, 187, 246
Wilson, Tom, 221
windfarms, 129
Wong Siew, 88
Wood, Charles, 36, 103
World Bank
commitment to livelihood initiatives in IDP camps, x
funding of IDP-focused projects, 273
funding of the Mumbai Urban Transport Project, 68
funding of the Sardar Sarovar Dam Project, 194
Global Internal Migration Assistance Facility, 280, 285
Global Program on Forced Displacement (GPFD), 281
Identification for Development (ID4D), 272
loans for Amazonian highways, 16
Operational Policy 4.12 on Involuntary Resettlement, 222
prominence of standards, 267
receptivity to critics, 149
role in healthcare, 233
World Bank Group
Independent Evaluation Group, 273
International Development Association, 281
Multilateral Insurance Guarantee Agency, 273
World Commission on Dams, 42
World Vision, 256
Wu, Alfred, 64

X

Xinjiang (China), 46, 181, 231, 298

Y

Yadav, Vineeta, 163, 164, 258, 259
Yakimova, Sonya, 140
Yakuts (Russian Federation), 61
Yang, Anand, 185
Yang, Yongjiao, 145
Yeltsin, President Boris of Russia, 61

Yoruba (Nigeria), 204
Young, Forrest, 232
Young, Helen, ix, 205
Yu, Shi, 40, 231
Yzerbyt, Vincent, 140

Z

Zaman, Mohammad, 276
Zea, Juan, 2, 221, 258
Zeccola, Paul, 40, 205
Zezza, Alberto, 102
Zhang, Dong, 145
Zhang, Heather, 19
Zimbabwe. *See also* Rhodesia
  expropriation of white-held land, 67
  Mugabe, President Robert, 43
  nativist violence, 181
  Sons of the Soil conflicts, 181
Zimmer, Andrew, 234
Zips-Mairitsch, Manuela, 279

SPRINGER NATURE

GPSR Compliance

The European Union's (EU) General Product Safety Regulation (GPSR) is a set of rules that requires consumer products to be safe and our obligations to ensure this.

If you have any concerns about our products, you can contact us on ProductSafety@springernature.com

In case Publisher is established outside the EU, the EU authorized representative is:

Springer Nature Customer Service Center GmbH
Europaplatz 3
69115 Heidelberg, Germany

FSC
www.fsc.org
MIX
Papier | Fördert
gute Waldnutzung
FSC® C083411

Kolibri 360 GmbH
Ferdinand-Jühlke-Straße 7
99095 Erfurt, Deutschland
produktsicherheit@kolibri360.de